BATTLEGROUND

BATTLEGROUND

AFRICAN AMERICAN ART 1985–2015

CELESTE-MARIE BERNIER

THE UNIVERSITY OF GEORGIA PRESS ATHENS

A Sarah Mills Hodge Fund Publication

This publication is made possible in part through a grant from the Hodge Foundation in memory of its founder, Sarah Mills Hodge, who devoted her life to the relief and education of African Americans in Savannah, Georgia.

Most University of Georgia Press titles are available from popular e-book vendors.

Printed in Canada

26   25   24   23   22   c   5   4   3   2   1

Library of Congress Cataloging-in-Publication Data
Names: Bernier, Celeste-Marie, author.
Title: Battleground : African American art, 1985–2015 /
    Celeste-Marie Bernier.
Description: Athens : The University of Georgia Press,
    [2022] | Includes bibliographical references and index.
Identifiers: LCCN 2022031923 | ISBN 9780820360478
    (hardback)
Subjects: LCSH: African American art—20th century. |
    African American art—21st century. | Art and society—
    United States—History—20th century. | Art and
    society—United States—History—21st century.
Classification: LCC N6538.B53 B47 2022 | DDC
    700.89/96073—dc23/eng/20220812
LC record available at https://lccn.loc.gov/2022031923

This book is written in loving memory of

Catherine Mary Nash
(1977–2019)

traveler, adventurer, artist, baker, life poet,
beloved sister-friend,

and this book is dedicated with all my love and heartfelt gratitude to

Earnestine L. Jenkins
Bill E. Lawson
George Lipsitz
Debra Priestly

inspirational intellectuals, pioneering historians,
trailblazing artists, visionary philosophers,
social justice campaigners
beautiful "whole-souled" friends.

CONTENTS

ILLUSTRATIONS

ACKNOWLEDGMENTS

I am very grateful to all the artists in this book for their wonderful generosity, exceptional support, and incredible kindness. I would like to give my very special, heartfelt, and lifelong thanks to Myra Greene, Lyle Ashton Harris, Lorraine O'Grady, Jefferson Pinder, Debra Priestly, Dread Scott, Clarissa T. Sligh, and Pat Ward Williams.

The editorial teams at I. B. Tauris (Bloomsbury) and the University of Georgia Press have been a joy to work with as they have wonderfully supported this project to completion. Every effort has been made to contact all the rightsholders and obtain all permissions to reproduce all materials included in this book. Information regarding any amendments that should be included in future editions of this book would be very gratefully received.

I am especially thankful to the U.K. Leverhulme Trust for a 2010 Philip Leverhulme Prize in Art History, which provided the vital funds that has made it possible to include full-color reproductions in this book. I am also deeply grateful to have received a 2020 Leverhulme Major Research Fellowship. As a result, I have been able to complete the final formatting and submission of *Battleground*.

I am forever indebted to the National Humanities Center in Durham, North Carolina, for the Senior John Hope Franklin Fellowship that made the final research and writing of this manuscript possible. I would not have been able to finish this project without the vital expertise and phenomenal support of the National Humanities Center's genius librarians, Brooke Andrade, Sarah Harris, and Joe Milillo, and their brilliant sleuthing that enabled them to track down hard-to-find resources. While at the center I had the privilege and pleasure of working beside and learning from so many fellows wonderful scholars and inspirational individuals.

I am forever grateful to all the inspirational members of the Frederick Douglass Honor Society and to the following "whole-souled" friends: Harriette Lowery, Childlene Brooks, Vickie Wilson, Brenda Wooden. I am equally indebted to a vast array of U.S.- and U.K.-based artists, academics, archivists, and activists who are a source of inspiration every day, including Ingrid Banks, Eddie Chambers, Ryan Cox, Maya Davis, Hannah Durkin, Walter O. and Linda Evans, Rachel Farebrother, P. Gabrielle Foreman, Diane C. Fujino, Christopher Haley, Kim F. Hall and the inspirational Hall family, Bernard L. Herman, Lubaina Himid CBE RA, John Howard, Sir Isaac Julien RA, Robert S. Levine, Stephanie Lewthwaite, Esther Lezra, Richard A. Lou, Grace Musila, Joey Orr, Sir Geoff Palmer OBE, Joanna Pawlik, Dora Petherbridge, Ernest Quarles, Geoff Quilley, Alan Rice, Barbara Rodriguez, Betye Saar, Emily Squires, Jeffrey C. Stewart, Fionnghuala Sweeney, Barbara Tomlinson, Vilna Bashi Treitler, Parisa Urquhart, Zoé Whitley, Lisa Williams, Deborah Willis, Sara Wood, Zandra Yeaman, and Rafia Zafar.

I finalized the research for *Battleground* during my last years at the University of Nottingham, England, and I am very grateful to all my undergraduate and postgraduate students for being an unending source of inspiration. I am especially grateful to all the students in my African American Art class in 2015–16. Since transferring to the University of Edinburgh, Scotland, I am very grateful to Sequoia D. Barnes and Zöe Charlery for their wonderful expertise as pioneering researchers, groundbreaking theorists, and inspirational writers of African diasporic art history. I am especially indebted to my past and present Edinburgh and Nottingham PhD. students—Nick Batho, Katherine Burns, Jimmy Brookes, Amy Cools, Christopher Counihan, Kiefer Holland, Hannah Jeffery, Hannah-Rose Murray, Andrea Nicholson, Aija Oskman, Carolina Palacios Guerra, and Paul Young—for their brilliant expertise.

Since I joined the University of Edinburgh in 2016, the faculty, professional services staff, and students have been a wonderful source of expertise and support. I am very grateful to everyone and especially the following wonderful colleagues and friends: Jackie Barnhart, Benjamin Bateman, Alan Binnie, Eleoma Bodammer, Jacqui Brook, Adam Budd, June Cahongo, Sarah Carpenter, Fred Carter, Frank Cogliano, Simon Cooke, Máire Cox, Véronique Desnain, Sarah Dunningan, David Farrier, Rhona Feist, Annette Gotzkes, Justyna Hajduczek, Fabian Hilfrich, Keith Hughes, James Gilmour, Katherine Inglis, Carole Jones, Ella Keam, Susan Kemp, Michelle Keown, Anouk Lang, Alexandra Lawrie, Christine Lennie, Ebtihal Mahadeen, Vicki Madden, Laura Mair, Robert Mason, Kara McCormack, Jane McKie, Dorothy Miell, Diana Paton, Chris Perkins, Gina Roberts, Julie Robertson, Jeremy Robbins, Vivek Santayana, Nacim Pak-Shiraz, David Silkenat, Jane Sillars, Leah Sinclair, Nicol Smith, Allyson Stack, Sheila Strathdee, Iain Sutherland, Olga Taxidou, Alex Thomson, Rebecca Tierney-Hynes, Laura Tomlinson, Gemma Thomson, Suzanne Trill, Anna Vaninskaya, Greg Walker, Lena Wånggren, Hannah White, Jonathan Wild, and Neil Young. I would not have been able to complete this book without the phenomenal support, wonderful generosity, and great friendship of Janet Black and Michelle Houston.

So many dearest family members and dearest friends have offered me their phenomenal patience, kindness, and support as a source of heart and hope during this time, including: Tina, George, and Jon Green; Claire, Ant, Charlotte, and Amy Freeman; Carla Hepburn; Ross and Christopher "the Incredibles" Lambert; Stephanie "Ern" Lewthwaite; Judie Newman; Dora Petherbridge; Gillian Roberts; Alan Rice; Barbara, Natalia, and Julian Rodriguez; Lisa Rull and Neil Roberts; Maria Ryan; Fionnghuala Sweeney; Tashki and Scarlet Waterman; Sara Wood. For always being a magnificent fount of all wisdom, a joyous source of fun, and a keeper of the most excellent tunes, I would like to thank Richard "Bestest Bro" Anderson. As always, a humungous heartfelt thank you goes to my magnificent Edinburgh family: Carole Jones and Jane Taube and Katherine Lymer, Marion Macpherson, and Emily Owen, bless you all.

No one gives love or offers hope like Andy Green, artist, poet, street historian, and musician: thank you for everything.

Finally, this book is in loving memory of Eric Lowery (1948–2020), my beloved "whole-souled" friend and our beautiful-in-spirit and beautiful-in-life sister-friend Catherine Mary Nash (1977–2019). Nothing would be possible without your courage, compassion, and creativity to inspire us all on. Your life force will never die.

BATTLEGROUND

"My artwork, ever since I been a kid, has always been my strength," declared Ronald Lockett in 1997, a year before he died at the tragically young age of thirty-three. "I've been going through a lot of hard times, where I've kind of lost my way," he confided, "but any time I kind of want to regain myself when I lose myself I go back to my artwork."[1] Eight years before his death, in 1990, Lockett, an Alabama-born African American artist, created *Smoke-Filled Sky: You Can Burn A Man's House but Not His Dreams.*[2] As Bernard L. Herman notes, this was not an isolated painting: "He produced at least seven variations in this body of work as he wrestled with the challenge of depicting the violence of the Klan."[3] The painting is an emotionally provocative and starkly minimal work. In it, the charred remains of a wooden building protrude from a salvaged wood surface. Lockett bears witness to untold stories of white racist violence by visibilizing the history of white supremacist atrocities enacted in the U.S. South. While he removes all obvious physical traces of a human presence, layers of black paint ripple and curl to suggest the singed skin and tortured flesh of wounded bodies. The flecks of blood-red paint splattered onto the cabin's burned-out wooden frame and bare tree branches powerfully represent his protest against mortal loss.

A monument to Ku Klux Klan violence, *Smoke-Filled Sky* functions as a surrogate memorial to the Black women, children, and men who were murdered and denied all burial rites at the hands of white vigilante mob rule. Lockett leaves his audiences no choice but to confront the human tragedy suggested by the tortuous trail of white smoke and the torn-apart surfaces of the cabin's broken walls. Lockett works with heavily laden

symbolism and emotively charged imagery. An important symbol in his radical visual lexicon, the white smoke assumes the contours of a fossilized, dinosaur-shaped skeleton. Lockett offers hope in the face of despair by imagining a world in which white racist violence is not only in the past but a remnant of a prehistoric era and doomed to extinction. The art of creation, the painting suggests, is an antidote to the act of destruction, a message that reflects Lockett's belief that artwork is his strength and is a means of finding his way back to a sense of selfhood in hard times. His practice of recycling salvaged remains breathes new life into discarded materials, giving the lie to the finality of death. Here and across his works, he demonstrates that, as he puts it, "you can burn a man's house but not his dreams.[4] As declarations of survival in the face of struggle, Lockett's works are weapons in his social justice arsenal. At the same time, they bear witness to his lifelong belief that "once something has lived it can never really die."[5]

More than twenty-five years later, in 2016, Clarissa T. Sligh asks, "Can hate be transformed?"[6] Sligh, a mixed-media photographer and installation artist, explains, "I am a black woman. I am an artist. For many years I have been creating work to bring issues of social justice into the public discourse."[7] Born in 1939 in Virginia, Sligh, like Lockett, uses art-making as a tool for social equality and political reform. She came of age at the height of segregation and during the civil rights and Black Power eras. In the work she is currently producing against the backdrop of a "new Jim Crow," and according to which people of color continue to be subjected to white supremacist and racist acts of torture, persecution, discrimination, and death, she asks an urgent, powerful, and serious question: can white racist hate be "transformed" through art-making?[8] She was prompted to tackle this issue directly in her practice by an invitation she received. "When I was 67 years old," she writes in *Transforming Hate: An Artist's Book*, "a proposal came from the Montana Human Rights Network asking artists to make artwork that would 'incorporate, respond to, or transform' pages from *The White Man's Bible*, / a white supremacist book."[9] "I SAID I WOULD," she states, and yet "the box of the books arrived, and sat for months / untouched." She is candid regarding her very real fear: "I was afraid to open that box, could not approach / White supremacy. / WHAT IF SOMETHING HAPPENED / to me? / a black woman / living alone."[10]

"When I was growing up / schools, / churches, / hospitals, / libraries, / restaurants, / and movie theaters, / were off limits to me because of my race," Sligh states in a hard-hitting exposé of the innumerable ways in which white racist hate discriminates and persecutes Black lives. She recalls her traumatic memories: "I never saw them, but I heard stories about the KKK / riding through our neighborhood at night." While she confronts her own fears as a "black woman / living alone," she celebrates family histories of Black female resistance in the face of white atrocity: "My mom said grandma could shoot a gun / straighter than a man." Just as Lockett's work was inspired by oral memories within his own family of exposures to Klan atrocities, Sligh's terror as a "black woman / living alone" is rooted in personal tragedy. She relies on blood-red lettering in describing her mother's witnessing of her brother's murder: "My uncle was lynched in South Carolina before I was born. / ROPE AROUND HIS NECK / His broken body was tossed from a wagon / to the yard in front of my mother." For both Lockett and Sligh, the quest for a new visual language in which to transform white racist hate reveals their shared determination to translate pain into beauty to effect social change. Across her works, she does justice to her conviction, "Violence has never stopped violence."[11]

In the search for answers to her question, "Can hate be transformed?," Sligh embarks on a physical and emotional journey: "I visited the Hiroshima Peace Memorial Park / and Museum in Japan. / Standing at that site of unbelievable suffering / I realized that we all participate. / Our separation makes it easy / to call each other enemy." Addressing the destructive consequences of internalized oppression, she observes that it is "easy to be complicit in acts of violence / committed in our collective name." In the midst of her desolation, she takes heart from an art installation: "In that sea of incredible dark sadness, / a small children's peace memorial / covered with thousands of colorful / paper origami cranes stood / brightly on one side of the park. / Origami cranes had become / an international symbol for peace." She finds an answer to her question "Can we find a way to live our lives / WITHOUT KILLING EACH OTHER?" by taking up the artistic practice of making origami cranes. She is newly able to "BREATHE LIFE / INTO EACH CREATION" in a ritual of art-making. For Sligh, the repeated process of "OPEN UNFOLD FLIP OVER OPEN" necessary to make an origami crane results in physical, psychological, emotional, and imaginative healing.[12]

"WHEN I WAS 75 / a young white man killed nine black people / at a church prayer service in Charleston, / South Carolina/," Sligh observes of Dylann Roof's massacre of Sharonda Coleman-Singleton, Cynthia Marie Graham Hurd, Susie Jackson, Ethel Lee Lance, DePayne Middleton-Doctor, Clementa C. Pinckney, Tywanza Sanders, Daniel L. Simmons, and Myra Thompson at Emanuel African Methodist Episcopal Church on June 17, 2015. "Despite a lifetime of living under the shadow of killings and murders, this man's actions were even harder for me to believe," she declares. Sligh's solace in the face of white hate is the redemptive possibilities of Black love. "I was deeply moved when the families, of the people who were killed, forgave the shooter right away," she says. "Their act became a gift of compassion, love and forgiveness for us all." Witnessing a public act in which state officials were breaking with tradition by working to right the wrongs of history, she recognizes her role as a conduit for the power of ancestral memory: "I watched a live online feed of the flag being removed by South Carolina state troopers. I thought of my mother's brother who had been lynched in South Carolina before I was born. I felt her looking through my eyes."[13]

For Sligh, *Transforming Hate: An Artist's Book* is a visual and textual meditation on her determination "to look at what it was like for me to turn hateful words into a beautiful art object." As she realized, "What actually evolved from that exploration helped me understand more fully the many levels of oppression and violence at the intersections of race, gender, class and sexual orientation." Across her experimental bodies of work, Sligh interrogates all kinds of discriminations, refusing to restrict herself to any one kind of hate. Hers is a lifelong quest to address inequalities. "Why do we keep each other from being who we really are?" she asks. "How can we begin to talk about what separates us?" Ultimately, Sligh denies safe ground to audiences of every race, gender, class, and sexuality. "The BOX— full of books, / the books full of words, / the words full of hate," represents "CONTAINERS WE ALL MUST FACE." As of 2017, she remains unequivocal in her protest against white racism, white supremacy, and all forms of persecution and discrimination: "I will not meet hate with hate." When she asks "AM I SAFE?", Sligh reveals that she is under no illusions regarding the very real dangers she faces. For Sligh, as for Lockett, the real issue facing humanity is, "Do we have the courage to live differently?"[14]

Sligh's call to confront the "many levels of oppression and violence at the intersections of race, gender, class and sexual orientation" is answered by the radical principles and dissident practices of all the artists working over the last three decades whose lives and works I trace in these pages. Twentieth- and twenty-first-century African American art, a tradition forged against white supremacist odds, interrogates formal boundaries, transgresses dominant conventions, and reenvisions vision in order to transform hate into love and forge a Black "lexicon of liberation."[15]

"Absence with a Capital A": African American Artists and the Battleground

In this book I map the paintings, drawings, and sculptures and the installation, digital, and performance art produced by more than twenty African American artists working over thirty years. As these artists' experimental bodies of work demonstrate, whether it is 1990 or 2022, the fight against white racist hate, let alone the battle for artistic freedom, is far from over. Just as white supremacist acts of discrimination and persecution continue to assume countless guises in the twenty-first century—bloody massacres, police shootings, housing segregation, economic impoverishment, suburban segregation, legal racism, educational discrimination, sexual objectification, physical violation, psychological trauma, media stereotyping, and government neglect, and much more—the battleground that is the no person's land of Western art history, art criticism, patronage, and exhibition remains. World-renowned painter Kerry James Marshall addresses this issue, stating that "the overarching principle" of his practice is "to move the black figure from the periphery to the centre."[16] He creates history paintings in which he represents all aspects of Black lives—social, political, imaginative, poetic, mythical, and cultural—on an epic scale. "I'm using African-American cultural and social history as a catalyst for what kind of pictures to make," he declares. "What I'm trying to do in my work is address Absence with a capital A."[17]

As I argue in this book, the battleground for contemporary African American artists represents a war waged on two fronts. First, theirs is a fight for artistic freedom as they hold steadfast to their commitment to developing experimental practices unfettered by Western art conventions. Second, they continue to endure the devastating consequences of their "Absence with a capital A." In 2022, Black artists still suffer from ongoing neglect, dismissal, and erasure at the hands of a white supremacist art world that repeatedly misinterprets, distorts, and invisibilizes their lives and works. The majority of African American artists continue to be written out of mainstream art history. In the exceptional cases in which Black artists are given representation in major galleries and exhibitions, the tendency is still toward tokenism—the inclusion of the few to the exclusion of the many—rather than any real engagement with individual artists and their practice. While a handful of the twenty-three artists examined in this book are renowned figures in the mainstream art world and some are represented by major galleries, many more create art in the margins. In nearly all instances, Black artists receive attention in significantly fewer retrospective exhibitions and catalogs, monographs, and scholarly essays in refereed journals and book publications than their European and American counterparts.

No more categorical confirmation of the bleak state of affairs confronting African American art and artists can be found than in their widespread dismissal in histories of contemporary U.S. art. Time and time again, Black artists are given only a truncated treatment , if they are not excluded altogether. As a painter repeatedly denied access to mainstream representation, Emma Amos observes that "there is very little criticism of the work of nonwhite artists which relates the content of their work to the work of white artists." Faced with this injustice, she exposes these deliberately segregated practices by questioning, "Why are black voices only compared to other black voices?"[18] She also notes that "there is NO criticism of the work of white artists which relates the content of their work to the work of nonwhite artists" and raises another powerful question: "Why are white voices only compared to other white voices?"[19]

As of 2022, scholars and curators provide damning evidence that the playing field is segregated, discriminatory, and tokenistic and that "Absence with a capital A" is still the order of the day. In contemporary histories of U.S. art authored in recent decades by leading scholars, African American artists and their practices continue to receive one or two sentences at best or widespread dismissal at worst. A source of hope in the face of despair, however, are the few volumes in which they have received far more extensive and in-depth treatment, authored by Erika Doss, David Joselit, Frances K. Pohl, and Eleanor Munro. Such works offer grounds for cautious optimism regarding future scholarly directions. Working against dominant tendencies to denigrate or devalue Black art-making traditions, these writers have produced inclusive rather than exclusive histories of U.S. art and artists in which Black and white voices are no longer segregated but interact in reciprocal patterns of influence and exchange.[20]

In comparison with white U.S. mainstream art histories, African American art historical criticism by Black and white writers and theorists is a centuries-old tradition that does not shy away from the stark reality that the persecutory practices facing Black women, children, and men in mainstream U.S. society are matched by the discriminations in the white dominant U.S. art world. At the same time that African American artists have sought to challenge white racist forms of oppression in white U.S. society, radical art historians and revolutionary theorists have produced seminal volumes, essays, and critical anthologies in which they continue the fight for control over the critical and theoretical language.[21] In the last few years, Lenwood G. Davis, Daniel Frye, Dele Jegede, and Steven Otfinoski have produced influential reference volumes on African American art and artists. They provide readers with vital information regarding names, dates, and titles for thousands of artists and their works.[22]

White racist strategies of discrimination, exclusion, and dismissal regarding African American artists and art-making traditions over the centuries have resulted in very real difficulties in accessing artworks. At the same time that these discriminatory realities continue to present ongoing challenges, many U.S. museums and galleries exhibit African American artists' work, and many institutions house collections of African American artists' work and unpublished archival materials.[23] Pioneering volumes for scholars working on the art of collecting have been produced by Halima Taha, John Hope Franklin and Alvia J. Wardlaw, and Patricia A. Banks in recent years. Over the decades, African American artists, activists, and curators have defied their "absence with a capital A" by producing groundbreaking art histories, artist monographs, essay collections, and exhibition catalogs. During this period, monographs have also illuminated the work of individual artists. However, African American women artists remain underrepresented in these publication lists. Emma Amos readily explained this absence, observing "a definite schism between Black male artists and Black female artists."[24] While all African American artists endure inequalities within the white U.S. art world, Black female artists continue to encounter "wrongs, and sufferings, and mortifications peculiarly their own."[25]

The publication of monographs, histories, and exhibition catalogs in the last few years notwithstanding, difficulties still remain not only in accessing works but in sourcing scholarship on contemporary African American artists and their art-making traditions. For example, of the twenty-three artists I examine in this book, only three—Kerry James Marshall, Mary Lee Bendolph, and Whitfield Lovell—have received extensive treatment across a range of well-researched monographs, collections, catalogs, retrospectives, refereed articles, and interviews. The majority, meanwhile, have suffered from a very real neglect, their work displayed only in underresourced exhibitions and addressed only in short publications with low print runs, if at all. Serious and almost insurmountable barriers face researchers of these lesser-known artists. In the years I dedicated to researching and writing this book, I experienced ongoing challenges and difficulties in gaining access to artworks and resources. The vast majority of the materials I consulted and which I list in the bibliography were only accessible with the support of specialist librarians and the generosity of artists, galleries, and museums. I urge readers wanting to undertake further research into these and other artists' lives and works to access the U.S. and UK archival collections and repositories that have been integral to the writing of this book.[26] Equally invaluable sources of information can be found on these artists' websites, which provide a treasure trove of personal writings, interviews, works, and criticism. In addition to listing their websites in the bibliography, I provide readers with further information regarding the private galleries that represent each of these artists—in some cases more than one—as they offer yet another vital source of artworks, catalogs, press information, and interviews. While cutting-edge scholarship and newly radicalized curatorial practices have succeeded in laying the foundations for a new African American art criticism and exhibitions policy, the fight for recognition and representation of and research into African American art and artists is a battleground that has only intensified in the twenty-first century.

"DON'T YOU MISS US WHEN WE'RE NOT THERE?"

The battleground that is the fight for equal rights, equal respect, and equal recognition for African American artists, art-making traditions, art movements, and art history remains a source of wounding and pain. While the increasing volume of African American and Black diasporic art scholarship published by major presses and endorsed by mainstream institutions is a source of hope, the entrenched white racist strategies of co-option, tokenism, misinterpretation, exoticization, and commodification persist. For African American artists, theirs is the burden of representation; but for historians, critics, and theorists, the burden is one of interpretation. Due to the destructive forces of a white supremacist ideology that continues to marginalize, appropriate, distort, and dehumanize Black lives and works within and without the art world, we are not there yet.

We should here recognize the real difficulties surrounding the use of mainstream art histories, catalogs, and essays to discuss Black artists and artworks. The reality is that the majority of white collectors, curators, and critics working in the dominant art world have received their training in elite institutions in which the histories of African and African diasporic art and artists formed no part of the curriculum. More damningly, in the rare moments when Black artists and artworks are included in such histories or catalogs, they are typically examined in intellectual and political isolation with a monodisciplinary reliance on the tools of art history as configured in Western terms. Just as African American artists embrace formal and thematic innovation as an aesthetic and political necessity on the grounds that no one form, medium, or practice fits all, so too no one scholarly paradigm alone can do justice to multitudinous rather than monolithic Black art-making traditions.

Working to find a "way out of no way" through these analytical minefields, compounded with the ongoing problems in obtaining access to works and writings by Black artists, in these pages I adopt a methodology in which artists' works, statements, interviews, and critiques are front and center. In mapping this art historical tradition, I recognize that African American artists have found a tried and tested method of answering to widespread dismissal within the white dominant art world: they assume the roles not only of sculptors, painters, installation, and performance artists but also of archivists, curators, researchers, and critics. As creators working in the crucible of racist inequalities, they have succeeded both in forging an alternative visual language and in laying the foundations for a new theoretical framework and pioneering critical discourse. For these reasons, the philosophies, critical paradigms, and theoretical frameworks established by individual artists must be placed at the heart of any history of African

American art. So I endorse an all-inclusive framework in which Black voices are no longer discounted but instead provide the catalyst to and inspiration for research into individual artists and artworks. This artist-centric approach offers an indispensable way of interrogating the inaccuracies generated by white mainstream myopia and gaining insights into each individual's practices, poetics, and politics on their own terms.

African American art histories and art-making traditions are not forged in social, political, cultural, historical, or aesthetic vacuums, and so a multidisciplinary methodology is necessary to begin to excavate and examine the self-reflexive practices of Black U.S. artists. Black artists rely on experimental techniques and materials to develop a new visual lexicon through which to bear witness to generations of survival, struggle, and suffering against a backdrop of enslavement, segregation, and lynch law. For the purpose of investigating African American art-making traditions in relation not only to art historical debates but to wider political, cultural, historical, and social contexts, I adopt a Black studies methodology. A critical practice informed by the intellectual and political priorities within Black studies and endorsed by numerous seminal scholars working on the self-reflexive strategies within Black visual culture generates an integrated rather than a segregated interpretation, analysis, and understanding of African American art-making traditions.

Battleground, a book written in the era of Black Lives Matter, is inspired by George Lipsitz's pioneering definition of "engaged scholarship."[27] Lipsitz urges researchers to shoulder the responsibilities of academic activism by undertaking fully accountable and fully usable research suited to meeting the needs of a twenty-first-century struggle for civil, moral, political, and cultural rights for all Black people. At the heart of Lipsitz's methodology and central to the practice I endorse in this book is a commitment to answering his key question: "What is the role of scholarship in a world that seems to be falling apart?"[28] Heeding Lipsitz's request that researchers "produce scholarship useful for meeting human needs and serving the cause of social justice," I have written this book to help not only experienced researchers but also general audiences embarking on studies of African American art history and Black diasporic visual cultures for the first time.[29]

More particularly, this volume introduces students of all backgrounds and specialties to new materials while immersing them in alternative methodologies. I have taken careful note of Robin D. G. Kelley's insistence that students in particular "are not fighting for a 'supportive' educational environment, but a *liberated* one that not only promotes but models social and economic justice."[30] As the artists in this book endorse malleable and above all liberated practices with which to interpret, deal with, and ultimately survive the physical, psychological, and creative damage exerted by a racist U.S. society, so must we construct an equally adaptable and emancipatory critical language that opens up interpretative possibilities. For this reason, not only artists and activists but academics must tackle Lipsitz's question: "What is the work you want your work to do?"[31] Scholars of Black visual culture must also work with every tool available to trace African American art-making traditions that have been forged against a backdrop of white supremacy in a determination to do justice to individual artists' experimental strategies of subversion, dissidence, and resistance. It is to the artists themselves that we must turn. Over the generations, African American artists have created transformative, empowering, and visionary "lexicons of liberation" in which the right to all artistic and political freedoms defines their practices, philosophies, and art-making traditions.

"Nobody really knows that much about black art," declared painter Emma Amos. "Critics and observers of the art scene write about what they experience through their limited Western-European-centered eyes."[32] As a contemporary artist who was under no illusion regarding the damage that white racist myopia generates in U.S. art history, she exposes a disheartening state of affairs. She asks, "If women and black artists are just now appearing in a few art texts, if books are segregated according to race, sex, and the dominant style of the period, then what scholars at which universities are learned enough to teach the total picture?"[33] She observes, "when minority artists are trained along with white artists in Western European male-biased college and graduate art programs, their work still may look 'different,'" explaining, "it is because black artists know or sense that what art historians, curators, and critics want to write and talk about as ART is only a fragment of the picture."[34]

For Amos, white racist failures to "teach the total picture" by working solely with a "fragment" is at the root of the exclusion of Black art-making traditions from official U.S. art history. "From the minority artist's position on the OUTSIDE, participation in what we see as an ART WAGON TRAIN FORMED IN A CIRCLE to exclude us is silly at best and apartheid at worst," she concludes.[35] Here Amos vocalizes her opposition to the social, political, aesthetic, and historical damage committed against Black artists by white racist ignorance on the one hand and a white supremacist practice of "apartheid" on the other. As Amos was all too painfully aware, white prejudicial and persecutory practices of exclusion and discrimination create an invisible yet impenetrable barrier around artistic creativity for all Black artists. While she readily acknowledges the destructive and damaging influence exerted on Black artists by white ignorance and supremacy, however, Amos insists that the only real harm done is to whites themselves. "Most gatherings of artists, curators, dealers, and critics at museums, galleries, art societies, and socials are without us," she observes, demanding: "DON'T YOU MISS US WHEN WE'RE NOT THERE?"[36]

Radcliffe Bailey, an installation artist, collagist, and painter, concedes that art world "labels don't bother me."[37] He admits, however, "when I walk into a museum and see my name, I want to be put around others; I don't want to be the 'other.'" At the same time that Bailey signals his refusal to be "othered" and celebrates his own freedom to "change the subject," as endorsed by Emma Amos, he also protests against any and all racially prescriptive definitions of his practice. "I see myself as making work that is universal," he explains. "First and foremost people say, 'You're this, you're that,' but I'm human." For Bailey, the human condition—irrespective of racial, gender, economic or national identities—defines his visual language. "These names and categories change across time and I want to make work that's timeless," he insists. "I want to make work that deals with who I am as a person, politically or spiritually."[38] At the same time, however, he provides a searing indictment of the ways in which African American audiences as well as artists are denied access to mainstream institutional spaces. He is all too aware that people of all genders "don't necessarily go to museums" for the simple reason that they "don't see themselves in those [art] objects."[39] While he refuses

to set any limits to his lexicon, Bailey's determination to ensure that African American and Black diasporic histories, memories, and lives are not only represented but above all seen defines his storytelling techniques and experimental practices.

"I didn't choose the 'black experience' as the basis of my œuvre any more than I chose the very race I was born into," observes Whitfield Lovell, an artist whose installations come to life through his charcoal renderings of Black subjects of all genders, ages, and backgrounds.[40] Lovell is disappointed by how the fact of his birth inspires reductive interpretations of his practice. Warring against biologically essentialist constructions of racial difference, he observes, "it's true that the art is constantly viewed through the 'racial filter,'" admitting, "It is a cross to bear, as my grandmother used to say." For Lovell, the racist tokenism of the dominant art world is a source not only of creative conflict but of psychological trauma. As he explains, "I find myself always having to comment on being black in America, or being a black artist. People want to know—if it is 'of', 'for', 'by', and 'about' black folks—then how does it relate to them?" He concludes, "It's a burden." He refuses to lose heart, however, instead taking a vehement stand against any and all such prescriptive definitions. "I have to say that not everything revolves around whiteness." Lovell rejects the legitimacy of an art world that defines quality exclusively on white terms by observing, "I decided long ago that I was not going to expend my artistic energy trying to show white people that we are the same or as good as they are, or our art is as universal as theirs."[41]

Despite Lovell's status as one of the few artists whose works are now included in national collections—he himself is often the subject of major sole exhibitions and monographs—he can be numbered among untold numbers of African American artists who suffered from an early exposure to racism during his formal art education. As he powerfully summarizes, "Art school can be such a battleground."[42] "I had one well-known instructor who was certain that I was stupid and continually made racist and insulting comments in front of the class," he recalls.[43] Lovell continues, "rather than take my work seriously, he talked about the 'black world' and the 'white world' and about anthropology being the 'lies that little brown men tell to big white men,'" adding, "he said that because I was from a lower social and economic background than he was, he could not relate to my work."[44] Lovell, however, refused to be defeated by his instructor's prejudice: "I stood up to him for the first time and some other classmates spoke up as well."[45]

Lyle Ashton Harris, Lovell's contemporary, encountered a similar battleground. "I had a white professor tell me that he couldn't understand my work because he didn't grow up in a black community," Harris remembers.[46] As an artist who is equally committed to showcasing his defiance, Harris shares Lovell's determination to transform such abuse into revolutionary dissidence. "I found myself coming up against and transgressing those institutions and challenging them," he says.[47] Harris offers no sanitized account of his struggle, instead readily admitting to the physical and psychological toll of exposure to these inequalities. "I guess what I fear will be exposed is that I hurt," Harris admits. "It is not easy being one of a few 'people of color' in a program with those who know very little about your culture, and do not care to know more."[48]

"My work is just not going to sell," concedes Pat Ward Williams. "You would be surprised how many people wouldn't want a lynched man hanging over their sofa."[49] Ward Williams, a mixed-media photographer and installation artist, draws on her own experiences to investigate the barriers African American artists encounter in trying to sell hard-hitting works in which they examine painful and powerful historical, social, and political issues within a private art market geared solely toward white privileged arbiters of taste. "Mainstream galleries completely ignore me," she adds, confirming her similar exclusion within public institutional spaces.[50] As with the difficulties facing Lovell and Harris, Ward Williams encountered these discriminatory practices decades earlier. During her time at art school, she remembers, "I was asked why I photographed mostly black people."[51] "Even though most of the people I knew and loved were black and I would naturally want to photograph them," she recalls, "my instructors saw the exclusion of white people in my photography as aggressive."[52] For Ward Williams, the answer to racist misinterpretations of her work lies not only in a wholesale rejection of the claims made by her instructors but in drawing newfound strength from solidarity with other artists. "Even

though black artists were and in some instances continued to be a segregated community, we are not and have never been an isolated community," she declares, jubilantly observing that the "inspiration we need to keep working we get from each other."[53] Across her body of work, she exhibits a dual commitment to a liberated aesthetics and a liberationist politics.

"What we don't need is the kind of unitary vocalization—one right point of view, one hip generation, that white culture seems to demand of us, so that it doesn't have to think about us so much, so that we're not too *complicated*," states Lorraine O'Grady, a performance and video artist.[54] A cutting-edge theorist no less than a self-reflexive artist, O'Grady denounces the monolithic, separatist, introspective, and static interpretations of Black art-making traditions favored by a white art world, according to which all artists' strategies of formal and thematic signification are rendered null and void. "We do not look at or produce art with aesthetics and philosophy over here, and politics and economics over there," she insists.[55] She issues a call for an integrated rather than a segregated investigation into African American art histories. According to O'Grady's intellectual, aesthetic, and political vision, "as these false barriers fall, we find ourselves in a space where more and more the entrenched academic disciplines appear inadequate to deal with the experience of racially and imperially marginalized peoples."[56]

O'Grady exposes the woeful inadequacy of western academia when it comes to the lives and works of "racially and imperially marginalized peoples," specifically condemning scholarly traditions born out of hierarchical classification systems that work only to divide and rule. She also denounces the white art world's racist tokenism by naming and shaming "the lingering truth of the folk wisdom of the black art world, that there is only room for one or two blacks of either gender to be successful at a given time."[57] As she contends, Black artists have been invisibilized within a mainstream art world not only as a result of outright exclusion but also through nefarious strategies of seeming inclusion. According to these disrespectful practices, small numbers of Black artists are given superficial and limited attention without any meaningful institutional reform. Hidden in plain sight, these tactics of exhibiting a handful of artists have succeeded in co-opting Black art practices only to perpetuate further injustices. "Up until five years ago I could confidently say that the entry of black artists into the mainstream art world had been safely bracketed: it didn't actually affect any of the theorizing, marketing, or role modeling that was going on; it was safe," she says.[58] While she acknowledges that "some things have changed since the events of the '80s," she remains despondent.[59] She freely admits that "other than a few black artists who've slipped under the radar to earn a living from their art, and an even smaller number who have landed in isolated sections of certain textbooks, it's difficult to say with precision what those things are."[60] Here O'Grady bears witness to the ongoing stranglehold exerted on African American artists and their practices by white racist strategies of tokenism and exclusion. The devastating reality that it is only a "few black artists" who can "earn a living" and an "even smaller number" who have made it into "isolated sections of certain textbooks" make it impossible for O'Grady to "say with precision" what, if any, "things have changed." Ultimately, O'Grady has lost none of her skepticism when faced with inequalities that make it "[m]ore difficult still to be hopeful."[61]

"Everything I do is racialized, examined, and questioned because of who I am. Our society hasn't gotten to a point where I can do otherwise. I don't know if it ever will," insists Jefferson Pinder, a video and performance artist.[62] He sheds light on the "black artist's dilemma" by observing, "if I'm doing black boxes that are about minimalism, people are going to wonder how those black boxes are connected to me as a black artist. I can't run away from it. It's an ambush for sure."[63] For Pinder, the repeated ways in which even his abstract artworks are unable to escape racially reductive interpretations constitutes an artistic "ambush" that is reminiscent of his experiences in the military. "Joining the Marine Corps was probably ill-advised," he observes, "But I learned a lot about the human condition." "One of the things they told us was never to run away from an ambush," he explains. "I always wondered why because you want to get away from the fire?" He soon understands: "The truth is, if they ambush you from both sides, there's a 90 percent chance you're going to die. The only way you're going to break through and maybe survive the ambush is to get to the line." For Pinder, as it was in his army experience, so it is in his artistic practice: "That's what I'm struggling to do—to break through that line so that maybe my work can have a larger interpretation." And yet, he recognizes the insurmountable barriers he faces by acknowledging his perpetual invisibilization: "I'm not there." "Society has to change and not just me as a black artist," he emphasizes, urging, "people have to be ready to look at a black artist and not always bring race into the conversation."[64] "I don't think we're going to be there anytime soon," he despairs. "There are hundreds (if not thousands) of unspoken rules of engagement in this never ending fight [against] racism in the United States."[65] For Pinder, the racism he endures in the art world is no different from the discrimination he faces in mainstream society. As he explains it, "When race is the first term of identification when you're pulled over on the street or interviewing for a job, why would it be any different when your artwork is on view?"[66]

"A 'white' power elite with the capital resources to build institutions, codify definitions and create markets, sets the parameters. Their bias determines what is good and who is best," summarizes Kerry James Marshall.[67] He lends further weight to Pinder's searing indictment of the omnipresence of white privilege and its devastating consequences, observing, "For people of color, securing a place in the modern story of art is fraught with confusion and contradictions about what and who they should be—black artists, or artists who happen to be black."[68] According to Marshall, African American art-making traditions will only survive if the white dominance of the art world is not allowed to continue. He writes that "without independent, resource rich institutions, controlled by black people, no serious challenges to the status quo can be mounted, and talented creators have to pray for recognition by the more progressive segments of a white dominated 'mainstream.'"[69] In this context, he communicates his lifelong protest: "I refuse to surrender the capacity to shape future art histories to people I don't know, and who have not, historically, had the interests of black people at heart."[70] Working to right the wrongs not only of institutional racism but of a discriminatory art world, Marshall's renown as a painter of epic-scale works in which he includes hyper-real, monumental-sized

African American subjects confirms his success in the "challenge" to "gain an uncontestable place in the pantheon of art history without surrendering the desire to make pictures with black figures."[71] Visibility rather than invisibility, creation rather than destruction, and presence rather than absence is the order of the day for twenty-first-century African American artists working not only to survive an "ambush" but to "get to the line."

Mapping "Invisible Histories"

Battleground: African American Art, 1985–2015, is the last of a trilogy of volumes in which I map African American and African diasporic art-making traditions across the last two centuries. The first, *African American Visual Arts: From Slavery to the Present*, explores the quilts, ceramics, paintings, murals, drawings, and installations of twenty artists. Each of these artists created self-reflexively experimental bodies of work in a lifelong determination to fight for all artistic and political freedoms. For all these artists, and for the vast majority working across the African Atlantic diaspora, a determination to preserve their right to an imaginative inner life in the face of white racist forces of dehumanization and destruction defines their practice.

The second volume, *Stick to the Skin: African American and Black British Art 1965–2015*, is the first comparative history of more than fifty artists working in the United States and United Kingdom. I begin by mapping pre-twentieth-century transatlantic and diasporic practices, providing a detailed investigation into eighteenth- and nineteenth-century African American and Black British art-making traditions. I work not only with printed sources but with unpublished archives held in personal collections and individual artist interviews wherever possible, offering readers access to little-known as well as renowned artists by examining their lives and works in relation to their otherwise elided aesthetic, political, social, and cultural contexts. Faced with the stark reality that untold numbers of Black artists working prolifically and experimentally on both sides of the Atlantic continue to be subjected to wholesale dismissal, I rejected an encyclopedic framework in favor of an in-depth examination of individual artists and their eclectic practices. The volume provides readers not with "a fixed, verifiable, and fully mapped canon, a definitive history" or "an all-inclusive reference work" but "a scholarly resource, an intellectual and theoretical point of departure, and an educational handbook designed to inspire further research."[72]

Battleground is informed by the same intellectual and theoretical priorities as the first two books in the trilogy. Mapping contemporary Black art-making traditions as sites of conflict, contestation, and creativity, I explore the formal practices, thematic preoccupations, and experimental practices of twenty-three artists on their own terms. I take inspiration from Abigail DeVille's powerful examination of African American lives and artworks as constituting "invisible histories."[73] In these pages, in which I focus on artists working during the last thirty years, I aim to do justice to their ongoing struggle on multiple battlegrounds for aesthetic as well as political, social, cultural, and imaginative freedoms. As I concede of *Stick to the Skin*, so can it be said of *Battleground*: "that for every artist I include, thousands more have been excluded" and that "for every artist I discuss, future bodies of scholarship are waiting to be written."[74] On these grounds, it is imperative to recognize that the exclusion of artists in *Battleground* is due solely to the practical demands of space constraints.

In *Battleground* I trace the lives and works of lesser-known and relatively renowned, as well as widely celebrated, contemporary painters, sculptors, muralists, and performance, installation, digital, and video artists. In these pages, I map their art-making practices and philosophies not in isolation but as part of centuries-old experimental and eclectic African American art-making traditions. Faced with the practicalities of producing a book-length study, I rely on a case study approach to trace the lives and works of a small number of artists in depth, offering close readings of the formal and thematic concerns of individual artworks, many of which have not previously been discussed. Ultimately, *Battleground*—just like *African American Visual Arts* and *Stick to the Skin*—is "a call to arms for current and future researchers" to continue the work of excavation and investigation into the lives and works of major yet still marginalized artists.[75] While in recent decades a number of pioneering theorists, critics, and historians of African American and Black diasporic art have written groundbreaking works, there is still much work to be done.

The second chapter, "'We Have Power': Visibilizing the Invisible," addresses issues related to memory, history, and the body in the works of Emma Amos, Alison Saar, Radcliffe Bailey, and Willie Cole. A painter and printmaker who has been subjected to widespread critical dismissal, Amos has produced a radical and experimental body of work through which she examines the politics and poetics of color, composition, and representation as she grapples with oral memories and personal witnessing. Saar is a sculptor working with salvaged wood, tin, paint, metal, and historical as well as found objects. The rites of passage embedded in the Black woman's body and centuries-long histories of confinement and liberation are at the forefront of her radical practice. Bailey is a visual storyteller. As an installation artist and painter who works with a collage aesthetic and family photographs, he does justice to imagined and lived histories of the Middle Passage, U.S. chattel slavery, Civil War, and Reconstruction. Cole puts salvaged domestic objects at the heart of his process. He repurposes an array of items such as household irons and shoes to testify to Black female dignity in the face of white racist oppression.

Chapter 3, "Memorials to 'My Skin:' Ancestral Storytelling in Slavery and Freedom," focuses on Nellie Mae Rowe, Mary Lee Bendolph, Whitfield Lovell, and Beverly Buchanan. A prolific artist, Rowe bears witness in her drawings to generations of creativity in her family. Play and fantasy are the guiding principles in her surreal dreamscapes, in which she visualizes innocence narratives, histories, and memories. Across her drawings, she works with intensified color as an antidote to physical confinement and psychological trauma. For Bendolph, one of the many now-renowned quiltmakers from Gee's Bend, Alabama, recycled materials are a canvas. She works with discarded fabric to create work-clothes quilts in which she honors intergenerational family stories. Bendolph embraces a visual language of abstraction to commemorate the buildings and landscapes that define her rural upbringing in the U.S. South. Lovell likewise works with salvaged objects. He includes found domestic items in his installations to add visual drama to his monochrome portraits of unknown women, children, and men created from historical photographs. As a sculptor, Buchanan takes inspiration from self-made family habitations, Black and white, in the U.S. South to create her diminutive shacks that function as portraits of hidden histories and missing lives.

The fourth chapter, "'Sites of Resistance:' Representing, Remembering, and Reimagining Struggle," traces the experimental practices within the mixed-media photography and installation art of Clarissa Sligh, Pat Ward Williams, Lyle Ashton Harris, and Myra Greene. For Sligh, the photograph fails in isolation. She juxtaposes text and image in her photomontage constructions in order to rewrite, reimagine, and reenvision family relationships as sights and sites of violence and violation on the one hand, and artistry and agency on the other. In her installations, Ward Williams uses photography to revisit histories of slavery and lynch law, emphasizing that nineteenth-century Black radical strategies of self-emancipation are needed to combat white persecution in the twenty-first century. As an artist who lives between New York and Ghana, Harris visualizes the traumatizing truths of Black diasporic social, political, and economic realities in his mixed-media photographs. For Harris, the devastation wrought by the Middle Passage during the transatlantic slave trade is on a continuum with the destruction of Black populations produced by mass incarceration. Myra Greene is an artist who is singlehandedly reviving nineteenth-century photographic traditions in which Black subjects were dehumanized and grotesqued in order to critique, interrogate, challenge, defy, and resist the iconographical stranglehold exerted by these Eurocentric conventions. Across her powerful portraits, Myra Greene works with her own face and body to visualize back to a white racist lens.

Chapter 5, "'Prepared to Die:' Empowering Beauty and Heroicizing History," examines the self-reflexively experimental paintings, installations, and mixed-media works of Winfred Rembert, Kerry James Marshall, Debra

Priestly, and Mickalene Thomas. A storyteller, memorialist, historian, social commentator, and political protestor, Rembert sees art-making as nothing less than a battleground. In addition to warring against the social, political, and cultural discriminations enacted by white racist hate against Black people in the U.S. and across the African diaspora, he waged a battle against his own personal exposure to trauma and tragedy, creating uncensored paintings of provocative emotional force and unequivocal imaginative power. His stories of slavery, sharecropping, segregation, lynching, cotton picking, chain-gang labor, domestic rituals, and civil rights activism are etched into dyed leather. Marshall is a virtuosic painter for whom mastery is a politically and ideologically charged concept. On the one hand, mastery is related to his cultivation of artistic prowess on Western terms—in line with the conventions of the grand master tradition—whose practices he then recodifies and reappropriates for use within a Black artistic context. On the other, he plays on the concept of mastery in an interrogation of U.S. white enslaving power—that of the white enslavers or master class—in order to arrive at a new visual language through which he dramatizes hidden histories of Black heroism. Hyperreal Black subjects dominate his monumental paintings, in which he celebrates historical and contemporary African American lives, enslaved and free, as the appropriate subject matter of fine art. In her delicately rendered charcoal portraits of individuals which she juxtaposes with traumatizing iconographies of slavery, Priestly examines the Black fight for freedom as waged on the battlegrounds of family history, domestic labor, and military service. Black female sexuality defines Thomas's visual lexicon. She works with various media—from photography to rhinestones—to create empowered and empowering meditations on women's beauty.

Chapter 6, "'A Tool and Weapon:' Monuments of Mortality, Performances of Protest, and Labors of Liberation," discusses the salvaged sculptures, performance and installation art, and dramatic reenactments of Lorraine O'Grady, Nari Ward, Chakaia Booker, Leonardo Drew, Jefferson Pinder, and Dread Scott. Working across photography, performances, and video installations, O'Grady uses her own body to denounce white art-world discrimination and condemn the complicity of mainstream Black artists. A cerebral, philosophical, and experimental artist, she examines topics related to interracial sex and family relationships in her artworks. Over the decades, she has also produced groundbreaking theoretical works that have laid the foundation for alternative aesthetic reimaginings and radical philosophical constructions of the Black female nude. Ward, an artist born in Jamaica but now living in the United States, recycles distressed and damaged objects he finds on suburban streets. His salvaged materials bear witness to the disposability of African American and African diasporic lives in an ongoing era of disenfranchisement, impoverishment, and martyrdom. He elegizes Black deaths at the hands of not only white racist members of the public but also the police force. Rubber tires form the foundation of Booker's practice. She transforms industrial objects into abstract sculptures as meditations on civil rights, poverty, hunger, and psychological despair. Drew works on an epic scale, producing aggrandized mixed-media installations that are made out of wood, cotton, metal, natural materials, and found objects and that are the result of a physically arduous process honoring rural and urban Black laboring histories. A performance artist, Pinder subjects his own body to extremes of physical endurance and psychological suffering. In so doing, he points to the social, political, ideological, and cultural forces that confine Black men in the twenty-first century. Scott is an installation, video, and performance artist-activist turned historical reenactor. He relies on his practice as a powerful means to expose and oppose the centuries-long histories of slavery, segregation, and lynching as the sources of the ongoing persecution of Black people in twenty-first-century United States. He draws on the lessons and lives of the past to effect revolutionary change and usher in a new world order based on freedom and equality in the present.

Battleground concludes with an examination of past and present artists' historical and contemporary "lexicons of liberation," a term first theorized by Black British artist Donald Rodney, for memorializing and monumentalizing the atrocities and abuses suffered by lynched Black women. As social justice artist LaShawnda Crowe Storm states, "Lynching is not just a black history; it's an American history." She urges, "we must begin to address it as a nation, or we won't be able to move forward."[76]

Written as a handbook, a guide, and a stimulus to further research, *Battleground* provides readers with an extensive bibliography of primary and secondary works, as well as a list of resources for further research. The bibliography and resource list include information concerning museums, collections, websites, and galleries in addition to printed source materials, many of which are unfortunately either no longer in print or difficult to obtain, as they were produced in small print runs and for a limited period only. The book also reproduces forty-five works as color illustrations in recognition of the ongoing difficulties confronting researchers and wider audiences in gaining access to these artists' paintings, drawings, sculptures, and installations. For twenty-first-century Black artists, activists, and archivists, the fight to create art and develop their practice in the face of a U.S. mainstream culture that dehumanizes and invisibilizes Black lives and works is never ending. As Lovell insightfully summarizes of African American art-making traditions of the past, present, and future, there is an "urgency to survive and make a statement about the human experience based on the here and the now."[77] Working to defy all limits, O'Grady encapsulates the vision of all the artists in this book: "I suppose the politics in my art could be to remind us that we are *all* human."[78] For all artists, irrespective of race, nationhood, gender, sexuality or class, the ultimate "battleground" in art-making is the "right to make it."[79]

————

"My work is dark, but there is always an element of hopefulness," declares Alison Saar.[80] Saar created *Hither*, an inspirational tour de force, in 2008, now over a decade ago. The large-scale sculpture of the monumental-sized nude body of an unnamed woman comes to life from wood, copper, tar, and paint (figure 1). A declaration of freedom and powerful testament to her belief in "hopefulness" in the face of despair, her figure is a celebration of Black female physical and psychological, no less than emotional and imaginative, power. Saar decorates the surface of this unnamed Black woman's body with white butterflies. The butterflies adorn her hands, face, breasts, arms, vagina, legs, and feet and appear in multiple sizes and in varying stages of flight. Saar's decision to sculpt their wings as alternately closed and open shores up her visual meditation on the

empowering relationship between the Black woman's body and spiritual liberation. Ultimately, Saar's butterflies bear witness to her commitment to beauty as an antidote to pain. These winged creatures evoke the immortality of the spirit realm while expressing her refusal to shy away from the frailty of human mortality.

Nowhere is Saar's exploration of Black female vulnerability more in evidence in *Hither* than in her decision to sculpt her figure's skin from the disused ceiling tin she salvaged from segregated housing in northern inner cities. She generates poignant visual drama by contrasting the intricate delicacy of the butterflies' wings with the dented, broken apart, ruptured, and scratched surfaces of her figure's tin skin. The damaged surface of the ceiling tin is marked by repeated holes that are suggestive of bullet wounds. Here Saar provides confirmation of the very real battles for existence facing Black people living in a white racist United States, where police shootings are a daily reality. *Hither* is a powerful visual testament to her declaration that, "I love the ceiling tin because it's patterned, and it becomes at once decorative and also this sort of scarification."[81] For Saar, the issue of emotional as well as physical "scarification" comes powerfully to the foreground.

Saar chose to construct the Black woman's body in *Hither* not only from ceiling tin but also from wood and tar. These emotionally charged materials memorialize centuries-long practices of lynching, tarring, and feathering to testify to hidden histories of white supremacist rituals of tortuous killing. Ultimately, however, Saar's *Hither* is a visual testament to Jacob Lawrence's lifelong conviction, "struggle is a beautiful thing."[82] According to her emotionally charged visual lexicon, butterflies are symbols of creativity and freedom because of their miraculous transition from cocooned chrysalis to creatures soaring in flight. She complicates her seemingly exclusive focus on violence and victimization, transforming her figure's incontestable wounding into a spectacle of spiritual healing. No voiceless victim, Saar's figure raises her hands to her face to suggest she is speaking out and beckoning her audience to come "hither." For Saar, Black women survive not by escaping but by living with wounded realities. Here and elsewhere, she celebrates an individual's power, within their skin, to find a way to transform mind-body-and-soul-destroying suffering into a catalyst for self-transformation.

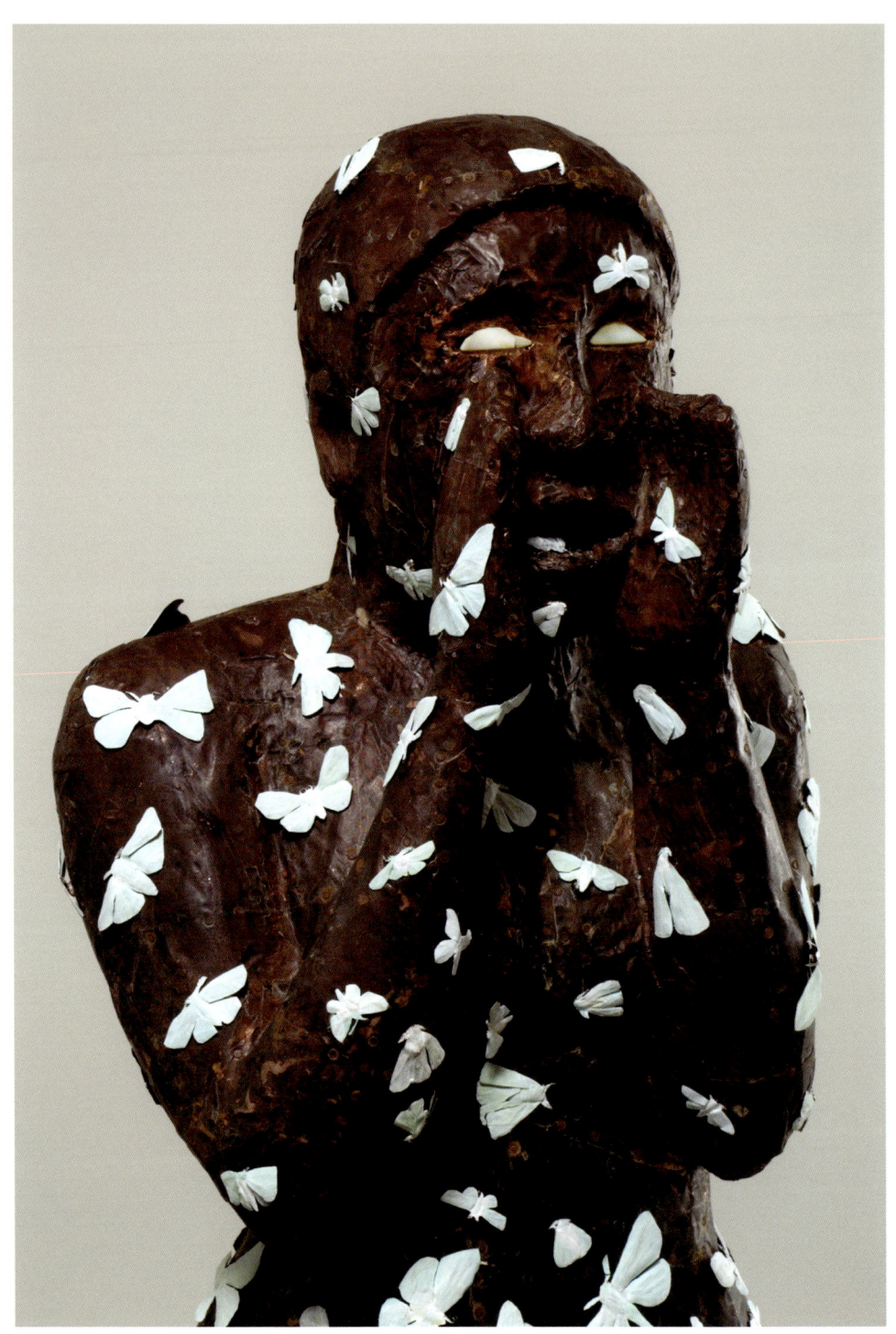

FIGURE 1 Alison Saar, *Hither*, 2008. Wood, copper, tar, paint (64 × 16 × 14 in.). Copyright Alison Saar. Courtesy of L. A. Louver, Venice, Calif.

Working to honor centuries of African American art-making traditions that signify, symbolize, and tell stories by any and every means necessary, Saar's practice is inspired by her belief that there are "constructive ways of facing tragic, painful experiences."[83] She believes that the "slaves survived all that pain—through creating, by making music, dance, poetry." We can also add art and art-making, as exemplified in Saar's own practice, to her revolutionary list as yet another transformative means of survival. Seeing herself as on a continuum with the struggle of her ancestors, she insists that creativity allows you to "somehow turn it around" when faced with the human tragedies of slavery, segregation, and lynch law over the generations. When "you're up against death," through a determination to make "music, dance, poetry" and art, "you make death this buffoon, this trickster." As she shares, "that's how you survive it, because otherwise you'd just lay down and die."[84] While Saar's wounded figure in *Hither* is indeed "up against death," she refuses to "lay down and die." The butterflies that rest on her skin transform the annihilating destruction of her scars into a source of art by functioning as symbols of the liberated and liberating power of a creative imagination.

Alison Saar's sculptures, drawings, and installation art are a powerful visual testament to Thornton Dial's lifelong rallying cry, "My art is evidence of my freedom."[85] She is not alone. All the artists in *Battleground* endorse creativity as a revolutionary means to corporeal, spiritual, and imaginative liberation. Working to transgress and transform artistic, cultural, political, racial, and national barriers, their art-making practices and philosophies are a powerful testament to her conviction: "I want to make sure that we can push beyond boundaries," she says. "It's the only way to survive."[86]

"WE HAVE POWER" VISIBILIZING THE INVISIBLE

▶▶ Emma Amos—Alison Saar—Radcliffe Bailey—Willie Cole

"Artists in Europe used Black models because either they were slaves or they were cheap." So Emma Amos, a painter, weaver, and collagist, summarized her findings following her extensive research into the damaging and dehumanizing practices that were dominant within white Western painterly traditions over the centuries.[1] Amos critiques the expendability and disposability of enslaved Black subjects for white artists and testifies to the traumatizing ways in which European artists whitewashed Black bodies out of existence by using racially diverse subjects interchangeably. "A good artist can transpose a figure from Black to white, just like that. Even if the body type is wrong," she explains.[2] Amos condemns all such uses and abuses of Black women's bodies as artistically, as well as politically, unacceptable and as morally heinous acts of atrocity. "In the work that I was doing when I did those few tentative Black nudes, I couldn't be comfortable with it. I did not want to see Black women with no clothes on. It means something else when a Black woman has no clothes on," she insists. "It means that you are for sale. It means that you are a whore. It means that you have 'got no class.' It means all these things, and I was not going to buy into it."[3]

For Amos, there is a political, historical, cultural, and ideological continuum between the buying and selling of Black women's bodies during enslavement and the buying and selling of Black women's bodies in the mainstream art world. Warring against white male tendencies to objectify and commodify Black women's bodies for financial gain and personal fame, she notes that "white artists, usually male, are free to draw on any image, white or black." She confronts the very real ways in which white male artists engage in deliberate acts of discrimination and dehumanization by declaring any "work of theirs that includes the dark body is seen as being more exciting, more provocative, more sexually charged, more noteworthy. Much of this art continues to be seen as groundbreaking in its expression of the will to cross boundaries." And yet when Black artists cross boundaries by engaging in equal acts of experimental play, she asserts, "we are often stopped at the border." Amos stages repeated declarations of independence across her mixed-media paintings. She testifies to her lifelong commitment to debating the "issue of freedom of expression in figurative imagery, particularly the symbolic use of dark bodies."[4]

Born into one of the many "upper-middle-class Black families" in Atlanta in the 1930s, Amos came of age against a backdrop not only of civil rights campaigns and Black Power activism but of segregation and Ku Klux Klan persecution.[5] Regarding one painful personal experience in particular, Amos recalls a "KKK march I witnessed on Stone Mountain as a kid." She describes it as "a very sad memory, because all of a sudden it came to me that my father, who I looked up to, who was a very important person in the black community, couldn't protect us in that situation." She was devastated to realize that "here he was nothing, had no power."[6]

For Amos, her early interaction with a white supremacist hate group remains on a continuum with her exposure to a white racist education in which Black lives were consistently denigrated and despised. "We ha[d] very little that we could hold onto that showed you were anybody," she explains. "There was nothing reproduced in books about African culture or what blacks had done."[7] As a result, she suffered from an internalized racism that caused deep psychological and emotional damage. "I would have to qualify as the prime case of a brainwashed person. You know, completely brainwashed. Not able to see anything beautiful in anything to do with being black," she states.[8] She further explains that she had no defenses against white racist hate in all its guises: "I swallowed all the other meannesses you know, all the other things— 'you're not as beautiful, your features are not as good, you have nothing to offer, you came from nothing and you are nothing.' . . . [I]t's the kind of insult that we live with every single day."[9] However, she soon discovered an antidote to her sense of powerlessness in the act of creating empowered paintings of Black women, children, and men engaged in acts of aesthetic, cultural, historical, and political liberation. Through her practice as an artist, she notes that she has "become aware of black people and that black is beautiful and there's nothing wrong with it; and that it's something to remark upon and to make a record of."[10] She is unrelenting regarding art making's capacity to right the wrongs of art history and racist society through a reenvisioning of vision itself. Among the seminal critics debating Amos's life and works are the following: Camille Billops, Gylbert Coker, Lisa Gail Collins, Lisa E. Farrington, Thalia Gouma-Peterson, bell hooks, Julia Hotton, Desiree Lewis, Lucy R. Lippard, Courtney J. Martin, Valerie J. Mercer, Albert Murray, Sharon F. Patton, Mira Schor, Mildred Thompson, Kimberly Wallace-Sanders.

"I was around 11 years old during the Watts Riots in LA," explains Alison Saar, a sculptor born in the 1950s.[11] She recalls, "Later I was living in New Orleans during the Rodney King beating and some kids were so into it," noting that they were "all 'burn baby burn'; and wearing berets."[12] "But I had already seen something like that and seen the aftermath and who was affected or even injured during the riot." A witness to the atrocities to which Black people were subjected in the aftermath, she argues that "after you see who really gets targeted you realize there must be a smarter way to deal with this." At the same time, she endorses the transformative power of activism and protest: "If there is something really outrageous you have to do something about it."[13] For Saar, like Amos, her personal exposure to racist inequalities has inspired her to endorse diverse forms of political and cultural dissidence. More particularly, she shares Amos's resistance against mainstream art practices, observing, "So much that Western culture idealizes I find so offensive—it's about men dominating women."[14]

Saar emphasizes her independence from Western art practices, stating that "a lot of my work is informed by African ideas."[15] She expresses a weariness for reductive accounts of African art-making traditions that distort or deny the multiplicity of their social, political, intellectual, and artistic contexts. "To assume that I know anything about African art would be the same thing as trying to study all of European art in one or two semesters—it would be equally ludicrous," she observes.[16] As an artist who repeatedly encountered the erasure of Black diasporic art and artists during her formal education, she embarked on her own research into multitudinous African art-making traditions as well as multilayered U.S.-based practices. "I got very interested in self-taught artists, specifically African American self-taught artists and seeking out traditions that carried over," she says.[17] Working to implode formal and thematic barriers, Saar creates heroic, symbolic, mythic, and monumental sculptures and prints of historical and contemporary Black figures, iconic and invisibilized. "My figures tend to be very dark, with strong Negroid features, simply because that's what [is] aesthetically pleasing to me," she summarizes, revealing an interest in the "symbolic use of dark bodies" that aligns her with Amos.[18] Saar insists on her right to a freedom of interpretation no less than of expression by confirming her reluctance to categorize her practice in racially reductive terms: "I consider all of those figures in the gallery Black, because they are my family," but she adds, "I'm not sure I'd call what I'm doing black art."[19] She refuses to limit her subject matter or set parameters on the interpretative possibilities of her work, stipulating, "it doesn't necessarily have to be about their struggle as African Americans."[20] Among the critics debating the artistic, philosophical, and political dimensions of her work are the following: Rebecca Altman, Abena P. A. Busia, Erin Clark, Jessica Dallow, Gabe Flores, Eleanor Heartney, bell hooks, Christine Y. Kim, Linda A. Kinnahan, Sidney Lawrence, Lucy R. Lippard, Julie L. McGee, Barbara C. Matilsky, Harryette Mullen, John David O'Brien, Fleur

Paysour, Mary Nooter Roberts, Elizabeth Shepherd, Franklin Simans, Judith Stoodley, Barbara Thompson, Mary Ann Unger, Judith Wilson.

"I'm an African American artist—proud of it! I'm someone who sits between generations," declares Radcliffe Bailey, a painter and installation artist.[21] Born in the 1960s in Bridgeton, New Jersey, and now living in Atlanta, Bailey not only "sits between generations" but works across north and south divides. At the heart of his collage aesthetic is a commitment to visualizing ancestral memory. Working with emotionally charged layering, Bailey combines oral testimony and family photographs with found objects, paint, and text to memorialize missing histories of creativity, resistance, labor, and migration. He shares Saar's commitment to working with Black diasporic art histories, explaining, "I enjoy combining African and African American cultural motifs with modern art concerns in order to send messages to multiple recipients."[22] "I think of my work as being able to create many stories," he explains.[23] No didactic artist, he works with multiple narratives to inspire multiple responses from audiences. Bailey celebrates an infinite number of interpretative possibilities by working to develop individual connections with his viewers so that "people can walk away with their own relationships" to his artworks.[24]

"I've learned I become comfortable with almost any mark I make," he says. "Tricky, but any mark I make, I have to live with it, I can live with it. It's just like being comfortable in your skin," he adds.[25] For Bailey, there is an inextricable connection between his art-making and his own body; he sees the creative difficulties of living with his practice as indivisible from the challenges of being comfortable in his own skin. "I try to erase everything I know about painting and sculpture when I go into the studio and I just try to *play*," he explains.[26] Warring against dominant traditions, he carves out a space of aesthetic and political freedom to "create art that genuinely articulates my message to African Americans and the art world."[27] Bailey also acknowledges his debt of gratitude to his forebears by disseminating his "message" to all audiences irrespective of race, class, gender, and sexuality. "I'm connected to a lot of older artists," he says. "And I understand their struggles and the fact that they didn't get a lot of opportunities that I'm able to get." He adds, "I have a lot of respect for them, so much so that I see myself as a vessel and things go through me."[28] In assuming the role of a vessel for Black diasporic artists' fight for aesthetic, political, and legal freedoms over the centuries, Bailey does not "take for granted their struggles. I don't see myself as a young cynical artist who rebels against, as much as I respect it."[29] He knows that this approach is not without its dangers. "Sometimes I feel I'm walking on a tightrope made of razors, where no matter which way I go, I'll get cut," he remarks. "I just try to take it in my stride."[30] Among the scholars coming to grips with Bailey's multifaceted symbolism and multilayered narratives can be counted the following: Anastasia Aukeman, René Paul Barilleaux, Manthia Diawara, Rebecca Dimling Cochran, Felicia Feaster, Lisa Fischman, Shannon Fitzgerald, Candace Jackson, Manuel Jordán, Lilly Lampe, David Moos, Michael Rooks, Hilarie M. Sheets, Edward S. Spriggs, Terrie Sultan, Carol Thompson, and Georgina Wells.

"The fact that I'm African American is obvious but in the art world I want to be seen as an artist first," declares Willie Cole, a sculptor and printmaker born in Newark, New Jersey, in the 1950s.[31] Working to come to grips with the spiritual rather than corporeal truths of human existence, he refuses to be imprisoned within biologically deterministic constructions of his identity or his practice. "My work is not about race. It's about spirit," he insists.[32] Cole's sense of urgency for his found object assemblages arises out of his determination to challenge the white supremacist stranglehold of the art world. And yet, his focus is on gaining admission not for himself but for his preferred audiences. As he explains, "My focus isn't to break through the color barrier or anything like that because in terms of the market place, I've already done that." Rather, he says, "I want to break back into the black world, to have my work seen by more black people." His commitment is to reaching African American and Black diasporic audiences who are systematically denied access to mainstream institutions due to entrenched economic, political, and cultural exclusion. "I'm trying to break back through the other side of the color barrier," he notes, explaining, "for years I've been exploring synchronism in cultural beliefs, mostly between West Africa and the Americas."[33] Like Amos, Saar, and Bailey, Cole takes inspiration from an array of formal and thematic art influences ranging across West Africa and the Americas to do justice to a "synchronism in cultural beliefs." At the same time, he refuses to lose sight of his own experiences and ancestral heritage: "I've attempted to filter these coincidences through events in my personal and family history."[34] All too aware of the overwhelming ways in which they have "no power," Willie Cole, Alison Saar, and Radcliffe Bailey share Emma Amos's revolutionary determination to resist by any and every means necessary.[35] Among the critics examining his works and practice are the following: Erin Belefski, Catherine Bernard, Jean Borgatti, Jacqueline Brody, Rebecca Dimling Cochran, Benjamin Genocchio, Elaine D. Gustafson, Leslie King-Hammond, David Moos, Matthew Guy Nichols, Marysol Nieves, Nancy Princenthal, Vivien Raynor, Mason Riddle, Sara Silvestro, Lowery Stokes Sims, Patterson Sims, Charles Wylie.

EMMA AMOS   *(Born in Atlanta, Georgia, 1937, died in Bedford, New Hampshire, 2020)*

An artist who has been physically discriminated against and psychologically persecuted by a white racist society as well as an exclusionary art world, Amos refused to surrender her power and instead pioneered a multilayered and multipurposed art "lexicon of liberation." She developed her art practice in defiance of an unequal playing field. As an artist coming of age in the 1950s and 1960s, Amos remembered, "when I became a figure painter, I was listening to all the rumbles of the civil rights movement." Her determination to do justice to these contexts of social dissidence and political protest directly informed her practice. As she emphasized, "there has got to be some way of doing this political concept and painting expressively."[36] The civil rights movement made her "more critical" about what she was doing: "I could not," she says, "in good conscience paint just lovely colored pictures with brushy strokes without having some of the pain and angst of the things that I wanted to say about women, black women in particular."[37] A defining feature of her practice, in which she works to visualize the pain and angst of Black female, no less than male, subjects, is her experimental interweaving of photographic fragments into her paintings. "Combining photographs with painting is making me use a sense that I don't even quite know how to articulate," she observes. "It's manipulating memory that's real, because it's painted, it's photographed."[38] Working with real and painted images of African American lives, Amos transforms white acts of destruction into Black arts of creation. Her works function as revisionist memorials in which she bears witness to myriad stories of activism and artistry.

Amos's commitment to manipulating memory across her mixed-media paintings is evidenced in her decision to integrate documentary photographs taken by her godfather, George Shivery, into her practice following his death. Celebrating his prowess as a "wonderful artist," she notes he was not only a photographer but "a painter and a sculptor."[39] According to bell hooks, Shivery journeyed across "Mississippi and Tennessee, photographing black people at play or working as cotton pickers or on tobacco farms" throughout the 1930s.[40] As hooks argues, the appeal of these documentary photographs for Amos lies in their exposure of U.S. chattel slavery's tragic aftermath: "Whereas Amos's photographs of her family . . . evoke a sweet sentimentality, the obvious poverty of the people in Shivery's photographs evokes the pathos associated with slavery."[41]

Amos's decision to include her godfather's visual testaments to survival in the face of mind-body-and-soul-destroying suffering provides emotional and political weight to her paintings. She refuses to lose sight of slavery's afterlife, or, more accurately, afterdeath; instead, she bears witness to the ongoing cycles of corporeal, emotional, psychological, and ideological violence visited on Black lives in a contemporary era. And yet Amos ultimately memorializes protest rather than pathos when confronted with these dehumanizing and

▶▶ "For me, a black woman artist, to walk into the studio is a political act."

destructive contexts. "Scarred and battered," to borrow a phrase from Langston Hughes, though they may be, her women, children, and men live on.

A hard-hitting case in point is Amos's reuse of Shivery's snapshots in her triptych *The Overseer*, which she painted in 1992 (figure 2). In this monumental painting comprising canvas, paint, and cloth as well as photographic fragments, she exposes how the legacies of slavery, segregation, and lynch law continue to have a devastating impact upon contemporary realities. Amos collages the first of these two sepia-colored photographs, which appears on the far left of the canvas, onto dense swathes of blue and white paint. These swirling textures of azure color in part reference the earth's surface, and all three parts of the paintings are accompanied by a blue-black horizon that appears in the backdrop. Their jagged layers also symbolize the tumultuous waves of the Middle Passage.

Shivery's unknown Black man assumes center stage as an unidentified and unidentifiable descendant of ancestors bought and sold in the transatlantic slave trade. No spectacle of subjugation, however, he stands with his hands on his hips in front of trees and wooden buildings that suggest a rural no-place in the U.S. South. Though he directly confronts the viewer, the grainy textures of the portrait's blurred reproduction work to invisibilize his facial expression. For Amos, Shivery's anonymous protagonist is both present and absent: he is revealed by the power of a Black photographer's lens at the same time he is concealed within the records of white official history.

Immediately to the right of the photograph of Shivery's unknown Black man, on the left-hand side of the work, Amos paints a figure she identifies as the overseer of the work's title and whom she describes in an interview as a figure that was the deliberate result of her determination to transform a Black male figure into a white male figure.[42] Here, she engages in an act of retributive justice. Amos, a Black woman painter, transforms a Black man into a white man in order to stage her protest against generations of white male artists who committed violations and violences against enslaved Black female models by whitewashing their bodies into European forms. In doing so, she makes some revealing changes. What was a declaration of Black male pride

in Shivery's subject, who has his hands on his hips, becomes for Amos' white man, who also adopts the same physical stance, a gesture of intimidation.

Amos's painstaking delineation of this white man's eyes, nose, and mouth results in a threatening gaze. He is no icon of invincible white supremacist domination, however. Amos inserts a pillar constructed from kente cloth into the painting, slicing this overseer's body in half. Yet more revealingly, she entombs his entire frame within thick slashes of red paint that assume the outline of a coffin.[43] Amos's white overseer is a representative of the living dead: he may be physically alive but he is morally and spiritually dead. While the pillar obliterates one half of his face, her decision to paint his remaining eyeless socket in meticulous detail not only compounds the cadaverous effect but also emphasizes his position as an unseeing witness to a white supremacist version of history.

Amos juxtaposes her own self-portrait in the second tableau of *The Overseer* with a detailed rendering of an unknown blond-haired white woman wrapped in the U.S. flag. Together yet apart, each woman looks away, belying an idealized vision of interracial unity and integration: the white woman's proprietorial ownership of the U.S. flag confirms her endorsement of a nationalism that is for whites only. In her final panel, Amos not only suspends another confederate flag above their heads but mirrors its iconography in a painted black cross shot through with strips of red color, naming and shaming white racist discriminatory practices. In a bold gesture, she cuts this last bloodied insignia of nationalism in half with yet another pillar made of kente cloth. Amos constructs her pillars out of kente cloth to insist that, white supremacist claims to the contrary, all the imitation classical columns that were a staple of the architecture of a white enslaver's house, as located on a labor camp in the U.S. South, were built by enslaved African diasporic laborers.[44] Kente is a non-Europeanized fabric she includes in her painting to appeal to Black audiences. As she explains: "kente cloth, for those who know it, resonates for black people."[45]

In the final panel and to the right of *The Overseer*, Amos includes another Shivery photograph showing a different stance for the unknown Black man. While his facial features are still difficult to decipher, his visibly

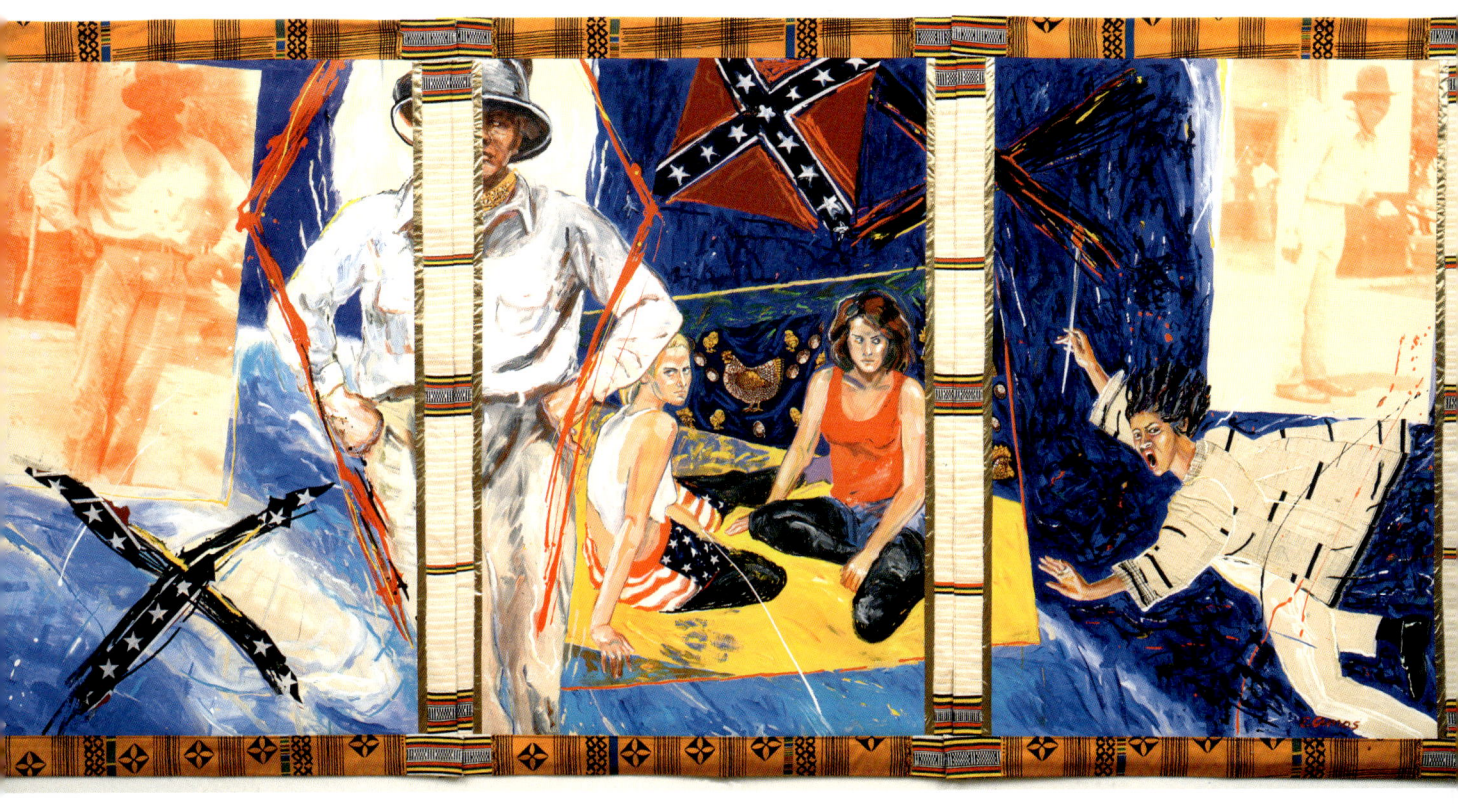

FIGURE 2. Emma Amos,
The Overseer, 1992. Triptych.
Acrylic on linen with African
fabric borders (84 × 168 in.).
Copyright Emma Amos.
Photo: Becket Logan.

broad smile compounds his vulnerability in this portrait. He visualizes back to, and fights against, white racist blackface minstrelsy caricatures by rejecting all persecutory demands that he perform servility to secure his survival. Blood-red spatterings mar the surface of this photograph to visibilize the very real threat of past, present, and future depredations against Black manhood by white supremacist forces.

In this final panel, Amos uses another self-portrait once again to suggest a dystopian view of race relations. This time, her body hurtles through a darkened sky while she directly confronts her audience with a traumatized expression, her mouth wide open, indicating screams of terror. She refuses to capitulate to despair, however, instead piecing together her dress from squares of cloth as she falls. This patchwork dress communicates untold genealogies of artistic dissidence by memorializing African American quilting traditions.

The falling Black woman motif is a defining feature of many of Amos's paintings. As she explains, it's "like a nightmare" through which she lays bare "an element of anguish." "I'm certainly not saying women artists are beginning to fall or artists are going to hell," she explains.[46] Rather, she relies on this trope to reject a status quo defined by injustice: "Our civilization, our way of life, our values, are up in the air."[47]

Equals, a painting Amos also produced in 1992, generates visual drama by bringing a self-portrait to life (figure 3). Once again, her traumatized facial expression holds the gaze of her audience while her body falls. This time she appears against a politically charged backdrop that consists solely of a hand-painted U.S. flag. Amos returns to Shivery's archive to visualize a national mythology that whitewashes Black lives out of U.S. history. She inserts a monochrome photograph showing family members of all ages living in Mississippi, dated 1937, and located in the top left corner of the U.S. flag.[48] Women, children, and men, appear in distant rather than close-up view, some standing and others seated beside mules and a plow and in front of a wooden frame house. Shivery's photograph renders visible centuries of back-breaking labor by situating the unidentified subjects next to a cotton field. Reflecting the dehumanizing impact of slavery and sharecropping systems, the mules are clearly delineated while the portraits of

his anonymous subjects are barely distinguishable. Amos replaces the stars signifying the U.S. states with Shivery's photograph as she testifies to her conviction that the nation's wealth has been built on the bodies of Black women, children, and men: enslaved, self-liberated, and free.

Equals was inspired by Amos's determination to shock white audiences out of their racist complacency and willful ignorance regarding U.S. slavery. Part history lesson, part oral memory, and part autobiographical story, *Equals* operates as a consciousness-raising weapon in Amos's protest arsenal. Amos replaces the white stars representing individual U.S. states with a photograph commemorating Black labor in order to bear witness to a traumatizing yet typically elided reality. Slavery has not only made contemporary white freedoms possible but guarantees the perpetuation of Black unfreedoms at every level—social, political, cultural, economic, and legal—of twenty-first-century U.S. society. For Amos, her commitment to offsetting the symbolic power of the white confederate stars by including multiple disembodied eyes functions as a fulfillment of her self-appointed role as a historian-witness-artist. No less forcefully, her reimagining of herself falling reveals to readers that the role of an artist testifying to racist injustices is not without its dangers. She reaches her hands out, braced for almost certain death: the U.S. flag is no parachute that will save her but rather the means to her inevitable destruction.

And yet Amos refuses to succumb to a dystopian vision in *Equals*. Instead, she inserts "Malcolm X photographs in the borders" of an "African fabric I found on 125th Street" in Harlem.[49] "They loved him in Africa," she notes; "they saw him as a beacon."[50] At the same time, the painting's border highlights the transformative role played by art making as a source of empowerment. Her falling body stands in counterpoint to icons, motifs, and symbols that celebrate the potentially transformative art of self-creation.

The title *Equals* functions as a satirical denunciation of a nation that trades in myths of freedom at the same time that inequalities are woven into the very fabric of the nation. Working with visceral imagery, she constructs the U.S. flag from layers of pink color, suggestive

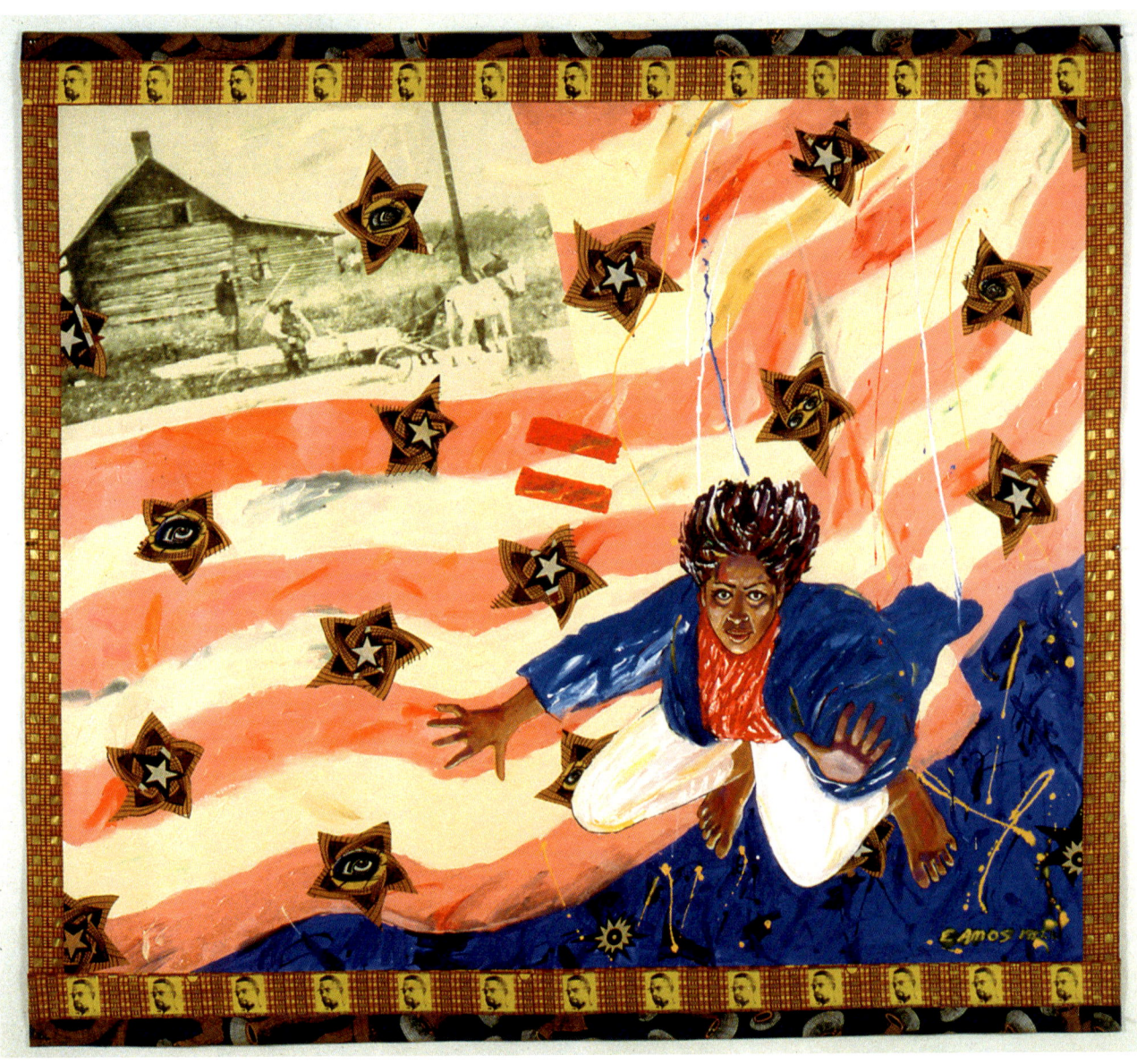

FIGURE 3. Emma Amos,
Equals, 1992. Acrylic on linen
with kente borders (76 × 82 in.).
Copyright Emma Amos.
Photo: Becket Logan.

of bleeding bodily organs and of no metaphorical but a very physical wounding. Here and elsewhere, she refuses to sanitize the realities of Black destruction that are the very real consequences of a white supremacist persecution.

In *Stars and Stripes*, a canvas Amos also painted in 1992, she revisits the iconography of the U.S. flag (figure 4). In this stripped-down minimal work, she again replaces the stars signifying the individual states with a Shivery photograph. This time, his snapshot provides no distant view of rural life but an intimate view of Black children of all ages as they stand on a street corner in an urban setting. The photograph celebrates their individualism; directly confronting the audience, each child assumes a different pose, displays a unique clothing style, and has a distinct facial expression. Through this group photograph, Amos challenges a stereotypical view that "blacks from the south are from some sort of plantation area."[51] Some white audiences "don't have a true picture of the metropolitan areas in the south," she insists. She pulls no punches regarding the abusive effects of white racist ignorance: "The assumption that you are unlearned, and that nobody in your family ever went anywhere or knew anything, was very painful."[52] Amos's reworking of Shivery's photograph serves as the radical antithesis of this white racist fiction that "you come from nothing, that you have no history" by memorializing missing family genealogies.[53]

Amos generates visual power in *Stars and Stripes* not only by representing the bars of the U.S. flag as violent gashes of bleeding red paint but also by inserting a white cross or letter *X* in the center of the painting. Amos does not concede to white enslaver power in *Stars and Stripes*. As an artist-memorialist-historian-witness, she defies white racist ignorance in all its forms by working with radical techniques and hard-hitting subject matters to interrogate aesthetic and political boundaries and arrive at a new "lexicon of liberation."

Amos' insertion of an "X" in *Stars and Stripes* reinforces the radicalism of her decision to collage photographs documenting Black lives onto U.S. flags. As she explains, "The 'X' means a lot of things to me, it means being censored, it means making a comment in my paintings and then crossing it out, before anybody else gets a chance to."[54] For Amos, the flag is no longer

a celebratory icon of nationalism for whites only but a memorial to Black sacrifice. She works with the X as a visual shorthand to diagnose a traumatizing reality: "hardly anyone gives a damn what I have to say as an artist or what black people have to say, period."[55] "I use [the X] in my paintings to erase, to cross out, to show that I am silenced," she adds.[56] And yet, while the X testifies to her erasure, it also provides Amos with a way to celebrate her own power in setting the interpretative parameters of her work. As she puts it, audiences "can't X the work out."[57] As an antidote to the widespread silencing she experiences, Amos develops an alternative visual language across *Stars and Stripes*, no less than across *Equals* and *The Overseer*, in which she does justice to missing histories, narratives, and memories of Black lives.

"Slave women were raped, or sexually coerced and degraded (in spite of having husbands and children) because it was the master's prerogative," Amos declares.[58] No more searing indictment of the physical and psychological depredations enacted against Black women's bodies during U.S. slavery, and as perpetuated by a white contemporary art world, can be found in Amos's work than in her painting *Measuring Measuring* (figure 5), a mixed-media canvas she created in 1995. Working with paint, collage, and cloth to present the traumatizing spectacle of a Black woman's mutilated nude body, she juxtaposes a headless, armless, and legless torso with a photograph of a nude Black woman—bound by measuring tape—with a classical sculpture of a white man to suggest the nefarious ways in which African diasporic women's bodies have been measured, classified, and categorized in inhumane and murderous Western iconographic traditions. According to a white racist dominant schema, they have been subjected to sexual violence at worst and grotesque caricature and stereotyping at best. Amos underscores the horror of the bloodied layerings of black and red paint that dominate the backdrop with a cloth border showing only silhouetted brown legs. There can be no mistaking their iconographic resonance with the silhouetted bodies represented on the 1788 diagram of the slave ship *Brooks*.[59] According to Amos, just as Black bodies were measured for the slave ship hold, so they continue to be measured according to white racist definitions of artistic representation. The canvas

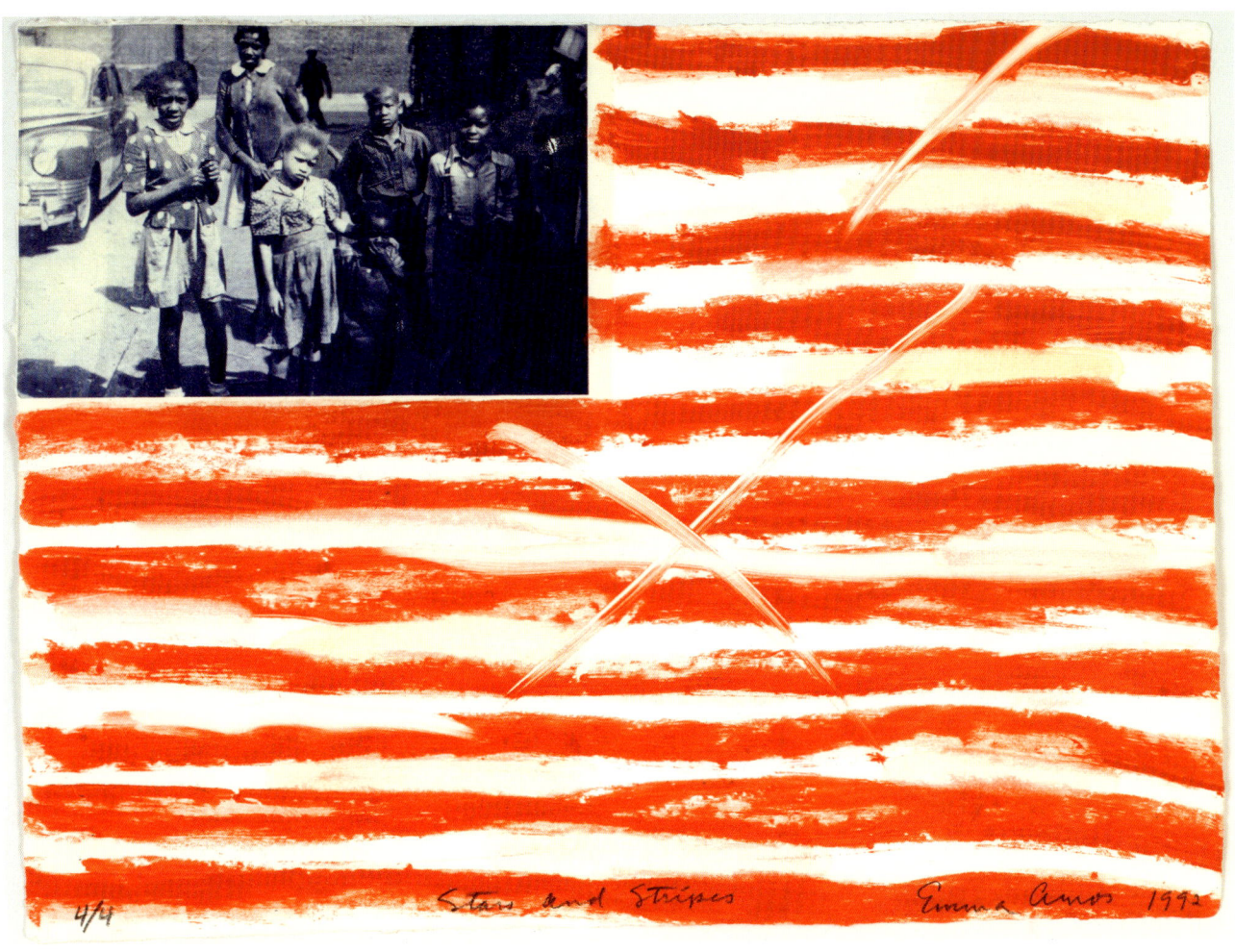

FIGURE 4. Emma Amos,
Stars and Stripes, 1992. Monoprint
(15 × 21 in.). Copyright Emma Amos.
Limited edition of four prints.
Photo: Becket Logan.

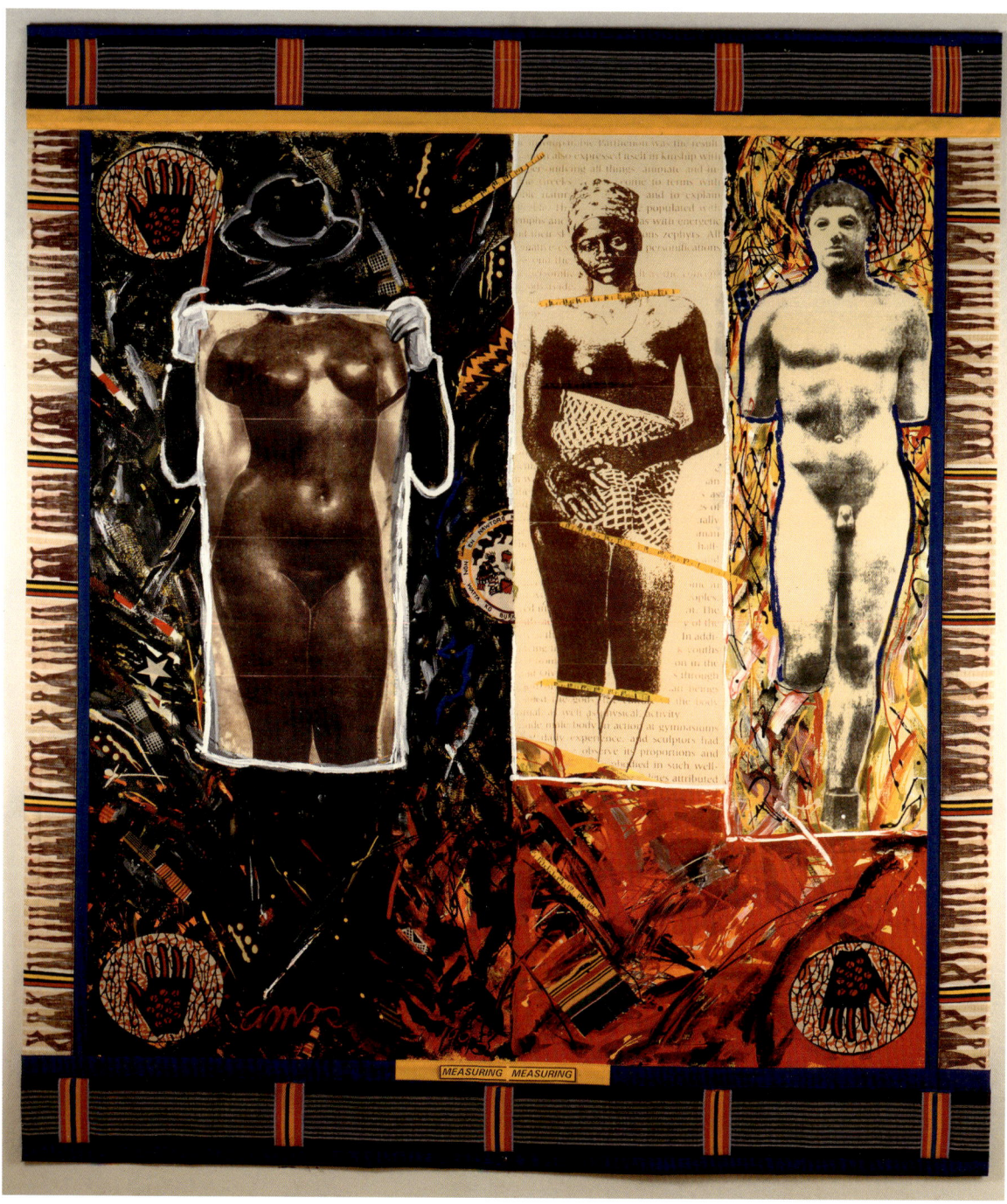

MEASURING MEASURING

FIGURE 5. Emma Amos, *Measuring Measuring*, 1995.
Acrylic on linen with kente borders (84 × 70 in.)
Copyright Emma Amos. Photo: Becket Logan.

offers yet another visual indictment of Amos's artistic convictions: "I had rejected the black female nude in particular. Their figures unclothed reminded me too painfully of the slave market, of black people as objects, of women as the powerless 'other.'" She bears witness,

"For me, a black woman artist, to walk into the studio is a political act."[60] Over the decades, Amos's experimental artistic practice has remained a hard-hitting testament to her self-reflexive development of radical and radicalizing language of liberation.

ALISON SAAR   *(Born in Los Angeles, California, 1956)*

"Lady Lazarus is a portrait of an ailing addict who despite her own suffering took it upon herself to care for other addicts, washing their clothes, preparing food, and late at night singing gospels in a deep rich voice," Alison Saar explains. "I saw this woman as a modern urban saint, a female counterpart to the biblical Lazarus, a beggar who though infected with the plague was able to cure others."[61] In *Lady Lazarus, 1988,* Saar represents a woman carrying a staff in one hand and begging for alms with the other. Standing erect, she is no servile figure. While her body is carved from wood, Saar inserts red tear-shaped jewels into the surface of her rough and lined skin to signal her inner emotional strength. Saar not only celebrates this unidentified woman's endurance of an unimaginable physical suffering but testifies to her transformation of her own pain into a spiritual beauty that heals others.

Saar's figure is distinctive for her shut eyes, suggesting her biblical, mythical, and prophet-like power to extrapolate existential truths from surface realities. Working to come to grips with "this blindness to being seen and not seeing," Saar explains that she denies viewers access to her protagonists' eyes in order to name and shame white racism while preserving Black autonomy.[62] "In part, it's about how all these women are always being perceived and viewed by the audience, and some of them take on freak-show sort of things, and again it's voyeuristic," she says.[63] Saar's aesthetic strategy rejects a white supremacist trade in Black women's bodies as objects for purchase, consumption, exoticization, and commodification. Rather, she foregrounds female agency and empowered subjectivity: "You're seeing her experience but you're not really understanding

her experience of being observed."[64] Working not to establish intimacy but to establish a "disconnection between the viewer and the subject," Saar indicts white racist ignorance in order to celebrate Black physical and psychological independence.[65]

In *Lady Lazarus*, Saar sheds light on the plight of an "ailing addict" who does not let her own exposure to unimaginable levels of human suffering prevent her from laboring for the survival of others. No invincible icon, this woman's body is pierced by jagged slivers of metal that have been inserted by Saar as a means of underscoring her unhealed and unhealable cuts. Here, she bears witness to her doomed struggle for survival. According to Saar's radical lexicon, while wounds have the capacity to heal, scars result only in more scarring. These lacerating metal strips that are cut into the woman's modern-day saint's body suggest an internal battle with addiction that has only one outcome: her self-destruction. "This is a piece about those who can comfort and heal others but cannot heal themselves," Saar explains.[66] Here and across her sculptures, prints, and installations, Black women's bodies testify to tragedy and trauma at the same time that they bear witness to artistry and agency. Saar rejects the threat of voicelessness confronting Black women artists by developing self-reflexive practices in which she establishes her artistic authority. Seeking to do justice to "a gut connection with a past that is completely downtrodden," she confronts long-standing histories of disenfranchisement and dispossession.[67]

As a sculptor, printer-maker, and installation artist who grew up in Los Angeles but who moved to Harlem in the 1990s, Saar was traumatized by the scale of

▶▶ "Women's Resistance to Pain"

suffering endured by the downtrodden people she encountered on New York City streets. "Unemployment was very high; a lot of people were homeless," she notes. "It was the first time in my life I was stepping over people to get through my front door."[68] Unable to unburden herself of this terrible reality and readily admitting, "I really felt the poverty 24/7," she sculpted unnamed protagonists through which she exposes the physical and psychological effects of the wholesale exploitation and abuse of Black people.[69] "My work is dark, but there is always an element of hopefulness," she states.[70] Working to bear witness to but not become consumed by her individual figures' personal exposure to loss, grief, and wounding, she takes heart from their resistance strategies. Saar's sculptures are not only artworks: they are memorials and monuments to the lives lived by her protagonists. According to her philosophy of art-making, inanimate materials are transformed through her radical practice to become agents and authorities, carrying and honoring the spirits, memories, experiences, and lived realities of individuals, in their own right. These run the gamut from self-adornment via beauty practices to self-defense via physical self-empowerment. At the same time that she holds nothing back regarding the corporeal dangers circumscribing Black lives, Saar's monumental and life-size sculptures also function as conduits to self-liberation. Through them, she explores the power of spiritual beliefs, imaginative release, and artistic expression as a means to defy human mortality. For Saar, no source material, form, or topic is off limits. "I want to make sure that we can push beyond boundaries," she maintains; innovation, she claims, is the "only way to survive."[71]

Creating sculptures and installations in which Black women as well as men live, laugh, love, and imagine at the same time that they grieve, suffer, and die, Saar urges. "A lot of the work is about women's resistance to pain and the ability to go beyond the pain."[72]

A searing indictment of the traumatizing ways in which Black women's bodies have served as sites of physical violence and sexual violation, Saar's *Strange Fruit* represents a contrast with the erect figure of an empowered-yet-vulnerable Black prophet as found in *Lady Lazarus*. In this sculpture she created over a decade later in 1995 and which was inspired by Billie Holiday's song of the same title, Saar's protagonist is suspended from a rope by her bound feet; her hanging body is not nude according to dominant Western art conventions but visibly naked as per white racist persecutory practices. In Saar's memorial, her unnamed Black protagonist demonstrates her "ability to go beyond the pain." When faced with the finality of death, she refuses to be defined by her victimization: she puts one hand on her breasts and the other in front of her vagina in gestures of self-protection.

In *Strange Fruit*, Saar works with emotively and politically charged salvaged materials, enveloping the figure's body in urban ceiling tin. As Saar explains regarding her process for creating this and other sculpted figures during this period, "They're all carved wooden figures underneath, but I like sort of putting a skin on them, and I love the ceiling tin because it's patterned, and it becomes at once decorative and also this sort of scarification."[73] The varying metallic hues of the ceiling tin produce rusted layers that testify to Black bodies as sites of erosion. At the same time, the "embellishment of the surface"[74]—via rectangular lines and swirling shapes—not only exposes a "sort of scarification" but visibilizes Black women's strategies of ornate self-adornment and beautification.[75] In *Strange Fruit*, the excessively red lips of Saar's hanging figure underscore her artistry. Against all odds, she uses her beauty as a source of imaginative survival in the face of fatal wounding. In so doing, she reinforces her multiple strategies of "women's resistance to pain" that may fail to protect the body but succeed in preserving the spirit.

For Saar, the history of the salvaged ceiling tin carries a powerful significance that is integral to her protest aesthetic. "A lot of the ceiling tin I found in New York," Saar notes, "was from the turn of the century."[76] "I'd realize this stuff was on ceilings since the Harlem Renaissance, and so it saw babies being born and people making love and people dying," she explains. She does not doubt that "it had this wisdom in that all my materials were new, but by putting this surface on it, in a way it's sort of like libations because it gives it a strength that the other materials sort of put on it."[77] For Saar, the ceiling tin carries a wisdom that derives not only from its historic imprint but from its spiritual energy as a found object carrying the memories of lived human experience. She clothes her figures in this material as a second skin to suggest that while her anonymous protagonists may endure unbearable physical traumas, they each bear within their own body a memory of genealogies of survival against all odds. The ceiling tin in this way functions not only as armor against white racist atrocities but as a portal between material and spiritual realities: "It also comes back to the idea of an exterior shell around this vessel, and the skin contains these spirits and holds all these things within them, too."[78] Saar expresses her commitment to doing justice to the invincibility of the human spirit in her repeated determination to award her lynched figure haunting power via her eyeless sockets. While this Black woman's hanging body is the "strange fruit" consumed by white supremacist hate, Saar denies her audiences access to the "windows to the soul" of her protagonist by retaining her imaginative inner life via her ownership of her spiritual freedom.

Saar describes a very different yet similarly unnamed female figure she sculpted in 1996 as follows: "*Sledgehammer Mamma* is about her physical strength and her spiritual strength and this power and how she has this sledgehammer attitude."[79] The antithesis of the mutilated bodies of *Lady Lazarus* and *Strange Fruit*, *Sledgehammer Mamma* iconically unifies corporeal, spiritual, emotional, and psychological strength. She stands erect with her hands balled into fists as she faces forward in a stance characterized by physical empowerment and readiness for militant combat. Like the figure in *Strange Fruit*, she is covered in a second skin of ceiling tin, although in this sculpture, the figure is not encased in a large sheet; rather, Saar inserts smaller patchwork pieces that she nails together, leaving the edges between the ceiling tin pieces visible on her nude body. In so doing, she inscribes into her very practice her determination to assume the role not only of an artist but of a preserver, memorialist, and resurrector: Saar sees herself as responsible for piecing together and breathing new life into missing Black lives. On the surface, the nails work in conjunction with the scarification of the ceiling tin to suggest the figure's vulnerability to bullets. On a deeper level, however, they testify to *Sledgehammer Mamma*'s mythic and superhuman capacity to withstand all forms of psychological and physical wounding: bullets may destroy her body but they will fail to penetrate her soul. Also, like the

figure in *Strange Fruit*, she is not only eyeless but almost entirely faceless. Saar sculpts her figure's features only minimally to convey the idea of her representative status for all women. *Sledgehammer Mamma* functions as a touchstone for all women resistors for whom a "sledgehammer attitude" is not only a state of mind but of being.

In a departure from her typical practice of representing the full figure, Saar renders *Sledgehammer Mamma*'s heroic status incontestable by replacing her feet with an actual hammerhead. "It's just about her physical strength and toughness," she explains.[80] The sculpture circulates as no fixed or static emblem of a reductive physicality, however. Saar's decision to rely on very literal devices to construct her female protagonist from a laboring tool speaks to a Black woman's "ability to forge" resistance strategies by celebrating her adeptness in "being malleable, being able to reform and re-create your environment."[81] For Saar, *Sledgehammer Mamma* is not only a builder, architect, and artist, but a visionary who sees beyond fixed realities and imagines alternative futures: "With her kind of physical strength she is forging her place in society."[82] Here and across all her works, Saar celebrates her heroic icon's success as a revolutionary defeating oppressive social structures.

Sledgehammer Mamma is only one sculpture in a series in which Saar challenges white racist stereotypes associating Black woman's bodies with tools of labor to assert power and reclaim moral, social, political, and cultural space. In *Clean Sweep*, which she produced in 1997, a year after *Sledgehammer Mamma*, she transforms her protagonist's body into a broom. As Saar explains of the rationale undergirding this sculpture: "the female figure that is this broom is very much subservient and domestic and having the same sort of power within the family but never being recognized as that power."[83] Saar transforms her figure's corporeal strength into moral, emotional, and political force. As she explains, the work is "about being the psychic strength within the family and being able to pull all these things back to the ground and clean up the mess." She invokes African diasporic belief systems to celebrate the importance of reclaiming psychic power over and above physical power: "I also like the idea—I don't know if it's true in African culture per se, but it's true in New Orleans and voodoo—about using the broom to clean out bad spirits." According to this belief, she argues, "by cleaning the house you're ridding yourself of that sort of thing, and you have the power to sweep all that stuff away, a sort of purification power."[84]

Saar's conviction regarding Black women's power to destroy bad spirits further informs her method for exhibiting *Clean Sweep*: "The way she's displayed—just sort of sitting in the corner of the room, she just leans in the corner of the room, like a broom would" is "about this power of sweeping and doing all these things, these grand gestures, which are never recognized." Warring against the ongoing ways in which Black women's bodies are "really just seen as this tool to do these things and never recognized as the power to mend and heal," Saar testifies to her commitment to a Black woman's self-appointed role as "being a healer." As with *Lady Lazarus*, the relationship between wounding and healing defines Saar's experimental practices as she celebrates her figures' "purification power." She, no less than her mythic figures, is dedicated to "cleaning up the mess" of white racist inequalities that maim, terrorize, and destroy Black lives.[85]

Saar continues her domestic theme, describing a series of mixed-media works in which she chose not to carve but to paint closeups of individual women's faces onto found objects. "They're just paintings that I did, and I give them names, a lot of them are either names of women that I've known or women who were domestics or names of friends of my grandmother's who were domestics or of that era when that was primarily what was available to them."[86] Working with salvaged skillets as heavily emotionally loaded domestic utensils that carry the imprint of Black women's labor, she does justice to missing histories, memories, and narratives in works such as *Skillet Black* (2001). No iconic sculpture, this work consists of five differently shaped frying pans on which she paints portraits of unmemorialized domestic laborers. Saar provocatively shackles these skillets together with interlocking chains, highlighting the indivisible relationship between Black women's labor and the history of chattel slavery. Saar uses blended textures and painterly layers as a way to make the faces of these anonymous laboring women alternately appear and disappear on the salvaged skillets. Her protagonists run the risk of disintegrating into the surfaces of these used frying pans as they are reduced to absent-presences and

present-absences. As Saar emphasizes, Black women undertook the denigrated and devalued domestic labor that was "available to them" at their peril. They risk the dissolution of their lives and the denial of their subjectivities by being reduced solely to the history of their labor.

While Saar celebrates Black women's undervalued histories in *Skillet Black*" by urging there is a "sort of glorification" in their memorialization of generations of Black female laborers she is in no doubt that that, "they're still invisible."[87] For Saar, the fight "to give them visibility" is a fight without end. While she acknowledges the threat of annihilation facing her protagonists, she does justice to the individualism of her subjects by confirming that her portraits either rely on "old-fashioned names" or "are island names since that was what a lot of the domestics in New York were, from the Caribbean, like Fiona, Hattie, Nesta, and Lyona."[88] "They're portraits of this invisible population within your household," she declares. Saar directs her ire toward discriminatory white family units by insisting that her Black women subjects are an "invisible population, and they're tools for the house, just viewed as being a utilitarian object; they're not really recognized as having a family or a life beyond that."[89] In contrast to the *Sledgehammer Mamma* figure, whose body is transformed into a weapon in a declaration of female independence, these unknown women circulate in portraits that succeed in exposing their utilitarian object status. And yet, her decision to reproduce Black female physiognomies on a salvaged object that resembles a "hand mirror" leaves her white audiences no choice but to "see your reflection." In *Skillet Black*, Saar celebrates African diasporic women's domestic labor by insisting that her white viewers not only own up to but face—in very literal ways—their responsibility and all-round complicity in disempowering systems that deny Black women's rights. With regard to her emotionally charged use of titling, she holds nothing back in naming and shaming white racist stereotyping strategies. Saar wrests control over denigrating language by artfully transforming "the term 'skillet black' or calling the skillet black" into a revisionist lexicon in which she honors and ends the harm to Black women's lives.[90] She seeks to inspire her white audiences to interrogate biologically essentialist categorizations of difference, encouraging them not to objectify her African diasporic subjects but to "see yourself reflected in the grease and grime."[91]

Saar also meditates on missing female laboring histories in *Blood/Sweat/Tears*, a 2005 monumental work she created from wood, copper, bronze paint, and tar (figure 6). Starkly contrasting to *Lady Lazarus*, *Strange Fruit*, *Sledgehammer Mamma*, and *Clean Sweep*, Saar's larger-than-life statue depicts a woman with her head in her hands, in sorrowful despair. The overwhelming emotional pain that grips her is poignantly conveyed by the enlarged black tear drops Saar carves into the surface of the statue's nude body. In an unflinching memorial to women's bodies as the locus of unrepresentable "blood sweat and tears," Saar forges her figure's frame from copper. As a result, the surface of her skin exhibits a luminous green patina, which suggests her body has been corroded and contaminated by her exposure not to the elements in the natural world but to those that make up the human experience. And yet, while tears bleed down her body as she experiences excruciating pain, she stands erect in a visual testament to her refusal to lie down and die.

Saar returns to ceiling tin to sculpt the plinth on which her anonymous figure stands. She opens up a space for hope in the face of despair by integrating this material into her sculpture that carries the imprint of missing Black histories. Here she suggests that her unidentified woman draws strength from ancestral memories of intergenerational survival. "Found metals and found pieces of wood have a history," she says. "They had another function at one time and that ghost is still hanging around."[92] Across her works, Saar reveals those hidden histories and silenced stories buried within abandoned artifacts. "Power," she adds, "is transferred to objects and as the 'experience' of an object accumulates, its power increases." According to her radical lexicon, sculptures such as *Blood/Sweat/Tears* function as power objects that obtain their social, political, and cultural force by translating elided experiences into revolutionary and radical subject matter for art.[93] More especially for Saar, this sculpture assumes heightened emotional and political urgency by visibilizing the "blood sweat tears" of the untold millions of people who were bought and sold during slavery and who

continue to be exposed to its mind-body-and-soul-destroying afterlife. On these grounds, the plinth may well represent an auction block, as Saar suggests that Black lives survive despite dominant histories of disfranchisement, torture, and persecution. Saar's inclusion of enlarged black tears recalls the blood-colored tear drops decorating *Lady Lazarus*'s body, suggesting a continuum across her bodies of work of women's survival in the face of wounding. The copper pieces of *Blood/Sweat/Tears*, nailed together and layered, suggest a body in the process of disintegration, yet still standing. Dramatically in the forefront is Saar's endorsement of the following refrain regarding Black women's lives: "I'll Bend But I Will Not Break."[94]

Saar readily admits the fundamental role played by racism in galvanizing her practice as an artist. "That's what got my blood boiling," she exclaims. "It's got me simmerin', so to speak."[95] According to Saar's practice, for Black artists the art of creation survives as a very real antidote to white persecutory acts of destruction. "There are constructive ways of facing tragic, painful experiences," she explains, insisting, "that's how the slaves survived all that pain—through creating, by making music, dance, poetry."[96] Just as formerly enslaved and self-liberated people of all genders turned to cultural production to make a way out of no way, the fight for survival in a contemporary era, she argues, is indebted to their resistance strategies. "You just somehow turn it around; you're up against death, then you make death this buffoon, this trickster," she says. "That's how you survive it, because otherwise you'd just lay down and die."[97] As she explains, artists engage in experimental play in order to keep on living and defy the mind-body-and-soul-destroying forces of white racist hate. Just as her unnamed protagonists refuse to "lay down and die," Saar herself refuses to surrender. She develops a wide range of formal and thematic tactics in her artistic arsenal in order to resist by any means necessary. In the wake of Barack Obama's election to the presidency in 2008 she articulated her heartfelt fear: "It's frightening for us because in the past when we have felt reason for hope, it has ended in disaster."[98] No more revealing an assessment of the current historical and political white supremacist context in 2022 can be found than in her declaration, "My kids think the civil rights struggle is over and it's not."[99]

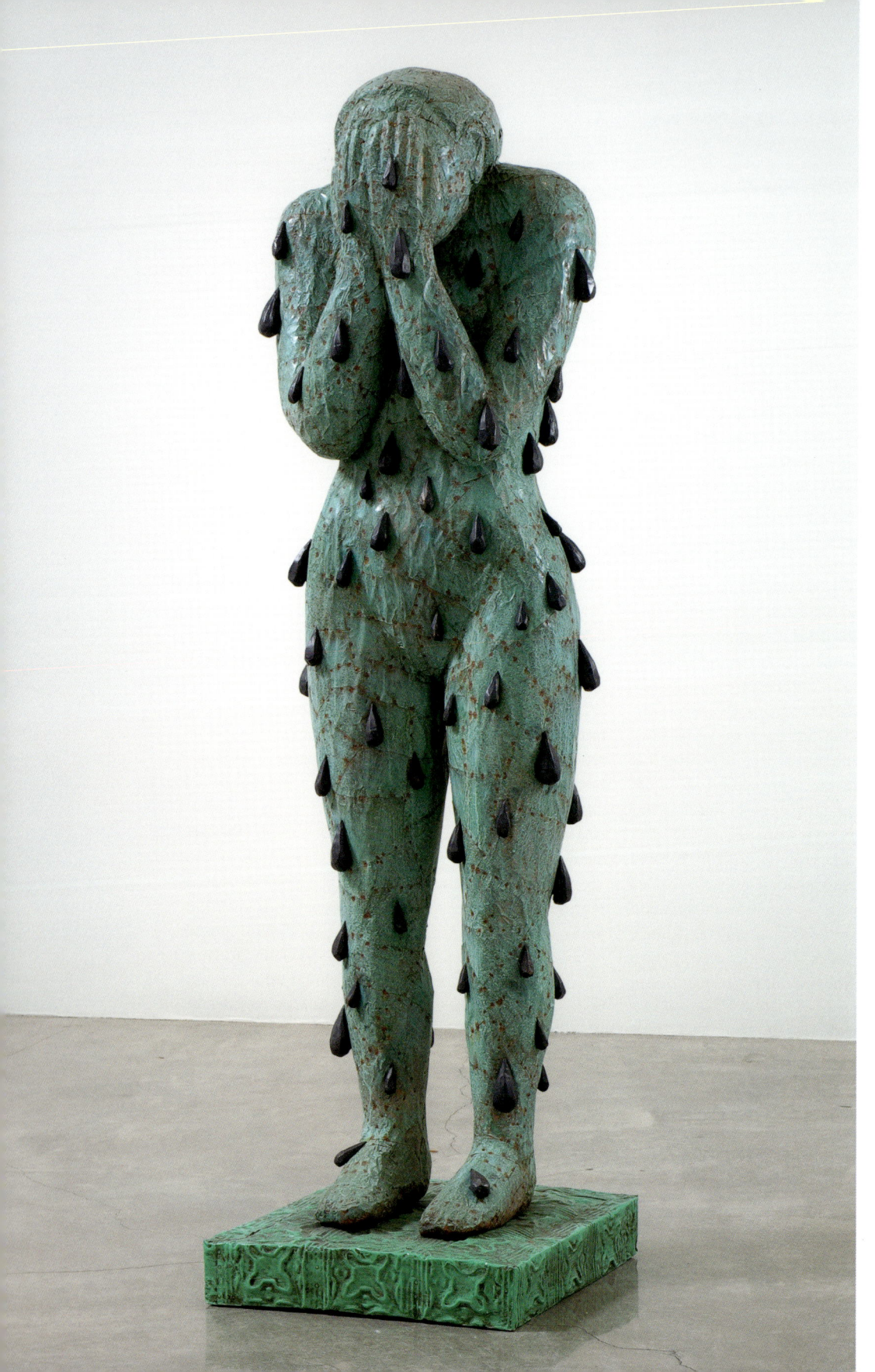

FIGURE 6. Alison Saar, *Blood/Sweat/Tears*, 2005, wood, copper, bronze, paint and tar (72 × 24 × 20 in.). Copyright Alison Saar. Courtesy of L. A. Louver, Venice, Calif.

RADCLIFFE BAILEY   *(Born in Bridgeton, New Jersey, 1968)*

"My art is about history and the mystery of history. Scientists, preachers, tricksters, they are my muses," Radcliffe Bailey declares. "I am also very much influenced by musicians, poets, inventers, and practitioners" and by "family members, by my mother, my children, and my grandparents."[100] As Saar honors invisibilized Black women's lives, so Bailey takes inspiration from the undocumented artistry of his family members: "My mother was quietly creating experiences for me to make art when I was a child. She was my first art teacher and is, today, my most important critic."[101] He adds that "while what [my grandparents] made may have had nothing to do with making art, I admired, for instance, how my grandmother made a quilt for someone who was sick and how my grandfather made bird houses."[102]

Bailey defines African American art traditions as encompassing practices that on the surface may seem to have nothing to do with making art, but that on deeper examination have everything to do with experimental creative practices. As a mixed-media painter and installation artist, he attests to his grandmother's formal influence over his layered constructions, which, he confirms, are "a reference to quilting, but also a reference to great composition and space."[103] "I often refer to my grandfather and the stories he told," he adds, explaining, "They came to me by watching my grandfather exist, by his actions and the way he lived his life."[104]

For Bailey, the art of storytelling as inextricably bound up with the act of living is at the heart of his practice. As he says, "I am not so much telling stories, but documenting every day."[105] No subject matter or source material is off-limits in his determination to grapple not only with the "mystery of history" but also with oral memories within his own family. Across his body of work, he translates his autobiographical experiences into visual narratives. "I believe that by making things that are very personal they become universal," Bailey insists.[106] Working in Atlanta, Bailey shares Amos's affirmation of the influence of the South on his

practice. "I am first and foremost an artist, a person of this world, and an artist of African descent who grew up in the South and has chosen to continue to live and work in the South," he explains.[107] And like Saar, he is also indebted to African diasporic influences. "By weaving together aesthetics derived from Congo, Nigeria, the Caribbean, and the African American roots culture," he explains, "I attempt to utilize these influences as starting points for visual and spiritual exploration."[108] His experimental processes are directly connected to his imaginative forays into the human psyche. "The correlations between my art and African ritual are at once direct and diverse," he says. "I take the basic tenets of many African and African-inspired belief systems and transmute them into a personal code."[109] As a self-reflexive artist, he develops his own visual symbolism in order to interrogate dominant modes of signification. "My work is like a never ending dream," he observes while describing the importance he places on psychic landscapes. Bailey defies straightforward explanations of his work by expressing his determination to create "very cryptic" paintings and installations.[110]

"The constant searching I engage in through the creating of my art acts as a meeting point that pulls scattered spirits back into a unified whole," Bailey declares.[111] He interprets his artworks as a "meeting point" for "scattered spirits" in order to reclaim, repair, re-create, and reimagine Black lives that have been all but broken apart and annihilated in a white racist imaginary. As he expresses it, "I'm interested in how people heal people."[112] He adds, "By using a symbolic language that invokes African and African American influences, I wish to show a continuum that leads directly to the modes of expression that we use to link ourselves to the past and steady our steps toward the future."[113] Over the decades, he has taken Western constructions of chronology to task by creating mixed-media works that defy temporal, national, emotional, and cultural divides in order to represent the present in the past and to imagine alternative and as yet unmapped futures.

▶▶ "The Discarded Ones That Nobody Talks About"

One figure that cuts across these various divides is the trickster. "The trickster comes up in references through so many different cultures," he observes. "I'm interested in those links. I try not to be very specific about one particular practice or one group of people, because I believe that I'm made up of a lot of different people and a lot of different practices." "I try to find the one common rhythm that runs through them and to put them together—that's been my method."[114] Bailey assumes the role not only of a historian, witness, storyteller, memorialist, and medium but of trickster: ever the satirist and shape shifter, he rejects interpretative fixity by engaging in improvisational play and creative dissidence.

"I'm sort of a family historian," Bailey notes. "Even though I don't know much of my family history, when I put one of the photos into an artwork it inevitably becomes a story."[115] *Returnal*, a multilayered painting he created in 2008, presents an intimate portrait of an anonymous Black man (figure 7). Bailey superimposes a photograph of the man, who directly confronts the viewer, onto a painted and collaged backdrop. Dense swathes of blue color dominate the canvas. Bailey positions a replica of a sailing ship, constructed from black glittered paper, onto the canvas to render the work's association with the Middle Passage incontestable. His work offers a powerful meditation on the difficulties and challenges experienced by a "family historian" with little access to "my family history" when it comes to representing, remembering, and reimagining the Middle Passage. An artist whose "maternal ancestors were from Sierra Leone and Guinea," Bailey recalls that in 2006, , "I went to Senegal and Dakar, specifically to Gorée Island, which is like a slave castle right off the coast of Dakar."[116] While he learned very little specific information about his ancestors, he remembers, "I did find where they may have departed from, and I went there."[117] He confronts his sense of loss by admitting that the gaps in his knowledge of his family members' lives meant that any artwork he created "was more like an understanding from the last point of touch."[118] In *Returnal*, Bailey assumes the role not of a family historian but of a family artist by providing a powerful memorial to the "last point of touch." Working not with historical facts but with emotional imaginaries, he creates layered visual stories in which he bears witness to African diasporic experiences of loss and mourning in the unimaginable and unspeakable tragedies of the Middle Passage.

No factual documentarian, Bailey works with paint, photographic images, and collaged objects not to record but to imagine the "last point of touch" and to do justice to his decision to assume the role of the "returnal." As the descendent who came back when his ancestors could not, the "returnal" bears witness to lost lives. "I don't read a lot, but I research, and I felt like I knew a lot of the history before I arrived" in Senegal and Dakar, he explains, observing, "What I got out of the experience was the beauty of the countryside and an understanding of current political struggles."[119]

Bailey's decision to incarcerate the Black protagonist of *Returnal* within a sheet of tarpaulin resembling the hull of a ship in which enslaved people were incarcerated comments on the socioeconomic, political, and cultural tragedies and injustices generated in the afterlife and afterdeath of transatlantic slavery. Black agency wills out, however. He collages pieces of red, white, yellow, and green cloth onto the tarpaulin's surface to suggest that the generations of African diasporic artistry that survive help to heal "scattered spirits."

The photograph of the anonymous man that Bailey collages onto the surface of *Returnal* is one of "400 photographs and tintypes from a family album" he was given by his grandmother "before she died."[120] "Some date from the time of the Civil War," he explains, adding that "some of my family members were in Northern cities, and they fought in the war."[121] This Black-created and Black-owned visual archive provides the catalyst for his experimental practices. In *Returnal* and his other works, he chooses to integrate portraits of unidentified figures only. "Even though they are family members, I pick the ones that are unknown," he states. "They are the discarded ones that nobody talks about."[122] Here and elsewhere he recovers lives that have been "discarded," dismissed, and denigrated to answer his own question, "how do you deal with these things?"[123] "It's hard to work with photographs of ancestors," he admits. "That's the reason why I don't necessarily put the images in my work at first, because it is so easy for the images to predict the painting."[124]   Bailey comes to terms with the psychological and political weight of these photographs

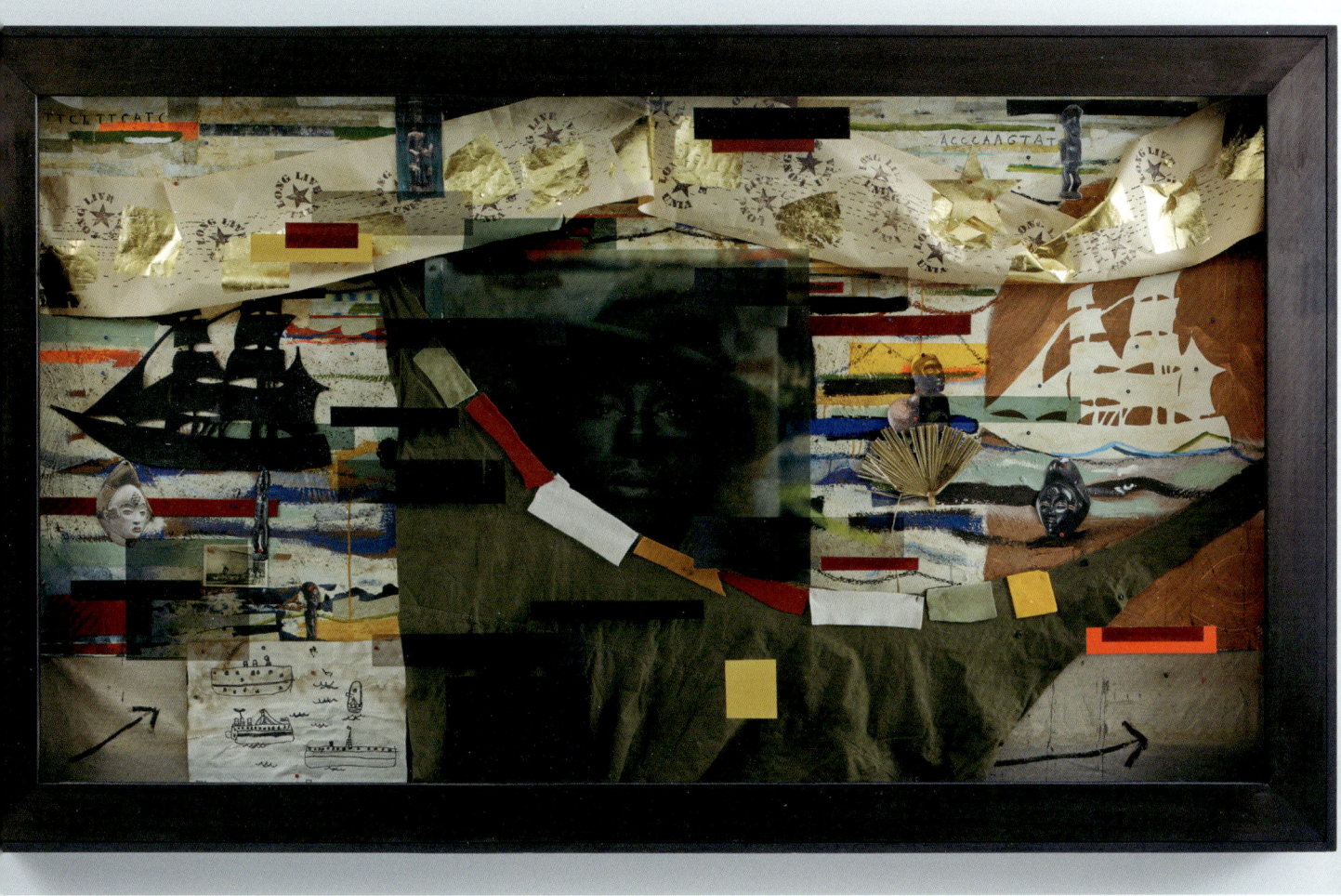

FIGURE 7. Radcliffe Bailey, *Returnal*,
2008. Mixed media (64½ × 96 × 5½ in.).
Inventory #RB08.001. Copyright Radcliffe
Bailey. Courtesy of the artist and
Jack Shainman Gallery, New York.

in mixed-media works such as *Returnal* by typically placing his visual archive at the center. This emotionally charged imagery catalyzes his exploration of issues related to racism and race relations, family, identity, belonging, nationhood, migration, spirituality, and creativity. Refusing didactic explanations of his work, he includes portraits from his family's private collection that function as protective talismans for his symbolism: "The photos are more like decoys to keep some things very private," he argues. "They serve as a visual element and hold the secrets of the paintings."[125]

For Bailey, his grandmother's archive was a lifeline in the face of the suffocating stranglehold of art school. "I pulled my inspiration from the first thing close to me, my grandma, rather than my art professors," he recalls. "That was to honor her, and my family."[126] Warring against exclusionary Western art conventions, he consciously inserts a Black presence into the U.S. mainstream art tradition. "I've always been concerned that art history—which we like to say is 'art mystery'—never really talks about all people, just a certain group of people. It was always limiting," he states.[127] As an "African-American artist, I want to know about my own family background in terms of religion, spirituality, DNA, all these things."[128] At the heart of his practice is his negotiation of history: "when I start to paint I think, 'Okay, I know art history but what about this other history that I don't know about that's so close to me?"[129] According to Bailey, African American artists must debunk the mythologies generated by "art mystery" to represent, reimagine, and re-create Black memories, histories, and narratives that have been invisibilized.

Working to do justice to this unknown "other history" that is "so close to me" while maintaining the "secret" of his mixed-media installations, Bailey constructed *Windward Coast* in 2009–11. A bold departure from his multilayered canvases, the work features a Black male figure's decapitated head on the crest of a wave and atop a sea of storm-tossed piano keys that deluge the gallery floor. The catalyst for this installation was the African mask collection Bailey saw at a Belgium museum.[130] He was shocked to encounter these masks not in isolation but alongside "body parts of different people," complete with "markings or scarification."[131] These artifacts not only reveal white racist systems of brutalization and violation but also Black artists' strategies of self-adornment and

beautification. For Bailey, they were Janus-faced objects testifying to suffering and survival. He was particularly moved by the "death mask" of an unidentified Black man, and it became the inspiration for *Windward Coast*.[132] "I got it and cast the bust," he explains. "The bust is about those lost at sea in the Middle Passage."[133] "In many ways, it is about being in a city, and the city as a sea; and it is about someone being lost at sea," he clarifies, speculating, "It could be yesterday or it could be tomorrow."[134] A memorial to the untold millions who died in the Middle Passage and who have been "lost at sea," he exposes his audiences to the enormity of these unimaginable "real tragic" losses by including only the barest trace of human life in the installation. Here he bears witness to centuries of African diasporic history by blurring the boundaries between past, present, and future tragedies.

Bailey's refusal to confine *Windward Coast* to the Middle Passage frees him up to do justice to contemporary devastations of and depredations against Black lives. Speculating on the potential interpretations of *Windward Coast*, he suggests, "It could be some of my first responses to all the recent devastations and the way the water washed up on land and moved things around in New Orleans and during the tsunamis."[135] Bailey began the work against the backdrop of Hurricane Katrina. In it, he interprets the socioeconomic injustices of a twenty-first-century human-made disaster as on a continuum with the untold, unimaged massacre of African diasporic peoples over a centuries long transatlantic slave trade.

While Bailey chose not to cast his own physiognomy for the protagonist's bust, he admits to an autobiographical component in this installation. "I don't want it to seem that it's a self-portrait," he insists. "However, in many ways, it *is* a self-portrait," one that "alludes to the condition of being overwhelmed."[136] Indeed, *Windward Coast* does powerful justice to Bailey's sense of "being overwhelmed" by past, present, and future tragedies. As he realized, the physical and psychological abuses and atrocities of the Middle Passage ultimately defy representation. For Bailey and many artists, the experiences of enslaved and emancipated women, children, and men across the African diaspora survive in the imagination as an artwork that cannot be made, a history that cannot be mapped, a memory that cannot be shared, and a narrative that cannot be told.

Searching for hope in the face of despair, Bailey generates drama in *Windward Coast* via his reliance, as Edward Spriggs notes, on using "keys that he collected from piano restorer shops" to represent ocean waves.[137] "Music," Bailey explains, "is a very important part of the work that I do." He adds that he is also interested in "how music has been connected to spirituality."[138] Offering a way out of no way and a source of spiritual survival in the face of physical destruction, he asks his audiences to "imagine all the pianos and all the different songs that each piano has played." "I am also interested in connecting the different time periods," he explains. "I am thinking about how music has been connected to spirituality."[139] While he concedes the mortality of the body, he celebrates the immortality of the spirit by memorializing "different songs" over "different time periods" to do justice to a multiplicity of individual lives. "I think about all the music that was probably played on those keys," he shares. "An ocean is something that divides people. Music is something that connects people."[140] According to Bailey's imagery, song has the power to erase differences, heal wounds, and confer spiritual salvation. Music not only "takes you somewhere else," he maintains, but it offers a way of "being at peace" with unknown and unknowable realities.[141] He turns a source of sorrow into an impetus for creativity, insisting, "I like stories about the past that don't necessarily have to have all the facts."[142]

Bailey's artwork relies on a self-reflexive lexicon to interrogate the divide between empirical facts and imagined fictions to extrapolate hidden histories of resistance. More especially, Bailey declares, "There is a part about fiction that is very real, and the escaping slave was very real, as were the thousands of other Middle Passage episodes."[143] Bailey relies on experimental techniques and a multilayered visual language to memorialize the missing memories not solely of the dead and dying—those who remain nameless, faceless, and bodiless in the persecutory records of white supremacist nations—but of the living and the plight of the "escaping slave." Gathering all forms of dissidence into his visual arsenal, he assumes the role of a self-appointed witness to individual and collective experiences across the African diaspora, explaining, "I am kind of making a visual history of a record of my past."[144]

In 2012, Bailey created *Vessel*, a mixed-media work consisting of tarpaulin, iron, a vintage model ship, three wicker baskets, and glass shards (figure 8). This work comes to life from the mottled and maimed textures of the tarpaulin sheet, which he suspends along the gallery wall. Bailey writes celestial coordinates in white chalk lettering onto its surface, suggesting the maritime course of ships in which enslaved people were incarcerated. Here he renders the symbolic and literary associations with the Middle Passage incontestable by mounting the diminutive replica of an actual sailing ship at the forefront of the work. He absents all trace of a human figure, photographic or sculptural, in favor of mapping a series of compass points next to a partially silhouetted outline of the African continent. In so doing, he unearths a missing maritime history in which the African continent played a central role. And yet, he refuses to confine himself to the tragedies of the slave trade as a site of unrepresentable human loss by drawing a blue arrow that points to a red circle with a white dot very close to the letter "N." Here he suggests the missing histories of self-liberated freedom fighters who successfully made it to freedom by following the North Star.

Bailey further dramatizes his narrative of Black liberation against the backdrop of transatlantic slavery by including the numbers "54th" and "55th," which refer to the renowned Massachusetts African American combat regiments that fought to great acclaim in the Civil War. The letters *U.S.* that appear here as well refer to the decorations on their belt buckles and serve as a categorical statement of Black belonging in U.S. narratives of nationhood, all white racist invisibilizations to the contrary. He hangs the diminutive ship above the three wicker baskets, in which he stores shards of white-colored glass that resemble cotton bolls in order to drive home the point that the history of enslaved labor in labor camps is a history of violence: if you touch these pieces your hands will bleed. "My work can be very direct," Bailey acknowledges. "I want to see myself as a vessel."[145] He not only creates an installation that operates as a conduit to missing genealogies of slavery and freedom but expresses his interpretation of the role of the artist as a spiritual, imaginary, and mythic "vessel." He visualizes the erased experiences of the untold millions who lived and died within the African diaspora

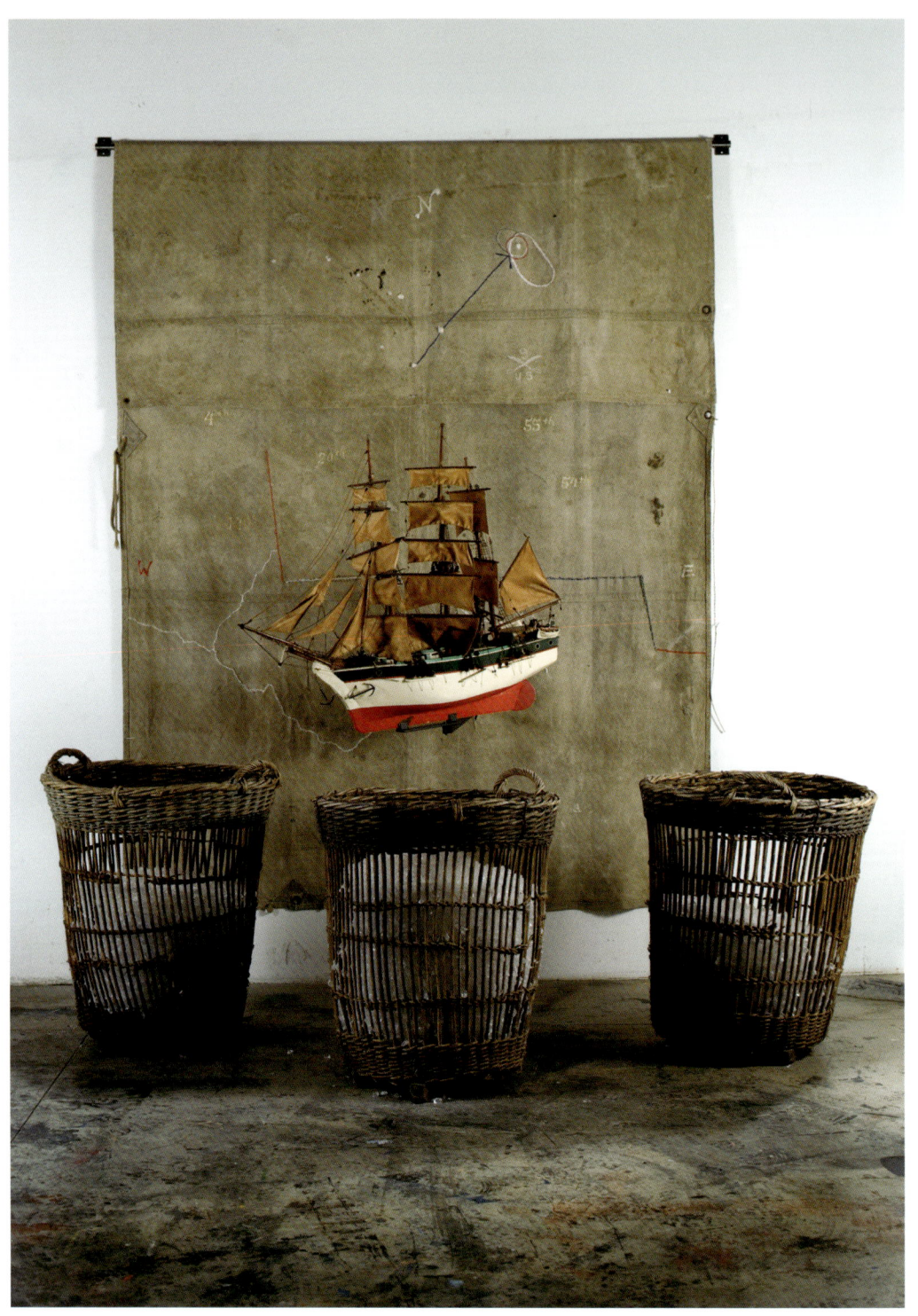

FIGURE 8. Radcliffe Bailey, *Vessel*, 2012. Tarp, iron, vintage model ship, wicker baskets, and glass (120 × 188 × 89 in.) (dimensions variable). Inventory #RB12.019. Copyright Radcliffe Bailey. Courtesy of the artist and Jack Shainman Gallery, New York.

to memorialize the "discarded ones that nobody talks about."[146]

In 2013, Bailey created *Congo*, an installation that like *Vessel* makes use of a tarpaulin backdrop (figure 9). This time he comes to terms with the Middle Passage as a site of mass burial by suspending three severed arms from a dark-blue colored sheet. To express the sense of horror he experienced on seeing "body parts of different people" in glass vitrines in the museum in Belgium, he names and shames early twentieth-century Belgian atrocities committed against Black women, children, and men living in what is now the Democratic Republic of the Congo. These mutilated limbs hang down while their hands gesture outward as if to suggest their refusal to succumb in an ongoing fight for survival against destruction. For Bailey, any denunciation of European inhumanity remains indivisible from an African diasporic fight for freedom.

The stars that decorate the tarpaulin sheet in *Congo* explicitly reference centuries of African American flights to freedom and testify to the resistance strategies of Bailey's own family: "My father's side of the family," he explains, "migrated north during the Underground Railroad. One family member kept letters and photos of the migration from South and North."[147] These acts of archiving within his own family encouraged Bailey to see the role of the artist as encompassing the roles of narrator, historian, and memorialist. "Making art is like writing a book. . . . Each work of art is a different page, but all are part of the same book."[148] Bailey's emphasis upon the extent to which individual images assume the weight of words reflects his commitment to storytelling. At the same time, he admits to feeling the enormity of the task by declaring, "I feel like I'm writing a book and I'm never going to be finished."[149] He is not writing just any book, but one book, a work in which his life story remains a defining source of inspiration: "Painting is like a page in my diary."[150] For Bailey, art-making is not a choice but a necessity that functions as his survival mechanism: "I don't paint to make paintings, but to get through life."[151]

Over the decades, Bailey categorically refuses to remain imprisoned either by "empirical facts" or material realities that can be evidenced. Rather, he draws on ancestral knowledge to argue that he is equipped with spiritual prowess. "Before I was born both of my great grandmothers were able to see me," he declares, revealing that his ancestors insisted he was born with a veil and was exalted as "someone who is born with a certain spiritual power."[152] This belief system derives from his multilayered identity: "In my family, on both sides, there is a mixture of Native American and African American heritages."[153]

Aiming not to divide but unite and not to destroy but create, Bailey defines his practice by his determination to defy all barriers: aesthetic, political, historical, emotional, political, and familial. "In my art, I try to restore some of the lost kinship between people," he declares, emphasizing, "I see painting as invocation and prayer. I see it as a medium where past and present are linked creatively, as ancestral alchemy and modern catharsis."[154] Bailey rejects all Western endorsements of linear time and celebrates his belief in the power of the ancestors and the past living in the present. "I truly believe that the ancestors dance in us daily," he says. "They dance and sing and whisper, hoping that we will hear them, and see them, and dream them back into relevant being."[155]

For Bailey, art making is a weapon in the daily fight for survival: "It is my belief that all true artists reach a point when their art becomes more than their art. When their art becomes a ritual of healing and transcendence."[156] It is a bulwark against wounding that he associates with the artist's "ability to transform the ordinary and pull the spiritual worth from subjects and objects often passed over by the general public."[157] His practice works to open up a space in which to imagine alternative existences. He maintains, "This pulling out forces the viewer to see something in a new way and travel to the emotional crossroads of their own being and point to their inner luminosity."[158] He inspires his audiences to "travel to the emotional crossroads" of their own existence rather than maintaining a safe distance as the only way in which to reinterpret sites of history and memory. "I tell your story, and it has many layers, it's fragmented," Bailey explains.[159] No simplifier or reductionist, he celebrates an eclectic practice and experimental form: "I pick fragments from here and here and here and mix them up and there's the gumbo."[160] Ultimately, Bailey denies himself or his audiences any safe ground, as his life and works offer no doubt of his resolution: "I like to get into trouble."[161]

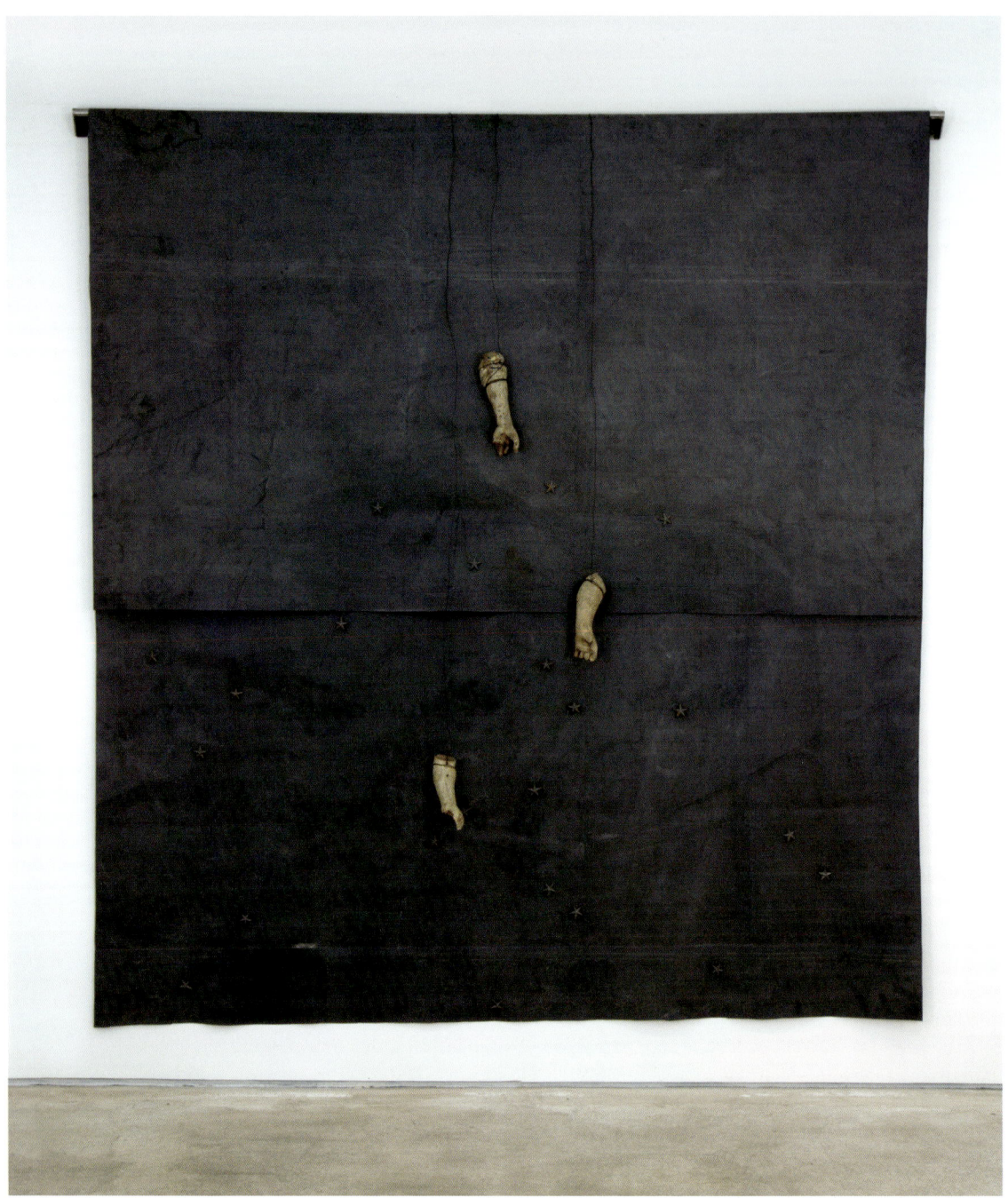

FIGURE 9. Radcliffe Bailey, *Congo*, 2013. Tarp, steel, wire, and wooden arms (111 × 101 × 8½ in.). Inventory #RB13.038. Copyright Radcliffe Bailey. Courtesy of the artist and Jack Shainman Gallery, New York.

WILLIE COLE   *(Born in Somerville, New Jersey, 1955)*

"Do 'cat faces' (wrinkles) in linen remind anybody other than me of women ironing in massa's house?" asks Emma Amos.[162] Over the decades, Willie Cole has proven Amos is not alone in her remembrance. He works with the domestic iron as a talisman, symbol, and vessel for memorializing the unmemorialized stories of enslaved, self-liberated, and free Black women's domestic labor. "I scorched a hot iron into the art world," he summarizes.[163] He explains that "iron imagery" motivates his commemoration of the struggles of women like his great-grandmother. "All her life she worked for this doctor and his family ironing their clothes," he explains.[164] For Cole, the iron is one among many mechanisms by which he memorializes political, social, cultural, and familial histories in his practice. He notes that "I made a conscious choice in 1989 to work with objects that had been handled—irons, doors, shoes, maps, hairdryers, windshield wipers." He uses them to tell the stories of women's struggles through the tools they handled.[165] More particularly, he declares, "I decided to become a scorcher to separate what the iron is and its function to see something else from it."[166] His assemblages come to life from broken and bruised irons of all ages, shapes, sizes, and designs as he visibilizes this object's invisibilized political, social, cultural, and historical contexts. A powerful conduit to Black women's labor, the iron is a defining feature of his visual lexicon in which he extrapolates the physical and psychological realities of Black women's lives. "I found myself in possession of a new vocabulary and new stories to tell based on the form and memory of objects," he states.[167]

"I was doing assemblage with a variety of other things," Cole explains when the "iron took over."[168] "I became so obsessed with steam irons that everything started to look like an iron."[169] Like Radcliffe Bailey, he creates art out of necessity rather than choice, stipulating his lack of free will: "the iron chose me."[170] "I brought the iron/mask into my studio and within two months,

started to use the iron exclusively in my work," he explains. "The rest," he says, "is mystery. I say mystery rather than history because for the next several months I was finding irons everywhere, so much that I felt they were finding me."[171] As Bailey reinterprets art history as "art mystery," so Cole defines his practice according to a mythically imagined rather than an empirically evidenced process. "I guess that experience could be called a kind of mythological union," he suggests.[172] For Cole, the iron is not only a catalyst to his experimental aesthetic processes but an artifact with hard-hitting emotional and political weight in a contemporary as well as a historical era. "My studio was in a sweatshop in a neighborhood called Ironbound," he explains of his location in Newark, New Jersey. He adds, "it wasn't until I begin making art with irons that I noticed a scorch on the floor."[173] For Cole, the "scorch" mark resonates as a symbol of destruction, via associations with burning, and as a testament to creation, via associations with hidden histories of labor. In Cole's radical lexicon, the salvaged iron bears witness to economic, social, political, and racial inequalities that endure across the nineteenth, twentieth, and twenty-first centuries.

Cole's reuse, reinterpretation, and re-creation of the iron as a found object is intimately tied up with generations of labor within his own family. "I had maybe 15 or 20 irons, because being the only male in the family through three generations, I was the guy who fixed everything," he explains.[174] The iron is no testament to Black women's work in isolation for Cole. He draws on a far longer family tradition than his assumption of the role of "fixer" by remembering that, "my uncle Freddy, my father's youngest brother, took me aside to show me a headstone" at "my paternal grandmother's funeral in North Carolina."[175] He was startled to discover that the "name on the headstone" of the "grave of my grandfather's brother" was "'Iron Cole.'"[176] While all the women in his family "[i]ncluding my great-grandmother, my grandmother, even my mother as a teenager" labored at

▶▶ **"A New Vocabulary and New Stories"**

domestic service, Cole immediately realized that, generations earlier, his paternal ancestor had gained such prowess as an ironworker and blacksmith as to have his profession integrated into his name and thereby rendered indivisible from his identity at his death.[177] His male ancestor's renown as a blacksmith signaled a major awakening for Cole by offering yet further ballast to his statement that the "iron came through my life."[178] As conduits for exploring the iron's multifarious importance in evidencing missing traditions of Black labor and artistry, his familial associations "became doors, you know, to explore the object."[179] No sanitizer of traumatizing realities, he confronts the disused iron's visceral power as an artifact carrying the memory of the pain of Black women and men, enslaved and free, within his own immediate family and beyond, as they labored under unimaginably inhumane conditions. "Something in my awareness opened up to the suffering of irons," he declares.[180] And yet he refuses to despair. Instead, he creates artworks in which he lays bare their—and his own—hidden histories of resistance. "Your iron becomes your weapon," Cole explains, insisting on the capacity of Black acts of artistry to transform a tool of oppression into a tool of liberation.[181]

Stowage, a work Cole created in 1997, is a visual meditation on the "idea of slave ships" (figure 10).[182] The monochrome print is an unequivocal testament to the suffering of humanity on an unimaginable scale during the Middle Passage as transmitted through the "suffering of irons." Cole explains that the work "is based on a diagram of a slave ship from a book I had in childhood, and since '85 I've been seeing it as an ironing board."[183] While he has never specified which diagram he used, the most likely source is the oft-reproduced woodcut of the *Brooks*, an eighteenth-century Liverpool slave ship.[184] Working with the dramatic tensions generated by the whorls in the wood, Cole highlights the transatlantic slave trade and the "sixty million and more," as the epigraph to Toni Morrison's *Beloved* attests, who died during the Middle Passage. As he explains, "I'm using a woodblock because wood represents water to me."[185] In a bold departure from centuries-old artistic interpretations of the *Brooks*, however, Cole replaces the faceless bodies of enslaved women and men crammed into the slave ship hold according to the nefarious policy of "tight packing" with a series of white dots inserted in a geometric formation.[186] Dispensing with any pretensions to realism, he rejects the idea of memorializing the lives of individuals on his ironing-board-turned-slave-ship. Rather, he works with a language of abstraction to cut to the heart of the magnitude of the transatlantic slave trade as an international atrocity committed by white U.S. enslavers that annihilated and devastated the lives of unknown and unidentifiable millions of people by tearing them from their homeland. "In that big slave-ship complex, those little squares of the ironing board are where the different tribes were housed. The ship would come up along the coast, gathering people," he explains.[187] For Cole, the little squares not only signify missing bodies but testify to the lost cultures, memories, beliefs, and families of different tribes.

Cole creates a space for Black agency, autonomy, and artistry by opting for a powerful strategy of visual resistance in *Stowage*. In so doing, he signals his opposition to the dehumanizing text accompanying the original eighteenth-century diagram of the *Brooks*, in which enslaved people were introduced to readers in a language of victimization, objectification, and subjugation. As per Cole's revisionist practice, he surrounds his slave ship with individually patterned iron plates. For Cole, these uniquely designed irons testify to his conviction that "any slave ship contained people from different nations or tribes."[188] These uniquely designed irons "represent different tribes," he explains: "The metaphor is Tribe of Silex, Tribe of G. E.—actually, it's the Fulani, Yoruba, West African tribes."[189] His decision to populate these waters not with the bloodthirsty sharks that typically followed slave ships in search of decaying and dying flesh but with visual surrogates for "the Fulani, Yoruba, West African tribes" celebrates African diasporic resistance strategies. No proof of subjugation but rather an empowering vindication of his commitment to the iron as weapon, the irons-turned-tribes stand guard around the slave ship. His iconography here and elsewhere is ambiguous; the iron not only "looks like a slave ship" but also "looks like a mask, whether it's African, Native American, Tibetan." He encourages his audiences to develop their own interpretations of his emotionally charged lexicon. "I think this print will definitely force the idea of these objects as symbols in a highly graphic form," he states, adding, "People will ponder. And the title—*Stowage*—will push them in a direction."[190]

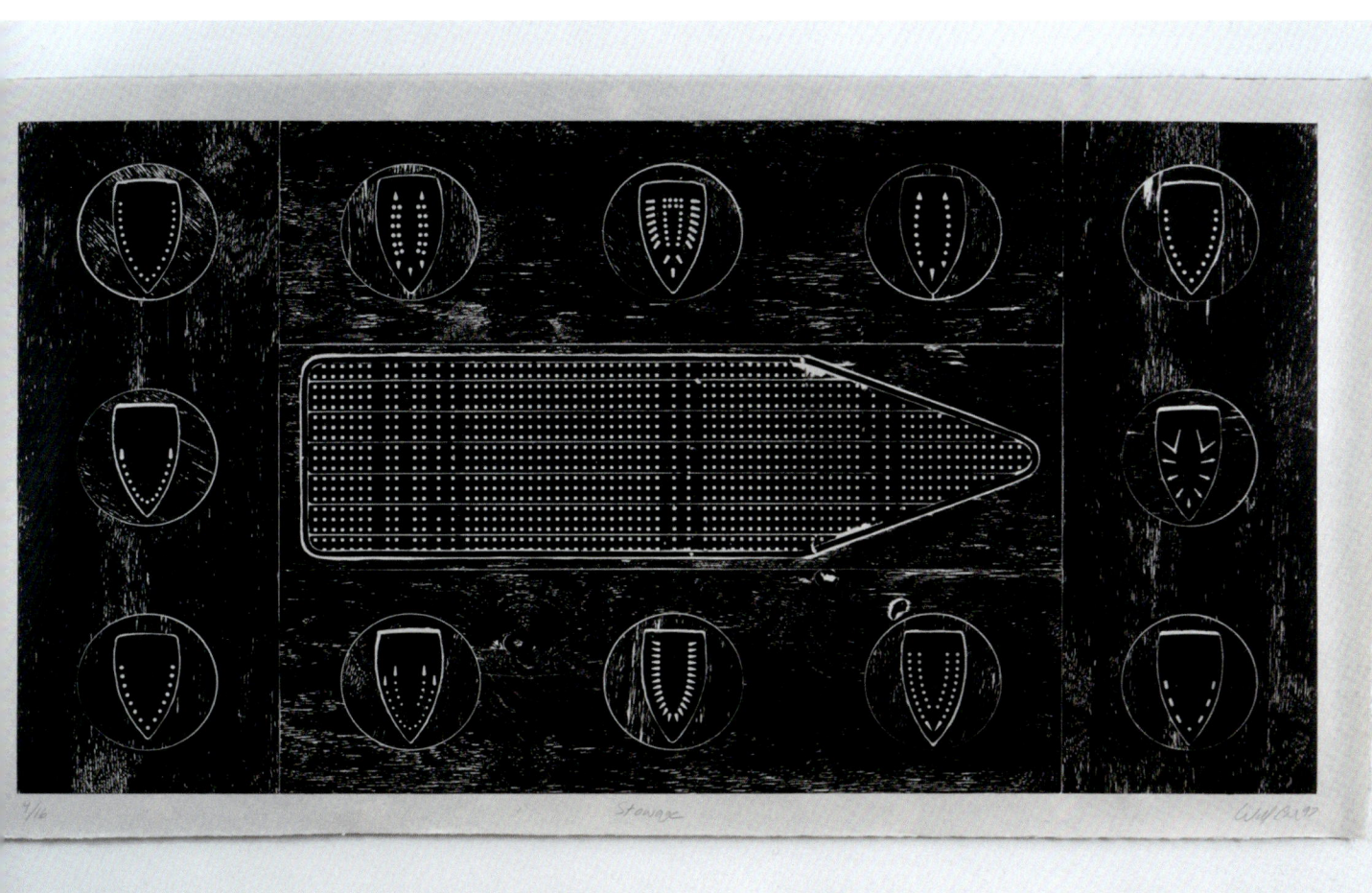

FIGURE 10. Willie Cole, *Stowage*,
1997. Woodblock on kozo-shi paper
(56 × 104 in.). Limited edition of
sixteen prints. Image courtesy of
Alexander and Bonin, New York.

Nowhere is Cole's use of the iron as a catalyst to a "new vocabulary and new stories" more in evidence than in his 1999 mixed-media triptych *Man Spirit Mask* (figure 11).[191] His definition of the iron not only as a tool of labor and an icon of racist oppression but as a weapon wielding spiritual, mythic, and religious power dramatically emerges to the forefront of the work. As he explains, his inspiration for creating *Man Spirit Mask* emerged from the following experience: "I saw a discarded iron. It had been run over by a car or a truck and left right in the middle of the highway. The magic occurred the moment I looked at it and noticed that it was looking at me too. I picked it up. It was no longer an iron but an African mask."[192] That the iron's triangular shape "will always make a face" inspires his symbolic and cultural transformation of this artifact into an African mask.[193] He takes an object that has been all but destroyed and transforms it into a source of creative energy, celebrating the power of the artistic imagination in a two-way process: as he expresses it, "it was looking at me too."[194] At the same time, he admits that his reinterpretation of African masks emerges from his own strategies of self-conscious mythologization and imaginative reinvention: "the closest I've been to Africa is Harlem."[195]

In contrast to *Stowage*, *Man Spirit Mask* dispenses with a language of abstraction. Instead, Cole features his own monochrome self-portrait in the first of the three prints. As the mythic embodiment of the man of his work's title, he confronts the viewer with an emotionally charged facial expression. The series of brown-colored markings he hand-painted onto his forehead, cheeks, nose, and mouth suggests ritual scarification or decorative adornment patterns and visibilizes his otherwise invisibilized belonging to one of many "different tribes."[196] In the second print of the triptych, he dispenses with the photographic medium and reproduces the silhouetted plate of an iron on a white backdrop. The blurred edges of the iron's brown-colored outline bleed onto the white background, suggesting the outline has been seared or even scorched onto the paper. If this is the case, the sepia tone may well be the result of the burning of the paper. Cole's decision to ensure that the pattern of this iron's plate is identical to the markings he inserts over his own face is revealing. The markings suggest that spiritual belief systems—ancestral origins and tribal affiliations—define his person. The final print, a mask, includes no photographic portrait of the artist and no silhouetted print of an iron. Rather, Cole creates a painterly rendering of an abstract mask, which very likely takes its contours from a compressed or even partially destroyed iron that he sets against a black backdrop. This artifact may no longer be viable for practical use but has new life as a catalyst to Black artistry. In contrast to Cole's revealing emotional expression in the first photographic portrait, this African mask foregrounds physical and psychological concealment in favor of focusing upon underexamined traditions of mask-making and performance.

"SAVANNAH. DOT. FANNIE MAE. QUEEN. ANNA MAE." So read the women's names that Cole inserts in capitalized lettering beneath *Five Beauties Rising* (2012), a series of monochrome prints representing individually patterned and vertically positioned ironing boards (figure 12). According to Mason Riddle, while the name of Lucy, Cole's great-great-great-great grandmother who had experienced enslavement, is not represented here, Cole was inspired to include some of the names of his "ancestors who worked as domestic servants over the decades" and of individuals who emerged from his "research of southerners, servants and slaves, or mammy names from cinema."[197] Cole translates his visual symbolism for his viewers, noting that "when the ironing board is horizontal, it represents a ship. When it's vertical, it's a shield."[198] Whereas in *Stowage* the ironing board clearly represents a slave ship, in *Five Beauties Rising* it inarguably resembles a shield. Cole subjected these already dilapidated and abandoned ironing boards that he had salvaged in no pristine condition to further physical abuse: "We destroyed them. We surfed them down hills and hammered them out. We even ran trucks over them to give them a little more history."[199] He also damaged them by using overheated irons to burn scorch marks into their surfaces. This scorching, he explains, symbolizes "'fleshmarking,' or branding practices." He sought to inscribe the tortuous enslaving histories not only into his subject matter but into his very process itself. Ultimately, however, these objects defeated his intention to "flatten them out."[200] Cole concluded, "I think of them as ironing board warriors."[201]

In *Five Beauties Rising*, Cole's "ironing board warriors" reject their exposure to suffering and instead

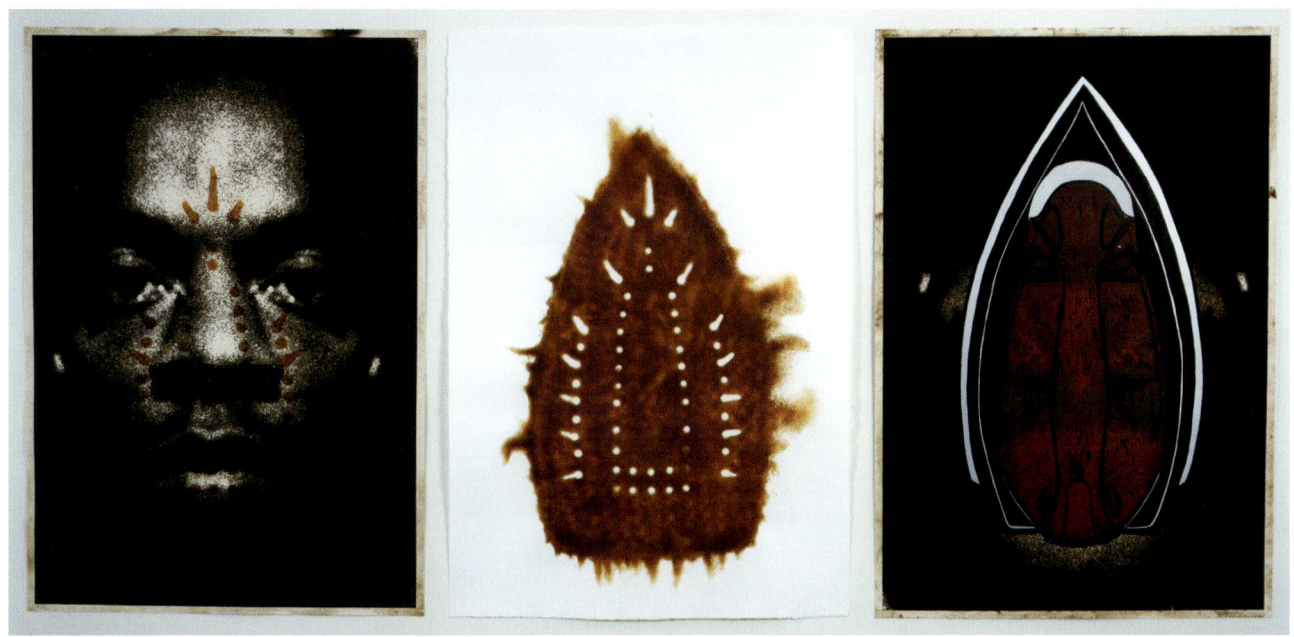

FIGURE 11. Willie Cole, *Man Spirit Mask*, 1999. Triptych. Photo etching; silkscreen; photo etching with woodcut (39⅛ × 79½ in.). Limited edition of forty prints. Photo: Orcutt and Van Der Putten. Image courtesy of Alexander and Bonin, New York.

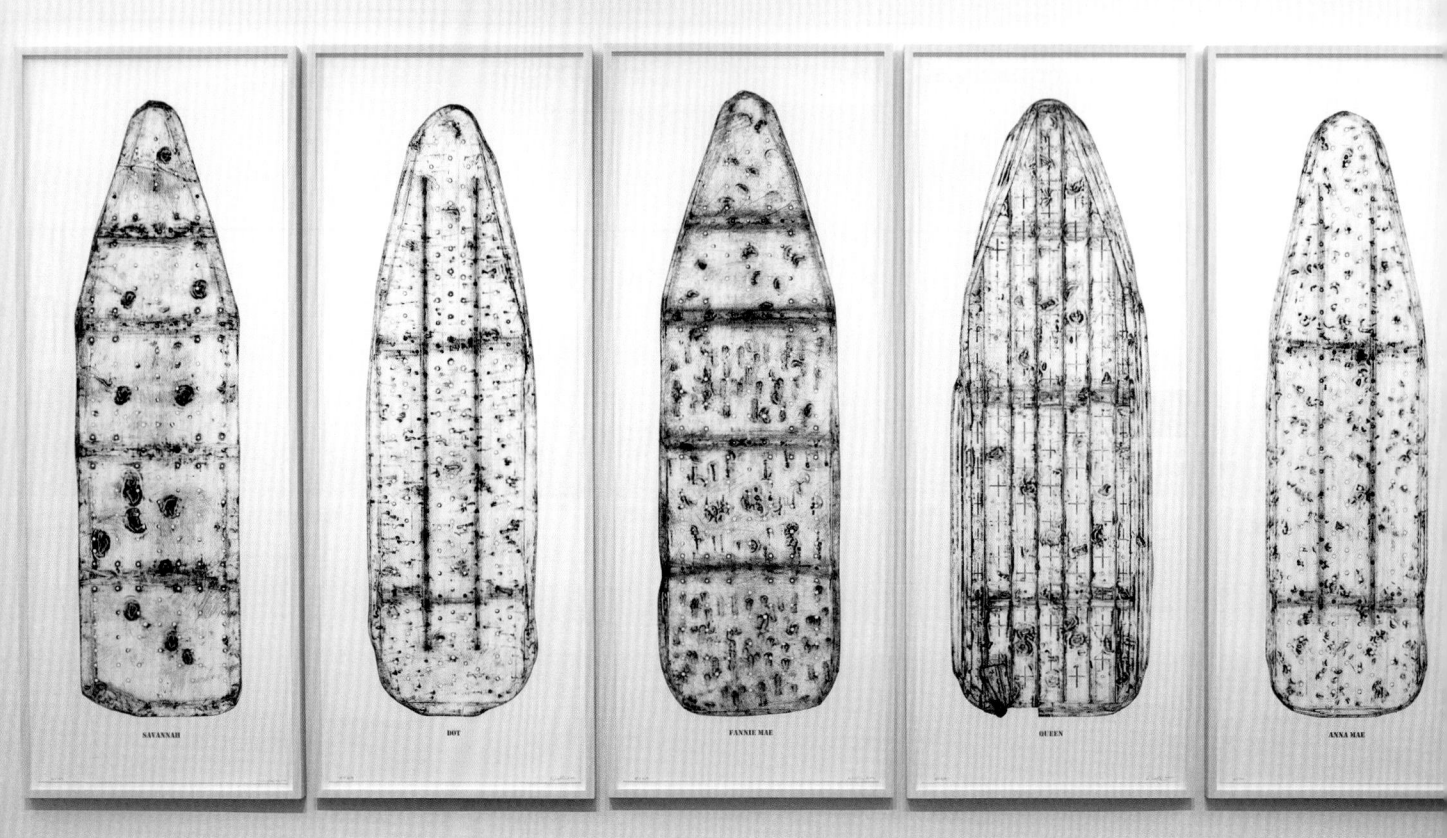

SAVANNAH DOT FANNIE MAE QUEEN ANNA MAE

FIGURE 12. Willie Cole, *Five Beauties Rising*, 2012. Intaglio and relief on paper in five parts (each 63½ × 22½ in.). Limited edition of nine prints. Photo: Joerg Lohse. Image courtesy of Alexander and Bonin, New York.

celebrate survival. The surface of Savannah's shield, the first ironing board on display, has been punctured by numerous black spherical indentations as a testament not only to a "little more history" but also to her "warrior" status.[202] The symbolic associations with bullet holes are unmistakable. Here Cole articulates the reality that Black women's bodies continue to be used as target practice in white mainstream U.S. society.[203]

Dot's ironing board includes two parallel vertical lines, forcefully speaking to the contemporary "stowage" of Black bodies in a white supremacist U.S. penitentiary system. The clearly delineated steam holes in this print suggest a call and response relationship with the holes in *Stowage*. In both works, they serve as surrogates not only for the missing and unnamed millions of people murdered in the transatlantic slave trade and Middle Passage but also for the missing and unnamed millions of people invisibilized by mass incarceration in the prejudicial and persecutory U.S. prison system.

The third print in *Five Beauties Rising*, Fannie Mae's shield, suggests the barest trace of human hands and feet in its markings. These severed limbs testify to the Middle Passage as a locus of physical mutilation. A series of horizontal lines suggests that the mass incarceration of Black women, children, and men is one of transatlantic slavery's many devastating afterlives. The combination of horizontal and vertical bars with a series of repeated crucifixes in Queen's ironing board underscores this theme further. Cole works with religious iconography by including these crosses to render the symbolic and spiritual associations between Black bodies and Christological martyrdom incontestable.

Finally, in Annie Mae's shield, vertical and horizontal bars continue his meditation on incarceration, but Cole also adds numerous diminutive bird-like forms. A source of hope in the face of despair, their partially open wings suggest the potential transcendence of mind-body-and-soul-destroying suffering through flight. Battle-worn yet victorious, all five "beauties" are "rising" as their names, in addition to their erect ironing board shields, testify to their individualism. For Cole, acts of Black artistry are triumphant against the dehumanizing realities of the transatlantic slave trade and U.S. chattel slavery.

At the same time that they signify as shields, however, these ironing boards do not lose their iconographic significance as surrogate bodies, coffins, and headstones due to their monumental scale. Cole refuses to lose sight of Black women's endurance and survival against all odds in the face of very real pain and creates a powerful visual testament to the untold stories of Savannah, Dot, Fannie Mae, Queen, and Anna Mae. These women's untold stories collectively testify to Langston Hughes' rallying cry, "I'm bruised and battered" but "I'm still here."[204]

According to Cole's radical lexicon in *Five Beauties Rising*, the ironing board functions as a symbol not only of white racist oppression but of Black liberation. "House negroes were domestic warriors," Cole declares. "Their ironing boards become their shields."[205] Here, his invocation of the historical term "house negroes" speaks to the complex histories of Black laboring experiences that existed during enslavement more generally but which are also traceable within his own family. "Once as a self-mining exercise, I processed my family lineage and classified the traits and lifestyles narrowly using the language of slavery into two distinct stereotypical groups: House Negroes and Field Negroes," he explains. Cole is painfully aware that the psychological damage and inequalities experienced by these two "stereotypical groups" are the result of the racist stranglehold exerted by a white supremacist society. He realizes only too well that "these are classifications that have a lot to do with how America treats black men and black women."[206] Ultimately, the histories and legacies of transatlantic slavery are integral to the form and function not only of *Five Beauties Rising* but also of *Stowage* and *Man Spirit Mask*. "I don't think I brought it [slavery] in," Cole observes. "It's what is there. I bring it out. The objects have a memory and history of their own," he adds.[207] "So if you have a slave, or just a domestic worker, people working for little money, their objects have a memory of that experience."[208] By reusing salvaged irons and ironing boards he activates these disused artifacts' memory of the experience of enslavement. At the same time, he reworks these found objects to expose the reality that human bondage has never ended, as he protests against ongoing global systems of modern slavery and human trafficking in the twenty-first century.

Working to fuse the spiritual and political power of utilitarian domestic objects, Willie Cole shares Radcliffe Bailey's determination to release emotional energy in his works. "Initially it's just spiritual, a buildup of energy," he explains, adding, "I want to get past language to the energy."[209] He argues further that "every action is political and spiritual as well as physical, of the moment." "I make art as a spiritual action, and because of the times I live in—or maybe the way I interpret it conversationally—it may appear to be political."[210] "I lived in Newark in the seventies and the eighties when assemblage was king, and discovered that the sudden addition or omission of a single 'thing' could render an assemblage dead or alive," Cole notes.[211]

In his layered art-making process, it is not only the energy but the history and even the memory of an artifact's use that can either be destroyed or resurrected. For Cole, a salvaged object such as the iron or ironing board signifies as an "anxious object" which he defines as "any object that already has a strong cultural identity and energy of its own."[212] The iron and ironing board are anxious objects not only because each is "an object that is anxious to express itself" but also because neither can "hide its own history, its own intent in the world, its past, present, future are all on its surface, and in the air around it, like an aura."[213] "Aura" here is equivalent to "trace"; Cole's experimental processes externalize missing historical, social, political, and emotional contexts to do justice to otherwise invisibilized human imprints. "I want the objects to have a life of their own: I think that it is what makes them real. They certainly do take a force of their own, a force that you feel," he declares. "When a piece gets to the point where all the parts are put together in the right way, it has a power of its own, and you know not to mess with it."[214] Willie Cole—no less than Emma Amos, Alison Saar and Radcliffe Bailey—bears witness to his lifelong commitment to art-making not only as a source of "power" but as an activator of the past. He no less than they insist, "I'm making history."[215]

———

Emma Amos summarized the philosophical, political, and personal priorities defining her experimental practice by stating, "My own work has centered on framed memory, divining and embellishing history, acting as witness, questioning the use of the black body in art, making art about art, exploring pattern, inventing images of face and figure, using irony and wishful thinking and fabrication."[216] As with the self-reflexive art-making processes of Alison Saar, Radcliffe Bailey, and Willie Cole, Amos defends the right not only to freedom of expression but to freedom of form, declaring, "As for style, combining abstraction with figure drawing, weaving with painting and collage is what makes going to my studio exciting and faintly dangerous."[217] While Amos has been doing the vital and "dangerous" work of visibilizing invisibilized lives over the decades, she not only received no support for the development of her practice, but the bodies of work she created have suffered from widespread neglect. "I am invisible as an African American woman artist," she stated.[218]

"I've been in so many different boxes," Alison Saar observes.[219] In stark contrast to Emma Amos, Saar grapples less with invisibility and more with the interpretative minefield confronting her practice, naming and shaming the oversimplified critical discourses surrounding her work. As she demonstrates, these overdetermined theoretical frameworks are reducible to essentialized constructions of her identity but have no bearing on her formal techniques or subject matter. "I feel like the African American artist box has opened up and I think the feminist box has opened up," she explains, insisting that "as the work changes the descriptions no longer qualify."[220] Working to use every material and means necessary, she creates ever-changing bodies of sculptures, installations, and prints that defy formal fixity and expose the myopia of one-sided critical models. As an eclectic and experimental artist working with a myriad of influences, she argues, "I have to do that, mix the sacred and profane in my work; it's a process of exorcism." She adds that "If I didn't do it in the work, I'd just jump off a cliff."[221] For Saar, the art of creation is a bulwark against the act of self-destruction. Her sculptures occupy liminal ground between dream and waking, reality and fiction, materiality and spirit, and proof and belief. She shores up her commitment to celebrating feats of emotional, spiritual, and artistic resistance over physical mortality. Any and all prescriptive attempts to categorize Saar's work only ever succeed in exposing the biases of curators, collectors, and audiences. "If someone has prejudice issues or feminist issues or racial ones they will bring those issues out in the work," she argues. She is ultimately immovable in her conviction that, "in a weird way it reflects more of the boxes that they are in rather than my own box."[222]

"I've always seen the artist as a trickster," Radcliffe Bailey insists.[223] Issuing a declaration of artistic and political independence, he challenges curators, critics, and collectors who are intent on closing down rather than opening up interpretations for his mixed-media paintings and multilayered installations. Working beyond the U.S. context, Bailey explicitly grapples with a Black diasporic context in his practice. "I am interested in an Africanism that permeates our contemporary world but goes unnamed, and is not talked about or fully addressed culturally," he states. "I am interested in the impulse of that mysterious African force that propels black people wherever they are in the world."[224] As an artist, Bailey is neither didactic nor doctrinaire: he refuses to restrict his works to any one symbolism, myth, history, or influence. "Through my work," he explains, "I am striving for the ability to speak to one's emotions without being specific to one root cause."

As an artist, he says, "I seek to evoke a mood from a realm of diasporic nostalgia and ambiguity."[225] Bailey cuts to the heart of spiritual rather than material processes: "I feel my works to be a form of visual magic that are almost shamanistic in their execution and result."[226] Bailey foregrounds this "ambiguity" and "visual magic" in a refusal to set himself up as an authoritarian figure defined on white dominant Western terms. "I don't want to talk for others," he says, insisting, "I'm not a politician, and I'm not interested in dabbling in issues."[227] Rather, he takes inspiration from his own and his ancestors' autobiographical histories in his practice. "I do see that I have an opportunity to speak of the experiences that brought me to where I am," he declares. "I feel a strange obligation to deal with my family history."[228] Ultimately, he dispenses with straightforward messages in favor of "ambiguity," endorsing narrative withholding as a source of empowerment, a vital component of his visual storytelling. "I think it's important that every artist keeps a certain level of secrecy in your work, which gives it a longer life too," Bailey observes. "Not everything should be known."[229]

"In my mind I see my use of single objects as material obsessiveness, as a new kind of Minimalism," Willie Cole summarizes.[230] "Now, I know that Minimalism is characterized by simple clean surfaces and pure forms," he concedes, "but I'd like to make an argument for the use of a single object multiplied as a new kind of Minimalism and introduce the term 'minimal maximalism.'"[231] Working with a stripped down aesthetic, he relies on a minimal use of materials to generate a maximum emotional effect. "I have chosen to use a single object" in "a minimalist approach to assemblage," he says.[232] Cole consistently sets himself the challenge of working with emotionally weighted artifacts, used only sparingly and with intense purpose. He provokes a psychological response from his audiences calling his practice "a mind game really; I call it 'perpetual engineering.'"[233] No less a trickster than Bailey, he interprets art-making as the "act of subverting the way people see things." "I want to challenge the viewers' sense of knowing, and the brain's ability to accept what it sees, kind of like a magician's," he adds. As an artist turned magician, he works with illusion, sleight of hand, distraction, and misdirection to inspire his audiences to engage with his works' multifaceted dimensions. He tempts his audiences away from an overadherence to reasoned argument and empirical evidence, arguing, "I want to break you away from your logical thought pattern and the comfort associated with knowing what's what and force you to see what I want you to see."[234] Cole's ultimate goal is for artist and audiences to come together. "In the moment of highest creativity," he observes, "the past, present and future converge into a single point called NOW" with the immediate result that "you suddenly see the past, the present, and the future at a glance."[235]

Over thirty years ago, Emma Amos recognized the urgency of celebrating an African American artist's "moment of highest creativity" by composing a manifesto of Black liberation which has lost none of its power today. Her stirring and provocative piece "Some Do's and Don'ts For Black Women Artists" ends with a message endorsed by Saar, Bailey, and Cole alike: "DO MAKE time to make art" and "DON'T GIVE UP."[236]

3

MEMORIALS TO "MY SKIN" ANCESTRAL STORYTELLING IN SLAVERY AND FREEDOM

▶▶ Nellie Mae Rowe—Mary Lee Bendolph—Whitfield Lovell—Beverly Buchanan

"I don't like to look at ROOTS. It makes me feel like I was back in slavery times. You see one and then another being whipped until the blood comes out and I don't want to look at it," states Nellie Mae Rowe, a Georgia-born artist.[1] For Rowe, a direct descendent of enslaved people who survived the mind-body-and-soul-destroying realities of "slavery times" in the U.S. South, a determination not to be destroyed by its dehumanizing legacies undergirded her life and life's work. As an individual who daily struggled with the emotional difficulties that derive from intergenerational trauma, Rowe refused to "look at" *Roots*, a world famous U.S. television miniseries based on Alex Haley's novel *Roots: The Saga of An American Family*, in order to reject, and emotionally disassociate herself from, the physical violences and psychological violations enacted against her ancestors by persecutory white enslavers.[2] "I think to myself, 'If I'd been living then it would have been my skin,'" she admits.[3] Rowe remained aware that were she not born in 1900, a few decades following the emancipation legislation of 1864, that had ended human bondage in legal name only, her own "skin," let alone her mind, body, and soul, would have been the site of atrocity and abuse.

Sam Williams, Rowe's father, was a firsthand witness and memorialist of slavery's tortures and traumas. "My daddy lived in slavery times," Rowe recalls. "He would sit down at night and tell us children, 'You think you are having a hard time, you ought to come up when I did.'"[4] "He said, 'just like you get a bucket and go out there and feed my hogs in the trough, that's the way I was fed coming up in slavery times.'"[5] Sharing his experiences with his family, Williams pulled no punches regarding

the traumatizing realities of slavery times when Black women, children, and men were treated like animals, bought and sold for white profit just "like getting a good stock of hogs or a good stock of cows." His oral testimony communicates a devastating reality: Black families were only allowed to exist if they served the interests of white enslavers' greed. "They'd pick out the good stock, just like if you's big and fat and healthy they'd see a man over there was healthy and they'd put them together so they'd have healthy childrens," Williams testifies.[6] Her father's painful stories were almost too hard for Rowe to bear: "Oh Lordy, Lord have mercy. That's mean. Seem pitiful, seem pitiful."[7]

Although Rowe's father was adamant that the self-liberated descendants of enslaved people would only really know what a hard time was if they had "come up when I did," she knew her generation too experienced very real suffering. "We had to work too hard when coming up all in our younger days. Work in the fields so hard, and wasn't getting nothing, but we was forced then. All day long in the hot sun, sunup to sundown."[8] She protested their ongoing poverty no less than the very real injustices they endured in having to work relentless hours in unlivable conditions. "When we came from school, we had to put our sacks on and if it wasn't cotton, you had to pick peas. If it wasn't peas, it was pull corn. If it wasn't corn, it was pull fodder. If it wasn't fodder, it was strip sorghum cane. Weren't that, haul the sweet potatoes. Wasn't time for potatoes, you have to go shell peas."[9] As an individual faced with the all-consuming reality that "there is somethin' to do all the time," Rowe understood that her fight to become an artist would remain a lifelong struggle.[10]

Neither Nellie Mae Rowe nor Sam Williams, her father, nor Luella Swanson, her mother, surrendered to white totalitarian rule, either at the height of chattel slavery or in its traumatizing aftermath. All their lives, they resisted systems of white racist subjugation and discriminatory hate that sought to annihilate Black families' lives as well as an individual's freedom of expression. Williams lived his life not only as a farmer but as a blacksmith and a basket maker. As Rowe remembers, he made the "finest baskets in Fayette County": "People came from all over to buy them."[11] No less creative, Swanson, who had been "born the year of freedom," was a quiltmaker."[12] Rowe readily admits to her mother's importance as her one and only art educator: "She made quilts and taught me to make them."[13] A multitalented self-made artist, Swanson was also a clothing designer. "Mama made our dresses," Rowe explains. "At Easter time Daddy would buy a bolt of cloth. We didn't want the dresses alike, but we could get the cloth cheaper that way. Mama made them all different."[14] Luella Swanson respected the individualism of her daughters by ensuring each dress was "different." Her powerful declaration of artistic freedom laid bare refusal to allow the practical realities of her own and her family's poverty to inhibit her creativity. Swanson's improvisational strategies transformed a financial necessity into a stimulus for innovative artistic design.

The emotional courage, physical endurance, wide-ranging creativity, and imaginative power of Nellie Mae Rowe's mother and father safeguarded her and inspired her expression of her own artistry against the odds. "When I was a little girl I would lay down on the floor and get my pencil and draw. I would draw all different things and after I finished drawing I would go in the kitchen and steal some flour, make it up into dough, and stick the drawings up on the wall."[15] "My sister would say, 'Mama, make Nellie quit putting those drawings up,' but Mama would let me go on doing it," she recalls, remembering lovingly her mother's early refusal to limit her creativity.[16]

For Rowe, art-making was a source of freedom from dehumanizing labor from a very young age: "I bet I wasn't 10 years old when I made my first doll. Sometimes when I ought to have been in the fields, I'd hide and go make dolls."[17] Joe Brown Sr., her nephew, narrates a powerful story concerning his aunt's artistic development: "she told me when she was a little girl she'd take the laundry, the dirty stockings and socks, and tie them up and make dolls out of them." And yet, in stark contrast to her mother's early support for her creativity in other contexts, these actions were punished. According to Brown Sr., "her parents'd whup her" because "they didn't know nothing about art.'"[18] While her parents were pioneering artists in their own right, their creativity aligned with use value, as in the creation of objects—baskets, clothes, and quilts—that had an everyday function. For Rowe, by comparison, a commitment to art for its own sake defined her practice. She lived the majority of her life haunted by an unfulfilled dream: "I wanted to be an artist but I did not have the chance."[19]

As her mother and father had refused to give up, however, so Rowe survived decades of back-breaking labor only to turn to art-making later in life. As she explains regarding her prolific outpouring of drawings, dolls, and assemblages, "I'm seventy-five years old and I'm like a child."[20] "I'm going to play in my playhouse and just keep playing," she jubilantly declares. "I've worked my days, now I want to play these other days out."[21]

For Rowe, the right to express her artistic vision through play and to live in her imagination represented nothing less than physical and psychological liberation from a life consigned to hard labor. Working with paint, pencils, and found materials, Rowe defined play as the right to improvisation and the expression of her own original aesthetic vision: "I likes to guess at what I'm doing."[22] As her mother had made each dress different, so Rowe had no interest in imitation or replication: "I don't want to copy what someone else do."[23] While she produced numerous mixed-media assemblages in her final decade, she preferred one artistic mode in particular: "I get a kick out of drawin'."[24] "I just take my pencil and see what I'm going to make out of it, and after I get the markings then it comes to me what I want to make out of it."[25] In the years leading up to her death in 1982, Rowe fulfilled her dream of becoming an artist while honoring her own and her family's lives lived in very real deprivation: "I take nothing and make something out of it."[26] Rowe has been an inspiration for a generation of artists, including contemporary painter Kerry James Marshall, who declares her influence in his "list of antecedent artists."[27] Among the pioneering critics who are dedicated to examining Rowe's life and innovative practice are the following: Judith Alexander, Linda C. Armstrong, William Arnett, Kinshasha Holman Coleman, Sterling Cook, Tessa DeCarlo, J. Richard Gruber, Lee Kogan, and Xenia Zed.

"In the winter it could be real cold, and she didn't have that many quilts to keep us warm," remembers Mary Lee Bendolph, a quilt-maker born a few decades after Nellie Mae Rowe in 1935 in Gee's Bend, Alabama.[28] Bendolph refuses to sanitize the financial destitution endured by her mother, Aolar Carson Mosely. She recalls her mother worked tirelessly to protect her family by putting "some old raggly jackets on our bed to help keep us warm."[29] "Here was some quilts, but they wasn't good quilts," she explains, painfully aware that the women of her mother's generation "didn't have nothing much to make quilts with."[30] In the spirit of Rowe's artistry as born of a necessity, Aolar Carson Mosely worked with what she had to "take nothing and make something out of it," becoming a quilt-maker and Bendolph's teacher and inspiration. "My momma, she always sit in the yard piecing quilt, or patching something like that, because we didn't have anything," Bendolph says.[31] At an early age and inspired by her mother's artistry, Bendolph made a life-changing resolution: "I decided I wanted to learn how to do it, too, and so Momma told me how you piece a quilt."[32] "She got some pieces and gave them to me. It wasn't anything but some old raggly pants. She gave me a needle and thread and showed me how to lay the pieces."[33]

As young Bendolph worked to piece together fragments of discarded clothing, an experimental relationship to color defined her early experience of learning how to make a quilt. "I put a red piece in there, and I put a brown piece in there, and if it didn't look too sweet to me, I'd take it back off," she recalls.[34] This call and response relationship between colors, which she uses to create "sweet" combinations, continues to define her innovative practice. Still working today, she summarizes her practice as follows: "I gather a lot of colors that might not look like they fit with each other and try to put them together and make them all work."[35] Bendolph's determination to create quilts from seemingly discordant and inharmonious color combinations and yet "make them all work" defines her artistic vision.

Working to wrong-foot, destabilize, and surprise her viewers, she explains, "What I want to have in my quilts" is "a color that would just take your attention away."[36] Now a world-renowned quilt-maker, Bendolph continues to honor her artistic indebtedness to her mother's creative influence: "Mostly all my quilts are a little like the quilts she made."[37]

Far from alone, Bendolph is one among hundreds of Gee's Bend quilt makers who exhibit their work worldwide. They include Ella Bendolph, Annie Bendolph, Emma Lee Pettway Campbell, Pearlie Pettway Hall, America Irby, Clementine Kennedy, Lucy Mooney, Arlonzia Pettway, Loretta Pettway, Lutisha Pettway, Liza Jane Williams, and Annie Mae Young. Despite the vast numbers of quilts these artists have made, researchers and historians working to learn more about this long tradition of quilt-making face challenges. The vast majority of the quilts created by these pioneering female artists have been lost to history. While scholar William Arnett takes heart that "of the few hundred women residents of the Gee's Bend area, more than 150 are now known to have made quilts of artistic significance," he is also candid regarding the irreparable damage done to this tradition: "for hundreds more women, there are simply no surviving quilts."[38] These statistics exposing the vast numbers of quilts forever missing testify to the unspeakable suffering endured by generations of Black families fighting to survive unbearable daily conditions: "It is likely that more than 95 percent of the quilts made in Gee's Bend during the twentieth century, and 100 percent of those from the nineteenth, are now lost to history."[39] For Kerry James Marshall, an artist dedicated to calling out a white dominant art world for its promotion of "absence with a capital A" when it comes to Black art history, this loss is devastating but not a source of despair.[40] He takes inspiration from the fact that the memories of enslaved people live on in the artistry of their descendants: "The history of slaves is woven into the very fabric of their lives."[41] Among the scholars doing justice to her experimental and innovative quilt-making practices are Matt, Paul, and William Arnett, Jarrette Barber, Dilys E. Blum, Glenny Brock, Elizabeth Brotherton, Patricia L. Brown, Stephanie Burak, Floris B. Cash, Cassie M. Chew, Bridget R. Cooks, Joanne Cubbs, Olga I. Davis, Chris Davis, Sally Anne Duncan,

Dana Friis-Hansen, Bernard L. Herman, Teri Klassen, Hugo Letiche, Jane Livingston, Peter Marzio, Mark L. McPhail, Maggi McCormick Gordon, Glenn McNatt, Eugene W. Metcalf Jr., Karin E. Peterson, Keith Plocek, John Ploof, Angela L. Roberts-Burton, Nancy Scheper-Hughes, Helen Silvis, Wes Smith, Vanessa K. Sohan, Amei Wallach, Alvia J. Wardlaw, Jessica Williams-Gibson.

"I have a collection of five or six hundred tintypes, cabinet cards, and photo-postcards of African Americans, mostly from the turn of the twentieth century through the 1950s," explains Whitfield Lovell, an installation, mixed-media, and portrait artist born in 1959 in the Bronx, New York City, over two decades later in 1959.[42] As an artist determined "not to focus on African Americans as victims of slavery and oppression," Lovell takes his inspiration from his photographic collections in which Black women, children, and men communicated their declarations of artistic independence before the camera lens.[43] In these collections, he notes, "these people were collaborating with the photographer in that they were going out and having themselves photographed the way they wanted to be seen." [44] A commitment to doing justice to hidden histories of agency and artistry defines his practice. For Lovell, these individualized portraits of Black women, children, and men emerge in direct opposition to the way their images circulate within a white discriminatory and persecutory imaginary. Rejecting the images of Black people that circulate within mass-produced, derogatory, and dehumanizing white racist imagery trading only in sensationalist and stereotypical iconography for centuries, Lovell relies on these visual testaments to Black empowerment to forge a radical "lexicon of liberation."[45]

Just as Nellie Mae Rowe celebrates play as a way out of no way and Mary Lee Bendolph memorializes creativity as a source of survival in spite of sacrifice, Whitfield Lovell relies on his mixed-media practice to reimagine the acts and arts of self and communal expression within the daily lives of unknown individuals. He aims to reclaim or re-create invisibilized rather than iconic lives. His work comes to grips with the "beautiful, sort of powerful aspects of their existence," reflecting his conviction that, "in spite of how they were viewed by

the rest of the world, their images of themselves were tangible, and critical for their survival."[46]

"Part of my process in making a work is to flip through the old photographs looking for ideas. This is how I begin each of my tableau pieces," Lovell explains. "They are referred to as 'tableaux' because they are not part of a full-scale installation, but rather they're individual pieces that incorporate two-dimensional drawings with three-dimensional found objects."[47] As per his mixed-media practice, he translates these photographic images into hand-drawn portraits, often monumental in scale, which he then inserts into his tableaux, also including salvaged artifacts, sound recordings, and material objects to reimagine the everyday domestic settings of Black families. For Lovell, these unknown women, children, and men do not remain anonymous subjects. Instead, he claims that they are "stand-ins for my own ancestors" because "these people were defining themselves through their ability to own and define their own space."[48]

In recent years, Lovell has also begun creating full-scale installations which interrogate "memory and heritage, and the markings that the past has made—and continues to make—on who we are." His work bears witness to missing rituals, traditions, symbols, and practices within the everyday lives of Black people living in the United States over the generations. "For me," he explains, "making an installation is like creating a shrine or setting a dinner table, carefully putting all the components in place, with each object having its own meaning and purpose."[49]

Lovell's tableaux and installations are visual testaments to the everyday struggle for survival of individuals and families. As for Bendolph, so for Lovell: material artifacts operate as powerful testaments to a life and lives as lived. Just as Bendolph creates quilts from disused clothing to honor an unknown individual's story, so Lovell relies on "objects that have been held and used in daily rituals by people who may not be here anymore but who somehow imbued those objects with their essence."[50] As a result, his installations, no less than Bendolph's quilts, varyingly function as altars, talismans, symbols, and touchstones for the human spirit or "essence." Lovell, like Rowe and Bendolph, is emphatic in his commitment to this practice: "As an artist, my priority is art. I'm not trying to change the world, and

I don't generally approach my work as protest pieces."[51] At the same time that he is not working to create "protest pieces," he confronts the reality that, "in many ways to be an African American artist at this point in time is unavoidably a political statement."[52] Among today's critics working to extrapolate and examine the defining forms and themes of Lovell's experimental practices are the following: Bartholomew F. Bland, Judy Collischan, Carla Hazel, Patricia Hills, Nandini Makrandi Jestice, Kellie Jones, Leslie King-Hammond, Dorothy Kosinski, Sarah E. Lewis, Lucy R. Lippard, Julie L. McGee, Melissa Messina, Dominique Nahas, Klaus Ottmann, Kevin E. Quashie, Lowery Stokes Sims, Elsa Smithgall, Jennifer Way, John Yau, Lilly Wei.

"My father came from a farm family in North Carolina," states Beverly Buchanan, a painter and sculptor who was born nearly two decades earlier than Lovell.[53] In contrast to Lovell, she grew up in Orangeburg, South Carolina, "on the campus of what was then the only state-supported school for Blacks."[54] "My father was dean of the School of Agriculture. I got a good education in Black history."[55] Buchanan shares the commitment of Rowe, Bendolph, and Lovell to working with salvaged materials. In her artistic beginnings as a sculptor she foregrounds her like-mindedness to Rowe by working to do justice to her declaration, "I take nothing and make something out of it."[56] "I lived near a program for college students where they had to construct mock houses," Buchanan remembers, noting the immediate benefits to her evolving artistic processes. "I had access, as a kid, to a lot of cast-off pieces of wood."[57] Working innovatively with such material until she died in 2015, Buchanan created vast numbers of small-scale and three-dimensional sculptures that she called "shacks." The small-scale exteriors and interiors of these "shacks" are the visual antithesis of the formalized order and symmetry of "mock houses." Inspired by a radicalized consciousness of race- and class-based inequalities in the human-made physical environment of impoverished communities, Buchanan honors the improvisatory, makeshift, and everyday rural architecture of families who have always been collaboratively working to "make something out of nothing."

"My early shacks are barns," Buchanan explains. She readily admits to the biographical inspiration of these sculptures: "I named them for family members and for people whose farms I knew."[58] She claims, "I had been travelling back and forth visiting family in North Carolina and I started to make structures and one day I said to myself, 'I'm making barns.'"[59] Buchanan was inspired not only by these visits but by her own work experiences. Just as Nellie Mae Rowe had labored in all areas of agricultural production, Buchanan recalls, "I worked as a tobacco field hand. Because I was a strong youngster I would help the men load the barns."[60] Buchanan's determination to visibilize an invisibilized history of unknown individual's artistry also inspires her small-scale barn sculptures: "I want to give people who can neither read nor write but made all the measurements and built their own barns and shacks a different way of looking at themselves."[61] She resists the indignities, abuses, and dismissals suffered by "people who can neither read nor write" at the hands of white dominant authorities by creating "barns and shacks" that live on not only as hard-hitting testaments to struggle but as empowered talismans of survival.

"Since I was a child I knew people who lived in shacks," Buchanan notes. "The fact that I went on trips with my father as a child and saw these shacks firsthand and met these families certainly was an enormous influence."[62] While she began her small-scale sculpture series with shacks that were barns, Buchanan went on to create not only farm outbuildings but also the domestic dwellings in which families lived. All too aware of the social, political, and economic inequalities reflected in the construction and materials used to build these physical structures, she embraces the emotional weight presented by the word "shack." As she emphasizes, "The term shack is offensive to some people because it has in the past meant a demeaning type of dwelling."[63] "Demeaning in the sense that people who lived in shacks were considered poor people, people who could not rise above the conditions in their lives," she explains.[64] While Buchanan's emotionally charged sculptures in no way detract attention from the devastating consequences of living in these cramped "shacks" for families struggling to survive on a daily basis, their intricacy and inventiveness also express the untold artistry, imaginations, and creativities of these families. "Shacks are reality. People lived in them, sometimes for generations," she notes. Despite these individuals' struggles with a daily mind-body-and-soul-destroying reality, they, as the shacks testify, "had dreams, and sometimes their dreams came true." Among the many scholars who have examined not only her shacks series but her site-specific sculptures and drawings are the following: Amalia K. Amaki, Max Belcher, Michael Brenson, Kimberley Frazier-Booth, Andy Campbell, Trinkett Clark, Karen Comer Lowe, Eleanor Flomenhaft, Susan Krane, Curtia James, Lucy R. Lippard, Jock Reynolds, Suzanne Slesin, Lowery Stokes Sims, Angela Son, Edward W. Waddell Jr., Rebecca Walker, Cassandra Von Weber, Chloe Wilcox, Marcia G. Yerman, and William Zimmer.

All her life, Buchanan urged that her shacks should not be interpreted along racially determinist lines. "These are not necessarily black or white structures," she maintains. "These shacks are not just about black people."[65] Even though "they are based on people that I knew growing up who were black," she points out that "once I became an adult I saw other people living in similar conditions."[66] No biographical exposé, anthropological investigation, or sociological assessment, Buchanan's series of shack sculptures endure as an emotive, empathetic and, above all, living memorial "to people and places."[67]

NELLIE MAE ROWE *(Born in Fayetteville, Georgia, 1900; died in Vinings, Georgia, 1982)*

"I draw what's on my mind," declares Nellie Mae Rowe. "What's important is thinking about what I'm going to make."[68] Shedding light on her cerebral practice, she explains, "I sit and study what I want to draw. / If I see a man's head, a woman's head, / a woman's feet or anythin', / I start from that."[69] To visualize "what's on [her] mind," she follows an improvisatory process: "I may make a start with a straight mark, / and it will come to me what I want to make."[70] The right to an autonomous expression of her creative imagination remained foundational to her aesthetic practice. She deliberately set no limits—emotional, cultural, or personal, let alone formal or compositional—on her bodies of work. According to Rowe's artistic vision, the medium is far less important than the matter: "I don't care if the color is ink, watercolor, crayon or pencil, whatever matches is what I will use."[71] At the heart of Rowe's practice is her commitment to the right to visualize her own internal landscape: uncensored, unedited, and unfettered by restrictive barriers.

In the final decade of her life, Rowe produced a vast body of emotionally charged, philosophically complex, compositionally experimental, and psychologically provocative drawings that give artistic expression to her kaleidoscopic imaginary worlds. "It is just like a dream when I see those things I drew," she explains, adding, "I don't know what it is, but I know one thing: it is in my mind."[72] For an artist who is a direct descendent of family members who experienced enslavement, the ability to draw what is in her mind constitutes a powerful act of self-liberation from external white racist forces that have sought to subjugate the imaginative inner lives of all Black people. All too aware of the daily depredations and devastations endured by her enslaved ancestors, Rowe avowed, "I have no energy to draw pictures about slavery times. It makes me feel sad."[73] Nothing could be further from "pictures about slavery times" than her surviving drawings of physical and psychological liberation.[74] All of the different themes within her work—labor, artistry, play, myth, and spirituality—have resonated powerfully with contemporary artists and critics. Most particularly, it is freedom—freedom of artistic expression, freedom of association, freedom of composition, freedom of color symbolism, and freedom of subject matter—that defines her artistic practice and visual language.

I Will Take You to the Market, a drawing Rowe created in 1981, is the closest she came to creating a picture of "slavery times."[75] In this emotionally unequivocal work, a nude woman's hunched over figure dominates the picture plane. Working with a deliberately nonrealist use of color here and across her other drawings, Rowe colors her body blood red to reinforce the association between this woman's physicality and

▶▶ "I Have No Energy to Draw Pictures about Slavery Times"

trauma. Her arms wrap around her body in a gesture of self-protection while her facial expression contorts in fear. She communicates the traumatizing reality that she has been exposed to abuse. The title of Rowe's drawing, "I WILL TAKE YOU TO THE MARKET," appears as handwritten and capitalized lettering immediately to the right of this woman's body. In her powerful use of emotionally charged written and visual language. She bears witness to pain and suffering. She renders the association of this unnamed woman's vulnerability with a history of the auctions of enslaved people incontestable. At the same time that she expresses this emotionally harrowing history, however, Rowe surrounds her figure with multicolored animals of all shapes and sizes. Here she no doubt recalls her father's testimony that enslaved people were subjected to dehumanization and persecution by being treated like "hogs." In accordance with this oral history, her female figure has been stripped of her clothing to be sold along with the farm animals at the market.

The drawing is much more than a narrative of sacrifice and suffering. These animals form a protective circle around Rowe's unnamed woman. Together, they are further surrounded by an explosion of abstract patterns (circles, stripes, crisscrossed lines, and geometric shapes) and colors (yellows, purples, oranges, reds, blacks, blues, and whites) that all suggest the potential for hope in the face of despair and for female agency in the face of annihilation. While there is no escaping the traumatizing reality that this woman has no control over the physical world she lives in, Rowe's abstract patterns and color explosions suggest that she does have control over her imagination. In this drawing, Rowe externalizes her female subject's internal landscape, revealing what is on her mind. The orange and purple flowers that look like balloons as they float to the sky serve as metaphorical emblems of liberation. As much a "picture of freedom" as of "slavery times," Rowe's drawing is a visual embodiment of her enslaved woman's interiorized subjectivity. Just as her unnamed subject keeps mind, body, and soul together through dreamscapes of liberation, so Rowe survives her own daily trauma by engaging in experimental practices that liberate her artistic expression. Here and elsewhere she honors her autobiographical struggle and expresses her conviction that she "had a hard time down here,

struggling and tussling, folks is so mean to one another, Lord have mercy. I wish everybody would love one another."[76] Neither fully a vision of dystopian reality nor of utopian possibility, *I Will Take You to the Market* is Rowe's meditation on what both a picture of slavery and a picture of freedom might look like. While a life lived in a white racist, classist, and gendered discriminatory society is a life of confinement, a life lived in the mind and in the dreamscape of the imagination, expressed via artistic experimentation, is a life of liberation.

In the same year, Rowe created *Picking Cotton*, a drawing in which a bent-over woman labors over a cotton plant. The woman seems to represent histories of women's back-breaking labor. However, her female subject's skin color is no longer blood red but brown, while rather than appearing nude, she is instead clothed in a beautiful orange dress. She also wears an ornately patterned blue, red, and white headdress and dainty blue shoes. This is not the clothing of an enslaved person or sharecropping worker. Instead, Rowe's Black female protagonist may very well be a surrogate for the artist herself. Though she hunches over the cotton plant, she may not even be holding a laboring tool in her hand but a pencil or even a paintbrush. Here Rowe introduces the idea that the drawing's subject is not only an imagined protagonist picking cotton but her own artistry.

Immediately to the Black woman's right, a well-dressed white woman in a purple blouse and checkered skirt sits idly, a passive onlooker to the Black female figure's bent frame. In the far left, a man, blue-skinned and attired in green pants and a yellow shirt, also sits and visibly lazes about. As embedded spectators, both the white woman and blue man are representatives of white U.S. citizens who have profited from Black laboring bodies over the centuries. And yet, as in *I Will Take You to the Market*, in *Picking Cotton* Rowe refuses to objectify Black women's lives by reducing their bodies solely to dehumanizing labor. Rather, she again celebrates this woman's imaginative internal landscape. She is bending over a cotton plant; however, manifestations of her imagination surround her in an explosion of abstract patterns and intense colors. As a potential surrogate figure for the artist herself, her Black woman protagonist is not only elegantly dressed but also has white wings attached to her back, suggesting she could fly away to freedom at any moment.

Across her body of work, Rowe rejects any and all easy explanations or clear-cut definitions. She aims not to replicate her everyday reality but to imagine a new utopian society into existence. She explains, "I draw things you ain't never seen born into the world and they ain't been born yet."[77] At the heart of her practice is a determination to safeguard the originality of her artistic vision. As she tells one interviewer, "You speak one way, but I come on and say it different. You can draw a mule, dog, cat, or a human person, I'm going to draw it different. 'Cause you always see things different. Each person's different."[78] Her drawings survive as visual testaments not only to her lived experiences but to her unparalleled ability to "say it different." "The pictures I am proud of that I have made are of my hand," she declares.[79] Rowe celebrates her artworks as memorials to her individualized artistry, insisting, "I'll be gone to rest, but they can look back and say 'that is Nellie Mae's hand.'"[80]

MARY LEE BENDOLPH   *(Born in Gee's Bend, Alabama, 1935)*

"I had a rough life. But I thank God that he helped me come through, and I ain't dead," says Mary Lee Bendolph.[81] Bendolph's quilts are material narratives in which she bears witness to the personal devastations she has endured in her life. In these quilts, she commemorates the sacrifices of past and present generations of Black women, children, and men living in destitute conditions in Gee's Bend, Alabama. "When I first looked at these quilts, all I saw were struggles and hard times, I didn't see art," Rubin Bendolph Jr., Bendolph's youngest son, states.[82] While the "world sees Mom's quilts as art," he sees them "as a reminder of what struggles my mom had to endure as a young woman trying to obtain just a small quality of life for her family."[83] As declarations of independence, Bendolph's quilts communicate her courageous determination to secure "a small quality of life" for herself and her family by creating visual stories and material histories testifying not to her own and her family's subjugation but to their emotional and cultural survival.

As Bendolph explains, quilts and quilt-making are not objects or traditions that are detached from everyday life. Rather, they are instead integral to every aspect of her lived reality: "I learned to talk around the quilts. I learned to sing around the quilts, and I learned to pray around the quilts. Everything I ever learned to do I learned around the quilts."[84] For Bendolph, quilt-making celebrates life in the face of existential, social, cultural, and artistic death.

Bendolph's artistic practices have emerged from "struggles and hard times," to which she has responded by becoming a storyteller-historian-witness-memorialist-quilt-maker. "The history is there in the quilts," she confides. "People can't help but feel the history because they see what their old parents went through in the old quilts. They see that resentment and hurt. It stick to the skin and that make them feel sad and sorry."[85] Bendolph's quilts respond to the untold histories of "hurt" that have devastated generations of Black people living in the United States by testifying to the tragedies that "their old parents went through" and memorializing the pain and persecutions that continue to be experienced by their descendants living with the consequences of intergenerational trauma in the contemporary era. As evidence of an individual and collective fight for survival in the face of mind-body-and-soul-destroying suffering, Bendolph's quilts endure as visual histories that "stick to the skin": they not only reimagine what "their old parents went through" but also materially carry that history by coming to life from their discarded clothing. As she confirms, "Old clothes have the spirit and I can't leave the spirit out."[86]

Working to find a way out of no way, Bendolph creates her quilts from torn up "old clothes" to safeguard the ancestors' "spirit" and ensure that "what they went through" will live on as a source of strength and a framework of survival for their descendants. "I put them together with love, then I know someone else will love them too," Bendolph declares. "That makes them

▶▶ *"History is there in the Quilts"*

beautiful."[87] As visual testaments to love, Bendolph's quilts protest against hate.

Bendolph sheds light on her lifelong commitment to artistic improvisation and creative autonomy in her quilting practices, explaining, "I say I'm going to cut out a quilt like something I see. I start it, but when I end up, I always got it going another way." Abstracting from rather than replicating "something I see," Bendolph creates complex quilts that consist of multiple social, political, and cultural layers. "I never make a quilt altogether like anybody," she observes. "It's better if you do what *you* are supposed to do than to try and copy somebody else."[88] As per Rowe's endorsement of an artist's individual right to freedom of expression, Bendolph remains committed to artistic originality and to safeguarding the uniqueness of her creative vision.

For Bendolph, the artistic struggle of making a quilt is a powerful testament to the lived struggle of an individual's daily fight for survival. As she explains to Essie Pettway, her daughter, in their sessions in which she shares her artistic practices, teaching Pettway quilt-making techniques is also the act of educating her on how to live: "Life is like making a quilt. Not just to keep warm, but to help her go through life, to understand life. Quilting ain't easy. It takes work. It takes time. It takes faith. It takes a mind to do it. It takes patience. Sometimes you have to give up pleasures of your life to make a quilt. Sometimes your hand gonna be stuck up with the needles. Sometimes it won't work, but you have to keep on and go on anyhow because you need to do that to help you go through life."[89]

Bendolph's insistence, "Life is like making a quilt," expresses the practical commitment and emotional dedication required of a quilt-maker, which is just as essential as the artistic skill. As her contemporary Lonnie Holley, an installation artist, sculptor, and musician, confides, nothing less than "life is at stake" in the artistic process.[90] Bendolph likewise insists that the process of making a quilt—which entails spiritual, psychological, and physical struggle, as well as emotional sacrifice—mirrors the daily struggles and sacrifices required of a Black woman living in a U.S. nation defined by the discriminatory forces of racism, classism, and sexism. For Bendolph, the practice of quilt-making is no luxury but a way to "go through life" and a source of self-liberation and self-empowerment within her tool kit for

survival. As she ultimately avows, "Life is like making a quilt."[91]

"It hurts me to see people waste up things," urges Bendolph: "Everything you throw away, it can be used and make something beautiful out of it."[92] Working with discarded clothing and disused fabric to "make something beautiful," she critiques the everyday wastefulness of mainstream U.S. society. She insists, "I see the value of the leftover cloth," performing repeated acts of salvage in her quilt-making practices.[93] "Almost everything I make," she explains, "somebody done worn the pants, the skirts, the shirt, or the dress first."[94] Nearly three decades ago, Bendolph created *Husband Suit Clothes (Housetop Variation)* (1990), now exhibited in galleries and museums worldwide, from a wide range of materials, including corduroy, denim, cotton, velveteen, and synthetic brocade. As Rubin Bendolph Jr. explains, his mother created this quilt by using "my father's worn-out church clothes."[95] Bendolph tore her husband's clothing apart after his death and patched triangular and rectangular shapes of browns, blues, reds, whites, blacks, pinks, purples, greens, grays, and yellows into a work of art that stands as both history and a living monument to his memory.

Bendolph generates powerful visual drama from the vertical and horizontal placement of strips of fabric of varying sizes, accentuating the varying textures of the worn-out clothing. She juxtaposes heavily used and worn fragments with material in pristine condition to heartrending emotional effect. The roughness of the corduroy and denim contrasts with the smooth surface of the velveteen and synthetic brocade, providing a visual testament to the different struggles her husband endured in his lifetime. Her sparse use of red and yellow creates a dramatic contrast with her reliance on blacks, browns, and grays, conveying the extent to which her husband's life and her own were defined almost exclusively by struggle but also miraculously punctuated by random, unconnected, and isolated moments of joy. In the center of the quilt is a sole piece of patterned blue fabric with a flower motif: here Bendolph may well be suggesting that out of pain, struggle, and death comes rebirth and a new life.

Husband Suit Clothes also eulogizes a marital bond that was far from peaceful or harmonious.[96] According to J. R. Moehringer, "Mary Lee misses Rubin, but not those beatings. Once, during a lull in the violence, Mary Lee dreamed that Rubin would apologize for every time he slapped her, every time he punched her, even the time he chased her with a shotgun. . . . People always ask Mary Lee about the U-shaped scar on her hairline, which resembles a map of the river bend. 'When Rubin did this to me,' she says, fingering her forehead, 'that was the worst day of my life, because my face stayed swollen, and I ain't had no money to go to the doctor.'"[97]

Bendolph lived a life in which physical, emotional, and psychological wounding was an ever-present reality. Her transforming of her traumatizing experiences with her husband into art not only reveals her spirit of forgiveness and compassion. Her art also expresses her painful realization that her husband's violence toward her was his response to, and mechanism for coping with, his daily exposure to white racist tortures. Her determination to reduce his recognizable clothing to abstract shapes by transforming it into torn-apart fragments ensures that his life becomes the subject matter for her art-making in a way that would not only allow her to cope with such experiences but also acknowledge the power of his love. Working with an abstract rather than a realist practice, she was able to remember his life within a detached framework and at a safe distance from her own exposure to ongoing psychological wounding. As a result, she remembers the life-sustaining force of their intimacy and honors her heartfelt conviction that she "loved him harder than anybody."[98] While he does not name Bendolph specifically, contemporary artist Jefferson Pinder undoubtedly refers to her practice and very likely even this quilt when he observes of one of the Gee's Bend quilts that it "used fragments" of the quilter's "dead husband's work clothes." It has "the power to keep you warm at night, and it also contains his blood, sweat, and tears," thus rendering it "sacred."[99] Pinder's contemporary art practice takes inspiration from Bendolph's emotively charged artistic process of transforming the reality of suffering into a ritual for spiritual redemption. "That's what I'm seeking to do with my work," he says.[100]

"The colors and patterns of *Mama's Song* reminded me of a piano," Bendolph says of a mixed-media work she created in 2005.[101] She departs from her earlier practice of quilt-making, using its formal principles to produce a color aquatint etching. Bendolph created this print to memorialize the artistry of her mother, Aolar Mosely. "Her desk was like a piano," Bendolph recalls. "She would be praying, singing, and piecing quilts. She would sit there and do this, groaning, moaning, asking, 'Who will watch over my children when I am in my grave?'"[102] A compositionally minimal print, *Mama's Song* juxtaposes black and white blocks of color of varying width and length. Interlocking with one another, they are directly reminiscent of piano keys in their rectangular dimensions. For her mother and for Bendolph herself, the spiritual act of prayer remains inextricably tied to imaginative art. Her mother's fear for her own mortality and her desire to ensure the survival of her children in the event of her death may have led her to see them as a way to protect her family even after she had passed away.

While *Mama's Song* is primarily a monochrome print, Bendolph generates visual drama by introducing blocks of red color in the center and at the edges of the work. She inserts a red square around a section of the print in which black and white shapes directly mirror piano keys, providing a visual representation of her protection and preservation of her mother's "song." The piece is not a hagiographic reimagining of this song, however: the red color interrupts the formal harmony of her monochrome palette. By introducing formal rupture, she provides an abstract meditation on the emotional complexity and dramatic intensity of a mother-daughter relationship that was far from uncomplicated. "Mama wanted to protect me, but there were things she didn't tell me about," Bendolph remembers. But "not telling me," she states, "is not protecting me." She reached a very different decision regarding the lives of her own daughters and sons: "I said, I won't be ashamed to tell my children what they need to know." For Bendolph, the physical and psychological power of her quilts ultimately derives from her determination to answer a lifelong question: "Could I walk free from fear and from shame, as those around me have? By having no fear, by telling what I knew, would this be what was in Mama's song?"[103]

WHITFIELD LOVELL   *(Born in the Bronx, New York City, New York, 1959)*

"Certainly the effect of slavery is something I can feel in my bones; it's a feeling I understand because I felt it coming off of my parents and emanating from my grandparents," explains Whitfield Lovell.[104] "I know so well how profoundly my grandparents influenced me; well, their grandparents were slaves, and that is a fact that had to have a huge impact on my grandparents, whether consciously or unconsciously. You can't just shake all that stuff off. Yes, the skin remembers."[105] As for Nellie May Rowe, Mary Lee Bendolph, and Beverly Buchanan, so for Whitfield Lovell: "the effect of slavery" endures as a source of individual and collective trauma for Black women, children, and men living with intergenerational legacies of psychological wounding, visceral pain, and emotional annihilation. For Lovell, it is an "effect" that is "bone" deep and a memory he carries in his "skin." "I believe that is why so many African American artists work with imagery from a generation or two behind them," Lovell states. "Our cultural memories and our identities are intertwined with a difficult history."[106] An experimental mixed-media artist, Lovell creates monochrome drawings of monument-scale Black subjects. He works with salvaged materials to reimagine destroyed domestic settings, and introduces powerful soundscapes to generate emotionally unequivocal and all-immersive installations in which he does justice to a "difficult history." For Lovell it is not only the "skin" but the mind, heart, and the imagination that "remembers."

"There is no way that I could draw someone's face without somehow feeling that person's spirit," Lovell admits.[107] In order to redress the wrongs generated by the exclusions of Black subjects from a white mainstream art world, he uses found photographs to create hand-drawn monochrome representations of unknown individuals that come to life on salvaged materials across his installations. Sensitive to the psychological interiority of his anonymous subjects, he establishes a connection not only with their corporeal reality but with their emotional complexity. "My process involves a back-and-forth method of adding and subtracting tones and markings that then get rubbed in or scrubbed out," Lovell explains.[108] He makes an important distinction: "it is not drawing in its simplest form because I'm removing any evidence of my hand."[109] Whereas Rowe sought to leave a direct trace of "'Nellie Mae's hand,'" Lovell actively erases any and all evidence of his artistry: "I didn't want these pieces to be *about* drawing."[110] In contrast to Rowe's celebratory affirmation of the uniqueness of her artistry, Lovell purposefully eradicates all visual imprints of his own "hand." Across his practice, he works tirelessly to ensure that nothing risks diluting or detracting from the power of each "person's spirit."[111]

"I don't think of my work as portraits," Lovell says, explaining, "I think of a portrait as being an artwork whose primary function is to depict a person's physical appearance."[112] According to his practice, the "physical appearance" of Black women, children, and men is of little significance in comparison with his commitment to dramatizing the emotional power of "each person's spirit." "I have to say that I did not want to make average or ordinary drawings. I wanted them to look as 'real' and alive as possible without having a 'super-realist' feel." He adds, "I think being aware of every edge and every nuance of tone is very important, not to mention stepping back and taking it all in to be sure the emotional character is right."[113] His determination to memorialize the interior lives of individualized yet unknown figures sheds light not only on the spiritual realities of his subjects but also on his own "emotional character." "I bring some of myself to how I'm interpreting this person's image, as well as whatever I'm saying with the objects," he admits, conceding, "I deal with a lot of my own emotions and ideas through these artworks, and so the images of these people sort of help me to express them."[114] As unequivocal emblems not only of their internal realities but of his own shifting emotional states, Lovell's subjects ultimately operate as conduits, talismans, and symbols of his own psychological landscape.

▶▶ ## "The Skin Remembers"

In 2002, Lovell created *Sanctuary: The Great Dismal Swamp*, a mixed-media installation first exhibited at the Virginia Museum of Contemporary Art Center in Virginia Beach (figures 13, 14, 15, and 16). Part monument, part history lesson, part spiritual, and part ancestral memory, *Sanctuary* is a visual and aural testament to generations of Black people who secured their self-liberation from enslavement to take refuge in the Great Dismal Swamp, a vast forest and swamp area located in southeast Virginia and northeast North Carolina. A sanctuary for enslaved individuals of all ages, the Great Dismal Swamp has been immortalized in Black and white antislavery literatures and U.S. mainstream culture for centuries as a locus of liberation. As Frederick Douglass wrote in 1855, "One of the most telling testimonies against the pretended kindness of slaveholders is the fact that uncounted numbers of fugitives are now inhabiting the Dismal Swamp, preferring the untamed wilderness to their cultivated homes—choosing rather to encounter hunger and thirst, and to roam with the wild beasts of the forest, running the hazard of being hunted and shot down, than to submit to the authority of *kind* masters."[115] More than one hundred and fifty years later, Lovell memorializes the powerful histories of liberty-loving and death-defying communities fighting for survival in this region. "Many of the images and objects that implied human inhabitants and the shingle industry were submerged in water," he explains as a powerful way to do justice to a traumatizing reality. "Somehow the legacy of those who lived hidden in the swamp to avoid slavery seemed to have been nearly lost, buried under that lake." For a people fighting to secure their self-liberation from an inhumane bondage in the U.S. South, the daily fight for survival within the Dismal Swamp—a living monument to hidden histories of Black resistance, rebellion and revolution—constituted nothing less than an individual and collective declaration of independence.

"The main inspiration for *Sanctuary: The Great Dismal Swamp*, aside from the readings and research I did, was visiting the swamp itself," Lovell notes.[116] "The people at the Dismal Swamp Wildlife Refuge hosted me for a day of hikes and a boat ride across Lake Drummond."[117] Ultimately, for Lovell, it was not the archival research or historical reading that was the source of his inspiration, but rather his physical and spiritual immersion within the natural environment. As he recalls, "Most important for me were the moments when I stood silently in the swamp and just listened to the sounds and felt the ambience."[118] He aimed to create an all-immersive experience for his audiences in which they would be able to imagine the ambience and experience the sounds of the Great Dismal Swamp for themselves. "It was important to me that I create an installation, an environment that the viewer enters into and becomes part of, as opposed to singular, discrete artworks that hang on the wall and are looked at from a distance," he explains.[119] By creating a mixed-media installation, he began to replicate the dystopian environment of this physical landscape. Working to deny his audiences any psychological safe ground, *Sanctuary* bears witness to the mind-body-and-soul-destroying realities of the Great Dismal Swamp as an "uncertain refuge" that required unimaginable courage of self-liberated women, children, and men, all fighting to survive by any means necessary.

Recognizing the impossibility of recreating the Great Dismal Swamp via "singular, discrete artworks," Lovell created a mixed-media installation that comes to life from "sculptural elements" that "thrust the figures into the viewer's physical space."[120] Both Black freedom-fighters and the natural landscape itself insert themselves into audiences' physical and psychological space. "For the installation we got thirty trees and stood them up in the gallery, with branches, leaves, and vines extending into the space, creating barriers and obstacles for the viewer," Lovell explains. "The floor was covered with mulch and there were sounds of crickets, cicadas, and barking hounds throughout."[121] His decision to bring actual "branches, leaves, and vines" into the gallery space works in conjunction with the reproduced sounds of "cicadas" and "barking hounds" to encourage his audiences to engage empathetically with the traumatizing "barriers" and "obstacles" faced by enslaved peoples fighting for their liberation. "Transforming the environment and using sounds, such as music and voices, and aromas—such as the scent of wood, clothing, and a decanter of whisky—engage the viewer from several directions," Lovell observes, emphasizing that "there is this space between image and object that is active and made active by placement and the relationship between the objects and the drawings."[122] Forced to be

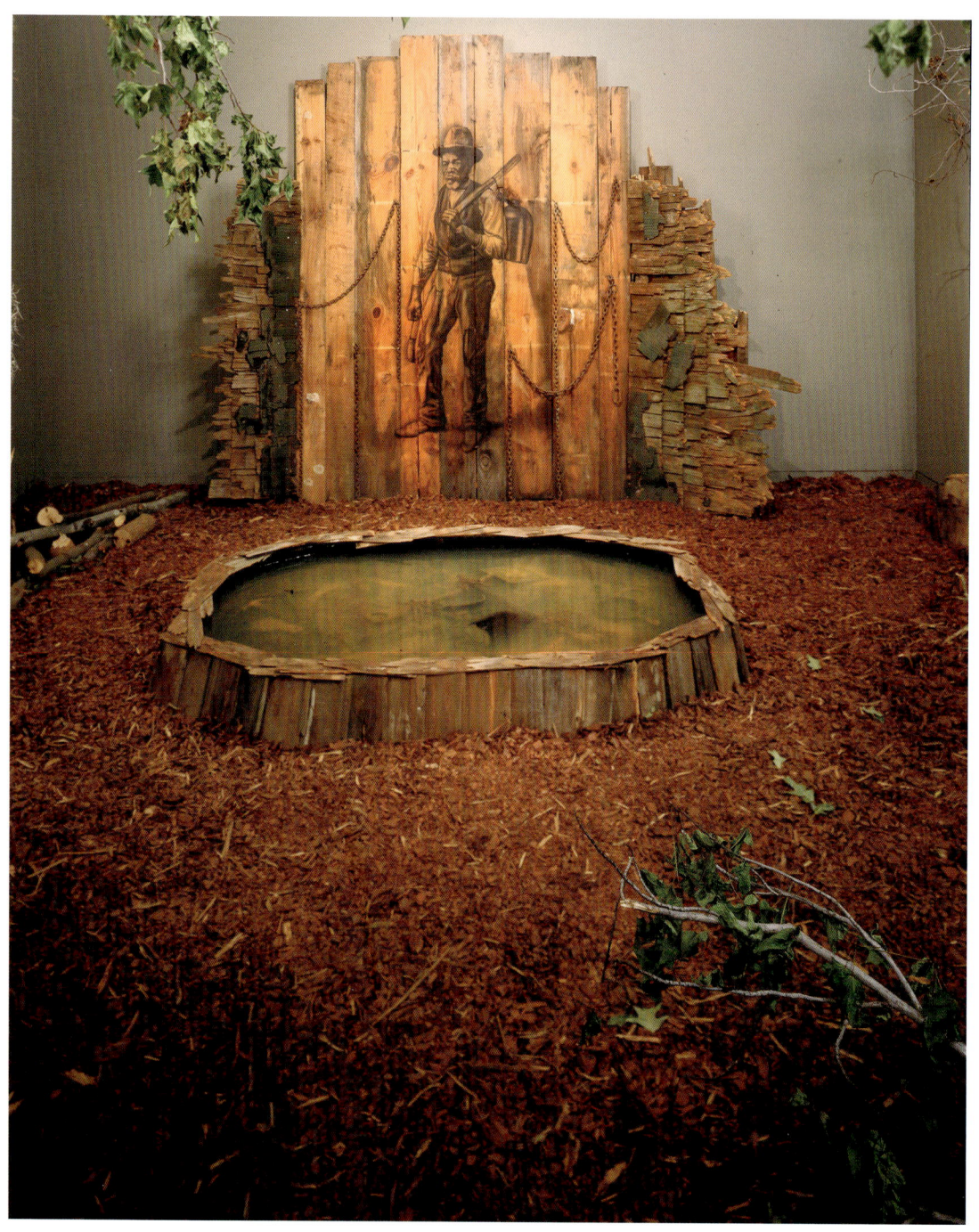

FIGURE 13. Whitfield Lovell, *SANCTUARY:*
The Great Dismal Swamp, 2002. Installation shots.
Courtesy of D. C. Moore Gallery, New York.

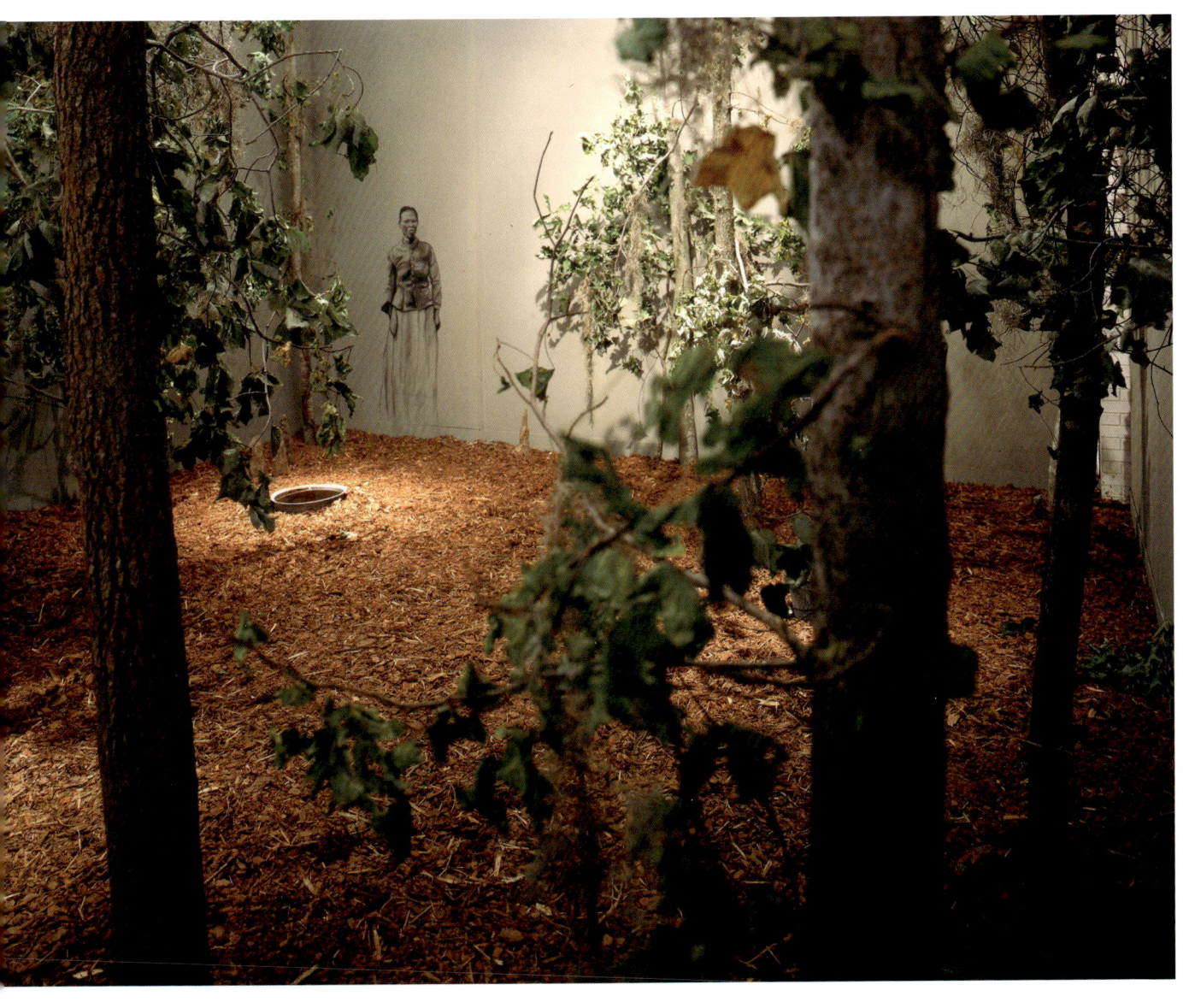

FIGURE 14. Whitfield Lovell, *SANCTUARY:*
The Great Dismal Swamp, 2002. Installation shots.
Courtesy of D. C. Moore Gallery, New York.

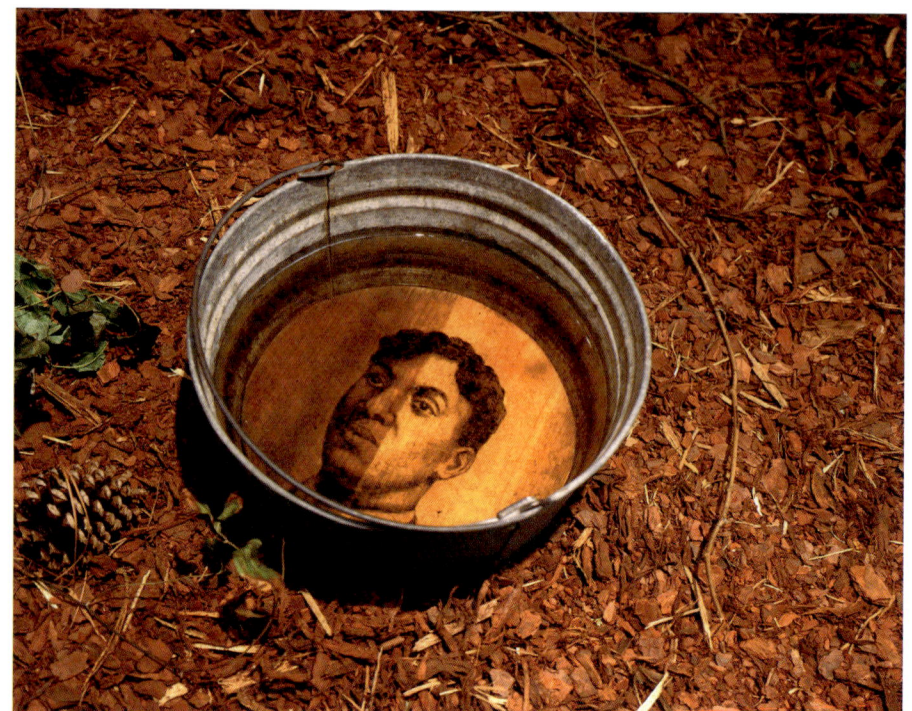

FIGURE 15. Whitfield Lovell, *SANCTUARY: The Great Dismal Swamp*, 2002. Installation shots. Courtesy of D. C. Moore Gallery, New York.

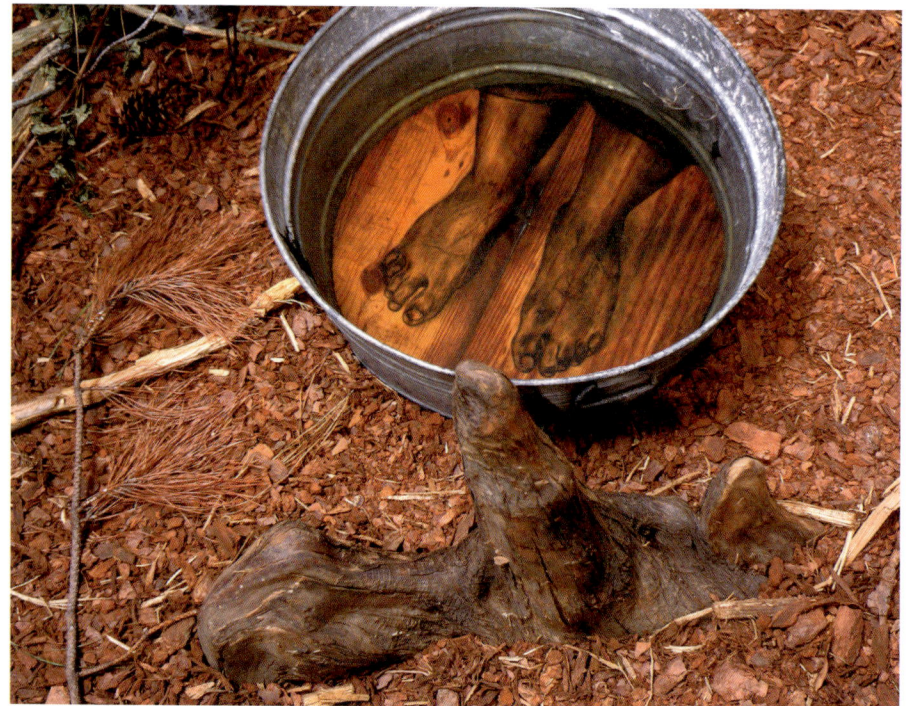

FIGURE 16. Whitfield Lovell, *SANCTUARY: The Great Dismal Swamp*, 2002. Installation shots. Courtesy of D. C. Moore Gallery, New York.

emotionally active rather than passive, psychologically immersive rather than detached, physically embedded rather than removed, Lovell's audiences experience *Sanctuary* as a living monument to a freedom struggle that is far from over.

On a salvaged wooden backdrop at the heart of *Sanctuary*, Lovell creates a monumental drawing of an unknown man. His heavily lined and emotionally charged physiognomy directly confronts the viewer as he bears witness to his own hidden histories of struggle and survival. He wears a shirt, vest, pants, shoes, and a hat and carries a bottle on a stick over his left shoulder. Scholar Carla Hazel explains that he is a woodcutter who is "traveling with a jug or water or moonshine."[123] This man's bottle attached to a stick recalls white enslavers' ads through which they sought to reenslave self-liberated people. In mass-produced, generic woodcuts that appeared in newspapers and broadsides and purported (yet failed) to represent enslaved women and men, faceless Black subjects were shown fleeing from enslavement while carrying a stick and bundle. As a young man who was himself still living in enslavement before he secured his world-renowned self-liberation, Frederick Douglass transported his belongings in this way. Writing in 1855 in *My Bondage and My Freedom*, his second autobiography, he remembered that he carried "my little bundle of clothing on the end of a stick, swung across my shoulder."[124] Additional visual signifiers betraying this unidentified man's formerly enslaved status can be found in the rusted chains that hang from nails Lovell has inserted into the wooden surface of a salvaged board. None of these shackles actually imprison the man's body, however. Rather, they drop down at his side as a visual testament to his self-liberation. The dehumanizing iconography of slavery in the depiction of this unnamed man highlights his fight for liberation and his success in achieving it through the new life he created for himself in the Great Dismal Swamp.

Lovell also memorializes the unknown lives of a younger woman and man in *Sanctuary*, creating larger-than-life representations of his subjects by drawing their figures directly onto the gallery walls. His unnamed protagonists are again distinctive for their emotionally complex yet ultimately unreadable facial expressions. However, this time they do not look directly at the viewer. Rather, they contemplate the far distance as Lovell works to do justice to their interior thoughts. Their remote expressions are hard to read, but they suggest that this woman and man are carrying spiritual burdens that cannot be adequately visually conveyed. Just as Frederick Douglass, Harriet Ann Jacobs, Sojourner Truth, and James W. C. Pennington, among untold thousands more, bore witness to their individual histories of suffering, Lovell's protagonists refuse to shy away from the emotional pain and psychological afflictions they continued to experience following their self-liberation. As self-emancipated women and men, they all remained burdened with the traumatizing reality that their family members and friends still living in enslavement were almost certainly going to die in enslavement. Believing that the "skin remembers" when it comes to the struggles endured across the generations, Lovell offers up individual minds, bodies, and souls as repositories of traumatic memory. He further emphasizes this trauma in his decision to only partially draw this woman's and man's bodies. While their faces and upper bodies are carefully drawn, their lower halves, including their feet, are entirely missing. In portraying his Black subjects as disappearing and dissolving on white gallery walls, Lovell testifies to histories of corporal and spiritual suffering and conveys the idea that the full extent of the atrocities and abuses experienced by all Black people living in a white supremacist U.S. nation can never be represented in visual imagery.

At the heart of Lovell's installation is a circular pool. Among the many objects he immerses in the water are spades, saws, chains, horseshoes, spoons, bowls, guns, and axes. Here he provides a visual memorial to survival. A history lesson in resistance, the work maps a continuum of Black strategies of liberation. These run a gamut from armed rebellion via guns—as in the heroism of Nathaniel Turner, a man who led a revolution against white enslaving tyranny in August 1831 in Virginia and who fled to the wilderness for sanctuary prior to his execution—on through to backbreaking labor undertaken by enslaved people on labor camps—represented by the spades and axes. Lovell's work also depicts acts of skilled craftsmanship in the blacksmithing trades and culinary arts—communicated by the horseshoes, spoons, and bowls—that endure alongside the survival of quilt-making traditions, hand dyeing techniques, ceramics manufacture, and weaving traditions, among much more, as testimonials to the fulfillment of Black creative expression against all odds.

A determination to honor the ancestors is a source of physical and spiritual empowerment for Lovell in *Sanctuary*. Working with no accidental numerical symbolism, he includes "Twelve basins and washboards filled with water," which he "placed around the room, with the faces of people looking out at the viewer."[125] As Nathaniel Turner defended his acts of liberation with the response, "Was not Christ crucified" (a statement he presented as a question to which he chose to add no question mark) so here Lovell evokes the symbolism of the twelve disciples to bear witness to the centuries long history of the crucifixion of Black people at the hands of white persecutors.[126] More specifically, the immersion of his Black subjects in water evokes the ancestors' endurance of the Middle Passage. At the same time, water signifies a conduit for enslaved peoples' strategies of survival within African diasporic spirituality, storytelling traditions, mythologies, and rituals. His determination to show only their physiognomies, rather than the whole story, however, operates as a hard-hitting testament to their fractured lives, betraying the corporeal realities of their dislocated and dismembered bodies. In an emotionally powerful image, another of the basins shows only the bare feet of an anonymous individual. In *Sanctuary*, Lovell honors the bravery of nameless untold millions of people who became fugitives from slavery only to suffer bodily injuries that made their escape from slavery impossible.

"Somehow the legacy of those who lived hidden in the swamp to avoid slavery seemed to have been nearly lost, buried under that lake," Lovell states.[127] Working to retell and reimagine this "buried" and "lost" history, he assumes the role of a historian, witness, advocate, storyteller, and memorialist in *Sanctuary*. His memorialization of the "legacy of the maroons who lived there for hundreds of years" is driven by his urgency not only to reimagine their "lost" lives but also to combat the devastating consequences of contemporary ignorance.[128] As he realized, "the people there who were working at preserving the swamp did not know that there were generations of runaway slaves who had lived there."[129] *Sanctuary* is a spiritual, emotional, artistic, and imaginative embodiment of Lovell's lifelong determination to memorialize Black presence in opposition to a dominant visual imaginary in which African diasporic lives are absent. "There was something haunting about the absence of surviving traces of black history," Lovell declares.[130] "One really has to use his or her imagination to conjure up palpable visions of cultural and historical memories."[131] For Lovell, the only way to honor traumatized and traumatizing "cultural and historical memories" is to find a new visual language in which to reimagine the "surviving traces of black history."

BEVERLY BUCHANAN *(Born in Fuquay-Varina, North Carolina, 1940; died Ann Arbor, Michigan, 2015)*

"My work is about response and memory," summarizes Beverly Buchanan. "It is a process of creating objects that relate to the physical works through perception rather than reproduction."[132] Buchanan's objects are not constrained by a narrowly defined material realism; rather, they are her emotive, spiritual, and imaginative responses to physical works. "Remembering the look and feel of structures has long been a strong focus in my drawings and sculptures—the house and its yard and the road behind and across."[133] At the same time, she explains, "Capturing the essence and something of the look and feel of now versus then is not easy. My shacks have always been situated in surrounding landscapes; the people who lived in them created and were sustained by gardens, yards, and fields."[134] For Buchanan, a determination to do justice to the "look and feel," no less than the "essence," of "shacks" defines her aesthetic vision. As Buchanan was all too painfully aware, the ability of her stand-alone sculptures, as typically exhibited in museums and galleries, to represent and remember their inhabitants' multilayered survival strategies via the creation of gardens and

▶▶ "I'm Still Here!"

yards, as well as the cultivation of fields, was only ever within set limits. She acknowledges, "My work is about, I think, responses. . . . My response to what I'm calling *GROUNDINGS*. A process of creating objects that relate to but are not reproductions of structures, houses mainly lived in now or abandoned that served as home or an emotional grounding."[135] Across her shacks series, Buchanan pays homage to the hidden histories, untold narratives, and unexamined artistries of their individual creators by painstakingly ensuring each domestic structure is unique and original in its design and execution. In so doing, she directly confronts the stark reality that these eradicated domestic spaces were a source of "emotional grounding" for their inhabitants living lives that have yet to be researched, let alone memorialized. Ultimately, their actual structures are honored in her shacks series not only as a physical reality but as imaginary sites of spiritual and psychological, no less than physical and material, salvation.

At the heart of Buchanan's visual practice is a determination to create shack structures that "are really portraits of individual people."[136] Across her works, she provides a "celebration of the spirit of people I had known who lived in dwellings called 'shacks.'"[137] "I'm making portraits of a family or person which may recall individuals or families I had met, and I would sometimes add traits from other families to a particular structure," she emphasizes.[138] At the same time, she explains, "I would look at shacks and the ones that attracted me always had something a little different or odd about them."[139] Her series honors the artistic individualism and unique creativity of the builders of shacks that were a "little different or odd." She summarizes her process as follows: "What I'm doing is taking parts of different family experiences from different people and putting them together into one thing."[140] These composite and multilayered portraits blend together the physical, emotional, and spiritual realities of multiple yet missing lives, giving them a compelling storytelling power.

While Buchanan honors "the spirit of people" by recreating "portraits of individual people" and even "families," she nevertheless shares Lovell's realization regarding the difficulties embedded in any and all attempts to recuperate, let alone reimagine, the "surviving traces of black history." She remembers with "great sadness the loss of a row of slave cabins in Madison,

Georgia." "There was nothing in that lot," she recalls, "They'd all been torn down. I was so devastated. I just sat in my truck and trembled and cried."[141] When faced with these unforgivable and traumatic erasures of the unknown lives of enslaved people, she confides that for her, "It's about loneliness."[142] Buchanan is no sanitizer of the repeated ways in which the physical objects and artifacts belonging to enslaved people are not only not held sacred but are actively destroyed within the U.S. Her shacks endure as empowering memorials. She honors unmapped traditions of Black artistry at the same time that she communicates her protest against the obliteration of any and all "surviving traces of black history" within a white supremacist U.S. imaginary.

"A lot of my pieces have the word 'ruins' in their titles," Buchanan observes, which, she says, "tells you this object has been through a lot and survived."[143] Working to do justice to untold stories of resistance rather than capitulation, she explains, "that's the idea behind the sculptures, really. Even with the 'Dwellings,' it's like, 'Here I am; I'm still here!'"[144] Her radical lexicon celebrates Black survival in the face of sacrifice, Black presence in the face of white absence, Black memorialization in the face of mainstream forgetting, and Black preservation in the face of widespread abandonment.

"I could write legends, and have written legends, that include the lives of people I met," Buchanan declares.[145] Among the many legends she has written to accompany her shack structures, which survive to this day, is a textual narrative for her series of three structures she created in 1989, titled *Three Families (A Memorial Place with Scars)*. A testament to suffering, struggle, and survival, her written legend reminds the reader that "like burnt clothing, remains carry the smell of danger past and present. Covering or patching (houses or garments) does not remove the memory. These structures, after being painted, were set on fire, left to burn and to be extinguished by friends. These shacks are a metaphor for what, then as now, was a tactic for enforced despair . . . despair from without."[146] A key starting point for interpreting Buchanan's practice is her conviction that her shacks "are really portraits of individual people." In light of her understanding of her shacks as portraits of specific people, we can see her decision to paint these shacks and then set them on fire as a determination to turn these structures into surrogates for the human body that speak to centuries of violence enacted by a white racist population against Black people, enslaved, self-liberated, and free. Buchanan shores up her visual meditation on the "danger" that faces all Black people, "past and present," by drawing a clear-cut analogy between these fire-damaged wooden structures and "burnt clothing." As visual signifiers of slavery and lynch law, Black bodies no less than Black-created buildings are sites of physical abuse, psychological wounding, and spiritual injury.

The conflagration of the shack sculptures in *Three Families (A Memorial Place with Scars)* operates as a visceral reenactment of the sufferings and sacrifices endured by Black people who have been and continue to be exposed to premeditated and opportunistic acts of atrocity and mob law by a white-dominant nation. However, the decision to ensure that the fires were "extinguished by friends" speaks to survival through solidarity.[147] If a white racist nation burns and destroys, then a Black radical population saves and heals. Buchanan's emblems of "enforced despair" and expressions of a "despair from without" offer a searing indictment of the systems of oppression that continue to dominate Black populations fighting for their lives within a white mainstream racist society. The insides of these domestic structures remain intact as testaments to the artistry and agency of all Black people, but their outsides are repeatedly damaged, a visual testament to Buchanan's conviction that Black lives do not matter within a white supremacist nation.

Three Families (A Memorial Place with Scars) consists of three shacks uniquely designed and individually constructed, but also visibly burnt and partially destroyed. The red paintwork of the first structure has been mottled and ruptured and the wood has been blackened and charred, but the flames have not consumed the building. A testament to resilience against the threat of annihilation, the corrugated roof and window shutters have both been preserved. Similarly, the second shack is only partially damaged by fire, as its wooden roof, chimney, window shutters, and red paintwork all remain intact. The third structure, a domestic habitation, has only minimal charring, and its brown paintwork and decorative woodwork remain undamaged. However much each structure has been damaged by fire, it retains its original design and survives as a testament to Black agency and artistry and to the psychological complexity and physical endurance of its anonymous inhabitants. While each structure operates as a locus of wounding—a "memorial place with scars"— each also endures as a site of empowerment. Together they testify to the hidden histories and anonymous lives of "three families." Here she honors individual and collective strategies of survival. The families that were subjected to slavery, segregation, and lynch law fought against white supremacist and white racist practices intent on annihilating and obliterating them by creating their own domestic spaces: spaces defined by a freedom from racism and a freedom to engage in artistic self- and communal expression.

In 1992, Buchanan created *Nellie Rush's House*, a diminutive unpainted one-story wooden shack. Her legend for this work again describes a history of empowerment in the untold stories of intergenerational resistance within Black families: "Nellie Mae went around the yard every day looking for the right stick to draw with in the dirt. The yard in front of their house was her favorite drawing spot. The road to town was too dusty and wide and busy. Her grandfather, Ollie Malcolm Rush, built this house for his family a long time ago. It's called a shotgun house."[148] Here Buchanan honors the improvisatory practices of one neglected experimental, trailblazing, and innovative artist in particular: Nellie Mae Rowe. According to her reimagining of Rowe's life, her domestic space and surroundings provided her with a studio and made her artistry possible. As she recreates Rowe's innovative techniques of "making something out of nothing," she also memorializes the architectural prowess of her ancestor, Ollie Malcolm Rush. The structure is a "shotgun house," an architectural design that, as John M. Vlach argues, is a visual expression of an "African architectural heritage."[149] The structure celebrates the survival of Black diasporic cultural practices despite the dehumanizing realities of the transatlantic slave trade.

"People lived in them, sometimes for generations, and they had dreams, and sometime their dreams came true and were realized in the form of their children," Buchanan summarizes regarding the untold narratives and hidden histories contained within her shack sculptures.[150] As intergenerational spaces not only of wounding but of creative rebirth, recreation, and reimagining, her domestic structures are "memorial places with scars" that testify to individual and collective feats of liberation.

In 2007 Buchanan created *Survivor* (figure 17), a shack which she constructed not from undecorated or burnt wood but from painted green walls as accompanied by a blue roof and red chimney. This structure is also a witness to survival. More especially, this work's painted exterior engages in call and response to a sculpture she chose to create one year later titled *Studio/Home* (figure 18). This work celebrates a hidden history of creativity as belonging not to unmemorialized families but to artists such as herself by coming to life from a vast array of colors: reds, yellow, blues, browns, whites, pinks, black-oranges, and greens. For Buchanan, this shack is a self-portrait. She draws her own face and body onto an external wall on which she writes "STUDIO/HOME." Her insertion of a separate drawing showing an enlarged silhouette of her own hand on this same wall likely celebrates a continuum of Black women's creativity, following Nellie Mae Rowe's conviction that the imprint of her hand would endure beyond her death as a memorial to her artistry. Buchanan may well also be bearing witness to her belief in the immortal power of her artistry. Art-making as a way out of no way is the explicit subject matter not only of this shack in particular but of her sculptures, drawings, and installations more generally. Across the decades, Buchanan remained unwavering in her commitment to art-making as a source of empowerment in opening up a new space for representing and reimagining unseen lives and untold stories. As she confided in her sketchbook, "ARTISTS SEE THINGS OTHERS DON'T."[151]

Ultimately for Buchanan, her shack structures are "memorial places." Here she bears witness to Black peoples' suffering through their ongoing exposure to material dispossession and psychological devastation. At the same time, she celebrates their spiritual empowerment via unmapped arts of creative expression. Across her emotionally charged sculptures, she shows how domestic spaces have been denied to Black people by the historical institution of slavery and its ongoing legacies. She names and shames dominant white supremacist, unequal, unjust, and unfair housing systems that institute, maintain, and perpetuate spatial segregation, racist persecution, and social discrimination. Buchanan walks a tightrope between exposing white racist abuses enacted by external structures of power and celebrating the redemptive force of Black interior imaginaries that are manifest in individual and collective subversive strategies of artistic expression. She works with inanimate objects to memorialize the lives of animate subjects: "Things, therefore, are reminders of what it took to survive."[152] She refuses to minimize acts of Black agency, artistry, and activism. Though they may be charred and blackened by smoke, each of her innovative and improvisatory domestic structures testifies not only to her personal conviction "I'm still here" but also to the collective cry "We're still here" that emanates forth from their unnamed inhabitants whose lives she is honoring. A song to survival, Buchanan's works echo Langston Hughes's proclamation, "I've been bruised and battered . . . / But I don't care! I'm still here!"[153]

———

"My home is on high and I'm going to reach it one day," Nellie Mae Rowe jubilantly predicted.[154] While she experienced real physical struggles in this world, she remained unwavering in her belief in a spiritual afterlife. Shortly before she died, she said, "I have to take time and get my breath. I'm growing short-winded."[155] Her increasing vulnerability in no way diminished her commitment to art-making: "I like to do my work; I enjoy sitting here drawing. As long as I'm able that is what I'm going to do."[156] Growing up in exceptionally difficult circumstances, she transformed her exposure to economic and social deprivation into a platform for imaginative possibility and creative fulfillment. "When other people have something they don't know what to do with, they throw it away, but not me," she proclaims. "I'm going to make something out of it."[157]

Mary Lee Bendolph's quilt-making practices are similarly inspired by a consciousness of the emotional, political, social, cultural, and imaginative weight attached to "making something out of nothing." "I see the value of the leftover cloth," Bendolph, who is still working today, declares. "Old clothes have the spirit, and I can't leave the spirit out."[158] "The spirit is all we had to lead and guide us, back in the day," Bendolph declares, insisting, "it still is."[159]

For Whitfield Lovell, it is not "leftover cloth" but abandoned photographs that speak to the enduring

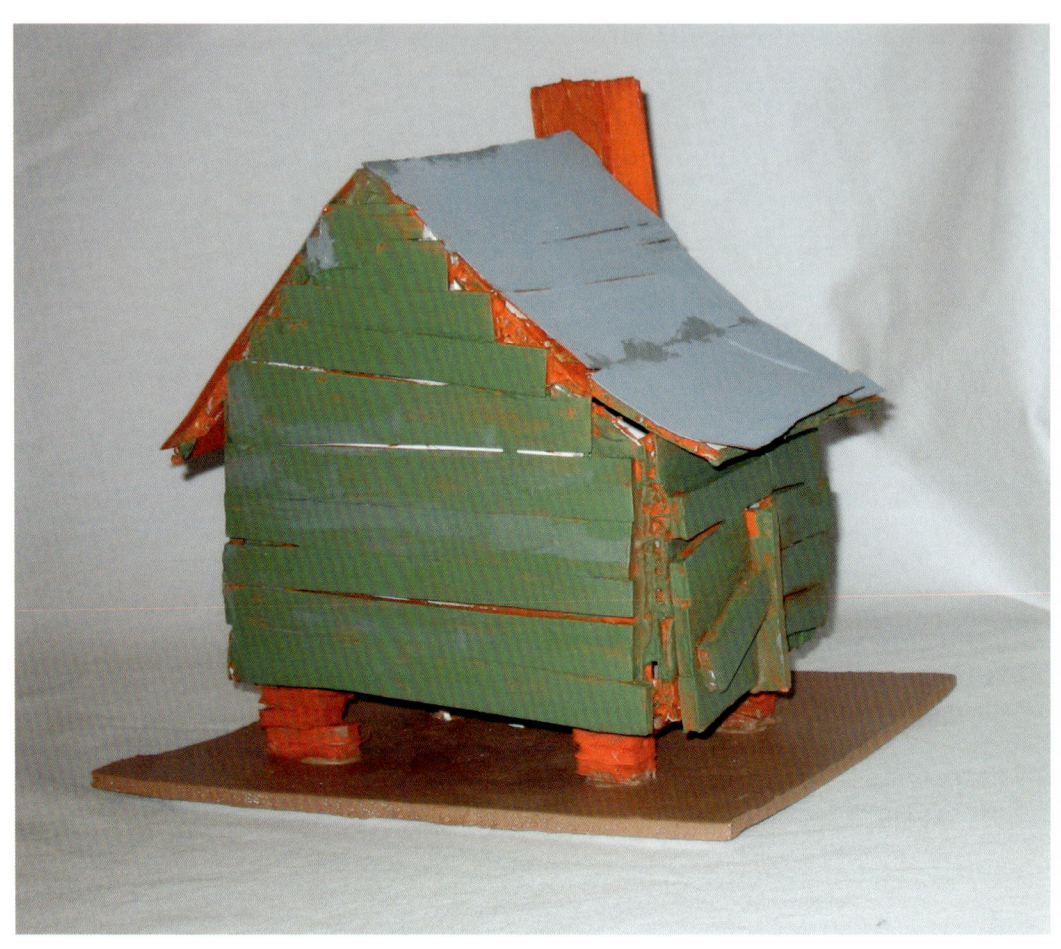

FIGURE 17. Beverly Buchanan,
Survivor, 2007. Gessoed foamcore,
wood, and acrylic paint (9.75 × 9.10 ×
9.10 in.). Courtesy of Jane D. Bridges.

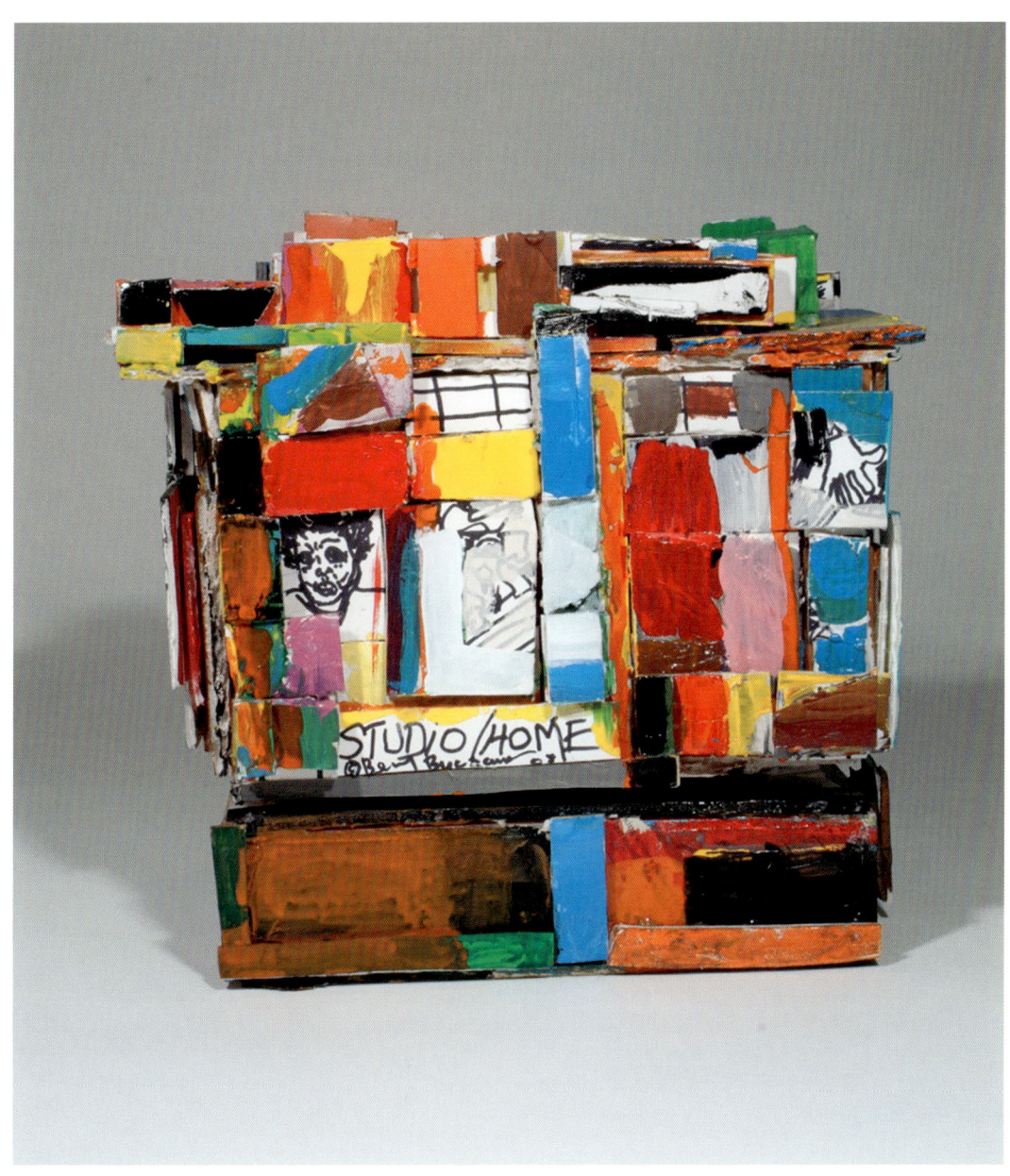

FIGURE 18. Beverly Buchanan, *Studio/Home*,
2008. Courtesy of Jane D. Bridges.

force of the "spirit." He explains that his drawings of Black women, children, and men who were personally unknown to him are "stand-ins for my own ancestors" and created in recognition that they "were defining themselves through their ability to own and define their own space."[160] His mixed-media and site-specific installations aim "to evoke a sense of place" in order "to be able to feel the spirit of the past for a moment" and "to feel the presence of these people."[161] Lovell's artworks, which celebrate intergenerational strategies of survival, are catalyzed less by the divine spirit and more by the human spirit in comparison to Bendolph. "In times of senseless manifestations of racial hatred, it is important to remember how vital awareness and consciousness of history is," he confirms, stipulating, "We have to acknowledge how we've come to where we are now, and how treacherous the journey was for some. We have to realize how pointless the hostility and violence are."[162] Lovell's radical practice fuses historical, social, political, and cultural contexts with individual and collective experiences and memories to expose the emotional realities facing Black people across the generations. Galvanized by the political urgency of using art as a stimulus to social reform and moral change, he insists, "In order to evolve as a society, we must teach every generation about what happened."[163] "Many positive strides have been made toward civil rights and equality in my lifetime," he claims, conceding, however, that "each generation has to be taught."[164] As he recognizes, "It is an ongoing process, and we have a long way to go."[165]

"I expected blacks not to like them, but they weep," Buchanan admits regarding the emotional responses to her shack sculptures.[166] As she explains, "what I'm hearing is people saying things to me like that, 'You're making me think about home' even if home doesn't exist anymore your idea of what home was."[167] For Black populations worldwide, Buchanan's shack series are visual testaments to unknown lives as lived in impoverished and improvised domestic spaces, not only as a memory, a reality, and an experience but as an imaginary in which each of the inhabitants have succeeded in protecting their minds and souls as well as their bodies from external acts of white racist persecution and discrimination. For Buchanan herself, her art-making practices are inseparable from her own civil rights activism. As a freedom-fighter who participated in a picket demonstration against Woolworths in Greensboro, North Carolina, in the 1960s, she faced terrible violence. As she remembers, "about five of us went and we went without escorts which was against everything we'd been taught to do . . . a little mob was waiting for us and beat the devil out of us with bats that had nails in it."[168] Carrying the scars of this experience into her later activism, she fought back when again faced with white racist barbarity during a subsequent demonstration. As she recalls, "another time a group amassed and attacked us and I jumped one man and tried to choke him to death."[169] She remembers of this traumatizing memory, "that was an extremely embarrassing situation" on the grounds that "I was asked to leave the line and not return because we were non violent."[170]

As visual memorials to struggle and conduits to emotional liberation, Buchanan's "bruised and battered" shack sculptures are a "tribute to the still strong spirit and to memories of that spirit in spite of blood and flesh and wood and fire."[171] Art-making is a salvation from suffering and an antidote to atrocity, for Buchanan as well as for Rowe, Bendolph, and Lovell. "That's what a real artist is," Buchanan explains, insisting, "'You have to do it. It's something that you have to do, no matter what.'"[172]

"SITES OF RESISTANCE" REPRESENTING, REMEMBERING, AND REIMAGINING STRUGGLE

4

▶▶ **Clarissa T. Sligh—Pat Ward Williams—Lyle Ashton Harris—Myra Greene**

"I grew up in a segregated, black community in Arlington, Virginia," says Clarissa Sligh, a photographer and mixed-media artist.[1] Sligh lived in Halls Hill, a "former slave enclave."[2] She remembers, "As a child, I would listen to the grownups talk about how everybody was kin to everybody else."[3] "They never exactly said if Mr. Hall had been the white man who had owned everybody," she explains, all too painfully aware that "they had a way of leaving out parts of the story that they did not want to remember."[4] Like artists such as Nellie Mae Rowe, who "did not want to remember" "slavery times," Sligh and members of her family found that the traumatizing history of the abuses and atrocities enacted against Black people at the hands of white persecutors defied any and all forms of communication or expression.

Ethel Mozelle Thompson, Sligh's mother, lived a life of terrible suffering not only in her intensive, back-breaking labor as a "domestic worker [for] most of her adult life," but also in the harrowing experiences she endured during her childhood.[5] As a young girl growing up in North Carolina, Sligh remembered, "Fear entered her life. Except that her parents had no money to place one, the obituary of her brother Council might have read: Council Jordan, age 12, passed away under violent circumstances on August 15, 1923, an apparent lynching victim. His body was brought back to his parents' homestead badly beaten. His arms and legs were bound, and a thick rope hung from his broken neck."[6] Still a young child herself, Sligh's mother was a witness to the terrible aftermath of her brother's lynching. As her daughter powerfully writes, "Mozelle was inside the house but saw the group of white men pull Council's body from a

wagon and dump it on the ground. As they exited down the red dirt road from which they had come, she ran out to help him." Mozelle's inconsolable grief traumatized her mind and wracked her body and broke her soul: "Not able to accept that her brother was dead, she cradled his lifeless body in her lap and rocked him back and forth." She held nothing back in expressing her protest to her parents—"she screamed over and over again: 'How could you just sit there and do nothing about it?' Their response is immediate and allows no dissent: "A huge hand came from out of nowhere and slapped her face. 'Shut up before the same thing happens to you!'"[7]

Mozelle's parents, who were Sligh's grandparents, were heartbroken witnesses to the repeated acts of white supremacist murder and barbarism that destroyed their lives on a daily basis. They understood the absolute impossibility and complete futility of protesting against this tragedy. A mother and father who were terrified of losing any more of their children to white racist murderers, they did justice to Council's memory and memorialized his violent death using the strategies they devised to keep the survivors in their family alive. Sligh records, "Each day before leaving the yard, the grief-stricken parents placed their sons Oscar and Crawford into separate burlap sacks. The bags were tied shut and hung from trees." She writes: "To protect them from their older brother's fate, the boys were hung in sacks. Hung to protect them. Hung from trees."[8] As children "hung from trees" and incarcerated in "bags" that were "tied shut," Oscar and Crawford paid a terrible price for their lives.

This traumatizing experience inspired Sligh's hard-hitting artist book, *It Wasn't Little Rock,* an emotionally provocative mixed-media work she created in 2004 (figure 19). On one page, Sligh includes a powerful image of a silhouette of a hanging human body. Immediately beneath this traumatizing outline sit four red chairs, one of which has the word "WITNESS" stenciled onto its back, while at the very bottom of the image run the names "GEORGE IRENE JAMES MOZELLE," an unequivocal testament to her family's experiences of unimaginable suffering and untold sacrifice in the aftermath of Council's lynching. On the facing page, Slight's emotionally powerful text bears witness to her family's intergenerational trauma: "Grief-stricken Irene and George built a pine box in which to bury their oldest son." Sligh refuses to lose sight of her mother's extreme pain, describing her as " furious, livid, unable to contain her anger and grief. Snot and tears ran down her face as she screamed over and over again: 'How could you just sit there and do nothing about it?'" Over the decades, these acts of individual and communal heroism were far from isolated incidents. Rather, they defined the intergenerational strategies of survival within Sligh's family, as well as those of African American families fighting for their lives in a white supremacist society dominated by segregation, persecution, and lynch law. Sligh does powerful justice to the history, memories, and storytelling traditions of past, present, and future Black families as sites of struggle, suffering, and sacrifice, as well as resistance, radicalism, and revolution.

"When I started working with photography I wanted to speak from my experience as an ordinary individual," Sligh explains. "From my experience with the Civil Rights movement, I learned it was ordinary people who made change happen."[9] She uses her photographs, installations, and mixed-media narratives as radical and revolutionary platforms for inaugurating social, political, and cultural change, but also to do powerful justice to the untold stories of everyday lives. Sligh's artworks are also inspired by her personal experiences: "I began by working with the family album and the family snapshot, to explore stories I grew up with."[10] Her reliance on her family album and the family snapshot constitutes a deliberate act of resistance to the widespread invisibilization of Black people within white dominant visual media. "Growing up, I felt that the reality of who I was as a person was missing from the mainstream picture of America," she declares.[11]

Sligh understood only too well that not only were her emotional, psychological, and physical realities missing, but that further damage was being done to Black lives as a result of the perpetuation and dissemination of dehumanizing, caricatured, and racist imagery. "The most important pictures in our lives, the ones that held center stage were the ones in the newspapers and magazines that told who we were and what our place was in all that," she observes. "It did not escape anyone's attention that most of the bad people were black."[12] As Sligh poignantly explains, the images that "told who we were and what our place was" visually embodied a white supremacist ideology that was and continues to be single-handedly responsible for destroying Black lives.[13] She holds white racism to account in her dissident practice by working with the "family album" and the "family snapshot" to reimagine, remember, and represent the distorted and denied subjectivities of individual women, children, and men in her family. "To my young mind, my father's photographs were the only material evidence that we were not what the media was always trying to make us," she observes. "I used them to create a site of resistance for myself."[14]

Sligh works in the revisionist photographic tradition established by her father to create autobiographically inspired works that operate as visual antidotes to the racist mythologies of white mainstream media. Her photographs, artist books, and installations constitute multiple rather than single "sites of resistance," not only for the artist herself but for the many photographers who are inspired by her practice today. And yet, Sligh's self-reflexively experimental and politicized practice continues to exert a terrible personal toll. As she admits, "I find that trying to express my real voice in my work often causes tremendous conflict, not only within other people's expectations, but within myself as well."[15] The psychological, social, emotional, and cultural forces of Sligh's practice are defined by the foregrounding of identity politics as a site of self and communal disintegration and recreation, and familial relationships as a locus of empowerment and disempowerment. At the heart of Sligh's work exists a determination to galvanize a sense of social responsibility in her audiences and inspire them to political action. As she declares, "I want each person to come to it as a witness."[16] In recent years, the many scholars investigating the formal

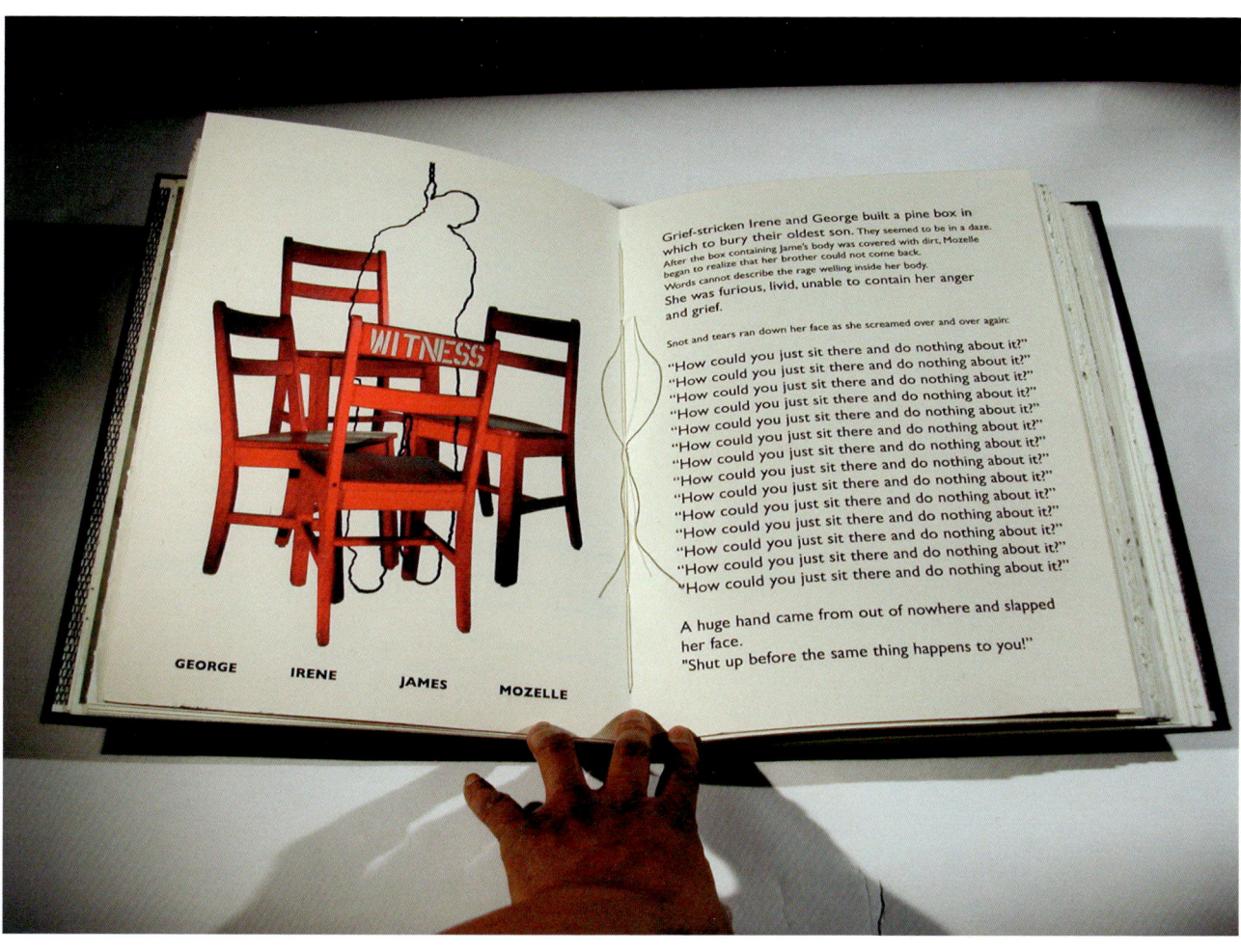

FIGURE 19. Clarissa T. Sligh, *It Wasn't Little Rock*, 2004. Ink jet pigment ink on arches paper (13 × 9 in.). Limited edition of five copies. Courtesy of the artist.

artistry, thematic complexities, and political radicalism of Sligh's works include: Angela Briggins, Robert Hirsch, Robert B. Menschel, Debra Singer, Maria Stephens, Jervette R. Ward, Carla Williams, Deborah Willis, Louise M. Wisechild, Janet Zandy.

Pat Ward Williams, a mixed-media photographer and installation artist, was born in Philadelphia nearly a decade after Sligh. A determination to ensure that her viewers respond to her work with the emotional, social, political, and cultural responsibility of "a witness" defines her practice. Just as Sligh carried stories of living in a "former slave enclave," so the hidden history of "slavery times," as recalled by Nellie Mae Rowe, endures as a source of trauma throughout the Ward Williams's family histories over the generations. According to scholar Linda Muehlig, "The artist herself can trace her history and name only as far as her great-great-grandmother Caroline, who was given with her husband and son as a wedding gift to the daughter of 'Mr Ward.'"[17] Muehlig explains that "Caroline's mother represents the point of disjunction in Williams' family history," and that "As the artist says, 'her name is not recalled'; she is lost, beyond the retrieval even of memory."[18] In her practice, Williams works to do justice to the untold story of "Caroline's mother" and to the lives of her ancestors—people who are not only "missing" from the archive but who are also entirely "lost" to "memory." Williams's art-making practices are informed by her knowledge that enslaved histories are not commemorated in white dominated official sites of U.S. history, and that Black lives continue to be invisibilized within white exclusionary archives. Williams creates her emotionally and politically charged works to fight back against this "exclusion tactic" that "continues today."[19] Her revisionist mixed-media photographs, in which Black subjectivities, memories, and histories are to the fore, reject the damage done by ongoing erasure tactics. Working with a radical politics of inclusion rather than exclusion and a visual poetics of presence rather than absence, she states her conviction in no uncertain terms: "Just leaving people out sends a message implying that these are the people who are not worth considering."[20]

Williams understands the challenges she faces in confronting a white mainstream media in which Black lives "didn't" and still don't "matter."[21] "There were aspects of the black community that weren't being shown," she states. She knows all too well that "it's a problem of African-Americans being effectively invisible."[22] Williams diagnoses the inequalities generated by ongoing white racist myopia, explaining, "White people often see a color instead of a person, they think that being black is a condition rather than a racial difference."[23] As an artist, Williams determines to make a way out of no way, against all odds. Though she acknowledges the reality that "Very often black people are lumped together in one category to facilitate people's handling of difference," Williams chooses to transform that pain into inspiration. That process represents "one of the reasons that I started making photographs."[24] Her artworks are "sites of resistance" and weapons in her social justice arsenal. She protests against a white supremacist ideology according to which "being black" is a "condition" and Black people are "lumped together in one category."[25] Ultimately, Williams's photographs memorialize her protagonists' emotional, imaginative, intellectual, and political complexities in order to represent their multiple rather than monolithic subjectivities.

"When I first started taking photographs, especially in the documentary tradition," Williams remembers, "I was trying to fight against what I thought was the negative message that photography had previously communicated to black people."[26] Williams's revisionist determination to use her empowering portraits of Black people as a means of undoing this "negative message," is a method similar to Sligh's righting of the wrongs generated by a white racist worldview in which "most of the bad people were black."[27] Just as Sligh emphasizes that "trying to express my real voice in my work often causes tremendous conflict," so Williams admits that "I also realized how easy it was to fall into the same trap and become my own oppressor."[28] To avoid becoming her "own oppressor," she resists relying solely on the photographic mode in her work. Instead, she endorses an aesthetic practice rooted in acts and arts of self and communal liberation. She creates mixed-media works in which she layers handwritten text onto her images. Understanding that a "single, documentary shot is usually too little to express a broader idea about racism," she arrived at a new solution.[29] "I started to make photographic constructions," she explains; "by giving my images a larger context I could say directly what I wanted to say."[30] Her multilayered, multi-imaged, and multivoiced "photographic constructions" juxtapose portraits of Black subjects with textual inscriptions and material artifacts, succeeding, through Williams's "lexicon of liberation," in providing the missing social, political, historical, and cultural contexts of Black lives.

"My work is drawn from personal experiences and collective spirit," Williams avows. "This means that my work relates and expresses a human condition as a Black woman living in America expresses it. It's how I see my family, my culture, and my world, and how I fit into those contexts."[31] Williams's subject position and autobiographical experiences are the catalyst to her practice. As an artist, she assumes the role not only of personal witness but of social commentator, political theorist, and philosophical analyst when it comes to representing the "human condition as a Black woman living in America."[32] She creates complex works in which her meanings are far from self-evident or one-dimensional: "I structure my work in layers of metaphor and ask my audience to get from it what they can," she says.[33] Working with a multifaceted rather than surface symbolism, she encourages her viewers to become active interpreters rather than passive responders to her mixed-media photographs and installations. "I don't expect my work to significantly change people's minds," she explains, "But I do want it to move them. I want the work to satisfy my viewers, even if it's made them dissatisfied about something."[34] Across her body of work, Williams emotionally engages her audiences through consciousness raising, revealing to them the social, political, economic, and cultural inequalities that have been and continue to be experienced by past, present, and future people of color worldwide. At the heart of Williams's practice is her role as a spiritual mediator and an imaginative interpreter of the oral traditions within her family history. Working against dominant mainstream documentary traditions according to which the creator's positionality is invisibilized in favor of a seemingly detached, if illusory, neutrality, she inserts her psychological perspective and corporeal reality into her work as the defining narratological lens. According to Ward Williams's radical vision, it is a Black radical and revolutionary woman artist

and each of her family members who hold the power of reimagining the African American family history that she holds in her hands. Among the many scholars investigating Ward Williams's psychologically charged and politically provocative practices are Mary Schmidt Campbell, Portia Cobb, Cathy Curtis, Kellie Jones, Elsa Longhauser, Linda Muehlig, Tony Pendleton, Moira Roth, Mel Watkin.

"Before traveling to Ghana much of my work since the early 1990s consisted of portraiture and self-portraiture," summarizes Lyle Ashton Harris, a mixed-media photographer and a collage and installation artist, born in the Bronx, New York, nearly two decades after Ward Williams.[35] He explains, "My desire in investigating these multiple selves was to try to find or create one that works for me."[36] Visualizing an array of "selves" within his self-portraits, Harris has, over the decades, developed a self-consciously radical "lexicon of liberation" in which he does powerful justice to his kaleidoscopic subjectivities. Working to explode any and all racial, national, sexual, and class barriers, he endorses the "return to the self as a site of interrogation."[37] For Harris, his realization is that the "self" is a "site of interrogation" and is not determined by external forces but is rather a potential source of utopian possibility. He applies this way of thinking to his sexuality in particular, explaining that "as opposed to thinking that because I'm queer my subjectivity lies on that side of the community," instead, "I'm interested in expanding the notion of what the community is."[38] For Harris, re-presenting and re-imagining competing versions of his autobiographical selfhood, undergirded as it is by shifting constructions of gendered and sexualized identity politics, plays a defining role in his commitment not only to his practice as an artist but to broadening definitions of community. "Coming from an African-American background, I understand the importance of tradition and continuity, cohesiveness, and that in itself has been a challenge," he observes. "I am clearly one for the expansion of that sense of tradition."[39] Shedding light on his myriad positionalities in his self-reflexively experimental bodies of work, he argues for an "expansion" not only of community but of "tradition and continuity" when it comes to the historical and cultural contexts, no less than the identity politics, of African American lives. Over the decades, Harris has argued for alternative art-making traditions in which a reimagining of "multiple selves" is newly possible.

For Harris, an experimental aesthetic practice as defined by a "multiplicity of images, ideas, possibilities and interpretations" is a source of imaginative, spiritual, and psychological liberation.[40] Working with a malleable aesthetic vision, he expresses a range of political perspectives and an array of thematic possibilities. He opens up rather than closes down strategies for reimagining Black subjectivities. As he summarizes, "I had finally found a means to say many things at once as opposed to distilling them into single images."[41] Recognizing the damage done by a white mainstream imagery that dehumanizes and destroys, trading in socially determinist and tokenistic images of Black lives, Harris creates layered and ambiguous visual constellations which "speak to the need for an immediate political, aesthetic, and psychic intervention."[42] As a result, his symbolically layered and emotionally charged works succeed in "providing a new framework in which to refashion the body and mind." "It is about expanding our horizons by working with the possibilities of pain and pleasure, trauma and excess," he explains.[43] As an artist who is in favor of malleability in all forms, he explains, "I've also been interested in liminality—of being on the border of multiple crossover points, such as race, sexuality, and gender."[44] At the heart of Harris's work is his all-encompassing commitment to providing a visual meditation on competing theories, shifting constructions, and multiple representations of race, sexuality, and gender. Harris refuses to shy away from what is at stake—socially, personally, emotionally, culturally, and creatively—in "being on the border." Here, there are no safety nets. Among the scholars examining Lyle Ashton Harris's works are Kwame Anthony Appiah, Robert Atkins, Deborah Bright, Cassandra Coblentz, Michael Cohen, Okwui Enwezor, Henry Louis Gates Jr., Peter Halley, Sarah E. Lewis, Claire Maxwell, Dinah McClintock, Gregory R. Miller, Senam Okudzeto, Anna Deavere Smith.

"There has been a shift in American culture I am not sure I understand," says Myra Greene, another New York city born mixed-media photographer and installation artist. More specifically, she says, "Those who want to talk about race are often called racists."[45] She names

and shames this contemporary moment, in which she is disheartened to realize that there is no space to "talk about race" without causing provocation and generating anger. "It is implied that when talking about race, bad tempers will rise," she observes. Disheartened by a cultural climate that "suggest[s] . . . we sweep all this under the table," she directly confronts the traumatizing reality that sanitizing and censoring debates on race within a dominant white U.S. society have mind-body-soul-destroying consequences.[46] In her work, she analyzes competing classificatory constructions of race and multiple systems of racism that continue to exert a political, national, emotional, cultural, and existential stranglehold over the lives of people of color. Among the many contemporary critics investigating the multiple social, political, cultural, and imaginative dimensions to Greene's practice are Tom Barrow, Lisa E. Farrington, Jeffreen M. Hayes, Deborah Jack, Bennie F. Johnson, Shawn Michelle Smith.

Greene's body of work debates a number of questions regarding white dominant and racialized constructions of Black selfhood: "where is this identity created? Is it on the surface—color of the skin—or what people read the color of the skin to mean?"[47] Greene is only too painfully aware the ways in which race has been defined within a white dominant and explicitly racist imaginary, she resists easy definitions, explaining that "when we talk about race, we can not only talk about the populations on the margins." Instead, "If we use race to describe, we must use it for all groups, including whites." Greene understands the United States as a multiracial nation in which whiteness must be recognized as a category within racial classificatory systems. She interrogates white privilege and white ignorance in order to denounce and challenge white racism. According to Greene's formulation, it is only by using "race" as a designator for "all groups" that we will all "become more mindful of how artifice and stereotype play into that act of describing."[48] As Greene, no less than Sligh, Ward Williams, and Harris, recognizes, "race has so many negative implications in society it is nearly impossible to not start a barn-burning fight around it."[49] For all these artists the only way to put out the fire and end the fight is by creating artworks that function as multiple "sites" of revolution, radicalism, and, above all, "resistance."

CLARISSA T. SLIGH   *(Born in Washington, District of Columbia, 1939)*

"My work is based on telling personal and community stories in works, photographs and drawings," explains Clarissa Sligh. "I work in the gaps between reality and myth, by speaking from my particular experiences and by inviting others to speak from theirs."[50] Her work establishes a call-and-response relationship with her audiences as a means of sharing her autobiographical stories and of opening up alternative spaces for "others to speak" from their "particular experiences." In so doing, she memorializes the ways in which traditions of storytelling and myth-making have provided and continue to provide Black women, children, and men with the necessary tools to keep their minds, bodies, souls, and imaginations intact over the generations. According to Sligh's "lexicon of liberation," she and they have not only engaged in politicized acts of civil rights protest all their lives, but they have also endorsed artistic strategies of creative empowerment. As a result, they have succeeded in holding onto their imaginative inner worlds against all odds. Sharing stories within supportive kinship groups, Sligh and her extended family members have given voice to their united protest against slavery's legacies that live on in systems and practices of persecutory legislation, social segregation, psychological abuse, and physical violence in the twenty-first century.

"Much of my work draws on my own family photographs, which I use to investigate intersections of the public and the private," Sligh explains.[51] She attaches great importance to the shifting boundary between personal autobiographies and public lives in her works. Her formal processes are as complex as her subject matter is confrontational: "Beginning with a photograph which already exists, I shoot, reassemble, and reshoot. Layer by layer a story unfolds."[52] Working with these multiple narrative threads, Sligh creates autobiographically inspired, emotionally complex, ancestrally influenced, politically conscious, and historically revisionist works. Here she explores issues related to childhood, family, domesticity, sexuality, identity, class, memory, and civil rights, among many more areas.

"My camera is important to me but I could not live without my pen," Sligh admits. "I see words as visuals similar to photographs, drawings, and paintings."[53] She explains that "words are meant to metaphorically complement and complicate visual images," and she sees the relationship between text and image as dynamic rather than static: "I want the image and text patterns to convey the energy and emotions behind the work."[54] Throughout her body of work, Sligh reveals the dehumanizing ways in which the written word and the visual image, when taken in isolation within a white supremacist imaginary, have created stereotyped and caricatured representations of Black lives. Sligh's hybrid practice, a multifaceted resistance strategy, testifies that it is only by creating works in which words and images are embedded, interwoven, and juxtaposed that we can begin to do justice to the invisibilized "energy and emotions" of people of color living in the United States. In this case, "the text is the 'witness-self'" according to Sligh's formulation: "It's like a fingerprint. I do consider it sort of like story-telling."[55] For Sligh, it is not only the text but the artist herself who becomes a "witness-self." The "fingerprint" of hidden histories, missing memories, and untold narratives newly come to life through her mixed-media works, in which she reveals her imaginative and philosophical indebtedness to centuries of African American "story-telling" traditions.

"In the neighborhood where I grew up," Sligh recalls, "stories were told at family and social gatherings and in the songs and music which where a big part of our lives."[56] She emphasizes that the written and the spoken word inspire her. She explains the motivation undergirding her visual and textual translations of these stories and songs into her work: "By reexamining my memories and experiences and collecting the stories of others, I aim to reclaim the flesh and blood reality of an era obscured by the impassiveness of official history."[57]

▶▶ *"Am I Invisible?"*

Moving beyond representation and reimagination, Sligh commits to politicized acts of reclamation and re-creation of a "flesh and blood reality." This reality has not only been "obscured" but annihilated by white supremacist "official history," in which Black lives and Black histories don't matter, and never will. Sligh is not one to concede defeat, however. Her question, "Am I invisible?," finds its answer in her empowering declaration: "We, the invisible people of this society, took our power and found our voice."[58] For Sligh, art-making becomes a "site of resistance" in which the "flesh and blood" imaginaries of Black people are newly inaugurated into existence. At the same time, Sligh's experimental creative processes ensure that her Black protagonists are equipped not only to take their "power" but to find their "voice."

"As a young Black child, before I could even think," Sligh remembers, "I was told how bad things are out there in the world, how there's no place for us, and how people don't like us."[59] Living in the United States, a nation in which persecution, social discrimination, and psychological and physical torture were and remain an all-encompassing reality, Sligh's family sought to prepare their children for the oppression that continues to be enacted and enforced against Black people to this day. "It was a fear put into us to prepare us—to toughen us up for the real world like a soldier is for war," she declares. "The history of American violence against Black people made our parents afraid that something awful would happen to us even before we grew up."[60] Grounded in the incontestable reality of the U.S. as a white racist nation steeped in centuries of bloodshed, Sligh's parents' fears were the result of their exposure to a "history of American violence" experienced by all Black people, a history which included the traumatizing lynching of Sligh's uncle, Council Thompson at the hands of white racist murderers. The tragedy of his death lives on as a heartbreaking memory that will never die for all generations of the Sligh family.

In Sligh's 1989 limited edition artist book, *Reading Dick and Jane With Me*, she visibilizes the "particular experiences" of her childhood that were defined by an individual as well as a shared exposure to white racist acts of terror (figure 20). "Using a memory of learning to read from elementary school textbooks called 'Dick and Jane Readers,'" Sligh says, "I combined photographs and 'the voice[s]' of my brothers and sisters and other neighborhood kids to engage in a dialogue that would interrupt 'the voice and authority' of the school textbooks."[61] Sligh interrogates and exposes the racist biases in evidence in the "voice and authority" of these white educational primers. She recognizes that these educational texts are a source of very real wounding for all people of color. She protests that these Western "stories portrayed the life of a white upper middle class suburban family and were touted as representative of the average American family" with devastating consequences. "As a young student I believed that they represented reality and that my own family was an aberration from the norm," Sligh recalls.[62] The racially offensive and persecutory Dick and Jane readers continue to masquerade as the "norm" as they were not only "used during the 1940s and 1950s as the standard reading textbook for American elementary schools," but have since been reissued in the twenty-first century.[63] As a result, they continue to be a mind-body-and-soul-destroying source of emotional trauma for and a catalyst for internalized oppression in communities of color worldwide.

Only one of these books, *Dick and Jane: We Play Outside* (2005), features any children of color on its cover. The cover's marginalization of an African American boy and two girls testifies to the endurance of a white racist mentality that shows no signs of abating. The Black children are shown in profile and in the background, while the white children, Dick and Jane, are front and center in a shameless fulfillment of the white American propagandists' dream: a white America for white American families only. Prophesying that the "'authority' of the old elementary school readers" would not only remain dominant but uncontested within a mainstream U.S. educational system, Sligh created *Reading Dick and Jane With Me* as a "site of resistance."[64] Working with the conviction that her newly inserted "fragments of family snapshots of children from my old neighborhood stand in for working class school age students and 'talk back,'" she disrupts and actively "interrupts" the white supremacist vision of these "old' and now newly reissued elementary readers in which only a rich, white, elite childhood is considered worthy of representation.[65] A radical site of Black empowerment that is still needed today, *Reading Dick and Jane With Me* is a weapon in Sligh's social justice arsenal.

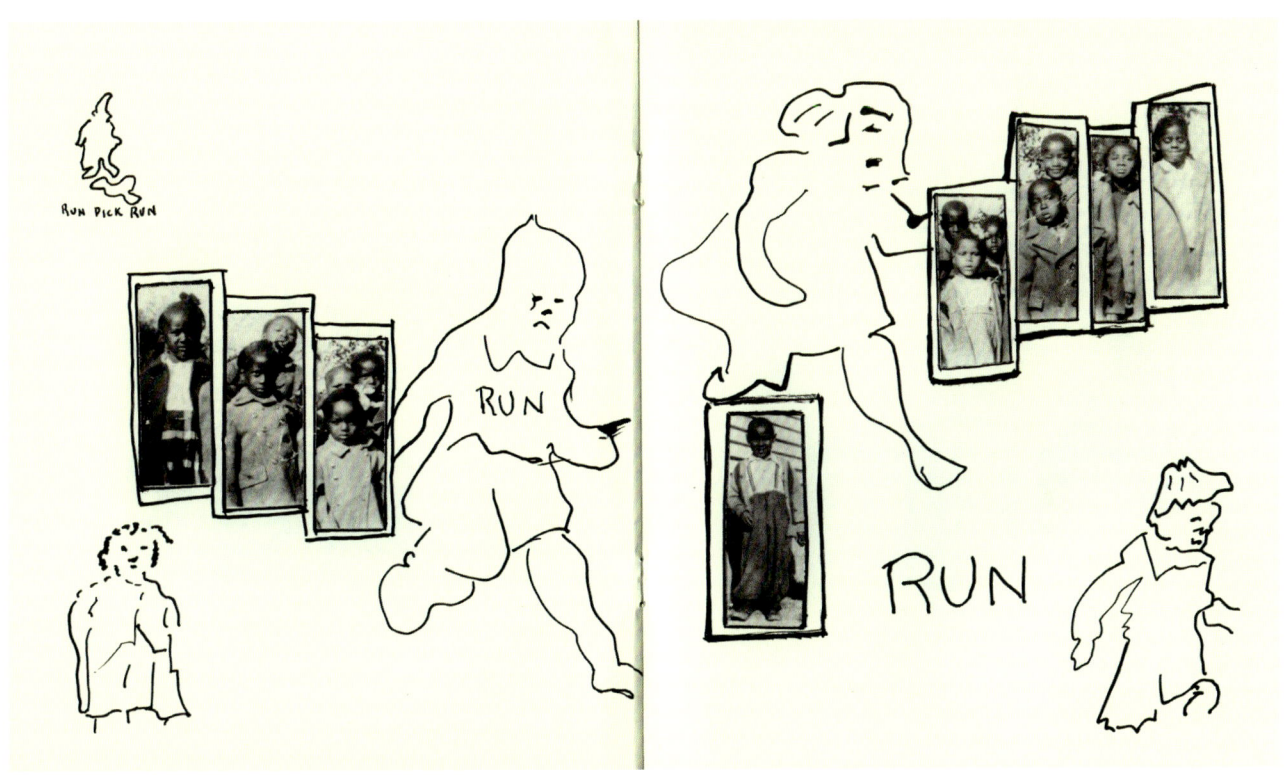

FIGURE 20. Clarissa T. Sligh, *Reading Dick and Jane With Me*, 1989. Stapled single signature offset paperback (8½ × 7 in.). Courtesy of the artist.

Even Sligh's choice of title—*Reading Dick and Jane With Me*—is a declaration of independence. Rejecting the white supremacist vision of what a U.S. family looks and acts like, Sligh insists that her audiences "read" the lives of white children not on their own terms or in isolation but "with me": and by "me" she specifically refers to her own familial context and personal experiences. She effortlessly succeeds in inserting her "witness-self" into the narrative frame, transforming the racist framework perpetuated by dominant white archetypes through a Black radical reinterpretative filter. According to Sligh's "radical lexicon," a Black female child's perspective becomes the lens through which it is possible to judge, interrogate, and critique white supremacist ideological dominance in mainstream U.S. culture.

Reading Dick and Jane With Me, a starkly monochrome work, contrasts the pastel colors characterizing the original readers' images—images through which their prejudicial white creators communicated their white supremacist vision of a white, rich, elite U.S. society for whites only. Sligh's emotionally hard-hitting and politically uncompromising cover replaces the brightly colored images of Dick and Jane with the silhouetted figure of a partially drawn young girl. Shown only in black outline, Sligh's unidentified and unidentifiable female protagonist is visible and invisible, present and absent, at the same time. According to her complex reimagining, childhood is not the source of unending joy or play displayed by the Dick and Jane books. Sligh's protagonist is the visual antithesis of the privileged white children of the old white primers: not only is her figure's physical form only partially rendered, but she is not shown playing with any other children. The unnamed and isolated girl is a powerful, incontestable embodiment of the artist as a "witness self." Confronting the viewer with an unreadable expression, she bears witness to the unspeakable stories and untellable experiences shared by Black people who are all fighting an intergenerational fight against the annihilating influences that have been generated by ongoing white racism across public and private contexts.

While Sligh produces "Reading," "Dick," "Jane," and "Me" of the book's title in a thick, bold type, she inserts "and" and "with" in italics and at an angle. She actively reinforces the idea that these words and the experiences they evoke—for Sligh and for children in her family and wider neighborhood—are only ever an afterthought. Sligh's placement of the title up against the incomplete portrait of her unnamed protagonist is a protest in itself. Her subversive strategy illuminates the ways in which Black children are, at worst, physically obliterated and psychologically annihilated within a mainstream western imaginary; or, at best, only appear as a tokenistic afterthought. Both result in yet further premeditated acts of violence to their personhoods. To encourage her readers to understand that both visual images and written words are sites of interpretative instability, Sligh creates a border of collaged layers of phrases in the book. Notably, only partial words are visible. She jumbles these textual fragments until they become unreadable. Here, she draws attention to the failures of visual no less than textual language when it comes to doing justice to untold Black lives. Using every means at her disposal, Sligh challenges the seeming neutrality of the all-white world as presented in these educational primers. Instead, she introduces interpretative instability as well as ideological and political uncertainty. Ultimately, Sligh's "lexicon of liberation" creates a radically empowered space in which she reimagines unrepresented Black family histories in all their psychological and emotional complexities.

Sligh's artist book subjects the mainstream "Dick and Jane" educational primers to a wholesale critique according to which she condemns their racist endorsement of an educational philosophy that is for whites only. She replaces the white supremacist vision of Dick and Jane with an empowered educational philosophy rooted in a celebration of Black autonomy, authority, and artistry. Sligh's Dick and Jane are the visual antithesis of the color-saturated poster children of the original book illustrations, thereby signaling her protest against the primers' heteronormative dominance. No longer rosy-cheeked, smiling, well-dressed, and privileged as they run, play, and jump within elite domestic settings, the Dick and Jane of her opening page have facial features that are all but obliterated. Their bodies are only partially visible, appearing against a gray backdrop and in an existential no place.

Sligh's decision to insert a fragment of primer text, "Dick and Jane and Spot," over and over again offers further categorical confirmation of her conviction that their dominance is in the process of self-destruction. Sligh starts with a large typeface but allows the words to descend into smaller and smaller print that becomes harder and harder to read. According to her revolutionary practice, Sligh's "me" calls the world of white privilege into question with the result that it falls apart. As she emphasizes, once the lives of "Dick and Jane" are read "with me," their white supremacist ideology—along with their white dominant power—fractures, splits, fragments, and dissolves.

Sligh sustains her psychological momentum and political provocation in *Reading Dick and Jane With Me* by repeatedly including her emotionally challenging portrait of a disappearing girl child from the cover. A surrogate for the artist herself, Sligh's unnamed protagonist reappears a few pages in and this time against an all-white backdrop. There can be no mistaking Sligh's symbolism: her surrogate self is all but obliterated in a sea of whiteness. Sligh's unnamed protagonist's importance as a "witness-self" is incontestable. When taken out of the context of a rich, elite, white-supremacist America for rich, elite, white Americans, the seemingly innocuous and innocent words, "Fun Dick Fun Jane Fun Spot Fun Sally Fun Puff," assume politically disturbing and morally offensive significance.

On the facing page, Sligh accompanies the exclusionary text "Fun Dick Fun Jane Fun Spot Fun Sally Fun Puff," not with a drawing of white children and their pets, but with a monochrome photograph of four Black children. The children directly contemplate the viewer. They are holding hands and standing in solidarity against the dehumanizing force of a violent and violating text that has been designed to eradicate their very existence. Here, Sligh exposes the devastating damage resulting from these children's exposure to a white racist ideological stranglehold, according to which they have no freedom for imaginative play but instead experience ongoing physical, emotional, and intellectual erasure within mainstream society.

Dramatically to the fore in Sligh's artist book is her determination to use the "photographs and 'the voice' of my brothers and sisters and other neighborhood kids" to "interrupt 'the voice and authority' of the school textbooks."[66] According to her radically revisionist vision,

while white children engage in acts of frivolous play, the unnamed Black children of *Reading Dick and Jane with Me* testify—via their emotionally charged and unreadable facial expressions—to the ongoing fight to survive, against the odds, a childhood dominated by an unspeakable and unimaginable suffering. Sligh refuses to lose sight of her protest aesthetic, ensuring that her Black protagonists have the last word and the last image and collaging their photographic portraits on top of the repeated fragments of the original white supremacist text. The work stands as one among many acts of dissidence for Sligh. She is categorical in her conviction that the white world of play is solely made possible by a Black world of physical, emotional, social, and cultural labor.

Among the most traumatized and traumatizing pages in *Reading Dick and Jane With Me* is a double spread from which Sligh removes all printed text, showing only close ups of Dick and Jane. Readers might expect Sligh to celebrate the demise of white dominance, and indeed the children have all but disintegrated, appearing only in sketchy terms. She subverts our expectations, however, by giving the figures unexpected power. Dick is no longer engaged in acts of lighthearted play. Instead, he holds a sharp object resembling a knife in one hand, while the word "RUN" appears on his chest. A dehumanized spectacle of terror, his head assumes the shape of a Ku Klux Klan hood while his minimally rendered nose, eyes, and mouth reinforce the idea that they are being partially concealed by a white mask. Jane is no less threatening: she may not appear to be wearing a Klan hood but her facial features are equally distorted as she runs, holding the photographs of Black children in her hands.

According to Sligh's reimagining, Dick and Jane are not innocuous white children engaged in innocent play. Rather, they are murderous white persecutors whose play is to torture Black children. Sligh's hand-drawn frames around each of these group photographs of Black children suggest her Black subjects are incarcerated in boxes that are visually reminiscent of coffins. The children are not yet murdered by white racists, but Sligh reveals the inevitability of her Black protagonists' experience of white violence. Sligh increases the harrowing resonances of this spread yet further by inserting another small drawing of the young girl from the cover. Again, the girl serves as Sligh's surrogate "witness self." Her role as a social commentator, political activist, and radical historian is here incontestable. While she has no agency to prevent the murderous barbarity of white people, her "witness-self" ensures that white mob violence is documented, dramatized, and never forgotten. Ultimately, Sligh's heartrending reimagining of the inevitability of white acts of violence against Black children in *Reading and Dick and Jane With Me* signals her transition from satirical denunciations of white supremacist privilege to hard-hitting meditations on the individual and collective fight for social justice and political reform as undertaken by Black families over the generations.

The hyper invisibility of Black people compared with the hyper visibility of white people lies at the heart of Sligh's radically revisionist protest aesthetic in *Reading Dick and Jane With Me*. In a later spread, she provides a powerful reworking of the group photograph of Black children she repeatedly includes throughout the book as a touchstone for Black presence in the face of white generated absence. On the lower half of both pages, the faces and bodies of the eight children all but disappear. Sligh substitutes the blurred lines of a drawing for the mechanical accuracy of a photograph, suggesting that their corporeal existence is all but annihilated. Here she includes a diminutive portrait of her "witness-self" directly above these all but disintegrated Black child subjects. This time her "witness-self" is represented in thin and barely delineated lines, a visual embodiment of the political statement of her handwritten text: "THESE STORIES SEEM MORE REAL THAN US EVERYBODY IS SO PERFECT EVERYBODY IS SO RIGHT WHO WE ARE BEGINS TO SLIP AWAY WHEN OUR SCHOOL BOOKS SOUND LIKE WE SHOULD BE THAT WAY COULD WE BE THAT WAY." Here Sligh directly engages with the pressures Black children face in fighting for their stories to remain "REAL" while working to hold onto "WHO WE ARE" in the face of white racist attempts to eradicate their personhood. Equipping her Black protagonists with the necessary revolutionary toolkit to "talk back" to white power, Sligh refuses to sanitize the traumatizing effects that have been caused by structures of internalized oppression over the generations.

Sligh's next spread argues that the only real way to eradicate white injustice lies in the acts of liberation undertaken by Black children themselves. She foregrounds their heroic feats of empowerment as they refuse to be subjugated by the dehumanizing tactics of white racists. Sligh includes an intimate close up of her "witness self" against a white backdrop. This time, however, she provides no visual capitulation to white supremacy; rather, Sligh's "witness self" directly confronts the viewer with a gesture of defiance. Sligh reinforces the image by collaging the group photograph of the Black children holding hands onto the girl's chest. On the facing page, she reproduces an enlarged copy of this same group photograph in order to give due space to her celebration of Black family traditions of survival. The handwritten text she inserts beneath celebrates the "voice" of these children as they "talk back" to white supremacist power: "WE KNOW HOW TO PLAY FUN GAMES TOO."

The final page of *Reading Dick and Jane With Me* includes no portraits of children, Black or white. Instead, Sligh draws a landscape with an intimate close-up of a tree marked by two spherical objects resembling eyes. Here it may be possible to argue for this tree's symbolic significance as a witness to the unmapped genealogical trees of Black families over the centuries. Ultimately, the ancestors' acts of witnessing through traditions of oral storytelling and myth-making make it possible for generations of Black families to survive the atrocities and tragedies that have defined centuries of slavery and centuries of a freedom that exists in name only. Sligh succeeds not only in interrupting but in actively destroying the supremacy exerted by white racists by repeatedly including the handwritten phrases "WE ALL HAVE DREAMS" and "WE ALL HAVE STORIES."

Declaring the independence of her protagonists, Sligh shares the conviction of Black children: that they themselves have power over their "DREAMS" and "STORIES." In so doing, she commits to righting the wrongs of white mainstream dominant educational history. She draws on centuries of Black oral storytelling and myth-making traditions to establish internalized systems of empowerment arising from strategies of Black intergenerational survival in place of the internalized structures of oppression generated by a white racist society. Sligh "knew my story was missing," but she translates the pain of that realization into a platform for the revolutionary reclamation not only of her own but of all erased narratives of Black lives.[67] "As I make visible, understand, forgive and heal the pain and hurt that I got just because I was me, I become more able to relax and reclaim pride and joy in who I am," Sligh jubilantly declares. "I regain my power and freedom as the healing occurs."[68] For Sligh, *Reading Dick and Jane With Me* testifies to the power of the "healing" act of art-making as a means of self and communal liberation for past, present, and future generations.

PAT WARD WILLIAMS   *(Born in Philadelphia, Pennsylvania, 1948)*

"I used to work in the documentary tradition, but I saw that people consumed these photographs without critical thought, often completely missing my meaning," Pat Ward Williams explains. Waging a war against the apathy of her audiences and their myopic misunderstandings, she developed an interventionist practice in which, "by manipulating the process, layering information, and using alternative presentation materials, I can put more of myself into the work and not just be a recorder of the facts."[69] Over the decades, she has endorsed a revisionist aesthetic, rejecting the seemingly dispassionate conventions of the "documentary tradition" that only ever pretend, and necessarily always fail, to be objective. Rather, Williams takes inspiration from her personal perspectives and lived experiences to create highly subjective, deeply emotional, and politically provocative photographic constructions and installations in which she invites her viewers into a "critical" as well as a self-reflexive engagement with her body of work. Instead of embracing a role as "recorder of the facts," she sees herself as a dramatist-historian-autobiographer-philosopher-artist who shares Sligh's determination to create multilayered assemblages and mixed-media photographs as "sites of resistance." "I like to construct an image, to reassemble and layer an image, to suggest layering of consciousness of layerings of experiences," Pat Ward Williams explains.[70]

Pat Ward Williams works with physical layers of materials to interrogate her own and her audiences' emotional, political, social, and cultural layers of consciousness. At the heart of her practices lies a commitment to doing justice to the untold and unimaged layerings of experiences within individual and collective African American autobiographical histories. For Williams, history—emotional, social, political, cultural, personal, and public—undergirds her "lexicon of liberation."[71] A social justice artist, she insists on taking up the "role[s]" not only of "participant" and "conduit," but of interpreter, investigator, analyst, re-presenter, and re-imaginer of all African American histories—personal and public as well as individual and collective.

Williams created the mixed-media assemblage *Ghosts That Smell Like Cornbread in 1986* (figure 21). She explains that "the piece is about the women in my family, women whom I never really knew except through oral histories and family photographs."[72] Working with a variety of materials, she creates an emotionally and politically complex memorial to untold family lives. She foregrounds closeup and long-view photographs of women in her own family as sources of imaginative and mythic power in order to celebrate her role as their living descendent.

In creating *Ghosts That Smell Like Cornbread*, Williams says that she "was really drawn to the tales of heroism and common sense that I heard about these women, so I made this as a shrine piece."[73] The piece is not only a "shrine" but an altar to which her audiences must reverently come to worship at the feet of Black female "tales of heroism." Williams defies her family members' human fallibility and physical mortality to testify to their spirit power that will never die. A complex work, this installation includes multiple photographic portraits of Williams's Black female ancestors and an interlocking grid produced by "curved

▶▶ *"DIG for My History"*

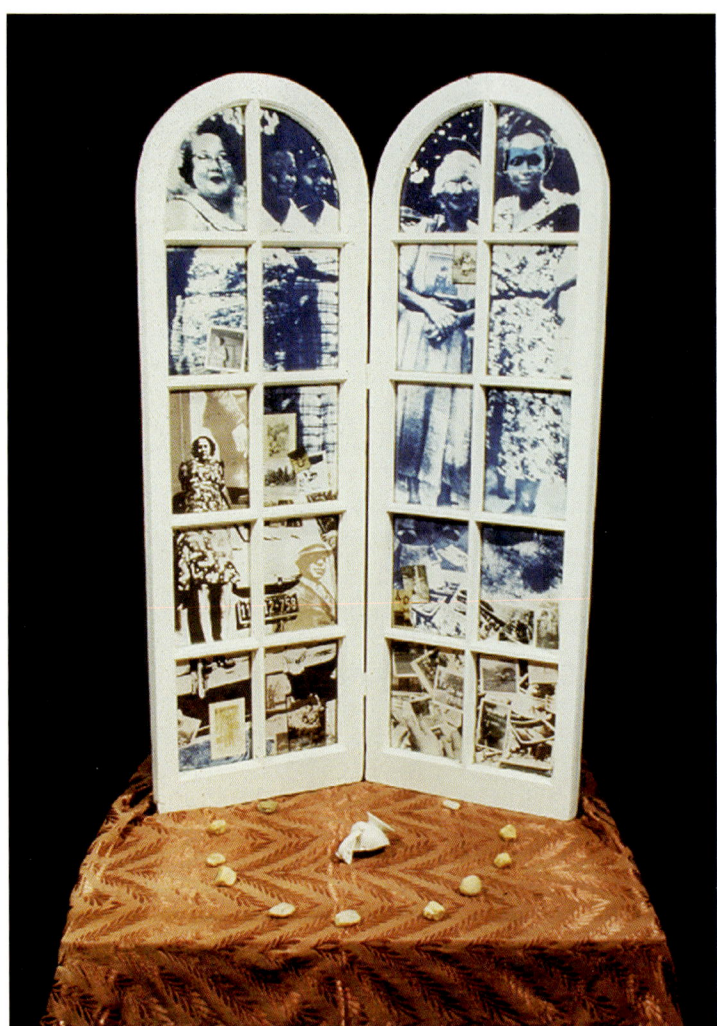

FIGURE 21. Pat Ward
Williams, *Ghosts That
Smell like Cornbread*, 1987.
Cyanotype photographs,
Vandyke photographs,
family snapshots, window
frames, fabric, stones,
broken cup (42 × 67 in.).
Courtesy of the artist.

windows."[74] Creating an "ecclesiastical look," these "curved windows" are visually evocative of the stained glass windows that adorn churches. Williams's "lexicon of liberation" is inspired by her determination to inspire her audiences to venerate Black female individual and collective histories of suffering and survival.

But the piece does not represent an idealized reimagining of her ancestors' lives. The portraits of Williams's female family members are literally split apart by these interlocking, white-colored bars, which run the risk of segmenting, fracturing, and even breaking apart their faces and bodies. With these frames, Williams exposes the traumatizing ways in which Black women's histories remain confined within ongoing social, political, and cultural systems of subjugation generated by oppressive white frameworks. Williams photographs her own hands holding numerous family portraits that are impossible to see because they are layered one over another in a hard-hitting testament to irrecoverable loss. She is all too aware of the painful reality that, in the lives of Black women across all families and generations, many individual and collective histories cannot be reimagined and personal and public memories cannot be memorialized.

Williams's work comes to life not only from the photographs in the curved windows but from the objects—including the stones and broken cup—she places before her altar. Shedding light on this mixed-media practice, Williams explains, "The stones arranged in a circle serve as a marker to the grave site of my ancestors. Very often in the African American tradition the last used article of the deceased or that person's favorite possession, like a cup, is placed on the grave for them to have for all eternity. But the cup must be broken, to make a break literally with its natural use in the world. The broken cup symbolizes its usefulness 'passing' from this world to the next. It's the same way that the spirit moves."[75] For Williams, *Ghosts That Smell Like Cornbread* is a conduit for ongoing communications, conversations, and collaborations with her female forebears. In recreating the "grave site of my ancestors," she generates a space in which the "spirit moves," defying the realities of physical passing to celebrate ongoing spiritual force through the emotional and political power of storytelling traditions and lived experiences. In very real ways,

the stones and broken cup function not only as "markers" but as symbols of the continuation of her ancestors' emotional, spiritual, and cultural lives in spite of their physical death. She insists that they are far from passive and powerless by foregrounding their very real presence in the lives of their descendants, including herself. Ultimately, *Ghosts That Smell Like Cornbread* is a visual testament to the enduring spirit power of Williams's ancestors in their own right and as emotional representatives of all Black women forebears. According to her radical aesthetic, these are ghosts whose real lives, including the culinary art of making cornbread, will never die but will live on as a source of inspiration for all generations.

In 1987, Williams created *Accused/Blowtorch/Padlock*, a mixed-media work constructed, like *Ghosts That Smell Like Cornbread*, from a combination of found and fine art materials (figure 22). Nothing could be more distinct from her shrine to the spirits of her female ancestors than this emotionally harrowing work, however. A psychologically disturbing juxtaposition of text and image memorializes the traumatizing photograph of an unidentified Black man's chained and roped body, shown just before he is lynched by a murderous white racist mob. A salvaged window frame consisting of four sections dominates this work. In the first frame Williams reproduces the heartbreaking photograph of this unnamed man, bound by a rope and chained to a tree. In the remaining three frames, she provides a series of closeups of different sections of the photograph, variously showing the man's hands, arm, and torso in an intimate perspective. She inserts capitalized lettering in red type across each of the three images in which this unknown man is horrifyingly reduced to a series of body parts: "ACCUSED," "BLOWTORCH," and "PADLOCK." *Accused/Blowtorch/Padlock* is a hard-hitting meditation on the sufferings, sacrifices, and struggles of the ancestors that are "always with us."

First and foremost, the dissection of the unknown and faceless man's body by the window frames is visually prophetic of his dismemberment by lynching. The accompanying text focuses on the barbaric injustice of this man's wrongful and murderous persecution as the "ACCUSED." Williams is incensed and deeply traumatized by the immorality of the centuries old

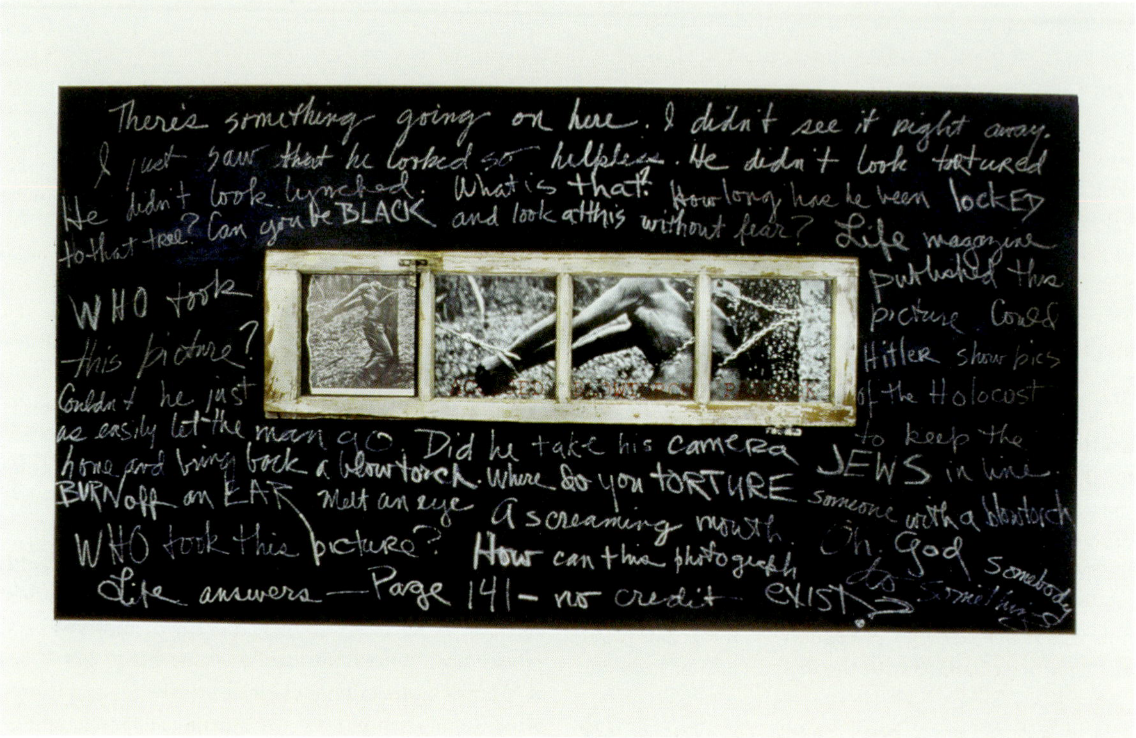

FIGURE 22. Pat Ward Williams,
Accused/Blowtorch/Padlock, 1987.
Magazine page, silver gelatin prints,
window frame, film positives, paint,
text (6 × 4 ft.). Courtesy of the artist.

practice of lynching, a white racist system of terror in which innocent Black people of all genders and ages were persecuted, tortured, and killed in the service of defending and maintaining white supremacist power. Here Williams is a radical memorialist and revolutionary witness to the atrocities and abuses experienced by generations of Black people within U.S. history. She denounces the shocking cruelty of the "BLOWTORCH" and "PADLOCK" to critique and condemn the persecutory weapons of white racist hate groups. The piece is calculated to instill a sense of anger in and inspire acts of protest from viewers. Williams makes her demands explicit: "I force the viewer to look at what is really going on, by dissecting the important body of information and by directing with text what the viewer should notice; the tied hands (accused), the scarred back (blowtorch), and the lock, chain, and tree (padlock)."[76] She deliberately denies her white target audiences access to any form of emotional catharsis, insisting instead that they "really look" at this psychologically disturbing photograph of the Black man's roped and chained body. Williams demands that her white viewers fully comprehend the tragedies generated by white supremacy, not only as a racist ideology, philosophy, and mentality, but as a practice of terror with the explicit aim of exterminating Black lives.

"I came across a book called *The Best of Life Magazine* (1979)," Williams recalls.[77] She identifies the source material for *Accused/Blowtorch/Padlock* by confiding, "I turned the pages and saw this photograph of a lynched black man, and I was horrified, as anyone would have been." "I put the book back on the shelf and left the bookstore." Afterward, she was unable to shake the photograph's power on her psyche. She explains, "This image stayed with me for weeks and weeks, until I felt that I had to go back to the bookstore and actually own that photograph so that I could really work out the feelings I had about it." Williams creates this mixed-media work to undertake an emotional process not only to "work out the feelings I had about it" but in order "to get it off my mind" and also "communicate to other people what I was feeling." She asks, "What is it exactly that I'm feeling when I see it? What do I think about when I think about this photograph?" Finally, she comes to a decision: "I thought that the best way to get all this across was with text—the writing on the wall,

so to speak—and to be as precise as possible about the questions it raised in me."[78]

Sharing Sligh's determination to work with an emotively charged relationship between word and image, Williams surrounds this photograph of a lynched Black man with handwritten text, white letters on a black background:

> There's something going on here. I didn't see it right away. After all, you see one lynched man you've seen them all. He looks so helpless. He doesn't look lynched yet. What is that under his chin? How long has he been LOCKED to that tree? Can you be BLACK and look at this? Life magazine published this picture. Could Hitler show pictures of the Holocaust to keep the JEWS in line? WHO took this picture? Couldn't he just as easily let the man go? Did he take his camera home and then come back with a blowtorch? Where do you TORTURE someone with a blowtorch? BURN off an ear? Melt an eye? A screaming mouth. How can this photograph exist? WHO took this picture? Oh, god. Life answers—Page 141– no credit. Somebody do something. [See figure 22]

Accused/Blowtorch/Padlock provides a psychological, political, and personal commentary on "what's going on here," provoking the moral outrage of audiences and galvanizing "Somebody" to "do something." Pat Ward Williams's textual denunciations bear witness to the violences and violations of this "image of a lynched man." They insist, too, on the photograph's typicality: "you see one lynched man you've seen them all." Williams asks the painful question "Could Hitler show pictures of the Holocaust to keep the JEWS in line?" in order to expose the lynching of Black women, children, and men in the United States as a traumatizing ritual of racial terrorism that is on a continuum with the acts of genocide institutionalized against people of Jewish descent and against "other groups singled out by the Nazis."[79] As Terese Pencak Schwartz writes, these groups "included LGBTQ individuals, the physically and mentally disabled, Roma (gypsies), Poles and other Slavic peoples, Jehovah's Witnesses, and members of political opposition groups."[80]

For Williams, both the physical violence caused by unnamed white lynchers and the visual violence enacted by the unknown photographer are sources of wounding. "WHO took this picture?" she asks, exposing the photographer's moral culpability. "Couldn't he just as easily let the man go? Did he take his camera home and then come back with a blowtorch?" Her outrage regarding the photographer's willful decision to play no part in ending this man's suffering is conveyed by an unanswerable question: "How can this photograph exist?" For Williams, the photographer's decision not to "let the man go" renders his "camera" synonymous with a "blowtorch" as a no less powerful weapon that is responsible for the torture and mass murder of Black people over the generations.

Because the photograph does not record the lynching itself, Williams relies on graphic textual language to testify to the visceral realities of the illegal practice of ritualized killing: "Where do you TORTURE someone with a blowtorch? BURN off an ear? Melt an eye? A screaming mouth." She asks, "Why is this photograph in *Life* magazine?" More importantly, "Is it information or terrorism?"[81] Ultimately recognizing the photograph's power as a tool of "terrorism" endorsed by white supremacist hate groups in their determination to injure, wound, and kill people of color, she asks and leaves unanswered a mind-body-and-soul-destroying question: "Can you be BLACK and look at this?"

By creating the handwritten text with a "chalkboard effect," Williams asserts her right to act as a teacher responsible for educating her white viewers regarding the urgent necessity of their political and intellectual, no less than their emotional and psychological,

engagement with this visual representation of a lynched male figure [82] "My handwriting acts as my voice, my own voice," explains Williams. "By using handwriting instead of print, I hope you can hear a tone and a human inflection."[83] She is painfully aware that the photograph is emotionally overwhelming. She asks her audiences not to detach themselves psychologically from her work's traumatizing and horrifying content, but to engage in emotionally responsible and thoughtfully meaningful ways instead. A key issue in Williams's aesthetic philosophy is her encouragement of her viewers to be self-aware of their reactions—emotional, social, political, and moral—to witnessing this man's body as a site and sight of violence and violation.

Endorsing the idea that "art can be a powerful weapon in the larger struggle against oppression," Williams insists on her audience's active engagement with her experimental practice.[84] "I like my work to agitate," she says, deliberately invoking the protest legacy of an earlier reformer. "As artists our continuous task is to, in the words of Frederick Douglass: 'Agitate, agitate, agitate.'"[85] As it was for Frederick Douglass, a freedom-fighter, revolutionary, radical, philosopher, writer, and orator living in the 1800s, so it is for Williams working in the twentieth and twenty-first centuries. The only way to realize the aims of social justice campaigns is to use language—textual, visual, and oral—as a tool of moral resistance and political agitation.

LYLE ASHTON HARRIS   *(Born in the Bronx, New York City, New York, 1965)*

"I began taking self-portraits in the 1980s to explore the dissonance and ambivalence I experienced in relation to my own image," Lyle Ashton Harris explains.[86] Harris uses the corporeal complexities and spiritual ambiguities within his personal constructions of selfhood as the thematic and formal departure for his work. "I'm interested in exploring the body as a site of both pain and pleasure in all of its ambivalence," he says.[87] Honoring the personal and political issues embedded within his own lived experience, he investigates both socially oppressive and emotionally liberating reimaginings of

racialized, gendered, classed, and sexualized identities, not only for himself but for people of color more generally. "I'm attracted to my subjects in a lot of different ways: in relationship to form, to power, to desire, and in relationship to the transgression of class," he explains. "All of my subjects have dealt with a certain amount of pain—I think we all have. It's part of the human condition."[88]

In Harris's visual meditations on the human condition, pleasure and pain are inextricably connected. He foregrounds the liberating potential of living and

▶▶ "A Conduit between History, Trauma, and Memory"

creating "on the border" as a means to reverse the damage generated by white mainstream U.S. racism. Harris works against hierarchies of inclusion and acceptability defined by a white dominant society in which all differences are persecuted, othered, and marginalized. As Harris summarizes, "I'm engaged in a democratization of the subject matter—equivalence, if you will."[89] Warring against reductive and prejudicial categorizations of experience or artificially dichotomous strategies of representation, Harris creates self-consciously interrogative and radically experimental works. His work explores what it means to live "on the border," and he endorses a practice which breaks taboos and raises consciousness. An individual's and a group's rights to freedoms remains at the heart of Harris's "lexicon of liberation."

Alongside photographic portraits and mixed-media installations, Harris repeatedly returns to collaging techniques, explaining that "through the art of the 'cut', collage, for me, acts as a weapon between history, trauma and memory."[90] Like Sligh, Williams, and Myra Greene, Harris understands the act of "cutting"—a formal strategy of layering and rupture—as a means to debate malleable physical and psychological relationships between "history, trauma and memory." For Harris, the acts of destruction and creation converge; he relies on fragmentation to break down all prescriptive barriers. Harris uses collage as a conduit of defiance against oppressive structures. Across his works, he imaginatively reconnects the fractured relationships between social and political histories, emotional and experiential traumas, and personal and public memories.

In 1994, Harris created three self-portraits with his brother, Thomas Allen Harris. They titled the piece *Brotherhood, Crossroads and Etcetera*. Harris explains that "the themes invoked in *Brotherhood* speak to the ambivalence around violence, betrayal, and abjection that is part of our collective legacy as African Americans."[91] The series of portraits is emotionally provocative and radically transgressive. Harris and his brother's complex strategies of representation—personally and in relation to each other—transgress socially normative taboos. Here, they debate issue of physical and psychological "dissonance and ambivalence" as they impact upon, constrict, damage, and dehumanize African American lives.

A sense of threat—corporeal, emotional, and spiritual—is powerfully to the fore in the portraits. In these works, the brothers defiantly pose nude and in various intimate positions. In recognition of the fact that they have denied themselves any safe ground, Harris describes their strategies of self-representation in spiritual terms, as both an "offering" and a "sacrifice." As he says, "We have been vulnerable in sharing our ambivalent feelings of desire, envy, fear and loss towards each other."[92] Dominate Western conventions of portraiture idealize white elite subjects and associate them only with political power and material wealth. The Harris brothers' psychologically charged and sexually provocative portraits reject such conventions and instead constitute an act of social protest as well as a spiritual, emotional, and cultural "offering": an association between Black manhood and issues of representation, reimagining, and resistance are a defining narratological lens.

In the first portrait of the series, Lyle Ashton Harris stands at the back of the photograph and directly confronts the viewer while his brother leans back, eyes closed, in a position suggestive of sexual ecstasy. Lyle Ashton Harris's right hand is outspread on his brother's chest. The second portrait represents another deliberate transgression of dominant sexual taboos. In it, Harris and his brother kiss on the mouth while they stand facing one another. This staging of physical intimacy remains complicated, however, as Thomas Allen Harris presses a gun to his brother's chest. This explicit inclusion of violence speaks to the series' preoccupation with representing the "ambivalence around violence, betrayal, and abjection" afflicting the lives of African American men in their daily fight for survival in a white mainstream U.S. society.[93] Compounding the emotional tensions embedded in their complex portraits of love and hate, the final image shows the brothers standing each with one arm wrapped around each other. Again, Harris offers his viewers no celebratory vision of uncomplicated love. While there is no gun, he and his brother each hold the end of a leather strap, suggesting the possibility of future acts of violence.

Harris interrogates the ways in which love and hate, desire and repulsion, empowerment and disempowerment, and "pleasure and pain" are mutually inclusive rather than mutually exclusive categories of existence for all generations fighting to survive the United States as a white supremacist nation that destroys, maims, and kills Black lives. He acknowledges that "these images are transgressive in their relationship to the pantheon of African American visual culture." Specifically, "they disregard bourgeois notions of propriety and morality" as a way of "combating hideous representations of blackness in American popular culture."[94] As "sites of resistance," Harris's controversial portraits imagine an emotionally vulnerable and radically nonconformist Black masculinity that is not only unconfined and undefined, but that actively challenges and rejects "bourgeois notions of propriety and morality." Sexually liberated, physically expressive, and emotionally provocative, these portraits are the visual antithesis of the "hideous representations of blackness" endorsed by a white U.S. imaginary.

Harris refuses to shy away from the harrowing reality that Black men have been and continue to be subjected to abuse within white mainstream U.S. society. He explains, "These images graphically mirror the violence and self-destruction that constitute our contemporary experience."[95] Courageously and compassionately, the *Brotherhood* series confronts the damage wrought by white supremacy as both a practice that maims and kills and as a mentality that creates internalized divisions within African American populations. Harris provides a poignant meditation regarding the portraits' message: "I often question if it is easier to reject or destroy those like yourself—someone who mirrors your shared history of lynching, terror, and the historical trauma experienced by the collective black body—rather than to love them."[96] White racist systems ruin Black lives by generating internalized structures of oppression according to which rejection, destruction, and hate are all-consuming and all-defining: as a result, any and all expressions of "love" to oneself or anyone else become impossible. Harris rejects these structures entirely.

Ultimately working with his own and his brother's portraits as a means to interrogate the dangers—emotional, physical, and personal—that are endured by Black populations more generally, Harris issues a warning to his audiences regarding his *Brotherhood* series: "If you read the photographs too literally—that these are two *brothers*—it obscures the larger idea of black-on-black violence as well as the resulting psychic

violence which is endemic to the culture at large."[97] Significantly, "such a reading compromises our ability to talk about how we are conditioned to kill that which we love and that which mirrors us—ourselves."[98] *Brotherhood* holds white supremacist acts of "psychic violence" against Black people accountable not only for generating "black-on-black violence," but for ensuring that self-hate rather than self-love is the defining psychological reality. As Harris explains, "These works are explicitly uncompromising while functioning as a form of exorcism against types of internalized social trauma that too often remain unseen and unspoken."[99] These portraits, in which Black men are emotionally and physically vulnerable, do not capitulate to white racism. Rather, Harris offers them as a "form of exorcism" that destabilizes socially determinist realities in favor of physically liberated and psychologically expressive Black male subjectivities.

"The red, black, green velvet backdrop we use in *Brotherhood* references Marcus Garvey's UNIA," Harris explains regarding his decision to foreground the "tri-color flag" of the Universal Negro Improvement Association, founded by the world-renowned Jamaican leader.[100] The "brotherhood" he is memorializing refers not only to his fraternal relationship with Thomas Allen but to the international "brotherhood" Garvey and his followers celebrated between African American populations in the United States and Black nations of Africa. Garvey's flag, an "icon" of association which endorsed a Black nationalist message and advocated a "Back to Africa" movement, has a long activist history in the U.S. and has "been taken up at different points since [Garvey], specifically by the Black Power movement in the late 1960s."[101] And yet, Harris's reuse of this flag is far from celebratory. He is careful to stipulate that "this collaboration with Thomas—using masquerade as our mode of transgression—is a way of expanding the notion of who can lay claim to the liberatory potential envisioned in the UNIA flag."[102] Spectacle and play are integral to both a theatrical "masquerade" aesthetic and to Harris's vision. The brothers' transgressive strategies of self-imagining open up an alternative space in which it becomes newly possible to visualize Black masculinity as a site of artistic agency and performative possibility. "We are challenging a construction of

African nationalism that positions queers and feminists outside of the black family, the Million Man march and other black institutions," Harris declares, adding, "I'm saying that this flag is my family's background too, both immediate and extended all the way, let's say, across the African diaspora."[103] Ultimately, his *Brotherhood* series performs this vital social justice work. At the same time, he carves out an alternative iconographic space in which he provides "a counter-memory, a memory of resistance," for his Black audiences.[104]

In 2010, decades after *Boyhood*, Harris created the mixed-media collage *Untitled (Miss Ghana)* as part of his *Jamestown Prison Erasure* series (figure 23). At the center of the collage is a handwritten poem in blue ink on white lined paper and accompanied by illustrations of a bird and flower. Signed "BY ALFRED," the poem hangs on the surface of a wall and reads: "I am a trap/ By my enemies/ Like a bird/ That had no course/ To be blame/ Oh! that I have wings/ Like a dove I will fly/ Away home," Emotionally and politically provocative, Alfred's poem relies on traumatizing language to describe his tortuous experience of physical incarceration and psychological confinement. Significantly, it does not appear in isolation. Photographs of semiclothed women and car advertisements hang pinned from the crumbling surface of this same wall. These emblems of escapist fantasy form a powerful contrast to Alfred's poetic meditation on his imprisonment.

The inspiration for the materials Harris selected for his *Jamestown Prison Erasure* series came in part from the "working archive of photographs" he amassed during his seven years in Ghana.[105] He further explains that he made a visit to a "seventeenth-century fort that once housed slaves awaiting transport and was used as a prison until 2007, when it fell into disuse."[106] He recalls, "Upon visiting this site before 2007 I frequently noticed long lines of local women and children waiting outside." He learned the tragic truth that "they were there to visit incarcerated family members who were serving their prison sentences in the former slave fort."[107] On a later visit, Harris and his New York University students gained access to the historic site and made a powerful discovery: "Scattered throughout we encountered the remaining fragile evidence of the site's recent inhabitants in the form of newspaper cutouts pasted on the rough-hewn wall surfaces."[108] Fighting not only to survive physically but to keep their bodies, souls, and minds intact, these men "left behind a compelling ghostly trace" via their artistic "cutouts."[109] Their juxtaposed words and images represented an array of themes related to identity politics, masculinity, family, racism, capitalism, sexuality, innocence, and freedom.

"Although the prisoners had been released or transferred, these abandoned artifacts—bearing witness to their desires and fantasies during incarceration—memorialized this lost time in the form of fragmentary wall collages," Harris observes.[110] Surviving against the odds, these incarcerated men-turned-artists transformed these "abandoned artifacts" into site-specific art testifying to their triumphs in preserving their "desires and fantasies" and in assuming the role of historians of and witnesses to their "lost time." Harris believes in the transformative power of art-making as a bulwark against self-destruction, self-annihilation, and self-obliteration. He recognizes the "redemptive power that creativity played in the lives of these incarcerated men."[111] To use the configurations of Clarissa Sligh, no more tangible "witness-selves" can be found than in these "fragmentary wall collages" they created while living in a former "slave fort" turned penitentiary. More particularly, as Alfred's meditation on his experiences of imprisonment testifies, these men refused to be defined by their incarceration. In their collages, they not only left a "ghostly trace" of their "desires and fantasies," but also protested against the moral, political, and social injustices of their confinement.

Alfred's poem is a living monument to Harris's conviction that "the art of the 'cut', collage, for me, acts as a conduit between history, trauma and memory." He writes, "I am a trap/ By my enemies/ Like a bird/ That had no course/ To be blame/ Oh! that I have wings/ Like a dove I will fly/ Away home." In these powerful words, he memorializes a hidden history of trauma in this "slave fort" turned prison that is centuries rather than decades old.[112] With this radical act, he is using the "art of the 'cut'" to create a "conduit" in which he opens up lines of spiritual and imaginative communication between the pain of his own and his contemporaries' incarceration and the suffering of the untold generations of women, children, and men living and dying by

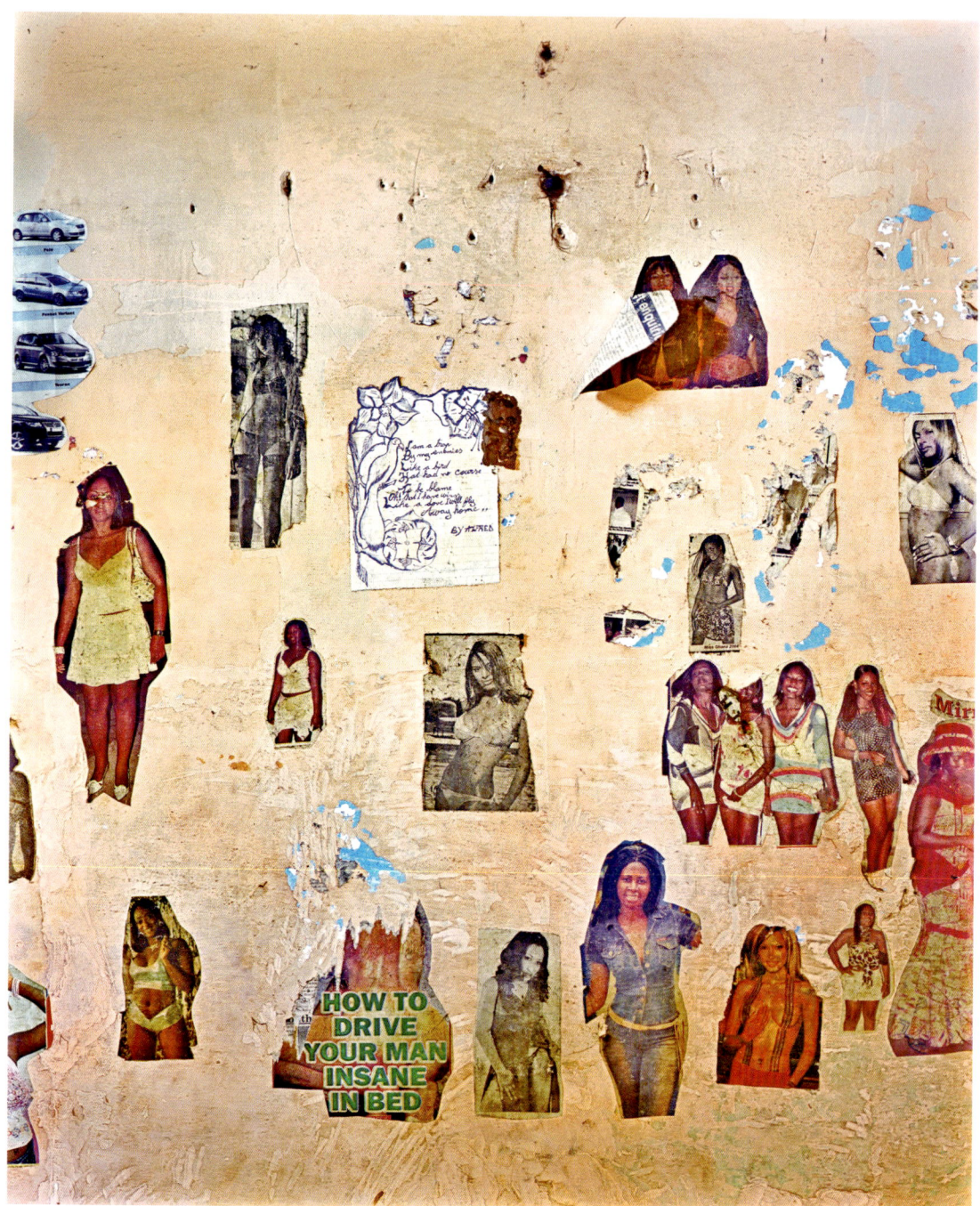

FIGURE 23. Lyle Ashton Harris, *Untitled (Miss Ghana)*, in *Jamestown Prison Erasure*, 2010. C-print on dibond (41 5/16 × 33 1/16 in.). Courtesy of the artist.

the untold millions of people within these walls during the transatlantic slave trade. Alfred's dream that "I have wings / Like a dove I will fly / Away home" invokes the belief system of his enslaved ancestors which taught that they would "fly / Away home" in death, leading many people to commit suicide on slave ships. Harris's collages honor the untold stories of men like Alfred in order to name and shame slavery's contemporary legacies. He memorializes the traumatizing reality that transatlantic slavery is not only not a distant memory but, for white European ex-enslaving and slave-trading nations, a site of willful amnesia, erasure, and denial. As he and Alfred are all too aware, the mind-body-and-soul-destroying realities of slavery persist in systems of racist persecution, imprisonment, and mass murder in the twenty-first century.

It is particularly significant for Harris that "in 2011 the World Bank declared Ghana officially a middle-class country."[113] An artist who is determined to interrogate the moral and social implications of this newfound financial status, Harris explains of his *Jamestown Prison Erasure* series, "I'm interested in tropes of modernity and consumerism, in what it meant for these incarcerated men to be imagining freedom, picturing life outside."[114] As artists, social commentators, witnesses, historians, and political theorists, men like Alfred are committed to "imagining freedom" in their war against wrongful imprisonment. Collaging, far from being a politically neutral act, is a weapon in their social justice arsenal. This powerful technique operates "as at once an aspiration on their part and also a critique of consumerism."[115] It is an anticapitalist, antimaterialist, and anti-imperialist act. Harris realizes that while the "act of the prisoners is in some way redemptive," it is also "a critique of the class-based culture that exists among the Ghanaians themselves as a former British colony."[116] These artists create consciousness-raising collages, "picturing life outside" as no halcyon state of existence but as mired in social, political, cultural, and ideological contexts of oppression.

While Harris confirms "a celebratory aspect" in his body of work, he is no less emphatic that "there's also the process of working-through trauma and grief."[117] Harris's practice is defined by a commitment to honor the emotional weight of art-making as a "conduit between history, trauma and memory," and as a source of Black diasporic resistance to centuries of white European systems of slavery, colonialism, and empire.

MYRA GREENE   *(Born in New York City, New York, 1975)*

"I made a lot of self-portraits and objects that related directly to my black body," Myra Greene notes, referring to her early autobiographically inspired photographs and mixed-media sculptures.[118] She later realized that "over time I struggled with the concept of commodified blackness and how an art object helps to promote that idea."[119] For Myra Greene, as for Clarissa Sligh, Pat Ward Williams, and Lyle Ashton Harris, the art object is not an ideologically neutral or politically safe space. Recognizing that Western art history has profited from and traded in a "commodified blackness," Greene's emotionally unequivocal practice exposes the traumatizing ways in which Black women's bodies have been repeatedly appropriated, violated, abused, exoticized, sexualized, stereotyped, misinterpreted, erased, and dehumanized within a white dominant imaginary over the centuries. "Some artists are interested in the taxonomy of looking at faces, while others try to draw narratives from the body," she observes. She is "interested in all of this," but adds, "I also don't want to be handcuffed to the parameters of portraiture."[120]

Greene challenges the parameters of portraiture in order to dramatize an array of psychologically ambiguous and politically complex subjectivities. A storyteller, memorialist, and witness to the hidden histories of Black women's experiences, she creates photographs and assemblages that "draw narratives" not only "from the body" but from the "taxonomy of looking at faces." Greene works with the corporeal realities and emotional narratives generated by her own face and body

▶▶ "I Look like a Slave"

as the catalysts to her visual language of self-liberation. Her aesthetic practice challenges and unsettles issues related to the politics of representation, identity, sexuality, power, beauty, memory, ancestry, and family.

In a radical declaration of independence, Greene created an experimental series simply titled *Self-Portraits* between 2002 and 2004. Working to free her practice, face, and body from the visual stranglehold exerted by a white racist imaginary, she rejects the appropriating and annihilating associations of the Black woman's portrait with self-evident narratives. Greene endorses a philosophically analytical as well as an emotionally and politically provocative radical practice. She explains that "in this series of contemplative portraits, I experimented with photographic techniques to create a random patterning and destruction of the photographic ideals of clarity and precision."[121] In creating materially ambiguous and emotionally ambivalent works, she rejects the art object's complicity in perpetuating the "concept of commodified blackness." She rejects the "photographic ideals of clarity and precision," denying her viewers ready-made access to her face and body in her self-portraits. Interrogating the formal strategies for reimaging and reimagining Black women's bodies, Greene adopts an ethic of anti-spectacularization, anti-commodification, and anti-exoticization. Her complex portraits are sites of concealment as well as revelation. She dramatizes her face and body by working with a visual language that is both abstract and figurative. By representing her own physicality in psychologically "contemplative" and spiritually empowering portraits, she renders null and void the damage to a Black woman's nude body resulting from "commodified blackness" and white audiences' tendencies toward voyeuristic consumption.

The titles of the nine inkjet prints in Greene's *Self-Portrait* series reveal a system of "random patterning" that provides a provocative investigation into only one part of her body at a time: *thighs, arm, belly, collar bone, face* (figure 24), *fleshy back* (figure 25), *head back, lower back,* and *shoulder.*[122] The prints come to life on heavy watercolor paper and rely on distinct formal dynamics. "The body is cropped and photographed as mass," Greene explains. She summarizes the formal dynamics of her process by emphasizing, "while murky, these images reward with the revelation of something, my body

and my presence."[123] Greene's rejection of "clarity and precision" speaks to a visual poetics of explicatory withholding rather than didactic explanation. Working with "murky" rather than crystalline photographic techniques, she generates formal ambiguities via layers of green, black, yellow, pink, and orange color that stream across each portrait's surface. As a result, the intimate photographs resembling abstract-figurative paintings foreground issues of psychological complexities rather than physical realities. While her titles promise her audiences a graphic exposé of her body parts, her obfuscating formal techniques deny access to her thighs, arm, belly, collar bone, face, back, and shoulder. Her nude figure is not only "cropped" but "photographed as mass," effectively invisibilizing the material trace of her body. Greene employs a politically dissident practice to reject dominant associations of Black women's bodies with "commodified blackness" or reductive corporeality in favor of imaginative possibilities and the spiritual, psychological, and emotional "revelation" of her "presence."

While *collar bone, head back, shoulder,* and *face* display an identifiable, if only partially recognizable, outline of her neck, the back of her head, her shoulder, and her physiognomy, *thighs, arm, belly, fleshy back,* and *lower back* defy realist conventions. These works' emotionally powerful close-ups have the hard-hitting result that her body has become all but indecipherable. A case in point is *arm.* Here, a mottled and "murky" surface consists of drops of yellow and red color falling onto the partial outline of her arm, incontestably associating the photograph with abstract painting. Greene does not endorse dominant systems of commodification and spectacularization. Instead, she resists the centuries-long history of Black women's bodies as sites and sights not only of appearance and disappearance but of appropriation, annihilation, and abuse within a white mainstream U.S. imaginary. She guarantees that *arm,* and her series of self-portraits more generally, "reward with the revelation of something, my body and my presence."[124] Black women's interior subjectivities (their "presence") rather than their corporeal objectivities (their bodies) define Greene's subject matter.

A psychologically provocative self-portrait in her series, *face* features an intimate yet partial view of Greene's physiognomy. Her face wears an emotional expression

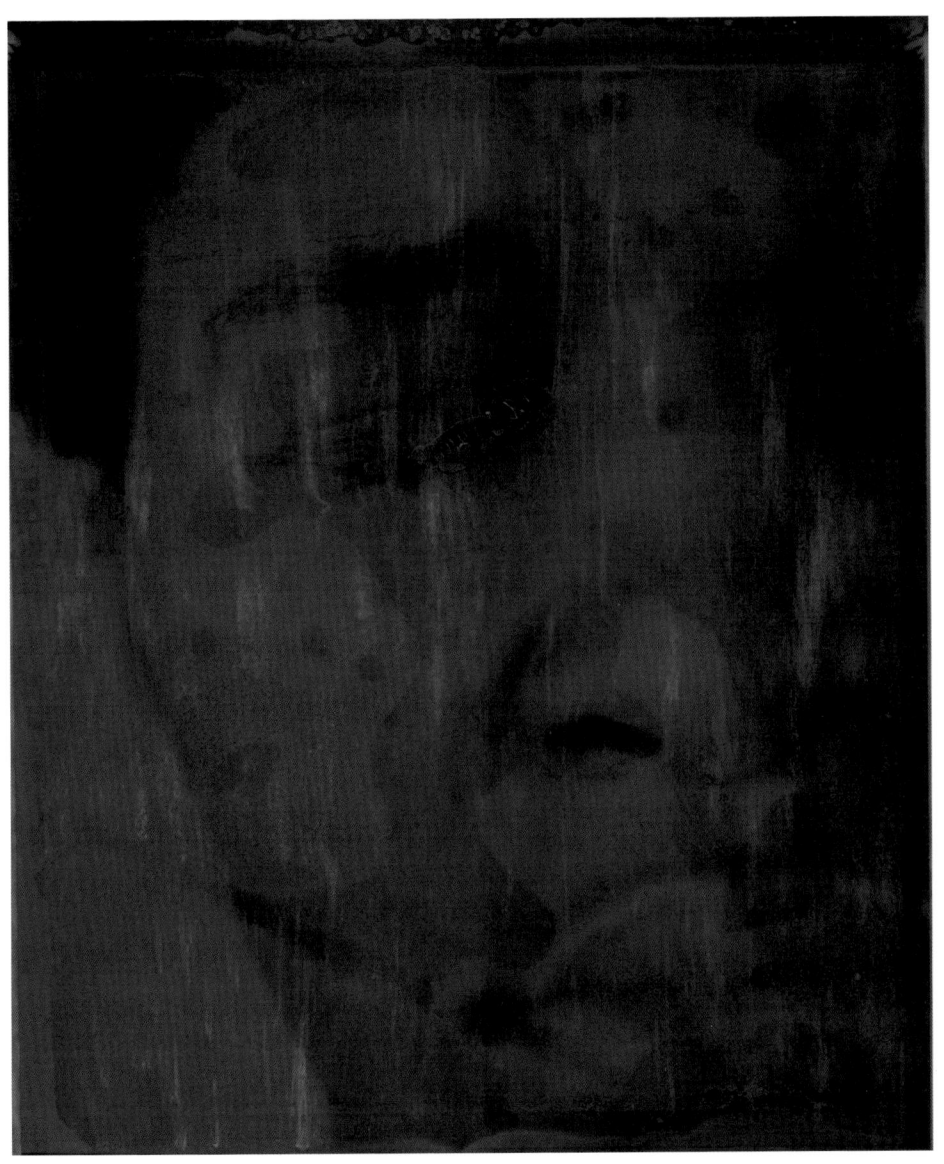

FIGURE 24. Myra Greene, *cropped face*,
in *Self-Portraits*, 2002–4. Inkjet print on
watercolor paper, 20" × 16", 1 of 3 with 2 AP's.
Courtesy of the artist and PATRON, Chicago,
and Corvi-Mora, London.

FIGURE 25. Myra Greene, *fleshy back*, in
Self-Portraits, 2002–4. Inkjet print on
watercolor paper, 16" × 20", 1 of 3 with 2
AP's. Courtesy of the artist and PATRON,
Chicago, and Corvi-Mora, London.

bearing witness to untold and unimaged experiences of despair and pain. Her eyes are resolutely shut to prevent her white audiences from participating in the voyeuristic consumption of Black women's lives, retaining her agency and authority over her psychological reality. Ultimately, the formal and thematic dynamics at work in *face*, *arm* and the other self-portraits in the series indicate that "[w]hen transformed by process, the body and skin transform into layers of sensibility and emotion."[125] Greene spurns memorializing her "body and skin" as a dehumanized spectacle, an object of financial exchange, a repository of sexual exploitation, or as an emblem of political abuse. Rather, she celebrates her "body and skin" as psychologically empowered and intellectually complex signifiers of her subjectivity. A call to arms, Greene's *Self-Portraits* reject the dehumanizing representations of Black women subjects dominant within western art history and resulting from the centuries-long institutions of slavery and the slave trade. The portraits instead offer psychologically charged and experimental reimaginings of individual lives, lived not only through bodies but through personal memories, individual narratives, autobiographical histories, and imaginative realities.

A few years later in 2006–7, Greene again protested white supremacist and racist systems of classifying, interpreting, and representing Black women's subjectivities in mainstream U.S. media through her radically revisionist photographic series, *Character Recognition* (figures 26 and 27). Battling the ongoing manifestations of a white racist discriminatory system, she candidly describes the catalyst for her new series: "Confronted with an up swell of bigotry both personal and public, I was forced to ask myself, what do people see when they look at me. Am I nothing but black? Is that skin tone enough to describe my nature and expectation in life? Do my strong teeth make me a strong worker? Does my character resonate louder than my skin tone?"[126] Greene condemns all prejudicial assumptions that originate in systems of racist discrimination. She names and shames a contemporary white supremacist context in which "bigotry," ignorance, and hate continue to dominate her daily existence. As she did in her *Self-Portrait* series, Greene again adopts experimental techniques to interrogate the devastating role played by a white racist persecutory ideology in reducing her

social, moral, personal, intellectual, and emotional "nature," in addition to her "character," to a biologically essentialist, socially determinist, and racially discriminatory definition, according to which she is "nothing but black." As she argues across her body of work, the basis for prejudicial misinterpretations of Black women's subjectivities lies in white racist endorsements of a "commodified blackness."

In *Character Recognition*, Greene demonstrates the devastating extent to which the language of contemporary racism has its political, ideological, and philosophical foundations in the centuries-long institutions of chattel slavery and the slave trade. For white enslavers and traders presiding over the auction block from the seventeenth century onward, all the body parts of Black women, children, and men—including not only their teeth but their legs, arms, hair, faces, and genitalia—were subjected to degrading examinations. Enslaved peoples of all ages experienced the violence of invasive physical examinations at the hands of white enslavers who adjudicated an individual's financial value by assessing their muscle capacity as well as their reproductive viability. In this context, it is no surprise that, as Shawn Michelle Smith explains, "in a workshop on early photographic technologies, the artist Myra Greene startled herself and her peers with her response to an ambrotype self-portrait: 'I look like a slave!'"[127]

Greene memorializes this painful reality in *Character Recognition*. She employs self-reflexively experimental art-making techniques to open up an alternative space for the imagining not only of the bodies and souls but of the hearts, minds, and intellects of her Black protagonists. She rejects a white supremacist iconographic system that makes her "look like a slave" to reconstruct the portraits that "people see when they look at me." Greene's triumphant declaration that "my character" will "resonate louder than my skin tone" reinforces her psychologically complex self-portraits. She liberates herself from centuries of white racist stereotypes and derogatory caricatures to endorse a dissident practice instead. In accordance with her radical art-making philosophy, she replaces her fear ("I look like a slave!") with a determination to investigate what it is to "look like" a person who is free. Ultimately, Greene makes a way out of no way in *Character Recognition*: she replaces traumatic images of enslaved people with psychologically liberatory envisionings of Black subjects whose lives she memorializes through radical portraiture.

Working with a highly aestheticized use of a medium that she self-consciously politicizes, Greene constructs *Character Recognition* from "black glass ambrotypes" as a way to "slip further and further into a historical past."[128] "Always fascinated by historical processes, I wanted to learn how to make wet-plate collodion," she explains. She describes her technical process carefully: "The glass is first coated with a thin layer of collodion, and then sensitized in a silver bath. While still wet, the glass is exposed using a large format camera. The plate is then developed and then fixed."[129] She summarizes her philosophical and political rationale for returning to nineteenth-century photography techniques, pointing out that by "using a photographic process linked to the times of ethnographic classification, I repeatedly explore my ethnic features in *Character Recognition*." Greene's reuse of oppressive photographic techniques is a harrowing experience that exacts an especially difficult, and very personal, emotional toll: "when I applied this old process to my interest in the black body and self, the imagery described my body in a way never imagined," she admits. Conscious of the fact that the "lessons learned are haunting and frightening in these modern times," she investigates this "old process" in her ongoing war against white racist definitions of the "black body and self" that continue to exert a dehumanizing stranglehold in the twenty-first century.[130]

Greene refuses to surrender to any and all persecutory practices, powerfully protesting these "times of ethnographic classification" in *Character Recognition*.[131] Revisiting a technical practice which was "popular from the 1850s through the 1880s" and which guaranteed the creation of a "singular unique image," she launches a political, social, and cultural investigation into white dominant systems of "ethnographic classification."[132] For Greene, a commitment to interrogating white racist misconstructions of her "ethnic features" galvanizes her practice. Working to educate her white audiences, she ensures that new lessons are learned by developing an alternative visual language that reclaims, recreates, and reimagines the "black body" not in isolation but in relation to a psychologically, emotionally, intellectually, and politically complex "self." More especially, Greene ensures that her "ambrotypes on black glass"

are "highly aesthetic but directly confront issues of racial description."[133] At the same time that she fights to eradicate the racist hierarchies at work within western systems of "ethnographic classification," Greene also takes "issues of racial description" to task. This series insists that its subject matter is the moral, social, political, and cultural "recognition" of "character" rather than the abusive history of white racist classificatory systems of inhumanity.

Greene's series exists not only as standalone works but also as images reproduced in a book. She focuses on individual body parts to divide her series into sections: *face, mouth (horizontal plates)* (figure 26), *ears, profile, nose, mouth (vertical plates)*, and *eyes* (figure 27). In a bold departure from her *Self-Portraits* (in which she cultivates "murky" color layers for each of her body parts), she relies on the wet collodion process to produce starkly monochrome works defined by the "photographic ideals of clarity and precision."[134] The images leave no room for audiences to misunderstand. They are anatomically accurate, meticulously realistic, and instantly recognizable visual representations of her face, mouth, ears, eyes, profile, and nose. Greene explains, "Tainted with the visual history of American slavery, these images point directly to the features of race": "Thick lips and nose, dark skinned; these contemporary studies link the viewer to a complicated historical past."[135]

Greene refuses to shy away from the dehumanizing realities generated by a persecutory white dominant imaginary, instead tackling the history of white racist stereotyping head on in *Character Recognition*. Rather than provide cleaned up or sanitized images, she uses the "photographic ideals of clarity and precision" established within a white dominant western imaginary to hold the visual language of racism accountable.[136] She exposes the "complicated historical past" informing her "contemporary studies" in order to confront the "visual history of American slavery."[137] Warring against the traumatizing reality that Black people were annihilated as well as abused within the "visual history" defined by the immoral precepts of "American slavery," Greene argues that there never was and never will be a "recognition" of "character" by a white racist dominant society when representing and reimagining lives, enslaved, self-liberated, or free.

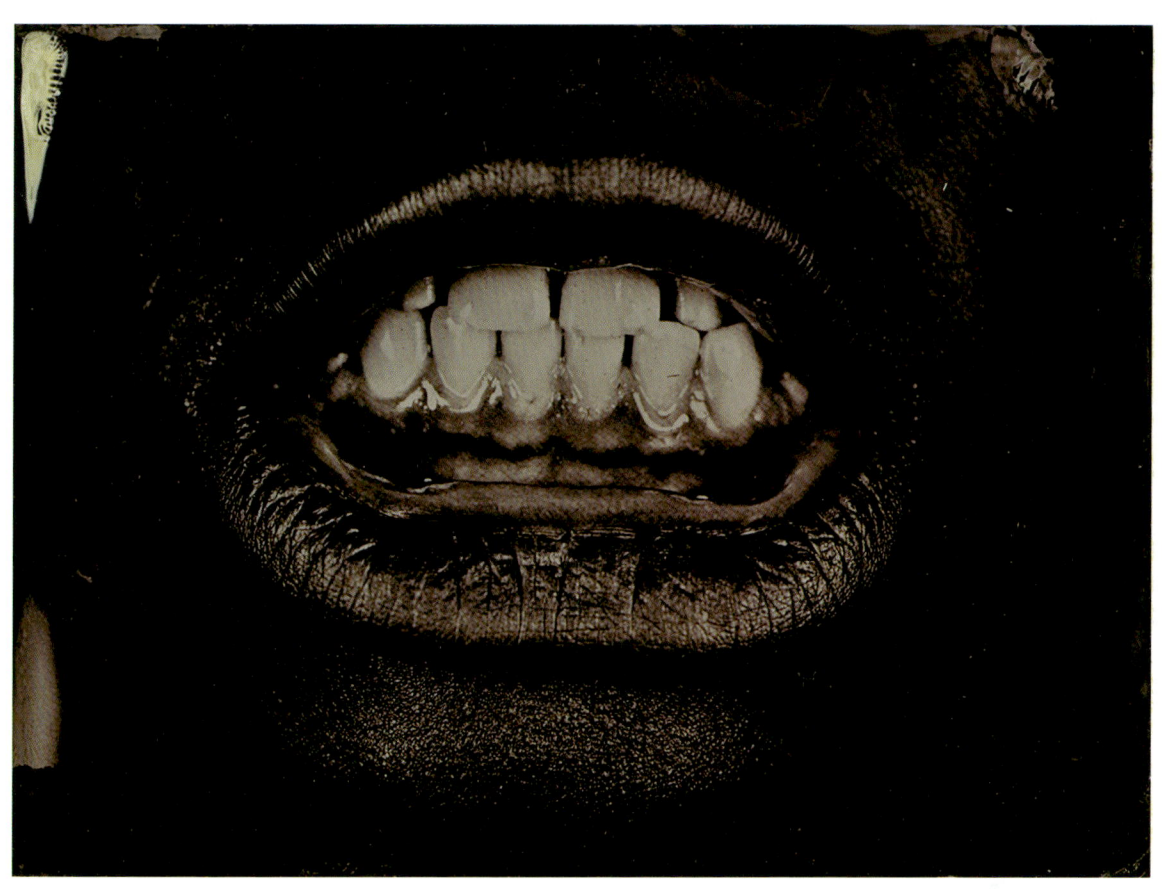

FIGURE 26. Myra Greene, *mouth (horizontal plates) from Character Recognition*, 2006–7. Black glass ambrotype. Courtesy of the artist and PATRON, Chicago, and Corvi-Mora, London.

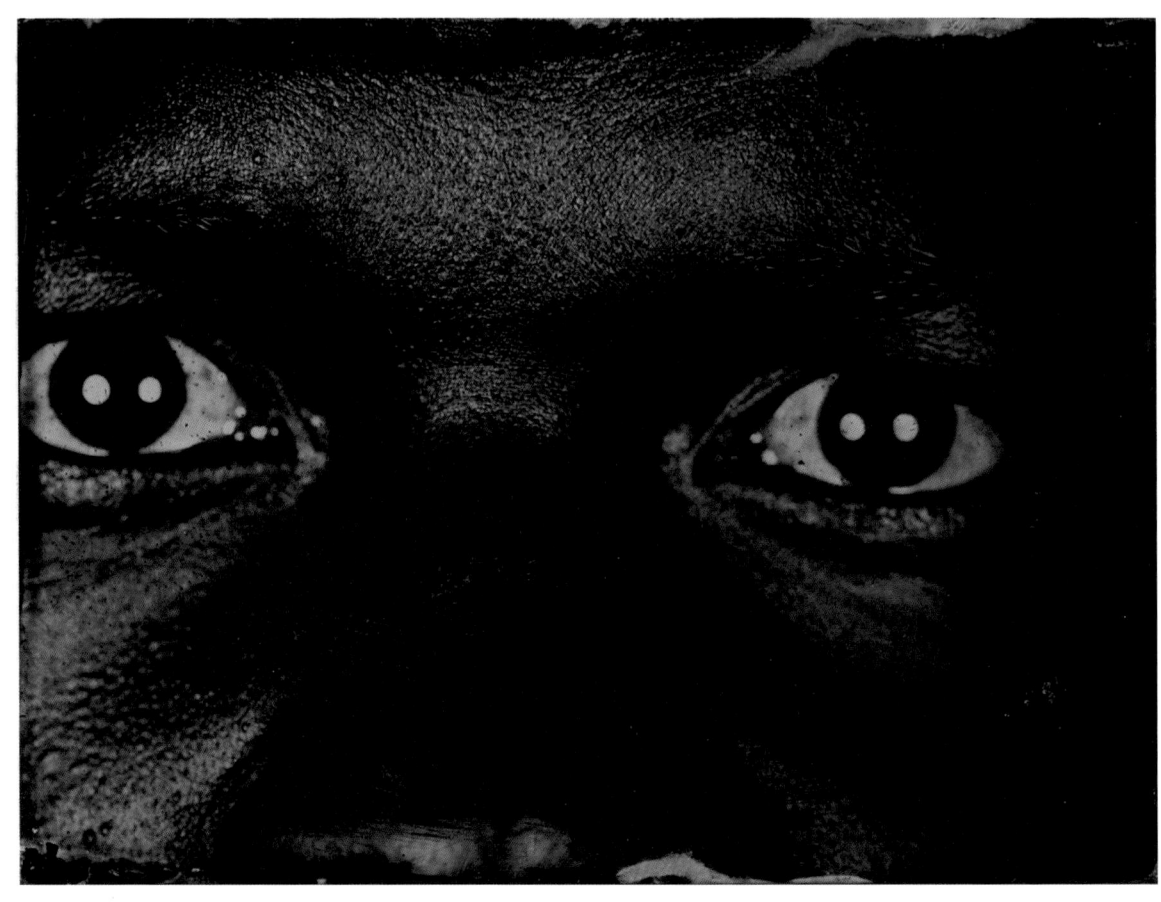

FIGURE 27. Myra Greene, *Untitled (Ref. #80) from Character Recognition*, 2006–7. Black glass ambrotype. Courtesy of the artist and PATRON, Chicago, and Corvi-Mora, London.

Character Recognition is not a site of surrender but a space of subversion and revolution. Greene explains that "while the process of wet plate codes the body in this work, the body is able to speak back."[138] She endorses Black acts of empowerment as antidotes to twenty-first-century white racist acts of macro and micro aggression. Greene is able to "speak back" due to the fact that "through small facial gestures the body reacts and rejects to these [white racist] modes and ways of classification."[139] In *mouth*, a work in which she signifies upon the "visual history of American slavery," she reimagines herself in the act of baring her teeth to communicate her endorsement of bodily gestures of defiance. Through her expression, she rejects racist classificatory systems that would otherwise consign all people of color to the status of specimens. As the visual antithesis of her question "Do my strong teeth make me a strong worker?" this image resists associations of her body with laboring strength in the service of white enslavers. Instead, this portrait represents her endorsement of strategies for self-empowerment in the service of Black liberation.

Greene testifies to the psychological complexities of her individualized subjectivity in *eyes* no less powerfully than she does in *mouth*. Telling the silenced story of Black female agency, Greene confronts the viewer with an emotionally expressive gaze, honoring the individualized psychological perspectives of all Black women, past, present, and future.

"For me the medium seems to fit the work, the questions, and potential metaphors," Greene summarizes. She adds that the "process is tactile and handheld and requires long examinations, something that I find as a thread throughout my work."[140] Greene's radical forms of self-portraiture transform Black female subjects associated with a dehumanizing history of commodification and appropriation into revolutionaries issuing a call to arms. Just as Frederick Douglass fought to retain his agency against the racist expectations of nineteenth-century white antislavery campaigners who insisted that he should "look like a slave and talk like a slave" in order to maximize his political effectiveness, Myra Greene rejects the political or artistic legitimacy of portraits in which she "looks like a slave." She instead establishes an alternative photographic lens, newly defined not only by her own autobiographical realities but

by the experiences, beliefs, emotions, and imaginations of enslaved, self-liberated, and free women of color surviving against all odds over the generations. Defeating temporal barriers, historical divides, and changing social contexts, Greene exerts artistic authority over her strategies of self-representation, reimagining, and re-creation. She reenvisions "how a slave" feels, thinks, looks, knows, and, above all, imagines.

————

Clarissa T. Sligh expresses a heartrending wish: "I longed for the voices of the slaves."[141] She explains, "I have traced my ancestry to 28 known people."[142] "I am looking for eight more on my mother's side," she adds, but "I've gone back to my father's great-grandmother. She was a slave who was sold three times and had two children sold away from her."[143] The genealogical search for her enslaved ancestors, known and unknown, is far from over. She succeeded in locating her great-grandmother in the U.S. "chattel records."[144] Devastatingly, however, her ancestor's voice is still missing: her personal experiences and lived realities remain unknown within the dehumanizing and racist space of white-dominant archives. Across Sligh's bodies of work, she remembers and reimagines the "voices of the slaves" and does justice to their personal, spiritual, and imaginative perspectives—a source of emotional pain, psychological drama, corporeal suffering, and political protest. She endorses a revisionist practice in recognition of the fact that in the white-dominant U.S. archives, Black lives do not and never will matter. Sligh explains, "through making art I give voice to these invisible narratives."[145] A determination to "give voice" to the "invisible narratives," hidden histories, and missing memories of Black people's lives as lived across the generations catalyzes Sligh's search for a new "lexicon of liberation."

"When we look around us, the past appears to be invisible but it is always present," Sligh observes. "For me memory is memory, whether personal or historical it is the same."[146] Sligh's understanding of artworks as "sites of resistance" reflects her understanding of the intersecting relationships between the past, present, and future. She meditates on the "personal" and "historical" struggle that will never be over for Black people fighting for survival in U.S. society. "I believe that the artist is a shaman, a spiritual medium, a way show-er and a poet, who draws on intuition, personal experiences, and things inherited from ancestral communal memories," she declares. "How could it be otherwise?"[147] Inspired by the "invisible narratives" in her own "ancestral communal memories" and beyond, Sligh assumes the role of a prophet, seer, and guide in order to transform sorrow into salvation and to do justice to the untold stories, unremembered memories, and unexamined histories of Black lives. "As I construct the unsayable, the unspeakable, and the unrepresentable through this reframing process, a healing occurs," Sligh concludes.[148] Traumas are emotionally, socially, culturally, and imaginatively healed as a result of her empathetic practice. Love in all forms is the way to liberation.

Pat Ward Williams shares Sligh's determination to memorialize the untold "ancestral communal memories" in her own family. As she says, "My work is drawn from personal experiences and collective spirit."[149] She explains that "there are moments when I feel political injustice, and I express these feelings in my art," adding, "I have other moments when I'm not angry, when I'm thinking about my family, about my daughter or my lover or God. Or I'm trying to work out the logistics of my own personal life."[150] Williams refuses to set any emotional boundaries, aesthetic limits, or political frameworks around her practice, insisting on her right to creative freedoms. "I don't see one subject as more important than the other,"[151] she says, but "even that's political, isn't it?"[152] Ultimately, she declares, "we as black people have to find different solutions to overcoming political and personal obstacles."[153] According to Williams, a Black woman artist's vision, philosophy, belief system, and cultural understanding has the power to heal.

Like Williams, Lyle Ashton Harris originally determined to work with a solitary image. "In my early work a lot of information got distilled into a single photograph," he explains.[154] Soon, however, he experiences the same realization as Williams of the inadequacy—formally, socially, politically, and culturally—of the "single photograph." As a result, his practice evidences a similar "formal shift from an iconic image to the accumulation of images" collected in a series. "There

was less of a hierarchy with the images, whether they were found newspaper clippings, media images, postcards, ephemera or some of my early photographs," he explains. Harris's work destabilizes social, political, cultural, and artistic "hierarchies" as he "opened the space of what was prioritized and categorized, and became much more about a multiplicity of images, ideas, possibilities and interpretations."[155] In his layered and egalitarian practice, Harris foregrounds formal ambiguity, thematic uncertainty, and subjective possibility. He asks but leaves unanswered a significant question: "How does one deal with an existential sense of isolation in the midst of acceptance?"[156] All the artists in this chapter agree: no single image and no single interpretation can begin to encompass the lived realities and complex imaginaries of Black people fighting for survival in a white, racist U.S. society.

Myra Greene addresses the issue head-on. "I have been in so many conversations, talks, lectures, arguments where people state that they are colorblind. They wish America would wash itself of its racial identity," she laments. "The differences are what make us all unique."[157] She argues, "Ignoring those differences or trying to assimilate them all seems to be a goal. But this is not what I want."[158] Greene's practice interrogates and investigates rather than sublimates or invisibilizes the "differences" that "make us all unique." "In the end," she declares, "race is a form of description."[159] At the same time, Greene refuses to ignore the devastating consequences of white racist mentalities. Calling out all forms of white racist stereotypes and caricatures, Greene explains that "the implications added to that description (strength, brawn, brains, sexuality, dancing abilities) are all human made."[160] Her experimental self-portraits expose the "human made" relationships between race, racism, and representation. In so doing, Greene not only denounces white racist ignorance but investigates all "differences": corporeal, spiritual, social, emotional, intellectual, and philosophical. For Greene, as for Sligh, Williams, and Harris, art-making is a "site of resistance" in which revolution is not only possible in theory but attainable in practice.

"PREPARED TO DIE" EMPOWERING BEAUTY AND HEROICIZING HISTORY

▶▶ Winfred Rembert—Kerry James Marshall—Debra Priestly—Mickalene Thomas

"It's all memory," declares Winfred Rembert, a visual storyteller, pictorial historian, and radical memorialist. "I work from images in my head of people and places from back then."[1] Born in 1945 in Cuthbert, a small town in Georgia, Rembert died in New Haven, Connecticut in 2021. Throughout his life, he deliberately put himself at risk emotionally, bearing witness to painful memories by creating paintings that testify to the sacrifices he and his family endured while living in a segregated South. They encountered daily acts of racist injustice, persecution, discrimination, torture, and death threats in their fight to survive the tragedies experienced by all people of color in a white supremacist U.S. society. Rembert memorializes their histories, narratives, and experiences in his emotionally powerful and radically experimental paintings.

"We would sit around the table. He would tell stories . . . about things that happened to him as a child," recalls Patsy Rembert, Winfred Rembert's wife.[2] She recognized the emotional, social, political, historical, and cultural importance of her husband's life experiences, and she warned him that "all these stories that you're telling me are going to be lost when you die."[3] Winfred Rembert began his new life as an artist determined to record the hidden histories of rebellion and resistance, suffering, and struggle within his own experiences as well as across his family and wider community. He created his paintings in response to Patsy Rembert's questions: "Why not do your life story?" she asked. "Why don't you take your history and put it on the leather instead?"[4]

Patsy Rembert's appeal that Winfred Rembert take his "life story" and put it on "leather" becomes even more urgent in the face of the traumatizing reality that the past, present, and future atrocities endured by Black people continue to be invisibilized within a dominant white supremacist imaginary. Patsy Rembert directly confronts the terrible reality that "there are some black people who don't have a clue of the struggle that blacks in the south went through."[5] "Those are the people Winfred is trying to reach as they don't know their own history,"[6] she explains. Winfred Rembert heeded his wife's call by creating hundreds of narrative paintings in which he translated his oral memories into visual stories, bringing them to life on dyed leather rather than on paper or canvas. He refuses to sanitize white racist acts of terrorism and tragedy. At the same time, he celebrates untold stories of the Black freedom struggle and revolutionary liberation movement.

As an artist, Winfred Rembert assumes the role of a historian, educator, witness, narrator, memorialist, and social justice campaigner. He visualizes the lives of generations of Black women, children, and men who fought and continue to fight racist inequalities. As his paintings testify, Black people of all ages have defeated the dehumanizing influences of white supremacy not only by leading civil rights protests, rallies, and sit-ins but by gaining an education, obtaining political power, undertaking agricultural and intellectual labor, protecting their families, and expressing their creativity in a variety of forms. Across his works, he memorializes the full range of empowered Black expression and radical performativity over the generations. He bears witness to the lives and works of untold numbers of women, children, and men who have been giving speeches, writing literature, singing songs, experimenting with foodways, and making art as just a few of their many ways of keeping their minds, souls, and bodies together over the centuries in their ongoing fight against white racism, white supremacy, and all forms of white discrimination and persecution. Rembert admitted to the enormity of the task he faces in memorializing both his own experiences and those of his family members and wider community, explaining, "there ain't enough time for me to do all the things that I remember growing up in Cuthbert Georgia."[7]

"Mama was a survivor. She came up under almost slavery time and she had this idea of you don't make waves, you can't change a thing, white people do what they want to do and how they want to do it and you can't do nothing about it and that was her thinking and that's what she tried to teach me," Winfred Rembert remembered of the defining role his grandmother, Lilian Rembert, played in his life. As a Black woman who grew up in a white supramacist era in which freedom existed in name only and in which legal segregation and lynch law were the ruling terrorist systems of the day, Lilian Rembert endured "almost slavery time," which led her to develop a very clear survival strategy. According to Rembert, her philosophy allowed for no expression of opposition or dissent to white authoritarian rule. As he recalls, she took the view that "if white folks do something to you you take it you take it and you live because if you rebel they going to kill you."[8]

Lilian Rembert's determination to live out her survivalist philosophy regardless of the emotional toll it took on her or her grandson powerfully surfaces in one of Winfred Rembert's childhood memories. He recalls, "One day me and mama was standing in the Wilson Brothers' store and one of the Wilson brothers said to her 'Lilian I see you got your grandson with you.' 'Yes sir Mr. Wilson I got my child with me.' And one of the Wilson brothers said 'Guess what, Lilian, he will never be a damn thing in his whole life is that right?' And she said 'Yes sir, Mr. Wilson you're right.'"[9] For Lilian Rembert, a woman who "knew nothing but work, work, work in the field" and who "didn't dream of nothing" because "she had nothing to look forward to," voicing her protest against the Wilson brothers' demoralizing, dehumanizing, and disrespectful acts of white racist abuse toward herself and her family was out of the question.[10] And yet, while the belief that if you "take it"

you will "live" defined Lilian Rembert's survival strategy, her grandson lived by a determination to "rebel" even if "they going to kill you."[11] As an artist-historian-memorialist-activist who came of age under a white supremacist regime that sought to limit and destroy any and all trace of his individual agency, Rembert understood that he "didn't have the power to make people do things."[12] Nevertheless, he chose to fight on, declaring, "I wanted it to be better for myself."[13] Over the decades, Rembert was determined to live a better life than the lives lived in a white racist South and experienced by his family members and members of his community.

Winfred Rembert's decision to participate in the civil rights movement even while he recognized his own powerlessness was the result not only of experiencing the psychological toll of his grandmother's survival strategy but also of witnessing harrowing acts of police brutality enacted against J.T., a member of his immediate family. Rembert remembers, "One day we was walking and he was holding my hand these two police men come up they grabbed him about his shoulder and snatched him around and they had this old big black jack made out of leather and they hit him right in the face and his eye fell down and then they looked at him and they said 'oh shit, this is the wrong nigger.'"[14] Rembert saw first-hand the horrifying physical assault of his mother's cousin by white racist police officers whose unjust actions were motivated solely by discriminatory hate. This experience led to an epiphany that laid the foundations of his political life as an adult. Rembert "decided to be a part of the protest" as his way of fighting the traumatizing reality that in a white racist mainstream U.S. society all persons of color are subjected to all forms of persecutory torture.[15]

In 1965, when he was not yet twenty years of age, Rembert remembers, "I was running around, making waves."[16] He voiced his opposition to white discriminatory practices by speaking before African American audiences. He immediately encountered difficulties: "nobody wanted to hear me," he says.[17] Just as Lilian Rembert had survived "almost slavery" by finding a way not only to navigate but to conceal her anger, so the vast majority of Black people living in the U.S. South understood that "if you rebel," a white racist population is "going to kill you." Black women, children, and men were living lives defined by terror during this period: "Everybody was scared in those days," Winfred Rembert admits.[18] While he respected his family and friends' survival strategies, Rembert was motivated by a determination not only to defeat but to eradicate the era of "almost slavery." "When I reached my teens, everything seemed so wrong to me about the ways that white people treated black folk," he remembers.[19] His sense of moral outrage against ongoing racist equalities only deepened in intensity. "It didn't take much for me to join in the civil rights movement," he explained.[20] While his decision to join the protest was hard for his grandmother, she made the courageous decision to support her grandson. "Mama used to be scared to death of white folk, and she'd say to me, 'If you follow those civil rights folks, I'm not gonna let you back in the house.'"[21] Rembert confirms Lilian Rembert's terror only to exalt in her bravery: despite her fear, "she'd be there, standing at the window, waiting for me each time I returned."[22]

Rembert refused to sanitize the dangers he faced or the sacrifices experienced. He recognized that his grandmother's fear was in no way exaggerated. "You go in these protests movements marches, you have to be prepared to die," he explained. "Because sometimes that's exactly what'll happen: you'll get killed. A black life didn't matter."[23] Rembert revealed the formative influence of his grandmother by explaining his survival strategies he shares with his own children: "Now I tell my kids, never argue with a police officer."[24] After centuries of civil rights protests led by African American freedom-fighters of all ages, Rembert confronted the traumatizing reality that a "black life" still does not matter. Life and death struggles are now experienced by a new generation, including members of Rembert's own family, fighting for both an existence and a life within a white supremacist U.S. nation.

"I was about nineteen when I heard about a demonstration in Americus, Georgia. A bus came around to take everyone who wanted to go, and I went."[25] So Rembert summarized of his willing participation in a civil rights demonstration in which Black protesters were subjected to violent and murderous reprisals by a vengeful white police force. "Things got out of hand and people started shooting at us," he remembered. "People were scattering every which way just running just trying to save their life you know."[26] Attempting to save his own life, he "ran down through this alley and when I looked back these two white people was running after me and they had shotguns and there was a car sitting there with the keys in it and I took that car."[27] No match for white villainy, however, he failed to make his getaway. He realized, "They must have had some kind of report out that the car was missing because I got caught."[28] He exposed the illegal white racist practices of a segregated South in which violations of Black civil rights were an everyday reality by stating that the "police arrested me and put me in jail with no charges and no trial."[29]

As Lilian Rembert predicted regarding the inevitable consequences of Black rebellion to white authoritarian rule, the police force illegally arrested Winfred Rembert and subjected him to physical assault. "One day, the deputy sheriff came into my cell and started beating me," Rembert recalled.[30] He recognized his powerlessness and attempted to follow his grandmother's advice: "I tried to brace myself and just take the pain, but it hurt so bad that I fought back."[31] For Rembert, the only way in which he was able to survive injury and pain at the hands of his white racist persecutors was not to capitulate but to engage in his own act of physical resistance.

Waging a war against his unjust incarceration, Rembert soon tried another tactic to effect his escape: "I took a roll of toilet paper and I stuck it in the john and when I flush it you know water goes everywhere. The deputy sheriff comes back and he kicked me he kicked me about three or four times so I grabbed him around his legs and I dumped him to the ground. He went for his gun. He and I was wrestling and I finally managed to take it from him. I locked him in the cell and I fled."[32] Yet again, his heroic act to secure his self-liberation was unsuccessful. This time, however, his heroism had even more harrowing, tragic, and shocking consequences, resulting in his mutilation and near murder by white "persons unknown." "After they caught me when I escaped they got a mob and they threw me in the trunk of a car and they took me for a ride. When they opened the trunk I'm staring them all in the face and they're just cursing me nigger this and nigger that," Rembert recalled.[33] As he immediately understood, the racist language of the white "mob" was just the prelude to the tragic and terrifying ritual they used to torture and kill him. "This was a beautiful place, just like a resort area with a well-trimmed lawn," he remembered.[34]

He recalled his panic, shock, and terror when he re-alized that this remote rural idyll had been staged for his bodily torture, followed by his execution. He later voiced his heartrending suffering: "the first thing I no-ticed right away was ropes hanging from trees."[35]

"I knew they was going to hang me," Rembert de-clared.[36] Over four decades later, the memory of his near lynching had lost none of its power as a source of unending psychological trauma and emotional devas-tation in his life:

> I seen a rope hanging from a tree a noose and then I looked and there was another one at least two or three trees that looked like the place designed for lynching people and the first thing on my mind when I saw it was I remember what mama told me she says white folk do you wrong let them do it don't you strike back that way you will live and they put a rope around my feet and they drew me up in the tree and they all standing around me just hitting me and they just kicking me and punching me and here come the deputy the one I locked in the cell he's got a knife in his hand and I can see it and he grabbed my private parts and when he grabbed them he took his knife and he stuck me I could feel the blood running down my butt cheeks down the back of my neck I was bleeding like you kill a pig or something another man grab his hand and he say "don't do that . . . we got better things we can use this nigger for. Let's use him as an example."[37]

As Rembert's heartbreaking testimony reveals, white southern men tolerated no expression of equal rights by Black southern men. The white deputy enacts murderous revenge against Rembert's heroic attempt to defend himself by instigating his torture: he is the one who took the knife to Rembert's "private parts," resulting in "blood running down" his body. Just as Lilian Rembert had survived "almost slavery," Winfred Rembert survived an "almost lynching." And as that experience defined her life, so did his exposure to the atrocity of lynching. For Rembert, this mind-body-and-soul-destroying memory lost none of its horror all his life. "They WERE lynching me," he declared decades later. "Not gonna. They were in the process of it, yes, lynching me."[38]

Rembert remembered that one of the anonymous white men saved him from death by lynching, but only at a terrible cost: "They shackled me up around my neck waist and feet with chains and they marched me through the black neighborhood."[39] He recalled, "They put me in shackles and walked me through black neigh-borhoods to send a message to other blacks."[40] Rembert was all too painfully aware that he was living in an era of "almost slavery time." The white mob's decision to put him in "shackles" and parade his body as a "message to other blacks" functioned as a direct reenactment of the abuses enslaved men had endured over a century before. Writing his second autobiography, *My Bondage and My Freedom*, in 1855, Frederick Douglass remembered the terrible consequences he and four men experienced at the hands of their white enslavers following their united attempts to secure their liberation from slavery. As punishment, they were all "drawn along the public highway—firmly bound together—tramping through dust and heat, bare-footed and bareheaded—fastened to three strong horses, whose riders were armed to the teeth, with pistols and daggers."[41] To the day he died, he never forgot that they were all subjected to "every possible insult from the crowds of idle, vulgar people," all of whom were white, "who clustered around, and heartlessly made their failure the occasion for all man-ner of ribaldry and sport."[42] As one of untold millions of enslaved people fighting for all freedoms, Douglass powerfully declared that he and these four men were "guilty of no crime, save that of preferring liberty to a life of bondage."[43]

Working to survive a contemporary context in which white racist systems of torture against Black people show no sign of abating, Winfred Rembert was equally "guilty of no crime" except that of "preferring liberty" to "almost slavery." As he emphasized, his punishment represented "a warning to other black folk of what happens if you try to think for yourself."[44] While the physical reality of legal slavery dominated earlier cen-turies, as Douglass himself had predicted, the "spirit of slavery" refuses to die, living on in legal, social, polit-ical, and cultural discrimination in the twentieth and twenty-first centuries.[45] Frederick Douglass was jailed in the 1830s after enduring his own white supremacist ritual of public humiliation; Winfred Rembert was im-prisoned again in the 1960s. As he remembered of his wrongful incarceration of nearly a decade, "I was prob-ably in an institution the first year and after that every-thing was chain gang."[46]

Such white racist terrorist tactics failed to subju-gate Rembert, however. Just as Frederick Douglass continued to resist his enslavement and ultimately secured his own freedom, so Winfred Rembert refused to surrender to white rule by using his time in the penitentiary as the foundation for his self-liberation. "I found some well-educated black men in prison, and they taught me to read and write," he remembered. "One guy, a trusty, was making leather things, and I watched how he did it and made some of my own. I looked through the bars at him working, and I thought I could do it because I'm artistic. I made wallets with a big rose in the center."[47] Rembert started by making wallets and soon discovered his exemplary abilities as an experimental artist, creating hundreds of paintings following his release from prison. Across his bodies of work, Rembert educates his audiences regarding the emotional and political realities of what "he went through" by memorializing his life stories of sacrifice, struggle, and survival.

Among the pioneering scholars who are committed to theorizing Rembert's practice are the following: Bartholomew F. Bland, Anne Dixey, Vivian Ducat, Michael Grossberg, Sarah Holder, Ellen J. Keiter, Chris King, Donna McClatchy, Owen McNally, Carol Millsom, William and Ann Oppenheimer, Jock Reynolds, Irma Watkins-Owens, Clifton Watson.

Kerry James Marshall, a contemporary painter and mixed-media artist born in Birmingham, Alabama in 1955, states, "As an African American, descended from a people enslaved to serve the interests and benefits of dominant 'whites,' I am acutely aware of the weakness of my position within the wider world, and even more so in the institutional structure of the art world." "We were not present at the creation," he observes, adding that the "numbers really matter because they validate a subtextual narrative of superiority."[48] Warring against the clear and ever present danger of a white racist hierarchy in which African American lives are rendered lesser, inferior, and other in Western societies, Marshall dedicates his practice to reversing the invisibilization of Black people as subjects within fine art. "I want," he declares, "to see more than a few images of 'black folks' every time I got to a museum."[49]

Marshall understands that the legacies of slavery incontestably dominate not only the "wider world" but the "institutional structure of the art world."[50] He condemns the gross negligence and willful perpetuation of inequalities endorsed by white supremacist U.S. society and a Western system of art patronage that is for whites only. Across his works, Marshall shares Rembert's determination to create paintings of protest in which he asserts a Black presence in the face of absence, Black historical realities in the face of white amnesia, and Black storytelling practices in the face of white-supremacist annihilations of Black lives. As one among thousands of Black artists working in the twenty-first century, he takes heart that he is not working in isolation. As he explains, "I am heartened that the culture of Africans in the diaspora still produces 'black' folks willing to aggressively assert their presence, power, and some kind of difference against tremendous odds."[51]

Marshall's protest aesthetic visualizes an African diasporic presence and power enacted "against tremendous odds" and is informed by his determination to memorialize the stories of struggle, sacrifice, and survival within his own family background as a form of protest. "I was born in Alabama in 1955 as the bus boycott there was beginning," he remembers. "We moved to Watts in 1963, just before the Watts race riots of 1965 that set American cities on fire."[52] As Marshall recalls, the family's constant movement was due to economic difficulties: "My father was trying to find better employment, and in the process kept us right on the edge of a number of significant conflicts."[53] Sharing Rembert's commitment to creating artworks in which he memorializes the freedom struggle, Marshall recognizes that "this obligation to articulate some socially relevant issue, a lot of that has everything to do with where I came from."[54] "You can't be born in Birmingham, Alabama in 1955 and not feel like you've got some kind of social responsibility," he observes, insisting, "You can't move to Watts in '63, and grow up in South Central near the Black Panthers headquarters and see the kinds of things that I saw in my developmental years, and not speak about it."[55] While Marshall does not share Rembert's experiences of wrongful incarceration or an "almost lynching," he is a first-hand witness to the persecutory discriminations endured by activists risking their lives in the Black Panther liberation and civil rights movements. Coming of age in the crucible of twentieth-century Black freedom struggles, he experienced a radical epiphany regarding the form and function of his practice that endures to this day. He explains, "I decided that whenever I painted an image of a person, it would always be a black image, and that image wouldn't be a personality so much as it would be an image that spoke directly to the issue of blackness."[56]

"The sentiment expressed in the United States Supreme Court's decision on the Dred Scott case of 1857, upholding the right of a master to retain ownership of a slave in any state or the union, slave or free, still echoes in the halls of most American institutions," insists Marshall.[57] As Frederick Douglass had prophesied, enslavement endures in "form" if not in "fact" through ongoing institutional structures of white supremacist dominance according to which Black people are not only invisibilized but denied their very existence. Marshall denounces ongoing white racist injustices, making a powerful distinction: "while chattel slavery was abolished some 150 years ago or so, the white supremacy it supported still conditions structural inequalities that are present in the United States, even in the world, today."[58] White supremacy's death-like grip is responsible for all the legal, political, social, economic, educational, financial, cultural, philosophical, and ideological "inequalities" that devastate and destroy Black lives today. It has not, however, gone unchallenged. As Marshall argues, "From the moment when the promises of liberty and freedom were inscribed in the founding documents of the country, black folks have been struggling to get the people who believe in these principles to adhere to them."[59]

Marshall recognizes the centuries-long presence of African American radical movements as the conscience of the U.S. nation and as a revolutionary and transformative means by which Black people are able to expose its whites-only "promises of liberty and freedom." According to Marshall, "If you believe that the struggle of the civil rights movement essentially revolves around the acceptance of black people as equals, and that non-violent resistance alone won freedom for black people, you essentially gloss over the history of resistance that black people have been engaged in from the moment they got here centuries ago."[60] Working as an activist-artist, Marshall dedicates his practice to reimaging, representing, and recreating the entire "history of resistance" by Black people as a centuries-long tradition.

For Marshall and thousands more, the "struggle" not only involved "non-violent resistance" but resistance by every means necessary, encompassing acts of legal, physical, psychological, intellectual, moral, and religious dissidence. "I'm interested in showing that such a history of resistance has always existed," he explains.[61]

Marshall acknowledges that "the mode of black figure representation I employ is a clear departure from most popular treatments of the black body."[62] He endorses a recuperative and radically empowering practice. He works against white racist distortions and dehumanizations of the "black figure" in his determination "to establish a phenomenal presence that is unequivocally black and beautiful."[63] Speaking of his use of portraiture, which dominates his visual lexicon, he declares, "It is my conviction that the most instrumental, insurgent painting for this moment must be of figures, and those figures must be black, unapologetically so."[64] Among the many scholars who are dedicated to examining Marshall's life and works are the following: Ian Alteveer, Kathleen S. Bartels, Angela Choon, Jeff R. Donaldson, Okwui Enwezor, Nav Haq, Cheryl I. Harris, Paul Hoover, Arthur Jafa, Nathaniel McLin, Kobena Mercer, James Meyer, Charles W. Mills, Helen Molesworth, David Moos, Amy M. Mooney, Terry R. Myers, John Neff, Richard J. Powell, Calvin Reid, Dieter Roelstraete, Charles H. Rowell, Raél Jero Salley, Deborah Smith, Susan Snodgrass, Robert Storr, Terrie Sultan, Lanka Tattersall, Luc Tuymans, Jeff Wall, David Zwirner.

Unlike Winfred Rembert and Kerry James Marshall, who were both born in the South, Debra Priestly, a portrait painter and mixed-media artist, was born in Springfield, Ohio, in 1961. An eclectic and experimental artist, she embraces all forms: "I make mixed media objects and multimedia installations, incorporating painting, drawing, digital imagery, readymades and sound."[65] While her choice of materials and media change over the decades, she is unwavering in her commitment to finding a "lexicon of liberation" with which to memorialize a "history of resistance" by enslaved and free Black people over the generations. In a bold departure from Rembert and Marshall's practices, Priestly represents, recreates, and reimagines a "history of resistance" not only through epic feats of heroism demonstrated through individual and collective participation in civil rights marches, Black liberation struggles, and militant warfare, but within everyday domestic rituals that are invisibilized within a dominant imaginary. For Priestly, these practices testify to the survival of African American traditions "against tremendous odds."

"The simple act of taking tea or the mere presence of a teacup, a spoon, or a canning jar can become an important vehicle in the preservation and transmission of personal memory, ancestral knowledge and historic events," Priestly explains.[66] In her radical and revolutionary protest aesthetic, domestic rituals assume center-stage as a powerful means not only for documenting and communicating oral storytelling practices but also for celebrating untold narratives of "historical events" and generations of "ancestral knowledge." "The power of association and the storytelling tradition can be invaluable tools," she explains. "I am interested in common rituals, such as the preparation and consumption of food, and the way in which everyday objects used in these rituals can inspire a dialogue."[67] For Priestly, "common rituals" and "everyday objects" are catalysts to conversation. They operate as ready-made portals through which she accesses the histories, memories, and experiences of intergenerational Black families.

"When my grandmother opened an aqua blue jar of homemade sweet pickles, it was as if stories flowed from it," Priestly recalls of a particular "everyday object" that became "an important vehicle" for the "transmission of personal memory."[68] "One thing would lead to another" she explains, remembering how "the elders would start talking about recipes, how rich or poor the local harvest was that season, who made the pickles, how she was related to us and how one could travel to her home via one route or another."[69] As an artist-witness-memorialist-historian dedicated to reimagining the "conversation" among her ancestors that "would take many turns," she celebrates "large family gatherings" as "immeasurable gifts" in which "an entire universe that connected the present with the past and the future unfolded."[70] Debra Priestly shares Winfred Rembert's determination to do powerful justice to the lived realities that define the struggles she and her family "went through." At the same time, she creates images in which she speaks "directly to the issue of blackness," just as Kerry James Marshall advocates.[71] For Priestly, the domestic sphere belonging to Black families is the ultimate site of untold acts and unmemorialized arts of resistance.

Mickalene Thomas, a mixed-media painter, photographer, and installation artist born in 1971 in Camden, New Jersey, summarizes her practice as follows: "My paintings and photography oscillates between the romantic notion of painting and engages conversation around art history as it relates to the positioning of African-American women."[72] Thomas is self-consciously dedicated to "celebrating female beauty and power." As she declares, "I like to think of myself as a visual thinker, a shape-shifter, an innovator, and my work is unpredictably consistent."[73] The key tenets of Thomas's protest aesthetic emerge out of the same conviction undergirding Kerry James Marshall's practice: theirs is a shared commitment to representing figures that "must be black, unapologetically so."[74] Waging the same war against the racist myopia of a white-dominant art world, Thomas maintains, "I want to use the black body because the idea of placing it in a context where it is not usually seen or spoken about enables comparisons to the Western ideology of beauty."[75]

Thomas works with photography, mixed-media painting, and installation art to challenge the traumatizing ways in which Black women's memories, histories, and narratives—let alone their bodies—have been subjected to white racist forces of distortion, dehumanization, and even annihilation within a dominant imaginary. "From my experience, in Western art history when you see images of black women they're generally depicted in positions of servitude or looked at through an anthropological perspective," she observes. "They are not seen in Western art history in the archetypal explorations of notions of beauty."[76] Working out of a determination to ensure that her Black female protagonists are "seen," Thomas recreates and re-presents Black women in positions not of subjugation but of empowerment. She liberates her subjects from an "anthropological" gaze by creating works in which they typically appear on a heroic scale. She liberates her Black female protagonists from an appropriating white dominant lens by endorsing an eclectic use of materials—photographic collage, paint, rhinestones, and textile pieces, among much more—to do empowered justice to their beauty.

Thomas deliberately challenges the caricatured assumptions of her white audiences to create works in which she defies the exoticization, commodification, and objectification of Black women's bodies within a Western mainstream iconography. As she explains, "I was interested in whether I could change those perspectives with the art that I made, if I could play with how people might look, not only on a stereotypical level but also maybe erase that and challenge viewers in their own perceptions of images."[77] She visualizes her protest against the ongoing unequal reality, in which "Black women are still today considered second-class citizens, or third, sometimes," by creating radically politicized and consciousness-raising mixed-media works.[78] She is adamant that "by portraying real women with their own unique history, beauty and background, I'm working to diversify the representations of black women in art."[79] Thomas rejects white racist stereotypes by dedicating her practice to visualizing the personal stories and biographical realities of "real women." She experiments with her choice of media and materials, photographic techniques, painterly devices, and site-specific installations to establish a new visual language celebrating Black women's identities, creativities, relationships, sexualities, and all forms of beauty. She commemorates Black women as psychologically, intellectually, and emotionally complex protagonists who are central rather than peripheral to Western art history.

"By selecting women of color, I am quite literally raising their visibility and inserting their presence into the conversation," Thomas declares.[80] She works to realize her heartfelt determination that, "I want the same kind of strength and tenacity to shine through all of my viewers," by intentionally and explicitly creating art for Black female audiences.[81] She emphasizes that "just as my muses insist on their visibility and identity, I want my viewers to feel present with fierceness and boldness."[82] For Thomas, a challenge to centuries-old white supremacist violences and violations of a western art world is as vital as her determination to carve out out an iconographic space within which to reimagine the elided experiences and subjugated subjectivities of her Black female muses. While the lives of an array of Black women who act as muses inspire her practice, an autobiographical perspective informs her "lexicon of liberation." As she says, "I'm using my art to articulate and express all the aspects of who I am."[83]

According to Thomas's revolutionary protest aesthetic, art-making expresses a multitude of emotional, psychological, existential, imaginative, and biographical realities. "I'd rather have my voice be powerful and profound and courageous and reach an audience through my art," she declares.[84] Among the leading scholars investigating Thomas's practice are the following: Naomi Beckwith, Andrea Blanch, Katie Booth, Gabrielle Bruney, Greg Cook, Ashton Cooper, Jori Finkel, Kenya Hunt, Joel Kuennen, Sean Landers, Sarah E. Lewis, Elsa Longhauser, Andrew Maerkle, Kerry James Marshall, Shane McCauley, Carmen McLeod, Suze Meyers, Madison Moore, Denise Murrell, Leah Oates, Barbara Pollack, Leigh Silver, Teddy Tinson, Kara Walker, Carrie Mae Weems, Lauren Weinberg, Carla Williams, Chloe Wyma, Lori Zimmer.

Ultimately, for Mickalene Thomas, as for Winfred Rembert, Kerry James Marshall, and Debra Priestly, art-making is the means to self-liberation. Their practices are a testament to Thomas's emphatic declaration: "My voice is my art."[85]

"I was kept in jail for several months before being tried and sent to the penitentiary at Reidsville, Georgia, the same one where Martin Luther King Jr. had served time," recalled Winfred Rembert of his wrongful imprisonment in the aftermath of his "almost lynching."[86] For Winfred Rembert, a vital connection exists between his damaging experiences in Reidsville prison and the incarceration endured by Martin Luther King Jr., a world-renowned civil rights leader, pastor, author, philosopher, and orator. He memorializes his unrecorded physical and psychological suffering as on a continuum with the corporeal and emotional pain endured by famous freedom-fighters. For Rembert, the civil rights movement was made possible by the acts of resistance committed by unknown and anonymous campaigners—individuals just like himself—as well as by celebrated, iconic, and legendary activists like Martin Luther King Jr.

"At Reidsville, they didn't call me by name, but by my number: 55147," Rembert recalled.[87] Not only was it the case that his name was taken from him and replaced by a number in which his humanity was all but annihilated, but he and the other male prisoners suffered further attacks on their individualism he will never forget by all being given the same clothing: "We wore white uniforms with a blue stripe down the sides."[88] Rembert speaks candidly about the backbreaking labor the men were forced to perform at the order of their white racist persecutors. As he later recalled, "I worked five days a week digging tree stumps out by hand and stomping on 'silo'—that's what we called plants that'd been chopped up and were being stored to feed the animals."[89] Always a freedom-fighter, however, he refused to be complicit in his own subjugation. Instead, he defied white dictatorial power by engaging in courageous feats of physical combat even when he knew his acts of rebellion would instantly be met with deliberate acts of persecution and torture by white authorities. "When I fought, I was sent to solitary confinement," he recalled. "We called it the Hole, and I spent a lot of time there."[90] Rembert sought

to destroy white supremacist power by every means necessary, and regardless of what it personally cost him. To the day he died, Rembert's life—no less than the life of Martin Luther King Jr.—was defined by an ongoing fight for all civil liberties and all equal rights.

"After a year at Reidsville, I was transferred to Leesburg. That was my first introduction to the chain gang," Rembert recalled. "We wore black-and-white striped suits."[91] He and the other men endured an unimaginably traumatizing and personally harrowing experience. They were subjected to the persecutory conditions of "almost slavery" by being denied all physical freedoms. "One leg was shackled to an iron ball," he remembered regarding his own bodily confinement. "Our work was to shovel sand out of ditches along the roads." But "sometimes, the ditches were full of water—freezing cold water, in the winter." Yet again, Rembert faced near-death consequences following his refusal to succumb to this mind-body-and-soul-killing reality. As he explained, all acts of rebellion by himself and the other men incurred immediate and extreme punishment: "If you fought or refused to work, the warden sent you to the sweatbox." Rembert recalled these inhumane sites of suffering: "Most sweatboxes were made of metal, and all were designed so that a person couldn't stand, sit, or kneel inside." His repeated acts of resistance were an unarguable testament to his undefeatable courage and had only one guaranteed result: "I spent a lot of time in the box."[92]

The sweatbox was an instrument of torture whose sole purpose was to break the mind, spirit, and body. Rembert refuses to sanitize the tragedies he and the other men endured. "They can keep you for 14 days, max," Rembert explained. Starvation conditions only exacerbated the terrible physical pain: "The only food was two slices of bread and a cup of water twice a day." Rembert betrayed no fear when faced with this unbearable suffering. As he recalled, "I was still angry at the system, the world, and white people." He refused to be controlled or contained by white totalitarian power

▶▶ "They didn't call me by name, but by my number: 55147"

even while he was incarcerated in the sweatbox. In an act of fearless bravery, he deliberately increased his suffering and exposure to bodily trauma by denying himself one of the means of survival: "I drank the water, but refused to eat the bread."[93] Rembert seized the right to exert his free will by wresting power from white authoritarian rule—regardless of the risk and damage it did to his own life. And yet, he persisted in refusing to single out his own heroism for any special commendation. As he readily admitted, while he withstood white supremacist systems bent on his psychological destruction and physical annihilation, he was one of the lucky ones. Rembert recognized that he was an exception to the rule, explaining, "A lot of kids lose their minds some die in there it's so tough of life."[94]

Even when denied the possibility of self-liberation from the traumatizing realities of a nonexistence in the sweatbox, Rembert still refused to surrender. "I got in a lot of trouble," he remembered. "I was in the sweat box 330-plus times in the seven years I was there."[95] While he failed to effect his liberation in the short-term, eventually his tactic of unending resistance met with success: "In my last two Georgia prisons, they finally stopped sending me to the box after I kept pretending that I didn't mind going there."[96] As Frederick Douglass explained when describing the brutality of white enslavers over a century ago, they "prefer to whip those who are most easily whipped."[97] Throughout Douglass's life, he remained adamant that "the old doctrine that submission is the best cure for outrage and wrong, does not hold good on the slave plantation. He is whipped oftenest, who is whipped easiest; and that slave who has the courage to stand up for himself against the overseer, although he may have many hard stripes at the first, becomes, in the end, a freeman, even though he sustain the formal relation of a slave."[98]

Rembert, like Douglass, understood that all philosophies and practices rooted in the belief that "submission is the best cure for outrage and wrong" ultimately run the mind-body-and-soul-destroying risk of resulting in self-harm rather than self-preservation.[99] As they were only too painfully aware, they ran the risk of further endangering the lives of Black people of all ages and genders as they fought for their survival in an era of "almost slavery." All his life, Rembert lived by his principles and practices as a civil rights campaigner, radical revolutionary, and social justice activist as he held to Douglass's opinion that the only way to become a self-liberated individual was by engaging in acts of resistance. "You gotta be a tough guy, mentally and physically," he emphasizes. "I felt like I had to be a thousand people."[100] Rembert was all too painfully aware that his mental and physical fortitude made him "able enough to endure," "hoping one day I'd be free."[101]

Looking for ways to be psychologically, imaginatively, and creatively—if not physically—free, Rembert learned the technique of carving pictures into leather during his incarceration. His teacher was a man named T.J. who had received "three life sentences."[102] T.J. survived the traumatizing realities of his incarceration and kept his mind, body, and soul together by making "wallets, billfolds, shoulder bags." Rembert recalled, "I stood there hour after hour watching him," adding, "something went off in my head." He soon realized that he "could do that." He remembers that T.J. felt threatened by his artistic prowess. "After he saw that I had the ability to draw different things and put different things on leather," Rembert remembered, "he took his tools away from me." Rembert explained that T.J.'s actions "didn't stop me" and were in no way a deterrent to his creative expression. "Things like that only give me the determination to go on," he maintained. He immediately found an answer to his problem by engaging in another act of creativity: "I made my own tools."[103] He explained that he "used nails—they come in all sizes, and all you have to do is shape the end the way you want it."[104] Rembert's creative process was nothing new: "I've been used to making things ever since I was a little boy."[105]

"First I sketch what I see in my head on paper, and then work on the leather with some 60 tools I have, sketching and raising the images, and then painting them with dyes," Rembert summarized regarding the various stages of his self-reflexive art-making process.[106] He explained that "you can't use paint when you're working with leather" because "it will crack." He advised that dye is ideal because it "soaks into the leather."[107] Working with leather as his canvas, he used dyes of all colors to create emotionally charged and politically powerful pictures in which private histories as well as public narratives of labor, civil rights struggles, and radical creativity come to life. "If leather is wet, you make any mark, and it comes right out," he observed.

"Once you put it down, you can't make a mistake at all."[108] His meticulous practice depends on technical accuracy. He created intricately layered compositions honoring equally intricate stories.

"Whatever picture I come up with, I draw it on paper first," Rembert explained. "I want it in my archives."[109] During his lifetime, he kept an original copy of each of his visual stories for his own records. In this context, his statement, "I work longer on the drawing than I do on the leather," is revealing.[110]

"The first lynching picture I ever did" is *Almost Me*, explained Rembert of a painting he created over two decades ago in 1997.[111] In a starkly etched outline, he traces the face and body of a man killed at the hands of a murderous white mob in this traumatized and traumatizing work. Rembert memorializes the tragic aftermath of the man's lynching: his head hangs down, his neck broken by the noose suspended from a tree limb. Rembert's title, *Almost Me*, works in conjunction with his powerful decision to etch the man's facial features in ways that resemble his own physiognomy. Rembert recalled that while "I hadn't talked much about being lynched then," the fact that "this picture was me" was self-evident.[112] "I don't know what conversation finally got me to start talking about it and doing art about it," he remembered, "but I never stopped thinking about it and having nightmares about it almost every night. Lots of times I'd get up out of the bed with Patsy and go in the bathroom and just sit there and cry."[113] For Rembert, the act and art of memorializing his own "almost lynching" in lines he carved into leather and in dye he soaked into its skin operates as a healing ritual of self-restoration, self-recreation, and self-preservation. While he would "never stop thinking about it" or experiencing "nightmares," Rembert used his art as a practice as a self-empowering means by which to visualize his experience, memorialize his pain, and bear witness to his survival.

Rembert carefully etched his surrogate self's facial features in *Almost Me*, ensuring his eyes are closed in a refusal to provide white audiences with voyeuristic access to his psychological interiority or private emotional reality. For Rembert, a determination to draw attention to this man's individualism and personhood works to reinforce his condemnation of the despicable beliefs and barbaric practices of his white murderers. In this work, Rembert denounced this man's white racist killers for operating as an anonymous group dedicated to the principles of racist hate according to which they failed to see Black people of all ages and genders as individuals and equal human beings. As an act of resistance, Rembert's refusal to sanitize the unspeakable suffering endured by this martyred man condemns the centuries-long white racist ritual of lynching people of color. Across his consciousness-raising paintings, he galvanizes his white audiences to a realization regarding lynching not as a historical but as an ongoing practice. Lynching rituals—morally depraved, psychologically destructive, physically tortuous, and emotionally harrowing forms of racist terrorism—continue to be perpetrated against innocent people of color by white racist persecutors and murderers.

"*Almost Me* is almost me," Rembert stated, explaining, "I never thought I would survive it but I did live to tell the story."[114] He lived not only to tell but to paint the story of his own suffering during his "almost lynching." At the same time, he memorialized the traumatizing reality that it was not only "almost me" but "actually us." As Rembert summarized, "I created this painting to honor those victims and everyone else who's been lynched."[115] Coming of age in a segregated South where white racist atrocity and abuse against Black people remained a dominant, widespread, and entrenched reality, Rembert not only suffered an "almost lynching," but he was a first-hand witness to a "real lynching" as a young child. "I was real little at the time, so Mama took me," he remembered of his firsthand experience of this atrocity. "We arrived at a little shack home and saw a man and his son hanging from a tree."[116] Rembert was a child witness to the double execution of a father and son. He knew from a young age that Black families were ripped apart, mutilated, and destroyed by white racist killers on a regular basis.

"When I was growing up, black folk were always worried about lynchings," Rembert poignantly declared. "Too many white people considered themselves above the law and might decide to hang a person without even a trial."[117] In *Almost Me*, he waged a war against the lynchings perpetrated against people of color over the centuries. At the same time, he condemned the mass circulation of white-owned and white-produced lynching postcards. His emotionally powerful and politically revolutionary painting lives on in radical opposition to these white supremacist, mass produced cheap postcards in which white women, children, and men of all ages appear beneath mutilated, tortured, and destroyed Black bodies in a propagandistic endorsement of white power. In *Almost Me*, Rembert removes all traces of white spectators to focus only on Black subjectivities, Black stories, and Black lives. In so doing, he denied lynching its white-supremacist function of racial terrorism. He assumed the role of a memorialist, historian, and witness to safeguard his role as judge of white barbarity. Across his works, he had not only the final word but, crucially, the final image when it came to visibilizing white racist atrocities enacted against peoples of color.

In the same year that Rembert created *Almost Me*, he carved into leather an equally emotional portrait he titled *A Slave*. In this psychologically hard-hitting work, he reproduced the same seminude body and identical facial features belonging to the Black male subject of *Almost Me*. But the figure is no longer dead and hanging from a noose: this time he stands erect with his eyes open rather than closed. The man directly confronts the viewer with an emotionally uncompromising expression, inspiring his audiences to a direct psychological engagement with his traumatizing subject matter. *A Slave* exists in a visual call-and-response relationship with *Almost Me*, not only due to the similar physiognomies of Rembert's male protagonists but in recognition of the fact that both men possess the same musculature. The Black man of *A Slave* wears the same green pants tied together with the same rope that not only encircles the man's waist in *Almost Me* but also resembles the cord that makes the lynchers' noose.

Rembert refused to shy away from the traumatizing realities of centuries of inhumane bondage, incarcerating the man's body in an enormous black iron chain attached to iron rings around his neck and ankles. While the title of the piece insists that protesting against the atrocities of slavery was his first priority, Rembert includes no background that would ground *A Slave* in a specific period. His enslaved man could be living in any era. Ultimately, his emotionally charged painting exposes slavery as a centuries-long institution, practice, and ideology that refuses to die. For Rembert and for millions of people of color, slavery and its nefarious legacies remain the dominant oppressive reality that inspires all past, present, and future freedom struggles.

"I was always scared in Georgia where white people had all the power to just hurt you for no reason," Rembert admitted.[118] He experienced a painful sense of powerlessness: "Watching black folks get beat up and called names and nothing you can do about it." He said, "I know it's forty years later but I still feel pretty much the same when I'm back in Cuthbert."[119] Rembert confronted his fear of "white people" who have "all the power" in his practice. This fear influenced his rationale for creating *A Slave*: "When I did a picture like this part of me is putting out my frustration and my scaredness, but secretly, and showing how I am always feeling—all chained up and powerless."[120] Although he bears witness to his own exposure to terror in a harrowing memorialization of Black manhood as "all chained up and powerless," he refused to consign his protagonist solely to the status of a victim. In *A Slave*, the unnamed Black male subject holds a hammer—otherwise a signifier of oppression through backbreaking labor—in his clenched fists in a deliberate gesture of militant defiance. Ultimately, for Rembert, only art-making is the way to self-liberation. Rembert's radical vision as a witness-historian-memorialist-artist transforms images of Black men as spectacles of subjugation into portraits of authority, agency, and power.

The Lynching. After the Lynching. The Burial. So read the titles of the traumatizing triptych of paintings Rembert created just two years later in 1999. The epic series of monumental works condemns and denounces white acts of murderous atrocity not in an individual lynching but in the mass murder of six men. In panel 1, *The Lynching*, rifle-wielding and baseball bat-touting white men occupy the picture's foreground. In horrifying contrast to the barbaric violence of these white men, the naked bodies of four Black men hang from a tree and are positioned next to two empty nooses in the background of the painting. Rembert depicts their bodies in various states of involuntary spasm and physical contortion as a visual call-to-arms. He refused to sanitize the excruciating torture that each of these men endured prior to their release from suffering in death. Rope heavily binds each of their bodies in Rembert's memorialization. Yet again, Rembert emphasized that cowardly white men succeeded in controlling courageous unarmed Black men only by tightly re-straining them prior to attacking them from within the anonymous safety of a vigilante mob.

While Rembert protested against white villainy in *The Lynching*, he ultimately focused on exposing the psychological and physical devastations experienced by Black women, children, and men because of these trag-edies. He shows the heartbreaking suffering endured by Black people of all ages in their shared witnessing of mass lynching. In a powerful contrast to the faceless, weapon-wielding white men, Rembert relied on care-fully delineated lines to memorialize the sorrowful and shocked facial expressions of his individualized Black women, children, and men. Rembert honored the fact that "all the black folk who lived in the plantation were likely to be forced to watch a lynching. The white mob was sending a message to us—just do what you're told or this will happen to you."[121] In spite of this warning, Black solidarity networks, rather than white racist ter-rorist practices, define Rembert's vision. Women, chil-dren, and men of all ages hold hands and support one another as they stand, kneel, and gesture toward his heartbreaking reimagining of "the struggle that blacks in the south went through."[122] As an artist who had not only been "almost lynched," but who had "been to a lynching after the fact," he had one enduring mem-ory he sought to dramatize here: "There was a lot of wailing and moaning from the family."[123] As he testified, "mothers was losing their sons and their husbands."[124] In Rembert's artistic protest, the focus is less on pro-viding his audiences with a graphic portrayal of a mur-dered Black body and more on bearing witness to the terrible grief experienced by Black families in the wake of these atrocities.

In panel 2, *After the Lynching*, Rembert continued to memorialize the sufferings and sacrifices experienced by anonymous mothers and wives. In this painting, his female protagonists lovingly hold their husbands and sons, whose bodies they have liberated from the white lyncher's noose. Rembert's recreation is not fictional. In this painting, he condemned southern whites for their atrocities in the wake of their heinous killings: "After a lynching the white mob went home, leaving the victim hanging."[125] As he remembered, grieving Black families did not tolerate this disrespect: "Black folk would cut the person down, place the body on a wagon, and have

the mules pull it to the grave site."[126] While Rembert me-morializes the heartbreaking reality that Black mothers and wives were unable to protect their husbands and sons in life due to the atrocities of enslavement and lynching, he provides a poignant meditation on the ways in which they were able to honor them in death.

Rembert visualizes the tragedy of the Black Pietà by showing mothers holding their dead sons and wives holding their dead husbands. Rembert's strategy of evoking the Western Christian iconography of the Pietà—the visual representation of the Virgin mother Mary holding the murdered body of her son Jesus after he died on the cross—carries powerful emotional and political weight. He rejects all white racist dehuman-izing stereotypes by instead associating lynched Black men with the murdered body of the Christian Christ. As Nathaniel Turner had proclaimed in the days be-fore his own execution at the hands of a white racist lynch mob masquerading as a governmental authority in November 1831, "Was not Christ crucified."[127] He also testifies to the strength generated by their shared solidarity. Warring against white supremacist strategies that effected the dehumanization, no less than the sub-jugation, of all people of color, Rembert meticulously rendered their clothing and carefully etched their facial expressions. Throughout his work, Rembert bears wit-ness to their individualism to provide an unequivocal testament to their personhood.

After the Lynching includes the same wooden cabins that appear in *The Lynching*. They resemble the homes belonging not only to twentieth-century sharecropping families but also to eighteenth and nineteenth-century enslaved families fighting for an existence. Rembert's decision to memorialize the untold stories of the com-munity's enslaved ancestors recalls Frederick Douglass's conviction that lynching was a form of racial terrorism that was directly dependent on the institution of slav-ery. Douglass's explanation of the psychology motivat-ing a white lynch mob in 1894 could just as easily read as a description of the beliefs of white racist persecutors living in 2022. He writes, "These people have not now and have never had any such respect for human life as is common to other men."[128] For Douglass, one reason and one reason only exists for their complete lack of "respect for human life:" "It is not the work of the spirit of liberty, but the work of the spirit of bondage, and of the determination of slavery to perpetuate itself, if not under one form, then under another."[129] Over a hundred years after Frederick Douglass's death, Winfred Rembert dedicated his life as an artist to the social justice work of protesting against the "spirit of bondage" in the ongoing fight to secure the "spirit of liberty" for all Black people still fighting for survival in the United States.

As Frederick Douglass and Winfred Rembert understood, it is not only the reality of slavery but also the "spirit of bondage" that has been responsible for teaching whites "no respect for human life and especially the life of the negro."[130] Though living centuries earlier, Douglass shares Rembert's pain regarding white disrespect for the sanctity of Black lives: "The sacredness of life which ordinary men feel does not touch them anywhere. A dead negro is with them a common jest."[131] Rembert memorialized persecuted, tortured, and martyred Black women, children, and men as not only the visual antithesis of a "common jest" but as a call to revolutionary arms and to the freedom struggle.

Rembert's final panel, *The Burial*, depicts seven anonymous graves surrounded by grieving and traumatized Black women, children, and men of all ages. They again give comfort and strength to one other in an emotionally powerful testament to Rembert's lifelong belief that survival is only possible through intergenerational systems of support. "I have seven graves here, six for the victims I've imagined and a seventh to bury hate," Rembert explained. "I figured that, if we bury hate, then maybe this won't happen again."[132] As for Douglass 150 years ago so for Rembert in the twenty-first century: a refusal to surrender to hate undergirds their past and present "lexicons of liberation." Rembert protests that the mass deaths of Black people endangers the future of the human race. "That empty grave is for humanity," he declared.[133]

A few years later, in 2005, Rembert produced a work he titled *Chain Gang (All Me)* (figure 28). Here he memorialized the harrowing experiences he endured during his period of wrongful incarceration. He refused to dye the picture in a bold departure from his characteristic reliance on an array of colors. Instead, he worked to ensure "that people could see the work before it's dyed."[134] He admitted to being especially anxious to provide his viewers with direct access to "every detail" to guarantee their full appreciation of his technical expertise. Bereft of all color, his careful carving of every line, dot, and incision that together make up the faces, bodies, clothing, and laboring implements of his unnamed men is dramatically to the fore. Rembert reported that he had "over a hundred tools that I use to this 3-D effect."[135] His technical virtuosity does justice to the individualized personhood of each of these men.

Rembert relied on intricate layers of lines to memorialize each of the men's facial expressions. He worked to remember their powerful emotions, including depression, distress, and resolution, out of a determination to ensure that his viewers would not only recognize but would respect their equal humanity. The men are shackled by their feet to iron balls and chains that dominate the foreground of this work. Rembert powerfully testifies to his male protagonists' complex subjectivities by creating a space for the expression of their individual agency and artistry. While the iron balls and chains are painful reminders of the damage wrought by a "spirit of bondage," each man's act of physical labor represents his power to survive through his will not only to exist but to live.

While Rembert refused to ignore the fact that the "chain gang is designed to mentally break you down," his male protagonists are far from broken.[136] They wield their hammers in various postures, kneeling, bending, and standing erect as they work. Rembert explained, "I'm trying to make these guys look like who they really were," and "I may not remember their names, but I got their faces." At the same time, he was equally working to realize the subtitle of his work: "All me."[137] "I'm so glad I had the strength to go through," he admitted, adding, "I had to be more than just myself to survive, so this picture is all me."[138] For Rembert, it was vital not only that he accurately visualize the faces of the men laboring beside him but that he foreground the extent to which he had to draw strength from their strength in order "to be more than just myself to survive."

"The chaingang is probably the worst thing you can ever do to a human being," Rembert declared.[139] He insisted, "They said slavery was tough but I just can't believe it was any tougher than being on the chaingang." For Rembert, the chain gang was the embodiment of the "spirit of bondage." "It's the place where all dignity

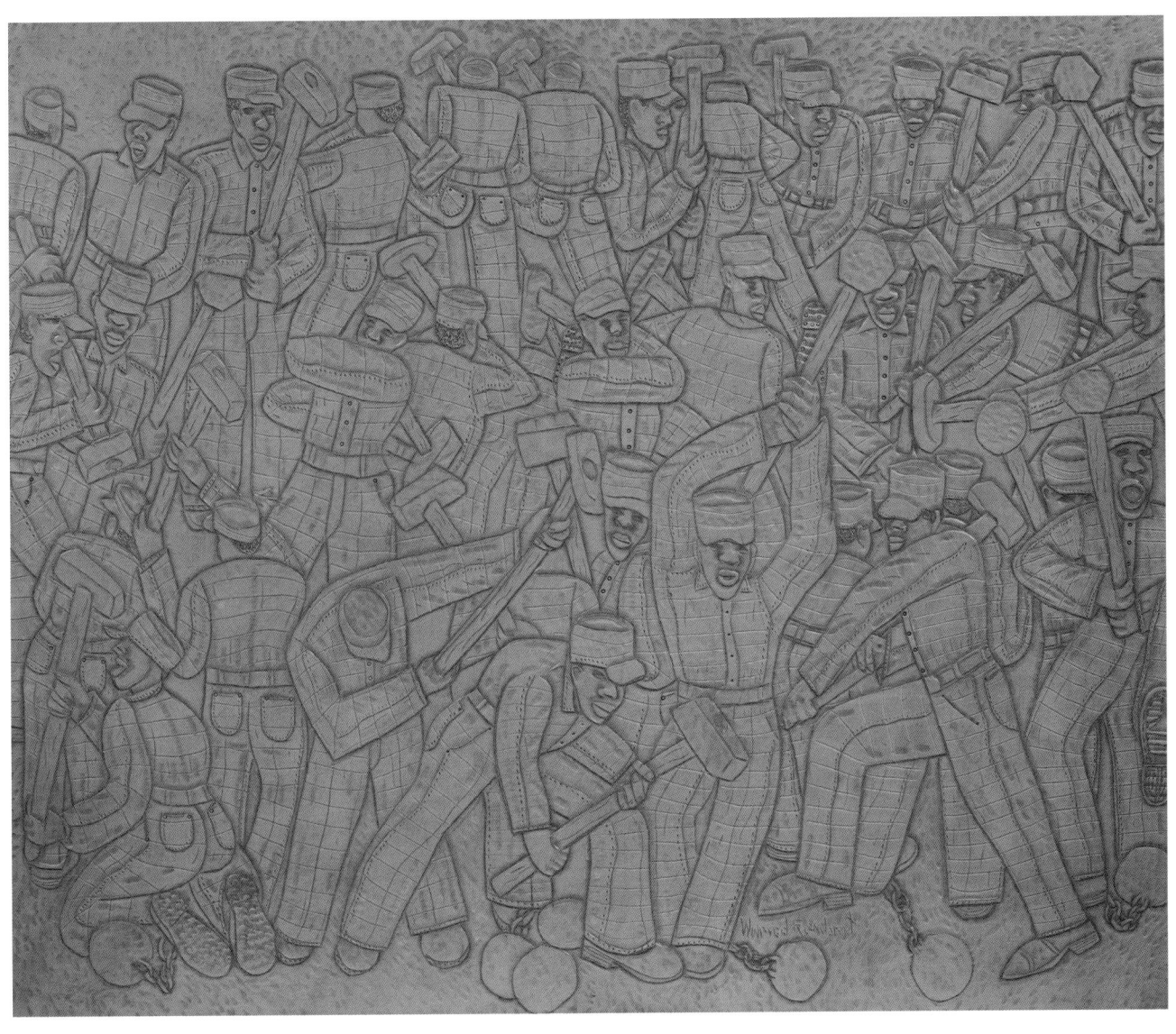

FIGURE 28. Winfred Rembert,
Chain Gang (All Me), 2005. Courtesy
of Adelson Galleries, Boston.

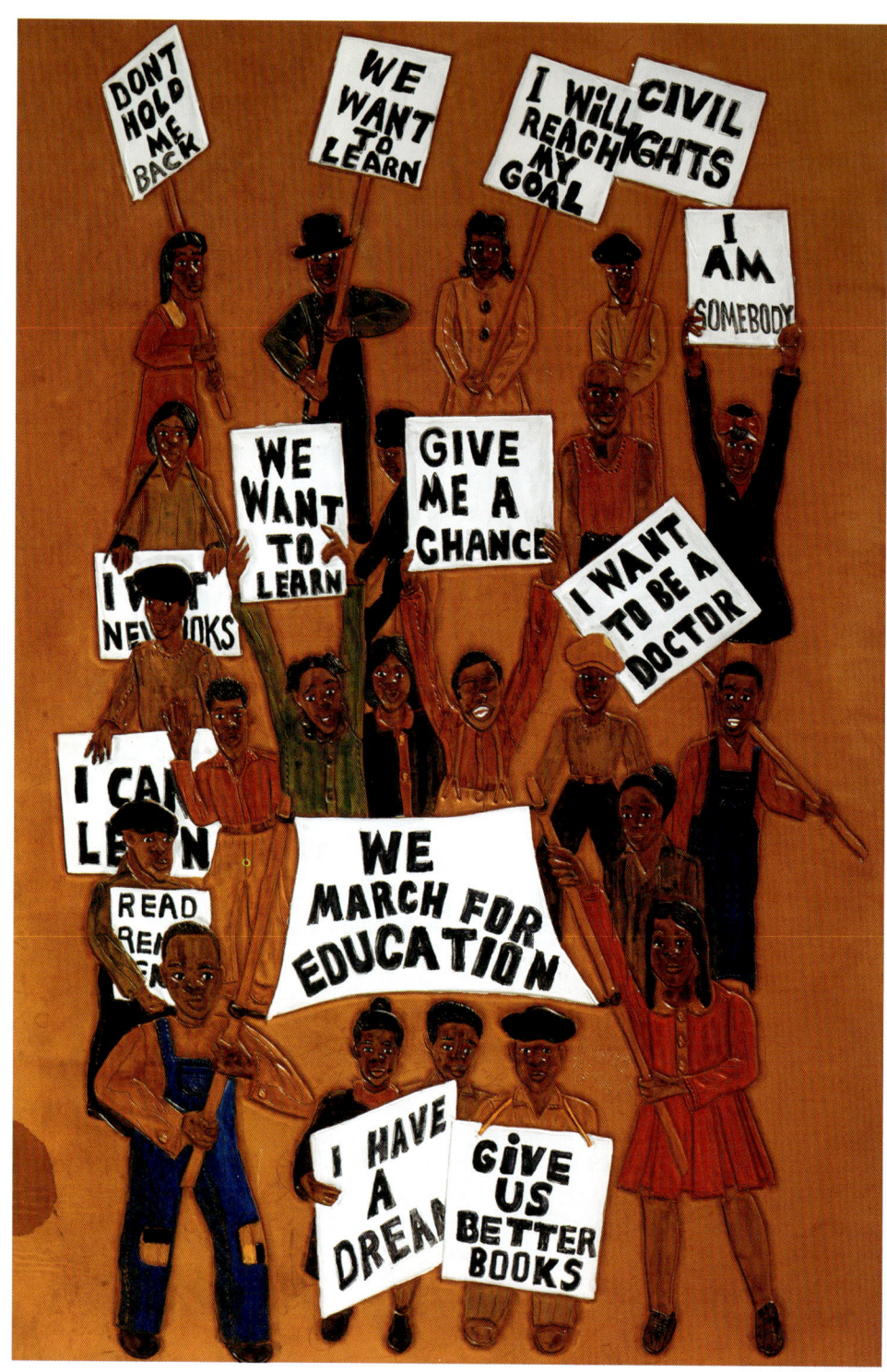

FIGURE 29. Winfred
Rembert, *Civil Rights
—I Have a Dream*, 1999.
Courtesy of Adelson
Galleries, Boston.

is taken from you," he explained. "You're not a man any-more." In a powerful reversal of the willful destruction of Black men incarcerated on chain gangs, Rembert restored the humanity, dignity, and manhood to all the complex protagonists he reimagines in this work. As a declaration of empowerment, *Chain Gang (All Me)* is a powerful testament to Rembert's conviction: "Thank God I was about to not let the chain gang take me over but I took the chain gang over."[140] Rembert issued a challenge to white racist persecutors, haters, and destroyers, then and now, by exclaiming, "You can't stop me."[141]

Rembert's 1999 painting *Civil Rights—I Have a Dream* (figure 29) depicts women, children, and men holding aloft white boards on which are written slogans in stark black capital letters: "DON'T HOLD ME BACK." "I WILL REACH MY GOAL." "I AM SOMEBODY." "WE MARCH FOR EDUCATION." "As I think back to my years in Georgia," he recalled, "I realize that what's most important is that every kid should have a fair chance and needs to get a good education."[142] Rembert knew that as far as his own experience was concerned, if he had "been able to stay in school, my life would have been so different."[143] *Civil Rights* is a painstaking work in which he memorializes the power of an intergenerational Black freedom struggle. Rembert again used intricately detailed lines to generate the individualized, emotional physiognomies of his civil rights protesters. Sources of hope for future generations, a young boy holds up a board that says "GIVE ME A CHANCE," while a young girl carries a poster that reads "WE WANT TO LEARN."

Rembert memorializes his own life story to educate the next generation regarding the realities not only of white racist hate and what "we went through," but also of a centuries-long Black freedom struggle and liberation movement. Rembert summarized: "I hope that the example of my life as told through my art will help children understand that they shouldn't be afraid to learn, that they need to keep trying, and that they have to find the courage to turn any anger they have into something positive."[144] Art-making provided Rembert with a transformative way in which he was able to turn his anger into "something positive." As he explained, he had one overriding goal for his younger audiences: "When they look at my art and read my story, I want each one to feel deep inside, 'Wow, me, too! I can do something with my life.'"[145]

Caint to Caint (Can't see when you go to work, can't see when you get back), created in 2008, is a painting in which Rembert visualizes the backbreaking work of "toiling, toiling, toiling" in the cotton fields (figure 30). In this painting, Rembert re-creates his memory of the cotton field as a site of struggle. He shows Black women, children, and men of all ages toting their sacks. They are bent over, leaning forward, or standing while they labor over the cotton plants. In this spatially claustrophobic work, Rembert's Black protagonists are surrounded by large cotton plants and baskets filled with cotton, while they themselves occupy only limited physical space. Here, he provides an emotionally unequivocal testament to the very real confinement experienced by untold numbers of unnamed individuals who had no choice but to live their lives surrounded by an "invisible fence." Rembert explained the painting's title by recalling, "When anyone asked, 'How long you all gonna work today?' we'd say, 'From can't to can't—you go when you can't see and you come back when you can't see."[146] He refuses to conceal the mind-body-and-soul-destroying realities that have resulted from the "spirit of slavery" and that live on in the persecutory practices endorsed by the ever-present and all-powerful white "plantation owner."

Caint to Caint celebrates its protagonists' individualism and collective agency. In the painting, Rembert carefully delineates each of his subject's facial expressions and meticulously re-creates their uniquely designed and varyingly colored clothing. While he refuses to sanitize the traumatizing reality that "we worked from sunup to sundown," he also commemorates the life-preserving strategies of solidarity endorsed by Black families and wider community groups.[147] "For dinner, workers would gather together, most times in groups of ten to twenty people. Usually, a group included the members of one or two families," he recalled. "Togetherness was a big part of black life in those days."[148] Rembert's practice is centered on educating his audiences regarding not only the sufferings and sacrifices endured by Black people but also their strategies for survival. Black agency survives despite white racist forces of discriminatory hate. As Rembert always remembered, "There was always lot of talk at dinnertime, especially about going north to make a better life."[149]

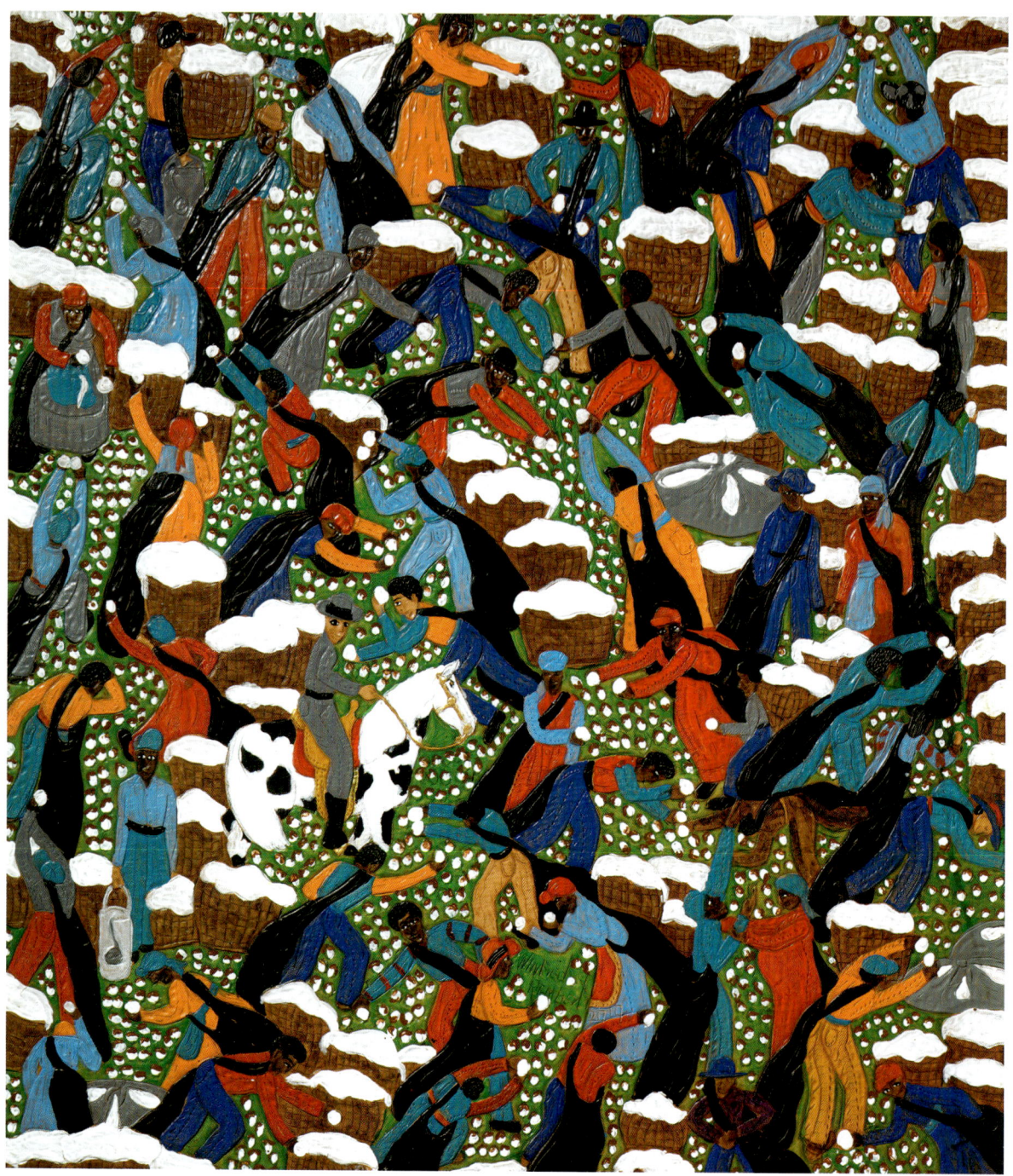

FIGURE 30. Winfred Rembert, *Caint to Caint (Can't see when you go to work, can't see when you get back)*, 2008. Courtesy of Adelson Galleries, Boston.

KERRY JAMES MARSHALL   *(Born in Birmingham, Alabama, 1955)*

"An imbalance of power exists between white people, in this world, and everybody else, in almost every sphere of human enterprise," observes Kerry James Marshall.[150] A social justice artist, Marshall dedicates his practice to documenting the racist inequalities, political discriminations, psychological abuses, and physical persecutions that result from a white supremacist world order. "No self-respecting people can accept such an imbalance and the marginality it sustains, without a fight," he maintains. "Against this backdrop I try to make some aesthetic inroads."[151] Marshall rights the wrongs of a white dominant society and art world by making "aesthetic inroads" into western systems of exclusion and erasure enacted against people of color. He insists, "When you find yourself, your culture and history" has "been subjugated, enslaved and colonised, you got to fix that."[152]

Marshall wages a war against deeply entrenched practices in western society that have been designed to subjugate, enslave, and colonize Black experiences, Black memories, Black cultures, Black art-making traditions, Black histories, and Black lives. He works to liberate Black women, children, and men from the dehumanizing legacies of U.S. chattel slavery, the transatlantic slave trade, and widespread systems of colonization. "Too often images of black people are associated with some sort of trauma," he explains. "It's often a historical trauma related to the narrative of slavery and colonialism, or some other deprivation."[153] Marshall interrogates and undoes the physical, existential, psychological, ideological, and cultural damage done to generations of Black people as a result of their exposure to an individual and collective "historical trauma." He has arrived at a new visual language in which Black power, Black beauty, and Black resistance dominate. Working against a tradition in which people of color have only ever been dehumanized or destroyed within a white racist imaginary, he is adamant that "I've always considered myself a history painter."[154] Marshall is a radically revisionist "history painter" dedicated to exposing the widespread whitewashing of the past to denounce centuries of white racist abuses and atrocities. Across his paintings, he creates "images of black people" as associated not only with "historical trauma" but also with contemporary healing and radical resistance strategies.

"I think it is important for a black artist to create black figure paintings in the grand tradition," explains Marshall.[155] He creates works in which the "black figure" is monumental in scale out of his conviction that "a foregrounded black figuration, powerfully presented, would have the most meaningful impact, inspirationally and experientially, on the whole art enterprise."[156] His practice of "representing black figures had something to do with their absence."[157] Over the decades, he has pioneered an alternative visual lexicon in his experimental radical practice in which he destabilizes as well as defies the overwhelming dominance of a "grand tradition" that is for whites only. As he explains, "What I'm really trying to do is to show that every level of mastery that underpins the master narrative of the development of art history can be easily understood, deciphered, and then deployed."[158]

Dedicating a lifetime of art-making to demystifying and destabilizing white totalitarian power at every level of mainstream society and within the "development of art history," Marshall reinterprets and redeploys the symbols, motifs, conventions, and practices from the oppressive "master narrative" in order to recreate, reimagine, and re-present liberated "enslaved narratives" of resistance. While Rembert protests the traumatizing consequences of a "spirit of bondage" that refuses to die, Marshall challenges the "spirit of mastery."[159] As Frederick Douglass had theorized the damaging impact of a "spirit of bondage" on U.S. society, so he also predicted the stranglehold that would continue to be exerted by white supremacy as a very real manifestation of this "spirit of mastery."

Marshall is as equally appalled by white racist systems of tokenism as by the invisibilization of Black cultures, memories, and histories within the art world. He recognizes the destructive consequences of a white western cultural milieu that remains committed to the inclusion of only a handful of artists of color. He

▶▶ "A Historical Trauma Related to the Narrative of Slavery and Colonialism"

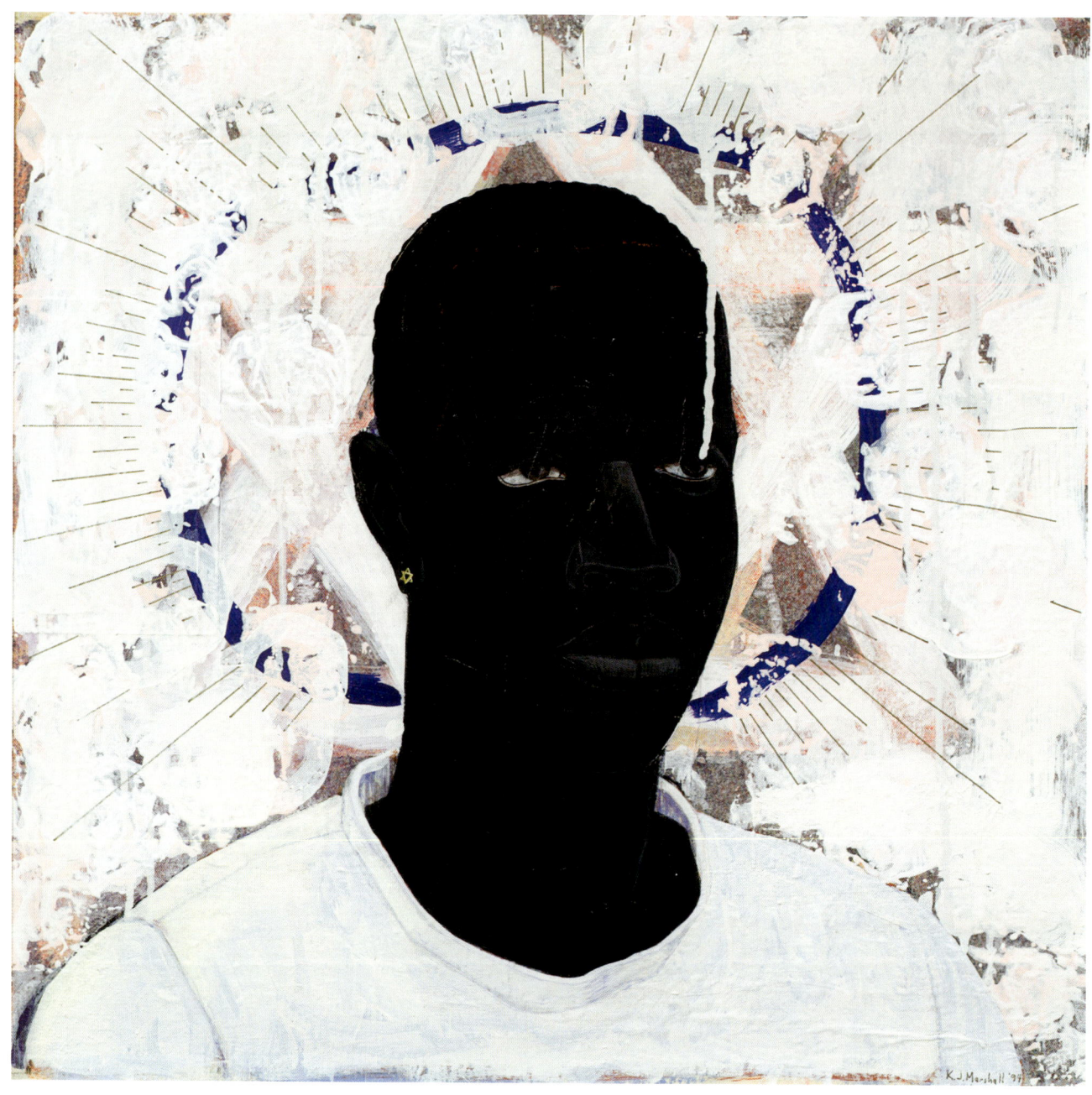

FIGURE 31. Kerry James Marshall, *Lost Boys: AKA Black Johnny*, 1995. Acrylic and collage on canvas (24¾ × 24¾ in.). Inventory #KM93.008. Copyright Kerry James Marshall. Courtesy of the artist and Jack Shainman Gallery, New York.

argues, "If you find yourself in the higher echelons of the culture and there's always just one or two of you, there's something wrong."[160] Ultimately, Marshall's categorical declaration allows for no dissent: "It should be unacceptable to any black person who had a measure of self respect."[161] Marshall allows for no violations or violences to be committed against his self-respect, dignity, or artistic vision. Instead, his "black aesthetic" is defined by his independence of subject matter, freedom of form, and liberation of iconographic language from the stranglehold of white western power.

"We've been under white domination too long," Marshall insists, emphasizing that the "idea of a black aesthetic is an important thing for me to explore."[162] As he maintains, only the exploration of the forms, techniques, and functions of a "black aesthetic" can expose a cultural criteria rooted in an exclusionary and violent white aesthetic. He creates experimental and emotionally hard-hitting paintings in which he rejects the scopic dominance exerted by white racist stereotypes of Black humanity. Marshall takes the view that, "If I, as a black man, can't construct an ideal of beauty wrapped in a black skin, then everything is lost."[163]

Lost Boys is "a series of nine 'funeral' portraits, embodying the concept of innocence and loss," summarizes Marshall (figure 31).[164] In these memorial paintings, Marshall mourns the premature deaths of Black male children whose lives prematurely ended through violence. These works assume heightened emotional power not only as memorials but also as surrogate headstones. Marshall explains that each of these portraits foregrounds the "birth and death dates of the children, to make it clear that they were teenagers or younger when they died."[165] He bears witness to "a period in the late 1980s and early 1990s when too many young kids were being killed in the crossfire of gang wars." As a painter, he says, "I wanted to address that tragedy within my work."[166] The series contains "pictures of young children killed before they have had a chance to grow up." Marshall's titles for the paintings are emotionally heartbreaking: *Lost Boys: AKA 8 Ball* (1992); *Lost Boys: AKA Baby Brother* (1992); *Lost Boys: AKA Black Tony* (1992); *Lost Boys: AKA Black Al* (1993); *Lost Boys: AKA Untitled* (1993); *Lost Boys: AKA Black Sonny* (1993); *Lost Boys* (1993); *The Lost Boys* (1993); *Lost Boys: AKA Black Johnny* (1995) (figure 31).[167]

Marshall creates "black figure paintings in the grand tradition" in a refusal to portray these children according to the destructive conventions of white racist stereotypes.[168] Rather, through his radically empowered "black aesthetic," he reimagines each of his protagonists as psychologically and emotionally complex individuals. His empathetic and dignifying portraits memorialize their humanity. Marshall not only includes each of these young children's names—Tony, Al, Sonny, and Johnny—but he also records their nicknames—8 Ball—as well as their family affiliations: Baby Brother. In *Lost Boys*, Marshall testifies to the terrible tragedies generated by a "historical trauma" that has very real contemporary ramifications for the survival of Black children in mainstream U.S. society to this day. His new visual language bears witness to a mind-body-and-soul-destroying reality: "For a lot of kids growing up in the city" in the twenty-first century, the "question isn't whether they want to grow up, but whether they will have the opportunity" to grow up.[169]

Marshall describes the paintings as "iconic images, like medieval icons in tone but with a contemporary backdrop, with suggestions of graffiti." He adds, "Some of the kids have a halo or nimbus. I used that as a sign of their innocence."[170] As one among the many emotionally hard-hitting works he creates from acrylic paint and collage on canvas for this series, *Lost Boys: AKA Black Johnny* is a powerful portrait of an intimate close-up of his subject's intense expression. Johnny appears against a "contemporary backdrop with suggestions of graffiti," shown in streaks of white paint, and surrounded by a blue halo which Marshall uses to communicate his innocence. Johnny retains his authority by refusing to confront the viewer.[171] Instead, he contemplates the far distance, suggesting that his mind, body, and soul are no longer part of this world but already in a spiritual realm.

Lost Boys: AKA Black Johnny is a poignant portrait in which Marshall refuses to shy away from the fact that a Black male child's struggle is always one of life and death. He exposes the violence of an omnipresent white supremacy that maims, mutilates, and murders. A white streak of paint in the background bleeds down Johnny's forehead and drips down into his eye, symbolically running down the child's brain and into his line of vision in a searing indictment of white racism's annihilating forces. As Marshall emphasizes, white supremacy destroys the lives of Black children, resulting not only in their physical death via everyday acts of violence but in their psychological torture and intellectual disenfranchisement. He condemns white supremacy as an ideology that seeps into an individual's cerebral faculties and corrodes their very act of perception by distorting their vision. Marshall interrogates one of white supremacy's devastating consequences: the extermination of all forms of self-respect, self-representation, and self-preservation.

The visual antithesis of the mug shot typically taken by persecutory police authorities, Marshall's portrait of Johnny foregrounds his emotional autonomy and psychological interiority. The political possibilities suggested by his stark juxtaposition of the white backdrop with the black skin of his protagonist foregrounds individuality. Marshall explains, "What I really tried to do, at the same time that I reduced their presence of their value, their color value, to an extreme black, was to try to always make sure that they all had individual identities, so that the only way you could say that they kind of all look alike in a way, was simply the fact that they were both black."[172] He visualizes back to white racist assumptions that all "black figures look alike," by emphasizing that it is the monumental presence and empowered beauty of his individualized protagonists that is the inspiration for his revolutionary Black aesthetic. Warring against the homogenized portrayals of Black people within a white Western imaginary, here and elsewhere he employs an "extreme black" skin tone for his protagonists as a testament to his conviction that "just as blackness is apparent, their beauty can also be apparent in their blackness."[173]

While Marshall ensures that each of his subjects has their own "individual identity" and "beauty" in *Lost Boys*, he also explains, "They are sort of composite portraits that are based on people."[174] In a deliberate rejection of white mainstream stereotypes of Black humanity, Marshall's protagonists ultimately come to life as "a kind of archetype."[175] In this series in particular, he refuses to adhere to realism in favor of providing a more abstract meditation on what it is to be "archetypically black."[176] Rather than reimagine a single person, he creates his protagonists as "composite portraits" in order to memorialize multiple lives at once. His

"composite portraits" of young Black male children assume a mythic, symbolic, and archetypal power in *Lost Boys*. Throughout the series, he memorializes composite lives to ensure that each of these murdered young protagonists exists not only as a recognizable individual but also as a touchstone, emblem, and representative for the atrocities and abuses endured not by one or two young people but by untold millions of children over the generations. Marshall admits that he took his inspiration from white British author J. M. Barrie's stories about Peter Pan in creating this series. *Lost Boys* is a visual memorial not to an isolated individual but to "a group of young boys who were lost down in Never, Never Land."[177]

"There has been a tradition of negative representation of black people and the counter tradition to that has been a certain kind of positive image," Marshall declares.[178] He acknowledges the destructive consequences of dichotomous and reductive representations of Black people, arguing that "both, in a lot of ways, end up being a kind of stereotype."[179] As an antidote to these oversimplified visualizations of Black lives, he works "to do two things at once" in order "to find ways that operate right on the borderline."[180] He resists fixed representations of his Black protagonists in *Lost Boys* to create portraits that occupy the middle ground. He creates an alternative imaginary characterized by formal experimentation and thematic ambiguity, visualizing his equal, radical, and revolutionary Black subjects through iconographic indeterminacy. Neither saints nor sinners, martyrs nor perpetrators, victims nor victimizers, the *Lost Boys* series embodies the psychological complexity, emotional ambiguity, and mortal fallibility of untold, unimagined, and unrepresented individual lives lived on the "borderline" not only of representation but also of existence.

Marshall's inspiration for his *Lost Boys* series can be traced to his family life. In his work, *Lost Boys: AKA Baby Brother*, he memorializes a traumatizing reality: his youngest brother "went into jail just shortly before I started the Lost Boys series."[181] "A part of the reason I started that group of paintings was a reaction to how I felt about him being incarcerated," he says.[182] But the emotional catalyst for this series is in no way restricted to his personal biography. Over the years, he has remained equally emphatic that his motivation to memorialize the tragedies and tortures facing his "lost boys" emerged because the "weight of the numbers of black men who end up going through a lot of traumatic experiences kind of sat heavy on my mind."[183] The work is one of mourning in which he provides a poignant visualization of the "concept of being lost: lost in America, lost in the ghetto, lost in public housing, lost in joblessness, and lost in illiteracy." Marshall refuses to censor the white supremacist realities that continue to damage and destroy Black lives—past, present, and future.[184]

In the *Lost Boys* paintings and in his practice, Marshall honors the "concept of being lost" in relation to the contemporary injustices, especially of white supremacist U.S. society's entrapment of Black people within segregated urban settings, economic inequalities, and discriminatory educational systems. At the same time, he also addresses the "concept of being lost" with regard to the "historical trauma related to the narrative of slavery and colonialism."[185] "Among a lot of friends and acquaintances of mine there has been this idea of a transitional moment in the experience of Africans being brought to the New World," he observes. "The moment of the Middle Passage was traumatic."[186] Marshall's practice bears witness to his determination to confront the "transitional" and "traumatic moment" of the Middle Passage as a centuries-long institution inaugurated and maintained by white Western avarice and greed, which resulted in the deportation of untold millions of peoples of color of all ages, genders, nationalities, belief systems, and cultures from Africa to live enslaved lives in the New World. Marshall develops a visual language of liberation within which to communicate that "many of the attitudes and personality developments in black folks in the diaspora are a consequence of this unresolved trauma."[187] Coming to grips with the painful relationship between "black folks" and "unresolved trauma," Marshall interrogates the harrowing realities not only of the transatlantic slave trade but also of U.S. chattel slavery. His paintings testify to the harrowing "matter-of-factness about a kind of violence that was part of plantation life." Marshall's description of "slavery times" recalls Lilian Rembert's survival tactics. He acknowledges the terrible price exacted of Black people for the preservation of their lives: "You had to negotiate it in silence. In that context, you were always powerless to resist it. You resigned yourself to being available to violence."[188]

Marshall is an empowered and in no way silenced "history painter." He refuses to be "available to violence." He rejects the dehumanizing influences of an ever-present white supremacist system and ideology that have been intent on effecting the subjugation of all Black people for centuries. An activist-artist, he dedicates his experimental practice to creating a revolutionary and radical Black aesthetic which celebrates first and foremost the beauty, power, resilience, and cultural agency of enslaved and free Black women, children, and men. Working to tell the stories of both the atrocities "we went through" and individual and collective acts of revolutionary heroism, he admits to a preoccupation with "looking back at African and African-American history and culture" to "locate moments of resistance and rebellion."[189] As he explains, "I'm always looking for ways to propel a black presence, forcefully, into the future."[190] For Marshall, a hidden history of "resistance and rebellion" offers a blueprint for future revolution. His portraits are an especially powerful means by which he is able to "propel a black presence . . . into the future." Marshall's portraits memorialize not only individual "moments" but individual subjects of "resistance and rebellion."

In 2009 and 2011, Marshall painted portraits of two historical liberators, David Walker (1796–1830) and Nathaniel Turner (1800–1831): *Believed to be a Portrait of David Walker (c. 1830)* (2009) and *Portrait of Nat Turner with the Head of His Master* (2011) (figure 32). As founding fathers of a centuries-old African diasporic freedom struggle, David Walker and Nathaniel Turner play a key role in Marshall's social, political, historical, and cultural meditation on "a long tradition of radical Black Liberation ideologues." In *Believed to be a Portrait of David Walker (c. 1830)*, Marshall asserts Walker's iconographic presence where before there had been only absence. Despite his importance as a historical legend, freedom-fighter, political theorist, social justice campaigner, philosopher, intellectual, historian, and civil rights leader, no image of Walker has survived in the official record or popular memory. Marshall addresses this staggering injustice through his title: the work can only ever be "believed to be" a portrait of Walker. In so doing, he deliberately introduces visual uncertainty into his imagining of this revolutionary freedom-fighter's portrait. As an exposé of white racist erasures of Black heroism, Marshall's empowered and empowering portrait represents an important truth. While Walker remains missing within white mainstream iconography, his life and works can effortlessly and easily be recuperated and recreated through a Black "lexicon of liberation."[191]

While there has been no physical trace of Walker in Western fine art or its visual culture tradition, Marshall candidly explains that he has been equally invisibilized by U.S. mainstream historical, political, and cultural memory. Coming of age in the 1960s, when "there wasn't such a thing as 'Black studies,'" Marshall recalls that "we were taught the history of slavery and so forth, but I didn't know of any stories of black heroism."[192] For Marshall, the erasure of "stories of black heroism" from the "history of slavery," endorsed as it is by white racist educational authorities, remains a source of psychological, social, and historical wounding. In a hard-hitting testament to his emotional pain, he poignantly summarizes "how I felt back then."[193] He experienced an overwhelming sense of existential nihilism and purposelessness, declaring, "I am nowhere and I have no idea where to go to from where I am." He communicates his despair: "I felt like I had reached some kind of dead end."[194]

For Marshall, portraits of "people like David Walker, an outspoken abolitionist from the nineteenth century" as well as of Nathaniel Turner, a leader of a Black rebellion, and, yet more recently, Harriet Tubman, a revolutionary freedom-fighter, assume heightened power as antidotes to his sense of hopelessness.[195] His reimagining of the "stories of Black heroism" and of the individual lives of Black heroes as portraits of power informs his radical Black aesthetic. Marshall paints legendary Black icons to generate new political realities and alternative imaginative possibilities for Black lives. He is a memorialist to the lives of Black heroes as eradicated by white national amnesia. He assumes the roles of artist-activist turned historian and educator to bear witness to a centuries-old African diasporic freedom-fighting tradition. "I want people to know that resistance has existed from the very beginning," he maintains, insisting, "Rebellion wasn't something that started with the civil rights struggle; it started in the eighteenth century."[196] Marshall's recognition of acts

and arts of Black resistance and rebellion as centuries old lends weight to his condemnation of contemporary injustices. The existence of a Black freedom-fighting tradition notwithstanding, white racist power has had devastating consequences by remaining so pervasive that "the goals of that struggle are yet to be realized."[197] As he understands only too well, and as Douglass, Walker, Turner, and Tubman themselves predicted, Black lives will never matter within a white supremacist U.S. society. On these grounds, the visual call for Black heroes in 2022 is more urgent than ever.

A monumental painting, Marshall's *Believed to be a Portrait of David Walker (c. 1830)* memorializes this revolutionary freedom-fighter in the guise of a war general. He appears against a black backdrop while his blue jacket is decorated with epaulettes and gold buttons. In accordance with Marshall's formal conventions adopted in his painterly practice, Walker's skin tone is an "extreme black."[198] Marshall relies on this powerful strategy to testify to Walker's importance not as a mortal individual but as a generic archetype and representative icon of missing generations of Black freedom-fighters. In this portrait, Walker confronts the viewer with a psychologically complex expression as Marshall bears witness to his heroic subject's emotional strength. An empowered and empowering portrait, Marshall's portrait honors Walker as a Black hero who waged a lifelong war against the transatlantic slave trade, slavery, and colonization. Living a life of protest in which he endured daily suffering and struggle at the same time he committed daily acts of resistance, radicalism, and revolution, Walker was unceasing in his opposition to entrenched systems of institutional, organizational, and legal persecutions that sought to enslave and colonize not only the body but the soul, mind, and intellect of all Black people worldwide.

An "outspoken abolitionist from the nineteenth century," Walker was also a military strategist, political thinker, social justice advocate, and an early denouncer not only of slavery and colonialism but of all white supremacist ideologies and practices. As one of the earliest works of Black philosophical and political liberation, Walker's manifesto, *Appeal, in Four Articles: Together with a Preamble, to the Coloured Citizens of the World, But in Particular, and Very Expressly, to Those of the United States of America*, first appeared in

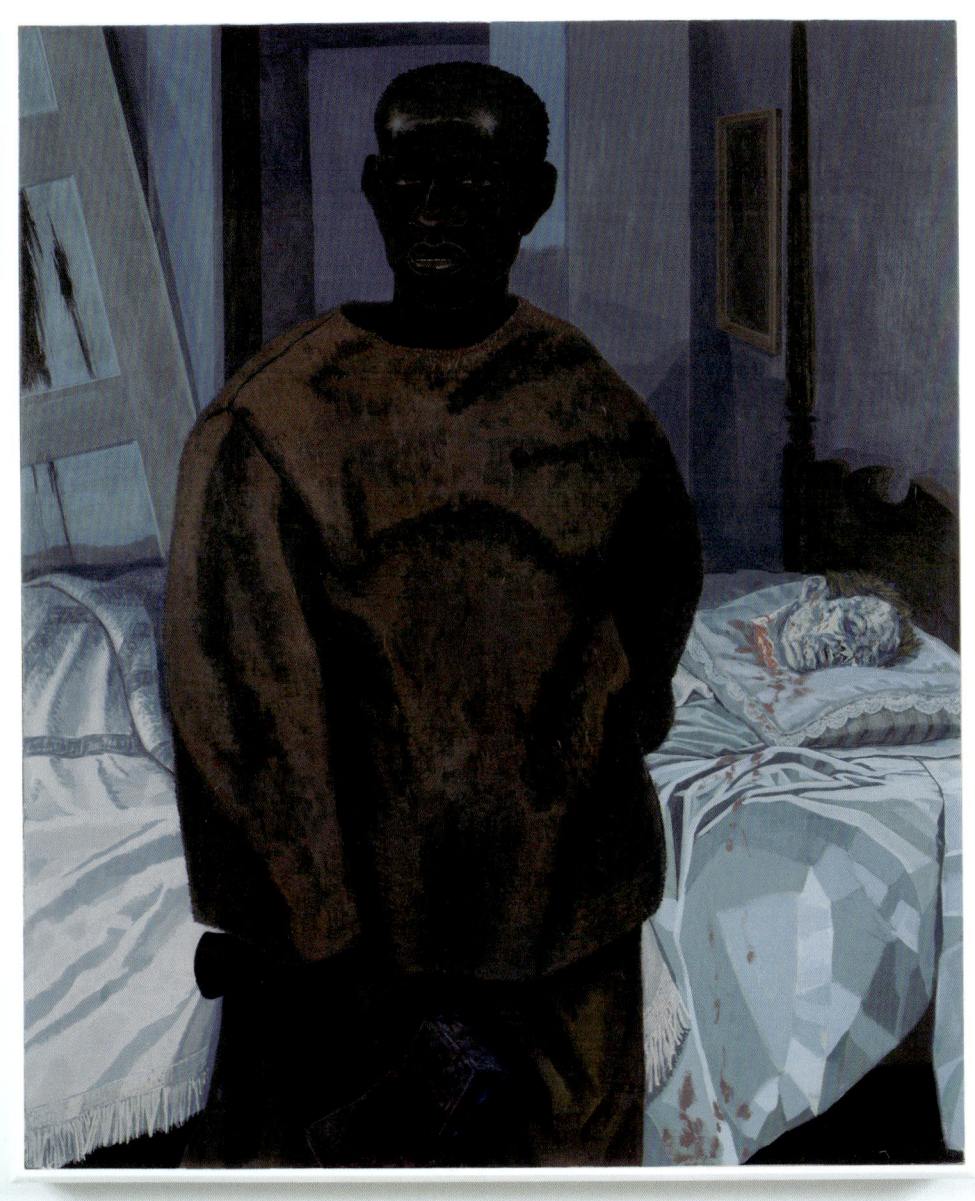

FIGURE 32. Kerry James Marshall, *Portrait of Nat Turner with the Head of His Master*, 2011. Acrylic on board (35¾ × 29½ × 3 in. framed). Inventory #KM11.002. Copyright Kerry James Marshall. Courtesy of the artist and Jack Shainman Gallery, New York.

Boston in 1829, a year before his tragically premature death.[199] In his revolutionary work, he issues a rallying cry to inspire Black people of all genders and ages to engage in individual and collective acts of liberation across the African diaspora. He rhetorically questioned his "Coloured Citizens of the World": "Are we MEN!!—I ask you, O my brethren! are we MEN?"[200] Never a conciliator to white power, Walker repeatedly condemned acts of white racist violence and violation by insisting, "The whites have always been an unjust, jealous, unmerciful, avaricious and blood-thirsty set of beings, always seeking after power and authority."[201]

Walker was a believer in divine retribution and an advocate of Black militancy. He used his text to issue a haunting prophecy: "As true as the sun ever shone in its meridian splendor, my colour will root some of them out of the very face of the earth."[202] He was in no doubt that whites "shall have enough of making slaves of, and butchering, and murdering us in the manner which they have," for one reason and one reason only: "the Lord our God, as true as he sits on his throne in heaven, and as true as our Saviour died to redeem the world, will give you a Hannibal."[203] According to Walker's prediction, "my color" will only ever triumph over their white oppressors by being led by an African diasporic leader whose exceptional militancy resembles the undisputed heroism of Hannibal (247–182 BCE), a military general from Carthage in northern Africa. Now ensconced in myth and legend, Hannibal's fight against the dictatorial power and despotic tyranny of the Roman Empire inspired Walker in his endorsement of a revolutionary military heroism for the "Coloured Citizens of the World."

For the vast majority of Black activists and authors living in the nineteenth century, including Frederick Douglass, only one person could represent the Hannibal of Walker's prophecy: Nathaniel Turner. Born into slavery in Virginia in 1800, Turner went on to become one of the most important liberators in world history. He lived his life by the conviction that God had appointed him as a leader, liberator, and emancipator of enslaved people. Two years after Walker published his manifesto, Turner experienced a vision. "I saw white spirits and black spirits engaged in battle, and the sun was darkened—the thunder rolled in the Heavens, and blood flowed in streams—and I heard a voice saying,

'Such is your luck, such you are called to see, and let it come rough or smooth, you must surely bear it.'"[204] Working to fulfil his destiny as a divinely appointed prophet and military general, Turner and his group of trained soldiers led a war on slavery in Southampton County, Virginia, on August 21, 1831. Their revolutionary actions, which they undertook according to the principles of war and military necessity, resulted in the deaths of approximately sixty white people from enslaving families. Bloodthirsty, vengeful, and discriminatory white supremacist authorities responded with the wholesale massacre of untold numbers of innocent Black people of all genders and ages. A fearless visionary, Turner faced death with dauntless courage in the months leading up to his execution on November 11, 1831. He recognized his importance as Walker's "Saviour" who must die "to redeem the world" by poignantly understanding the necessary sacrifice of his life in biblical terms: "Was not Christ crucified."[205]

Marshall's *Portrait of Nat Turner with the Head of His Master* is a stark contrast to his painting of David Walker, in which he offers a visual confirmation of his status not only as a military figure but as a free man. In poignant comparison, Turner wears the poor quality, ill-fitting, and shapeless clothing that reveals his enslaved status. Unlike Walker, Turner is not alone. Standing in the foreground of this painting, Turner holds a bloodied axe while the severed and blood-smeared "Head of His Master," complete with a terrorized expression, lies behind him.

While Walker appears against a black backdrop indicating no specific time or place, Turner exists within an immediately recognizable setting. The "Head of His Master" lies on an ornate white lace pillow resting on equally elegant white sheets and expensive tasseled blanket that together make up his bed, while a gold-framed painting hangs on the wall. In this scene of Turner's revolutionary actions, the inhumane and barbaric white enslaver's bedroom becomes the enslaved liberator's battleground. Turner's act of war transforms a domestic space celebrating white male power—featuring opulence, luxury, and wealth made possible solely by enslaved labor—into a place celebrating the heroic militancy of Black male power.

Marshall does not focus on Turner's upper body and facial features, as he does in Walker's portrait.

Rather, Marshall paints a three-quarter-length portrait of Turner as a monumental figure. According to Marshall's radical reimagining, Turner appears not as a subjugated enslaved man but as a self-liberated war hero. He visualizes Turner in the aftermath of his revolutionary act to exalt in his exemplary moral character as judge, jury, and executioner of white enslavers. According to Marshall's Black aesthetic, Turner's revolutionary actions, and Walker's radical philosophy, whites and whites only are the "unjust, jealous, unmerciful, avaricious and blood-thirsty set of beings," and their atrocious and inhumane acts are nothing less than a declaration of war.

In this painting, Marshall is careful to stipulate that the severed head belongs not just to any white man, but to Turner's enslaver or "Master." For Marshall, a domestic interior that was formerly the scene of the physical and psychological violations and violences enacted against Turner and his family has become the site of white execution. In his powerful portrait, Marshall reimagines Turner not only as a "Savior" but as a military general who takes no pleasure in undertaking acts of warfare. No ad hoc militant who relishes in bloodshed, he directly confronts his viewers with an emotionally unreadable and psychologically charged facial expression. As an individual who kills solely out of necessity and who knowingly sacrifices his own life to the cause of liberty, Marshall reimagines Turner's militancy as the direct manifestation of his divine mission. In this imagining and according to Turner's conviction, God appoints and instructs Turner as a prophet who will end the immoral acts of white enslavers, an "avaricious and blood-thirsty set of beings." As he remembered, God appeared to him and declared, "Such you are called to see, and let it come rough or smooth, you must surely bear it."

In his emotionally and physically empowering portrait in which he stands between his audiences and the "Head of His Master," Turner is not only a soldier and saviour but a witness, historian, and protester against white enslavers' atrocities. By his self-sacrificial act, he declared slavery a state of war on the minds, bodies, and souls of women, men, and children. According to Marshall's Black aesthetic, Turner assumed the role of a war general for one reason and one reason only: to transform the white "master narrative" of totalitarian power into an "enslaved narrative" of revolutionary resistance. A portrait of a Black hero prophet, Marshall's painting of Turner is a fulfilment of his mother and father's conviction, remembered by Turner himself only days before he was executed, that "I was intended for some great purpose."[206]

Marshall painted portraits of Walker and Turner because, as he observes, "critical to each of their beliefs is the need for a complete reformation of the enslaved black mind, body, and spirit."[207] The rhetorical art expression of Walker and the revolutionary act of war performed by Turner foreground the urgency of military resistance. They shared a commitment to ensuring the radical undoing not only of the "enslaved body" but of the "enslaved black mind" and "spirit" in order to effect the wholesale liberation of all Black people. As these freedom-fighters understood, and as Marshall emphasizes, enslavement was and remains a corporeal, spiritual, psychological, emotional, cultural, social, and ideological state of war inaugurated by a tyrannous white enslaving power in order to eradicate and exterminate all areas of all Black lives.

Marshall is an artist who continues to wage his own war against the survival of the "spirit of slavery" and the "spirit of mastery" in the twenty-first century. He issues a revolutionary call-to-arms in his portraits of historical Black heroes Walker and Turner. No sanitizer of ongoing systems of racist persecution, he is dedicated to a lifelong protest against the systems of physical violence, legal inequalities, social injustices, and cultural eradications that continue to oppress all Black people in U.S. society. As it was for Walker, Turner, and Douglass so it is for Marshall, Rembert, Priestly, and Thomas: their lives and works are defined by a determination to sacrifice everything in their fight for all freedoms on the "field of battle."[208]

DEBRA PRIESTLY *(Born in Springfield, Ohio, 1961)*

"My research led me to the Library of Congress, where I observed countless images documenting the transatlantic slave trade," summarizes Debra Priestly regarding the emotionally challenging archival investigations that influenced her 2001 mixed-media series, *Strange Fruit*. [209] Working with psychologically harrowing and physically traumatizing images, she recalls that she "was compelled to present them as matter of fact." Priestly memorializes the tragedies of the "transatlantic slave trade" by relying on an emotionally empowering visual lexicon across her entire series. The second work in the series, *Strange Fruit 2*, contains "40 life-size jars are spaced evenly on a tall narrow vertical." Working not with paint, dye, collage, or craft materials but with computerized manipulation techniques, Priestly explains that she "digitally superimposed graphic black-and-white images onto my colour photographs of canning jars." An experimental artist, memorialist, witness, and historian, she inserts some of these "countless images," consisting of "diagrams of human cargo and torture devices, handwritten slave manifests and bills of sale, and etchings," onto the jars. [210] In Priestly's revolutionary strategy of representation, these "diagrams" of atrocity are no static icons of abuse. Instead, she relies on a self-reflexive relationship between text and image to transform this historical iconography of suffering and struggle into an active platform for political resistance and a catalyst to a radical artistic imaginary.

Across her practice, Priestly relies on the canning jar as "an infinitely versatile prism where narratives unravel." She works with multilayered visual and textual narratives in which she incorporates "diagrams of human cargo and torture devices, handwritten slave manifests and bills of sale, and etchings" in order to memorialize a multiplicity of Black historical realities and oral storytelling traditions. Here and elsewhere, she emphasizes the canning jar's importance not only as a means of accessing her own autobiographical experiences—the "jar has great personal significance"—but as a ready-made way to build an emotional relationship with her audiences through "a familiar object to which most viewers readily connect." A domestic emblem of the everyday and a symbol of family rituals, the jar is simultaneously a "container that can seal and preserve matter for consumption or display" and a "versatile prism" of private and public narratives and histories. As a way of "preserving" not only "matter" but memories, the jar ultimately allows Priestly to interrogate temporal boundaries. "Metaphorically, it functions as a portal or a time capsule that can preserve anything for reconstitution or safekeeping," she explains. [211]

In *Strange Fruit*, the jar opens a physical and psychological "portal" through which Priestly bears witness to the intergenerational struggle for survival across the African diaspora. She recognizes the social, historical, and political significance as well as the contemporary relevance of the images of "human cargo," "torture devices," "slave manifests," and "bills of sale." As she emphasizes, the canning jar operates as a "window that provides a bearable distance for the viewer, or even myself." [212] A vessel working to protect both artist and audience, the jar enables Priestly and her viewers to gain access to reimagings of these "sorrow objects"—traumatizing testaments to the sufferings of enslaved people—from a position not of emotional danger but of psychological safety.

Priestly's memorialization of the "torture devices" of slavery and the transatlantic slave trade rejects dehumanized spectacles of Black people reduced to "human cargo," "slave manifests, and "bills of sale." They do not appear in isolation in *Strange Fruit 2*. Rather, she assumes the role of a revisionist historian, radical storyteller, and subversive memorialist to place these harrowing images in a call and response relationship to her "photographs of notable abolitionists, many of whom had escaped slavery: Toussaint Louverture, Harriet Tubman, Sojourner Truth, Frederick Douglass, John Brown, Henry Box Brown, Sergeant William Harvey Carney, and Peter (formerly known by the name of "Gordon"), a formerly enslaved man whose photo revealed a back covered in keloid scars formed after several whippings." [213] Priestly protests against white

▶▶ **"Unintended Martyrs in the Fight"**

racist acts of atrocity, abuse, and annihilation as enacted against Black people. In her *Strange Fruit* series, she visibilizes an invisibilized history of Black resistance, radicalism, and revolution.

Priestly memorializes a call to arms in the lives and works of revolutionary leaders such as the founder of the first Black republic in the western hemisphere, Toussaint Louverture; the world-renowned liberator of enslaved people living in the South, Harriet Tubman; and the social justice campaigner and radical reformer Sojourner Truth. While she memorializes enslavement as a site of corporeal, spiritual, intellectual, and emotional mutilation and murder over the centuries, she eulogizes Black heroism as a hidden history of agency, activism, and artistry that necessarily contains the blueprint for resistance in a contemporary era. While Priestly includes the horrifying visual record of Gordon's back, she does powerful justice to the revolutionary reality that his "keloid scars" from "several whippings" were the result of his dauntless courage. They are the incontestable proof of his undying resistance to the inhumane punishment he received from white enslavers for his repeated attempts to secure his self-liberation from the "prison-house of bondage."[214]

For Priestly, Black heroism is defined not only by the epic feats of militancy, warfare, and reform work that have been undertaken by renowned leaders but also by everyday acts of rebellion of anonymous Black women, children, and men. These include acts of self-liberation, withholding labor, psychological empowerment, sacrificial martyrdom, creative self-expression, and domestic resistance through the preservation of family relationships against all odds. Across her series, Priestly shares Rembert's determination to memorialize the untold stories of "what we went through" by juxtaposing the celebrated portraits of empowered and iconic leaders such as Louverture, Peter, Douglass, Truth, Tubman, and Carney with images documenting the invisibilized lives of unknown individuals. Priestly includes nameless and dateless photographs, engravings, and drawings of the following in *Strange Fruit 2*: unidentified women laboring over washboards; anonymous men exposed to invasive physical examinations on the auction block; unknown women who had no choice but to nurse white enslavers' children; and most traumatically, unnamed individuals hanging from nooses. Priestly's

choice of title for this series reveals her determination to memorialize the tragic centuries long history of the lynching of African Americans of all ages and genders at the hands of white racist and murderous mobs. As she explains, she names "*Strange Fruit* after Abel Meeropol's haunting American classic poem"—a work he wrote to protest against lynching—and "recorded in song by Billie Holiday" in 1939.[215]

Strange Fruit 2 reproduces an empowering eighteenth-century portrait of Black heroism featuring Toussaint Louverture in his decorated military uniform. The portrait, however, is juxtaposed with a twentieth-century lynching photograph as a harrowing memorial to the mutilation and murder of untold numbers of unnamed Black people over the centuries. For Priestly, the tragic subject matter of Meeropol's "Strange Fruit" and the hard-hitting power of Billie Holiday's performance attests to the dystopian vision and protest aesthetic undergirding her series. Priestly, like Rembert, Marshall, and Thomas, does not sanitize the legacies and realities of white racist injustices in the contemporary era. Ever the freedom-fighter, she transforms "Strange Fruit," a song that laments the lynching of African Americans, into a work of art in which she is not only lamenting previous acts of atrocity but also providing a searing indictment of modern-day lynchings.[216] Contemporary manifestations of white racist terrorism endured by Black people still consist of murderous rituals enacted by white racist mobs. They also include systems and practices related to police brutality, legal injustice, social ostracism, educational inequality, cultural annihilation, and economic deprivation. According to Priestly's "lexicon of liberation," the lives and works of historical freedom-fighters, known and unknown, are needed now more than ever.

"Betsey." "$410.00." "Nancy." "515.00." "Harry." "1200.00." "Mary." "600.00." "Lucinda." "467.00." "George." "510.00." These are just some of the names of the enslaved women and men and their accompanying financial amounts legible on a slave ship manifest that Priestly includes in the first jar of her mixed-media work, *Strange Fruit 16*. Revealingly, their names and financial value, as determined by white "traffickers in human flesh," do not appear in isolation.[217] In this same jar, she includes a reproduction of the eighteenth-century Liverpool-owned "*Brookes* slave ship."

A historical illustration commissioned by white abolitionists, this image shows "454 enslaved bodies arranged on the ship's lower decks in accordance with the Regulated Slave Trade Act of 1788."[218] In recognition of the *Brooks*'s political and emotional power, Priestly reproduces this traumatizing image in all the jars in *Strange Fruit 16*. This historical drawing provides a visual accompaniment to the jars that variously contain an advertisement for the sale of enslaved people—"TO BE SOLD on board the Ship *Bance*"—as well as financial information regarding enslaved property—"SLAVE TAX RECEIPTS for State of Virginia—1860 and 1862." Priestly's determination to reproduce the slave ship manifest, auction notice, and financial list next to repeated drawings showing "454 enslaved bodies" operates as an emotional shock tactic in this work. Her powerful decision to provide a hard-hitting juxtaposition of physical bodies with abstract commercial lists exposes the real cost of the European transatlantic slave trade. What is a source of economic profit for "avaricious" and "bloodthirsty" whites is a source of inhumane damage and unimaginable suffering for the millions of people bought and sold across the African diaspora.

Priestly sheds further light on her political rationale for including multiple reimaginings of the slave ship *Brooks* not only in *Strange Fruit 16* but across her series as a whole by explaining, "I repeatedly layered these diagrams, in some cases creating dense, barely discernible blots, to suggest how difficult it is to fathom the number of journeys this ship actually made and the number of humans actually transported before and after the Regulated Slave Trade Act."[219] As Priestly layers one image over another, this diagram transforms into an indecipherable abstraction. As a result, the illustration is divested of its ability not only to communicate the "number of journeys this ship actually made," but even to represent the physical outline of an enslaved person with any degree of realism. With this visual tactic, Priestly underscores that the only way in which white murderous traders were able to justify their horrifying, barbaric, and inhumane institution was by effecting the wholesale eradication and dehumanization of enslaved people, making them no longer people "with bodies and souls akin to their own."

The historical documents authored by white enslavers fail to do justice to the lives of Black women, children, and men as individuals. They include only their partial names at best or, at worst, remove their humanity entirely by focusing only on their financial value as determined by white capitalist greed. Priestly's radical and revolutionary visual lexicon wars against the atrocities committed by these injustices by exposing the mind-body-and-soul- destroying ways in which Black memories, stories, and histories are reduced to an absent-presence in the white supremacist archive and white racist imaginary. By including multiple diagrams of an imagined aerial view of the *Brooks*, she focuses her viewers' attention on human beings barbarically reduced to "dense, barely discernible blots."[220] Here she memorializes the traumatizing reality regarding the failures not only to know the "number of humans actually transported" but the names, beliefs, families, cultures, and thoughts of the untold millions of enslaved individuals who experienced the Middle Passage.[221]

The unimage-able and unimaginable scale of human suffering experienced on a single ship, let alone on the untold millions of people that crossed over during the centuries of the Middle Passage as a result of the transatlantic slave trade, defies visual or textual representation. In *Strange Fruit 16*, Priestly continues to focus on legendary Black heroes by memorializing Harriet Tubman, Sojourner Truth, Toussaint Louverture, and Gordon. At the same time, she made the decision to insert repeated "diagrams of the *Brookes* slave ship" into their portraits as a visual manifestation of Betye Saar's statement: "the slave ship will never wear out because its imprint is on all of us."[222]

"My gaze shifted from the transatlantic slave trade to modern-day lynching and other current events," Priestly explains regarding the change in political direction undergirding many of the mixed-media works she includes in her *Strange Fruit* series.[223] Working to memorialize the physical trauma, psychological pain, and spiritual suffering caused not only by the centuries long histories of slavery and the slave trade but also by "modern-day lynchings," she protests against one recent act of white U.S. racist terrorism in particular in *Strange Fruit 15*. "In 1999," she recalls, "Amadou Diallo, a 23-year-old immigrant from Guinea, was killed in front of his home in New York City. Four plainclothes officers mistook Mr. Diallo's wallet for a gun." This tragedy confirmed testified to Black innocence and condemned

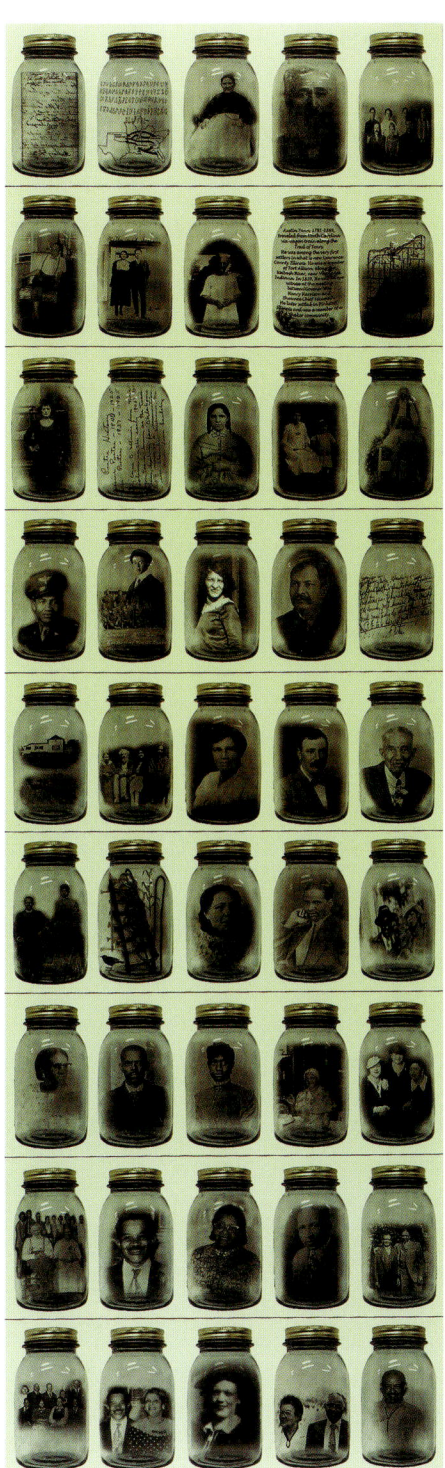

FIGURE 33. Debra Priestly, *Mattoon 5*, 2002. Paintings, Photographs, acrylic, photo transfer, ink, resin on wood (80 × 24 in.). Courtesy of the artist.

white murderous guilt: "The officers fired a total of 41 shots at the unarmed man and were later acquitted."[224]

For Priestly, both the terrible injustice of the officers' wrongful acquittal and the mutilation and murder of Amadou Diallo's body was a source of ongoing trauma. "During the trial, a leading New York City newspaper published the autopsy reports on the cover page," she states. "I was moved by the lyrical colour illustration of the brown nude bearing 19 entry and exit wounds," she emotionally remembers. At the heart of Priestly's protest aesthetic here and elsewhere are her powerful meditations on the unimaginable numbers of Black men sacrificed and destroyed at the hands of white supremacist torturers and killers. "I incorporated these reports into *Strange Fruit 15*," she explains. "It is a tribute to the memory of Amadou Diallo and a reminder of the countless Black men who become unintended martyrs in the fight against police brutality, racial profiling and Stand-Your-Ground laws." While coming to grips with the atrocities contained within "countless images documenting the transatlantic slave trade," Priestly does equal justice to the deaths of "countless Black men" who are not only "lost," as per Kerry James Marshall's lexicon, but who continue to be the "strange and bitter crop" of white supremacy.[225]

"*Mattoon* is named after a town in Illinois where we often visited elders," recalls Debra Priestly. "Works entitled *Mattoon* relate directly to my personal ancestry."[226] Dedicated to visualizing the untold stories within the history of the transatlantic slave trade and U.S. chattel slavery and within her own family, she recalls that "my passion for family ancestry began as a child and I often studied our archives."[227] Priestly's *Mattoon 5 (2002)* (figure 33) is an emotionally charged work and a testament to her preservation of personal and collective autobiographical narratives within her family over the generations. She describes *Mattoon 5* as "a genealogy record." The mixed-media work resembles a human body. "The spine is the central vertical column," Priestly declares, adding, "It displays nine portraits of grandmothers from six generations." "The ribs are the horizontal rows," she explains. "In these jars, migration maps, handwritten records, historical documents and photographs chronicle the lives of my ancestors."[228]

Alongside the many photographic portraits of family members that she includes in *Mattoon 5*, Priestly includes a metal object consisting of seven nails and seven rings. The form and function of this artifact would be impossible to decipher were it not for her decision to share her autobiographical testimony. "Great-Great-Grandfather Priestly forged a wrought-iron patience puzzle he used to win his wife's freedom," she remembers. At a family gathering in recent years, "we were introduced to the iron puzzle and we took turns learning the pattern that releases a shuttle from seven rings and horseshoe nails."[229] Revealing a hidden history of resistance, she focuses on the fact that her Great-Great-Grandfather Priestly's invention of this "patience puzzle" met with success as a liberation device: he was able to "win his wife's freedom" by his artistic ingenuity. Priestly's revolutionary practice centers on memorializing Black acts of artistry and agency to defeat white-enforced systems of subjugation and suffering. Here and elsewhere, she creates a revisionist U.S. history. Black strategies of resistance not only encompass heroic feats of revolutionary warfare, martyrdom, and corporeal suffering, but also no less dissident practices related to the preservation of spiritual beliefs, storytelling traditions, material cultures, and experimental foodways.

MICKALENE THOMAS   *(Born in Camden, New Jersey, 1971)*

"Any depiction of woman as 'beginning' is philosophical, spiritual, and powerful," declares Mickalene Thomas, a photographer, painter, filmmaker, and installation artist.[230] In her practice, she defies white Western heteronormative and masculine art historical traditions that exoticize, other, dehumanize, appropriate, objectify, commodify, and essentialize Black women's subjectivities. Thomas creates portraits in which she reimagines Black women's lives as lived across all social backgrounds, identities, sexualities, positionalities, economic classes, and political affiliations. She testifies to the importance of personal autobiography, explaining, "With my work, I'm the beginning."[231] Interrogating arbitrary and artificial boundaries between public and private experiences, she confides, "I'm relinquishing and revealing my most intimate self."[232] Just as Thomas provides an emotional meditation on her psychological realities, she also commits to finding a "lexicon of liberation" through which she reimagines not only her own self but Black women's selves more generally.

Interrogating white racist mainstream representations, Thomas is adamant that her practice is "really about me searching, a discovery of myself, trying to understand some of these stereotypes that were a little mysterious to me, how perception is put onto the black body."[233] Working to defy the iconographic stranglehold exerted by stereotypes that are attached not only to the Black body but to her own physicality and sexuality, she states, "I'm black, you can see. I don't hide."[234] Thomas is a portrait painter and photographer who holds herself accountable to no dominant social, political, or artistic order. "I don't feel the need to say, 'I'm a lesbian.' I'm living my life, and involved politically. I speak out," she declares.[235] She is an aesthetically complex, politically empowered, sexually inclusive, and social consciousness–raising artist. Thomas's lifelong commitment to portraiture emerges out of her conviction that "we are not validated until we see ourselves."[236]

Thomas is a radical and revolutionary witness, memorialist, historian, and storyteller of Black women's realities. She declares, "Not only are we present, we demand that we be seen, be heard, and be acknowledged."[237] And yet, just as she celebrates her empowered aesthetic practice that centers Black women and their individual and collective determination to "be seen," she is all too aware that "African-American women" have been "largely absent within the history of figurative painting" that has dominated western art history.[238] Thomas rejects the deliberate exclusion of Black women subjects by the white mainstream art world. She shares Kerry James Marshall's determination to foreground an empowered Black presence where there has been only absence in white-owned museums and galleries. At the same time, she sets herself the task of intervening into the white-centric parameters of European portraiture. Thomas protests against a traumatizing reality: Black women have not only been excluded but have been visually violated through the discriminatory conventions of a white supremacist iconography that continues to commit terrible acts of violence against their subjectives by denying, denigrating, and dehumanizing their equal humanity. She admits, "I felt a kinship and desire to interact with pivotal figurative painters of this style," referring to the artists working within the "history of figurative painting."

Thomas's 2007 mixed-media portrait of an unnamed, nude Black woman, *A Little Taste Outside of Love* (figure 34), is executed on a wood panel and comes to life from acrylic and enamel paint as well as from meticulously glued on rhinestones. Thomas's nude Black woman rejects the commodification, appropriation, and objectification of her face and body as a spectacle within a white supremacist iconography and white racist imaginary. Instead, Thomas's radical and revolutionary practice liberates her autonomous individuality. According to her radical lexicon, her Black woman subject is positioned in no exoticized location, placed in no servile position, engaged in no act of physical labor, and available for no white audience member's sexual gratification. She visually embodies liberation.

▶▶ I'm Here; I Exist; See Me"

Thomas's protagonist reclines on a richly patterned couch decorated with a luxurious array of floral and geometric textiles that offer visual confirmation of her elite status in this monumental portrait. No passive object packaged for white consumption, Thomas's Black woman bears witness to her empowered subjectivity. Here she directly confronts the viewer with an unreadable gaze that gives the viewer no access to her emotional, personal, or spiritual interiority. Thomas's work resists the iconographic stranglehold that has been exerted over Black women's bodies not only by western art history, but by Western anthropology and centuries of European scientific racism and entrenched systems of colonization. Thomas rights the wrongs of centuries of sexual, emotional, spiritual, and physical abuse by introducing an "exchange of gazes as a metaphor for an honest conversation, rather than . . . an exchange of sexual appeal or lust."[239] Thomas's protagonist in *A Little Taste Outside of Love* is no equivocator or conciliator to white dominance. Instead, she offers a visual embodiment of the artist's commitment to representing Black women subjects as psychologically, politically, emotionally, personally, and intellectually self-liberated individuals.

"All of the women in my work have a profound sense of inner confidence, and recognize themselves as the visible subject," Thomas states. "Their directness is filled with agency and self-knowledge."[240] Thomas's portraits free her subjects from an incarcerating, white mainstream lens, and her pantheon of Black women defy white racist stereotypes to assume the roles of heroic icons, myths, and imaginary muses. As she maintains, "They have all the power and control to demand the viewer to meet them in their own space, rather than being exploited or scrutinized."[241] Ultimately, Thomas's power over the violating practices of Western art derives from the fact that "the gaze in my work is a female gaze from my perspective as a Black woman."[242] As one contemporary commentator writes of *A Little Taste Outside of Love*, Thomas's aesthetic practice "turns the historic nude on its head and ousts the white European woman from the bed where she often lounges, attended by a black maidservant, in Western art."[243] Working with a revolutionary iconography, Thomas calls out the discriminatory myopia of Western art history. Here and elsewhere, she celebrates Black female

protagonists whose lives and bodies—and memorialization in mainstream portraiture—depends neither on a "white European woman" subject nor on a white European male "figurative painter," but rather on the vision of a Black woman portraitist. "When both artist and muse are both black women, the dynamic is different," Thomas explains. "It's sensually more powerful."[244]

Rhinestones are at the heart of Thomas's radical reframing of white mainstream representations of Black women subjectivities in *A Little Taste Outside of Love.* She breaks new ground by meticulously attaching black, silver, gold, brown, and white colored rhinestones onto the surface of her subject's body. These multicolored gems not only animate her subject's hair, eyes, mouth, and nose, but also the nipple on one of her breasts as well as the entire outline of her body. Here Thomas uses the rhinestones' kaleidoscopic shifting of light and color to create her Black woman subject's visually arresting physical outline. The result celebrates a Black female presence in the face of absence, a Black female visibility in the face of invisibility, and a Black female endorsement of life in the face of death.

"I serendipitously stumbled onto the rhinestones," Thomas explains. "What I was attracted to when I first decided to start working with them came out of working through notions of beauty—particularly related to French impressionism."[245] Interrogating as well as interacting with the practices of "pivotal figurative painters" in general, and of French impressionists more particularly, Thomas found that rhinestones "allowed me to treat a surface completely (like pointillism) in place of paint."[246] Whereas turn-of-the-century white European artists such as Georges Seurat created portraits of white men, women, and children solely from a meticulous layering of painted dots, Thomas creates her pantheon of Black women subjects from intricately positioned rhinestones juxtaposed with layers of paint. Starkly contrasting to a white French impressionist whites-only "notion of beauty," Thomas's rhinestones result in a pointillism that celebrates the exceptional beauty of her Black female subjects.

All too aware of the white racist myopia undergirding the aesthetic philosophy of white European painters, Thomas declares, "We can't escape the societal ideals of what beauty is, [and] that it stems from

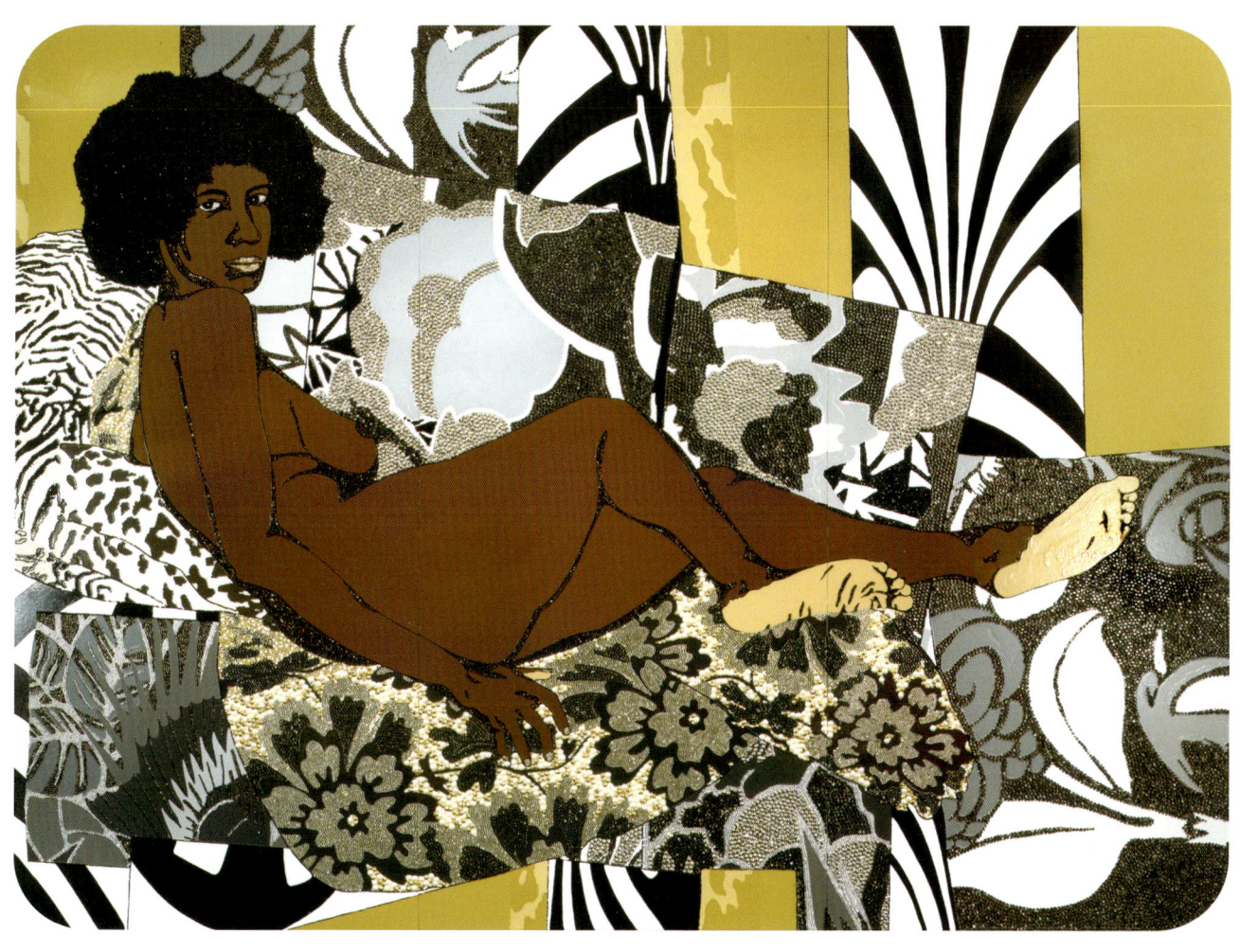

FIGURE 34. Mickalene Thomas, *A Little Taste Outside of Love*, 2007. Rhinestone, acrylic and enamel on panel (72 × 108 in.). Courtesy of the artist and Lehmann Maupin, New York and Hong Kong, and Artists Rights Society, New York.

the ideologies of white women."[247] Thomas condemns dominant "societal ideals" that annihilate and reject all definitions of a Black woman's "beauty." She explains, "Out of necessity, black women have always had to consider others' perceptions of a certain beauty ideal, just starting with the skin color."[248] She resists the deliberate exclusion of Black women from a whites-only "beauty ideal" by offering her own version of pointillism to signal her declaration of independence from the incarceration of Black women within a white-dominant western imagery. "I was interested in the play of craft materials—decorative or outsider art materials, materials that were considered secondary or on the peripheral—and how to bring those to the likes of a high art," she emphasizes.[249]

For Thomas, introducing rhinestones as "secondary" and "peripheral craft materials" into the domain of "high art" provides her with a means to grapple with a "larger western canon idea."[250] Just as she rejects western conventions that favor one material over another, she opposes discriminatory ideologies that place one idea of beauty over another. In a reclamation of power from white European "masters," Thomas effects a radical reversal in her works. She turns the tables on white-dominant structures within Western art history not only by rejecting the white-dominant canon but also by inserting her own practice and her Black women subjects into the "larger western canon idea."

Thomas reveals her interrogation of a "western canon idea" not only in her choice of materials and composition, but also in her title, *A Little Taste Outside of Love*. According to white Western art traditions, Black women have been subjected to strategies of exclusion at best and, at worst, practices of abuse and violence. Regardless of whether they experience annihilation or alienation, as Thomas argues, they have always existed "outside of love" and beyond the scope of the "western canon idea." As Thomas explains, "My work is rooted in the tradition of portrait painting," adding, "This is essential to me because I want to insert the women into the history of art and to thereby shift the existing canon that has historically under or misrepresented black women."[251] According to her radical practice, Thomas creates works inside of love in which she succeeds in reappropriating, reclaiming, and recreating dominant art historical conventions for the reimaging and reimagining of Black women's lives.

"I believe that history is important whether it is art history, political history, or cultural history," Thomas declares. "It allows you to gain an understanding of the language that has developed and where you might contribute to the discussion."[252] Thomas works across all types of history not only to obtain control over the dominant language and iconography but also over the parameters of the "discussion." Ultimately, Thomas succeeds in her determination "to portray the beauty and sexuality that I see from women that I surround myself with" in the domain of western art history. She explains, "My work is about a sense of empowerment and celebration of self. Beauty, sexuality and sensuality—these are components of how we feel about ourselves."[253]

At the same time that Thomas memorializes Black female strategies of self-representation and self-imaging across her practice, she explains, "was interested in making the audience see these women not just as characters, but as signifiers."[254] She works not to create individualized "characters" but mythic and representative "signifiers" of an array of female subject positions, experiences, backgrounds, and stories. She insists, "They are no longer characters, but representations of women throughout different generations."[255] Thomas fights a never-ending fight to end all forms of persecution and discrimination enacted not only in U.S. mainstream society but also on the battleground that is art history. "I am constantly contemplating or challenging various stereotypes around Black women," she explains. "It's crucial for me to flip these types of perceptions by making images of women who are full of energy and confident to declare their space."[256] Ultimately, Thomas and her Black women characters-turned-signifiers urge their viewers not to appropriate or authenticate but to accept and acknowledge and respect their individual and collective subjectivities. As she and they declare, "I'm here; I exist; see me."[257]

⸺

"Ideas crowd in on me so much I almost died last year," Winfred Rembert poignantly declared. "I'm in prison every night or else running for my life. I can't sleep."[258] As an artist who experienced all forms of physical, emotional, and spiritual suffering, he refused to hide his lifelong exposure to pain. "My life, at times, has been very difficult," he admitted.[259] Rembert memorialized his painful experiences and traumatic memories through his art: "It's important to me for people to know that my work is nonfiction," he explained.[260] "These pictures are my true memories of my childhood growing up in Georgia," and "I don't know if I've got time to tell them all."[261]

One of the areas of Rembert's "very difficult" life that remained a defining source of inspiration was his mind-body-and-soul-destroying experiences as a laborer working in cotton fields. "I have no memories of anything good about picking cotton," he declared. "Toiling, toiling, toiling is what picking cotton is about."[262] Rembert recalls that "at six years old, I was picking cotton for fifty cents or a dollar a day."[263] He was all too aware that it was his labor as a cotton picker that resulted in his loss of education: "That's why I couldn't go to school—'cause the plantation owner wanted me to work," he explains.[264] Rembert recalled not only his own suffering but also his grandmother, Lilian Rembert's heartbreaking experiences. "Mama made only two dollars for every hundred pounds she picked," he remembered. "She usually worked five days a week and sometimes, a half-day on Saturday." Growing up in a segregated and persecutory South, he saw the devastating damage inflicted on Black families by white racist authorities. Survival was all but impossible. "You never had enough money to pay all you owed and the owner liked it that way, 'cause you were always in debt and couldn't go work for anyone else," Rembert observed. "It was like the owner had an invisible fence around you—you couldn't get out, and nobody else could get in."[265] Rembert's paintings are powerful memorials to the stories of women, children, and men who lived lives as defined not only by white external forces intent on their physical and psychological incarceration but also by their individual and collective fight for liberation from "an invisible fence."[266]

"I wanted to find a way to make sure that when young black kids went to the museum, that they didn't just have to be inspired by the work of European artists but could also be inspired by the work of a black painter and by work that didn't have to be segregated into a black section of the museum."[267] So Kerry James Marshall summarizes the overall motivation that defines his aesthetic practice. Working not only to ensure that "young black kids" had access to works by a "black painter" in mainstream museum spaces, he seeks to educate white European and U.S. critics regarding Black art as a site of formal experimentation and self-conscious innovation. Over the decades, he has continued to be appalled by a discriminatory tendency among white scholars: "the moment a black artist presented images of black people, then the issues in the work seemed to always collapse into simply social and political issues."[268] An exclusive focus on "social and political" debates has resulted in the terrible consequence that "any sort of aesthetic value that the work could have seemed to slip out of the discussion, so that the work was seen as a social phenomenon rather than an aesthetic phenomenon."[269] Working to right these wrongs, Marshall creates thematically challenging, experimental, and formally complex works inspired by his conviction that "what I'd always wanted to do was really to make work that operated in very complex ways, aesthetically, formally, and also content-wise and conceptually."[270]

Just as Rembert memorializes the legacies of slavery, segregation, and lynch law in his paintings, Marshall exposes the collateral damage generated by white racist amnesia. He creates consciousness-raising, politically revolutionary, and historically commemorative paintings. He foregrounds the fact that when it comes to the history of slavery, "most white Americans prefer to avoid the topic altogether, but, when pressed, deny having profited directly or indirectly from slavery."[271] A legal institution profiting a white U.S. enslaving nation for centuries, slavery did not end with its legal abolition. To this day, slavery continues to exert a political, legal, social, economic, and cultural stranglehold over U.S. society, contrary to white racist denials. Marshall uses his practice to come to grips with the traumatizing reality that "slavery was an extreme manifestation of racist ideology, and its legacy is evident in the glaring unequal power differential of blacks and whites today."[272] Warring against the widespread whitewashing not only of the history of slavery but of the survival of its spirit in the U.S. national imaginary, he argues that "this denial remains a source of great friction between black and white Americans."[273] Marshall uses his practice to cut to the heart of this "great friction." As he urges, the fight against the "spirit of mastery" is "field of battle" to be fought on all fronts, not least in the white supremacist domain of western art history.

Dedicated to memorializing a past, present, and future African diasporic tradition of resistance and rebellion, Priestly relies on superimposed images that she inserts into canning jars as a means to collapse temporal, geographical, historical, social, political, and emotional boundaries. She does not, however, rely on isolated images of Black heroism to commemorate the lives of Black women, men, and children who are all "unintended martyrs in the fight." Rather, she works with multiple representations of iconic and invisibilized lives, explaining, "Multiples have the capacity to connect microcosms and tell a larger story." The works in the series coalesce around a determination to tell "a larger story" that is no respecter of white racist hierarchies of knowledge, power, or representation. A visionary creator of "a multifaceted memory map that traces personal and collective narratives," Priestly defines the personal and the collective as political.[274] For Priestly, intergenerational narratives of liberation necessarily have their beginnings and their endings in the storytelling worlds of her family.

Mickalene Thomas observes, "I kind of discovered art through an art therapy course. I took it during college to deal with a few issues that I had with my family and my sexuality."[275] Art-making continues to play a key role in Thomas's life as a way of dealing with "very difficult" personal experiences. She explains, "I first started delving into photography in the early 2000s as an arts student, and started photographing my mother, who was my very first muse and model."[276] Among the many powerful works in which she honors her mother, Sandra Bush, as her "muse and model" is her 2009 mixed-media piece, *Ain't I a Woman (Sandra)* (figure 35). The work includes two portraits of Thomas's mother. In one, she reproduces a photograph showing Sandra Bush seated on an ornately decorated couch but with her head partially bowed. Through her mother's posture, Thomas associates her Black woman protagonist with vulnerability and struggle.

Nothing could be further from Thomas's imagining of her mother in this sorrowful photograph than the other portrait she includes in this work. Working with paint and rhinestones rather than with photography, Thomas creates a mixed-media portrait in which Sandra Bush directly confronts the viewer. In this iconic painting, she celebrates her mother's exceptional beauty. Thomas uses red, pink, silver, white, black, purple, blue, and brown rhinestones to draw her viewers' attention to Bush's self-conscious strategies of self–representation and self-creation. Bush's multicolored eye shadow, luxuriant hair, and affirmative pose all attest to and emphasize her empowered acts of self-liberation. "Growing up, watching my mother work as a professional model during the '70s and '80s, I was always galvanized by her glamour, tenacity and gracefulness," Thomas recalls.[277] She explains that "working with her as a model really helped me to understand how her charisma related to me, to my own femininity."[278]In these dual portraits in which she not only does justice to her mother's "femininity," "glamour," "tenacity," and "gracefulness," but also to her vulnerability, Thomas juxtaposes a realistic with an idealized imagining of Sandra Bush. Here she lays bare her refusal to shy away from the physical and psychological complexities experienced by her Black women protagonists across her works.

Thomas's decision to title this painting *Ain't I a Woman (Sandra)* is revealing. She directly references not only her mother's life but also a speech that was delivered over one hundred and fifty years ago, in 1851, by one of the most world-renowned, self-liberated, and historical freedom-fighters in U.S. history: a woman born into slavery as Isabella Baumfree and reborn into freedom as Sojourner Truth. In a speech Truth delivered at a Woman's Rights Convention in Akron, Ohio, in 1851, she provided her white audiences with an unequivocal declaration of Black female liberation. She stated, "I am a woman's rights."[279] For Truth, speaking in the antebellum period and at the height of chattel slavery, the fight to end centuries of human bondage was a life and death struggle. For Thomas, working today, Truth's endorsement of a Black woman's entitlement to all of a "woman's rights" bears witness to the revolutionary political priorities of her portraits of power. Thomas creates monumental Black female subjectivities in her mixed-media works in which she asks and answers her lifelong question: "Who is a black woman? What is a black woman?"[280] Thomas dedicates her life as well as her practice to protesting

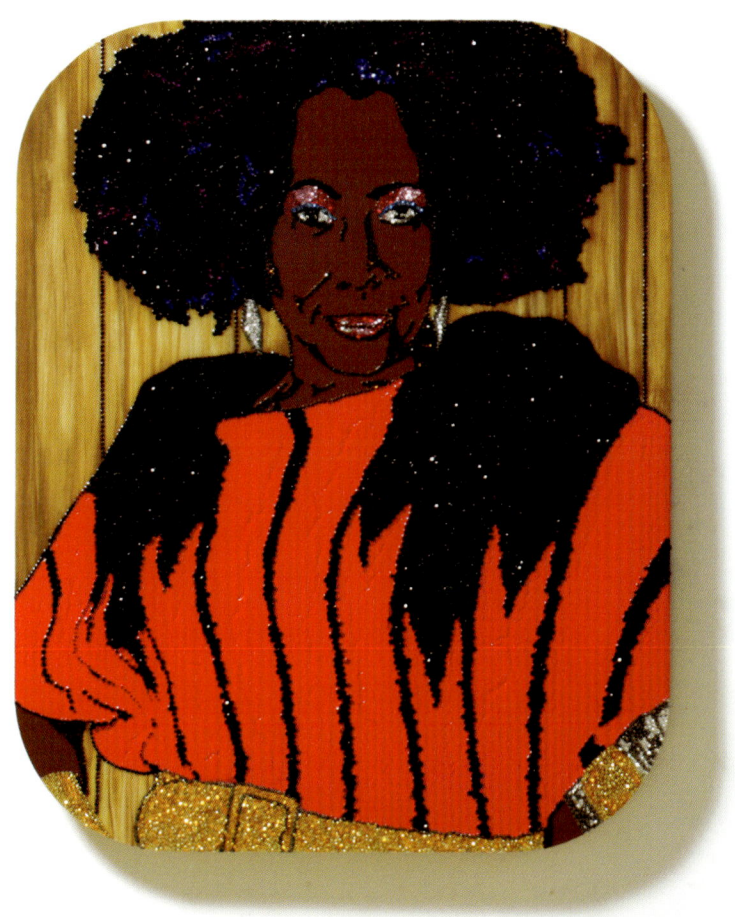
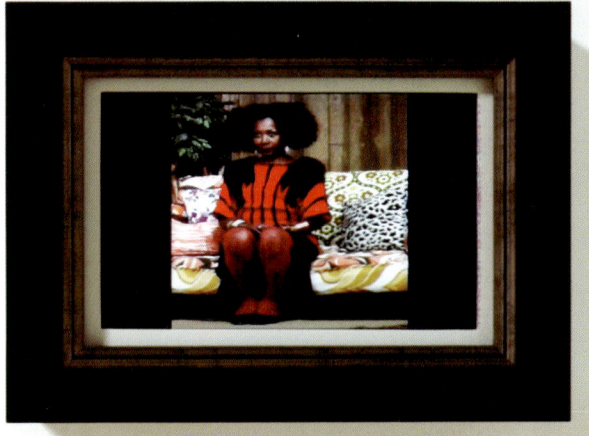

FIGURE 35. Mickalene Thomas, *Ain't I a Woman (Sandra)*, 2009. DVD, rhinestone, acrylic, and enamel on panel, diptych (painting, 36 × 28 in.; framed monitor, 18 × 24 × 5 5/16 in.). 45.7 × 61 × 13.5 cm. Edition of 3. Courtesy of the artist and Lehmann Maupin, New York and Hong Kong, and Artists Rights Society, New York.

against the economic, social, political, imaginative, and cultural inequalities endured by Black women who are all still fighting for equality in a white supremacist era. Her revolutionary body of work is "a way of tracing that lost history of African-American women, that sense of self-empowerment, beauty and embracing their own sexuality."[281] She relies on her art works as a means to endorse her conviction that "We are a woman's rights."

Ultimately, Thomas's admission that "dealing with the black body is already a rebellious act" reflects the experimental protest aesthetics of Winfred Rembert, Kerry James Marshall, and Debra Priestly.[282] As it is for Thomas, so it is for Rembert, Marshall, and Priestly, "We are survivors, and most artists are survivors."[283]

"A TOOL AND WEAPON"   MONUMENTS OF MORTALITY, PERFORMANCES OF PROTEST, AND LABORS OF LIBERATION

▶▶ Lorraine O'Grady—Nari Ward—Chakaia Booker—Leonardo Drew—Jefferson Pinder—Dread Scott

"An upper-middle-class black woman, making art that insists on cultural equality, performs just one necessary political function," declares Lorraine O'Grady, a performance, collage, and installation artist born in 1934 Boston.[1] O'Grady is a political philosopher, radical thinker, revisionist historian, and social justice artist. She creates artworks in which she insists on all forms of legal, economic, intellectual, ideological, social, and cultural equality. "I confess, in my work I keep trying to yoke together my underlying concerns as a member of the human species with my concerns as a woman and black in America," she explains. Working to express her personal emotions, she readily acknowledges the difficulties she experiences in communicating her concerns as a Black woman living in the United States: "It's hard, and sometimes the work splits in two—within a single piece, or between pieces," she admits. O'Grady produces textual, pictorial, and performative pieces as psychologically powerfully and politically dissident art works. She describes her practice by summarizing, "I keep trying, because I don't see how history can be divorced from ontogeny and still produce meaningful political solutions."[2] For O'Grady, any understanding of U.S. history in particular, and world history more generally, is only possible via an investigation into the principles and ideologies undergirding a nation's foundations. As she argues, it is solely by examining and excavating a country's historical account of its origin that it can become possible to reach "meaningful political solutions" regarding a society's past, present, and future political, social, cultural, and philosophical realities.

O'Grady is a cerebral artist who asks and answers complex philosophical and theoretical questions. She also sees art-making as a cathartic process: "I experience art as a way of discovering what I really think and feel," she explains. She relies on her aesthetic practice to navigate her understanding of the relationship between her own psychological reality and her commitment to political protest. "The main reason my art is 'political,'" she says, "is probably that anger is my most productive emotion". Warring against the repeated acts of persecution and discrimination perpetuated against all people of color by a white supremacist U.S. society, she understands that, as far as her revolutionary practice is concerned, "politics will always be more a matter of emotion than ideology." As an artist who creates works of civil rights protest, she explains, "I find it so much easier to know what I'm *against* (monopoly capitalism, personal and social cruelties of every kind) than to know what I'm *for*." And yet "the achieving of aesthetic form frequently gives me something in which I can believe, about which I can feel, 'This is true.'" Offering a way out of no way and a source of hope in the face of despair, O'Grady develops an eclectic and experimental practice that produces not just one but many aesthetic forms. As visual and textual "lexicons of liberation" that are emotionally true and politically real, her works of art operate as necessary counterpoints to the unconscionable immorality of a U.S. society built on white racism, violence, hypocrisy, illusion, and make-believe on the one hand, and on lies, pretense, and deception on the other. O'Grady favors no one material, mode, or practice over another: rather, she says, "I'm convinced the struggle for a just society is a kaleidoscopic one that has to be fought in all shapes and colors simultaneously."[3]

Performance art is one of the weapons in O'Grady's social justice arsenal. "The reasons I go on with Performance are two," she explains. "First, because I'm stuck with it. It's the only art form I feel capable of both mastering and expanding aesthetically. And second, because I believe it is an acceptable political option."[4] For O'Grady, performance art is not only a radical means to articulate her political convictions and a way to access alternative imaginaries but a self-reflexive process through which she builds new worlds. She emphasizes that "'performance' artists are explorers, primarily motivated by the sense of play."[5] No politically didactic, socially prescriptive, or historically reductive artist, O'Grady rejects all forms of fixity in favor of endorsing a myriad of strategies by which she celebrates all kaleidoscopic forms of creative arts. "'Performance' is dedicated to uncovering possibilities, to enlarging what is known about both old and still-unnamed art forms" she explains.[6] But the practice does not "uncover possibilities" without the artist herself experiencing very real challenges. O'Grady insists that "'performance' is a matter of artists shifting *dimensions*, putting themselves at risk by changing their accustomed relation to space/time."[7] For O'Grady, performance art generates new perspectives on emotional, imaginative, historical, geographical, spatial, and temporal contexts in order to create new ways of seeing and being. At the same time, she is only able to assume the role of an explorer and fulfill her "sense of play" by dispensing with safety nets for either herself or her audiences: viewers must enter at their own risk.

As the "child of Jamaican immigrants," O'Grady remembers, "I understood from the beginning that as a first-generation black American I was culturally 'mixed.'"[8] She found herself bereft of means by which to express the realities of her autobiographical history. "I had no language to describe and analyze my experience," she explains, noting that it was "not until years later" that "words like 'diaspora' and 'hybridism'" would "gain currency for the movement of peoples and the blending of two or more cultures."[9] In light of the role these ideas came to play in O'Grady's understanding of her biography, her insistence that the "governing aim of my work is the reconciliation of opposites"

can be no surprise.[10] While painfully aware that as a young person she was equipped with no textual language through which to communicate her multipositionality, she has succeeded in arriving at a new visual lexicon though which she reimagines and re-presents her complex identity. "I can see that the *diasporian* experience, however arduous, has been critical for my life and work," she notes, adding that the difficulty lies "not so much in the mixed details of my background as in the constant process of reconciling them."[11] O'Grady's practice emerges from a determination to arrive at an alternative "lexicon of liberation" through which to grapple with and gain control over the psychological complexities, emotional barriers, existential challenges, and social difficulties she experiences. As she understands, her commitment to a "constant process of reconciling" the "mixed details" of her identity necessarily fails to attain a halcyon state of existence for either herself or her audiences. "I undertake the quest for 'wholeness' and 'meaning' knowing that it's doomed," she admits. "But I can't help harboring a secret hope that I will be able to achieve psychological and artistic unity."[12] Throughout her body of work, O'Grady articulates a lifelong determination to secure emotional and aesthetic wholeness.

O'Grady explains that "in my work, 'miscegenation,' the pejorative legal word for the mixing of the races, functions as a metaphor both for the mixed media I employ and for the difficulties and potentialities of cultural reconciliation."[13] Confronting the heartbreaking reality that the quest for psychological, existential, political, and artistic wholeness and "cultural reconciliation" is never ending, she consciously interrogates the explicitly racist term *miscegenation* as a means to conjoin the ambiguities and ambivalences she experiences in her identity with those she endures in her practice. She fuses her personal biography with an experimental language of aesthetic protest in order to expose this "legal word for the mixing of the races" as a deeply offensive term. O'Grady's decision to use miscegenation as a metaphor for her "mixed media practice" reveals her art-making process itself as a means by which she bears witness to and resists—in corporeal, spiritual, and emotional terms—the centuries of abuses inflicted upon Black women's bodies by a white supremacist, enslaving U.S. nation.

O'Grady adopts this "legal word," *miscegenation*, in an explicit refusal to shy away from the traumatic acts of violence and violation that have accompanied the "mixing of the races." For O'Grady, no topic is taboo: she names and shames miscegenation as a term that exposes the sexual assault, rape, and torture Black women experienced at the hands of a barbaric, murderous, and persecutory white population. O'Grady examines "miscegenation" through the lens of centuries of white racist violence against Black lives to reveal that what is a "blending of cultures" from a white-dominant perspective is nothing less than an act of appropriation and co-option, at best, or eradication and extermination, at worst, for African diasporic people. Among the scholars undertaking in-depth examinations of O'Grady's installation and performance art in conjunction with analyses of her philosophical essays are Cecilia Alemani, Maurice Berger, Connie Butler, Laura Cottingham, Theo Davis, Jarrett Earnest, Andil Gosine, Amanda Hunt, Heather Kapplow, Lucy R. Lippard, Andrea Miller-Keller, Linda M. Montano, Karen Rosenberg, Moira Roth, Stephanie Sparling Williams, Judith Wilson.

"Although my work seems very politically charged, it actually starts from a very personal spiritual place," confirms Nari Ward, an artist who was born thirty years later in 1963.[14] Working to communicate his individual beliefs while refusing to lose sight of his radical convictions, he emphasizes, "I like to think of the works as a meditation or prayer, which addresses my angst, frustration, or anger."[15] Ward transforms his emotional struggles into site-specific installations and stand-alone sculptures that foreground his search for spiritual healing and inner peace. Working with a call-and-response relationship between artist and audiences, he is emotionally dedicated and politically committed to establishing a connection with his viewers. "The challenge," he explains, "is how to mold the emotional, political, and material form in a manner, which tells a uniquely poetic story for each viewer to interpret."[16] Just as O'Grady dedicates her life to developing an experimental practice in which no topic is off-limits, so Ward insists that no one "material form" or "poetic story" fits all. His psychologically powerful and politically charged works gain heightened power when interpreted through the lens of his audiences' experiences.

Ward's assemblages and site-specific installations operate as spiritual touchstones for his viewers, allowing them to arrive at their own "uniquely poetic story" by speaking to the difficulties they endure within their own lives.

While O'Grady is the U.S.-born child of "Jamaican immigrants," Ward was born in St. Andrew Parish, Jamaica. "I came to the U.S. from Jamaica when I was 12 years old, first to Brooklyn, then to New Jersey, and finally to Harlem," he recalls. "I really loved Harlem. It reminded me a lot of Jamaica, in that it has its own third world and so many communities together—like African and Caribbean."[17] At the heart of Ward's love for Harlem was his realization that "I felt a little bit less like an outsider" there.[18] His life in Harlem—a familiar geographical location populated by so many communities of people of color—led to a socially and emotionally transformative epiphany for Ward. For the first time, he experienced the benefit of "still feeling a connection to my place of birth, the small island of Jamaica."[19] At the same time, this connection in no way diluted or detracted from his very real "sense of belonging to dual identities."[20] Across his practice, Ward does justice to each of his "dual identities" individually and in their own right.

Ward pioneers an alternative visual language through which he not only represents and reimagines his dual identities but also memorializes African Caribbean social practices, political beliefs, and cultural systems more generally. "Caribbean people have the ability to identify their own moment, their own life," he declares. "They understand the need to be in different places, to pivot, to move, and enter into new realities where you can take your past with you, in you."[21] Ward creates psychologically complex, emotively charged, and politically confrontational mixed-media assemblages and site-specific installations. He creates multilayered and self-reflexively experimental works through which he simultaneously occupies "different places" in order to extrapolate "new realities." According to Ward, who endorses no artificial boundaries, your past can never be repressed, denied, or erased: it is not only "with you" but "in you" as a source of emotional and spiritual rejuvenation.

For Ward, Jamaica influences not only his personal history but also his improvisational aesthetic. "There is a way of using materials over there with which I feel a kinship," he explains. "People use available things, and they make them function as their form dictates."[22] Rather than working with costly and traditional fine art materials, Ward takes inspiration from people living in Jamaica who create objects from readily available things. Above all else, these artists refuse to superimpose their own vision on their art, instead prioritizing a respect for their found objects' original form. Ward's sculptures and installations reveal his determination to create artworks by cultivating a respectful relationship with the "available things" he collects from urban environments. Ward shapes his practice in recognition of the people living in Jamaica who understand that "you may not have everything, but you make do with what you have, so it works." Ward's assemblages and sculptures honor an improvisational aesthetic as born of an economic necessity. In so doing, he not only honors Jamaican traditions but he joins thousands of African diasporic artists dedicated to "making something out of nothing" and "mak[ing] do with what you have." "Visually it doesn't make sense," he concedes of this longstanding Jamaican practice. All the same, "on some deeper level it really hits."[23] Ward succeeds in generating a variety of emotional, visceral, and spiritual connections with his viewers by cultivating this "deeper level" through the re-usage, re-creation, and reconstruction of "available things."

"I am really trying to do traditional sculpture, using non-traditional objects and materials, and a non-traditional set of information—my own set of information," Ward summarizes of his practice. He issues a powerful declaration of artistic independence from national, racial, cultural, or formal affiliations. Instead, he urges that his sculpture "isn't necessarily Jamaican, black, or mainstream." Rather, he says, "I am most successful, I think, when I am able to tie all these things together."[24] While he may foreground the importance of separate and "dual identities" on a surface reading, on a "deeper level" he shares O'Grady's commitment to searching for a political and aesthetic unity which will "tie all these things together." Recognizing the power of salvaged artifacts as "non-traditional objects and materials" in their own right, he finds their usage integral to his practice. As he summarizes, these disused artifacts provide him with "an opportunity to allow history to be built and written not just by the victors: now it can include other voices, which can interject necessary counterpoints."[25]

These "non-traditional objects and materials" previously owned by dispossessed and disempowered people fighting for survival across the African diaspora form the building blocks of Ward's protest aesthetic. He reworks, re-creates, and reimagines these objects to communicate the traumatizing reality that not only have they been dismissed, unvalued, broken, and abused—so have the women, children, and men who used them. Ward is ideally equipped to develop alternative histories in which the "other voices" of African diasporic people are no longer voiceless but are instead valued in a mainstream U.S. imaginary. For the first time, the vanquished and not the "victorious" "interject necessary counterpoints" to an official history that is, according to Ward's radical reimaging and reimagining, no longer for whites only.

Ward relies on dramatic conventions to liberate his practice from the constraints of the official exhibition space. "My work as an installation artist has always flirted with the theatrical, creating works for specific sites that inspire reflection and dialogue and bypass the trappings of the gallery white cube," he explains.[26] As an anti-elitist artist, he refuses to allow his assemblages and installations to be co-opted or contained within the white supremacist privilege of a white dominant art world. Rather, he liberates his practice by creating works that generate "reflection and dialogue" from his viewers due to their situatedness within "specific sites" that are revelatory of their social, economic, and political contexts. "My work isn't about an abstract society, but is about making us all aware of our role in authoring that society," he avows.[27]

Ward prevents either himself or his audiences from abdicating their ethical, moral, and emotional responsibilities as complicit inhabitants of a Western society that is rooted in the perpetuation of very real injustices. As he maintains, "we are all creators rather than passive receivers" when it come to our participation within dominant hierarchies of power.[28] Ward's conviction radically contrasts O'Grady's realization of the limited revolutionary impact available to her. While she argues that "no one is going to go out and man the barricades after seeing a piece by me (at least, none that I've produced so far)," Ward maintains, "My faith lies in the belief that the actions I take can produce a meaningful contribution to effecting another individual's expectation of the world."[29] He insists, "I want the work to change the viewer on some level."[30] For Ward, art as a site of innovation and experimentation, and as a platform for social and political change that happens in the hearts, minds, and behaviors of all individuals, defines his many "lexicons of liberation." Among the many critics investigating Ward's self-reflexively experimental acts and arts of protest across his bodies of work are Naomi Beckwith, Jan Garden Castro, Kimberly Chou, Olukemi Ilesanmi, Scott Indrisek, Erica Moiah James, Brian Keith Jackson, Ralph Lemon, Alessandra Pace, Lowery Stokes Sims, Judith Stoodley, Philippe Vergne, Chloe Wyma.

"My sculpture continues to evolve and change," states Chakaia Booker.[31] She is an artist who was born over a decade earlier in 1953 in Newark, New Jersey, and she shares Ward's commitment to working with salvaged materials as the defining catalyst to her experimental processes. Booker describes an ever-shifting and developing practice in which "changes in tools, different materials, varying work spaces, and installation sites all bring about the creation of different forms of sculpture." She remains unwavering in her lifelong conviction, however, that regardless of processes, tools, or results, "it is always public art."[32] Both Booker and Ward prioritize creating artworks that will be prominently on view in the public arena and freely accessible by all members of society, rather than consigned to the private space of the gallery for consumption by the elite few. While Ward works with a vast array of found materials, Booker relies almost exclusively on one disused industrial artifact in particular: "I usually start with the rubber tire."[33] "Sometimes I find special places on the street," she explains. "I also gather materials from local gas stations as well as auto body shops and recycling centers."[34]

Working with disused rubber tires is thematically, politically, culturally, and ideologically vital to the construction of Booker's sculptures. "A wall or relief using old tires suggests archaeological finds and the deciphering of patterns and textures into new languages or new symbols," she declares.[35] Cultivating a deliberate iconographic association between these "old tires" and "archaeological finds," she takes on the roles of examiner, excavator, and representer of social, political, and emotional realities. Booker assumes many identities as an artist turned spiritualist, alchemist, myth-maker, archaeologist, symbolist, translator, and interpreter. As such she transforms dominant "patterns and textures" into "new languages" and "new symbols" in order to build new physical, psychological, existential, and imaginative worlds. "These same patterns may have been a means of communication some time in the past," she observes, adding, "they may translate into a way of writing, a language or physical tool that actually performs."[36] By transforming these rubber tires into a "physical tool," Booker reinterprets the individual "patterns" on each of these tires as potential "writing." Over the decades, Booker's political philosophies and experimental artistic practices remain indivisible from her lifelong commitment to social justice. According to her vision, these patterns generate a blueprint for a new language of protest. Across her epic-scale works, Booker not only translates but provides a means of communicating about and protesting against economic, legal, social, political, and cultural inequalities.

Booker transforms the role of a traditional painter who "has a palette and the palette has color." For her, "each color has energy and that is how the painter begins the composition; part of it is through this energy." Booker describes herself as a painter working with a very different palette, however.[37] "My palette has the textures of the tire on it instead of color, and these textures and the energy embodied within them is what I use to create the work," she explains.[38] Booker takes her cues from the psychological power and imaginative force generated by these discarded rubber tires, which are individually distinctive for their "many variations of textures from being busted and worn." She explains that "all of that feeds my energy, which in turns helps to inform me on how this energy can be used to create the composition of the sculpture."[39] For Booker, the tire's "energy" derives from its importance as an emotionally hard-hitting, politically weighted, and socially revelatory touchstone, talisman, and emblem. As material objects that are subjected to yet somehow endure purposeful and accidental damage, extreme physical stress, and elemental weather conditions, they are powerful symbols of human suffering, struggle, and survival. The many seminal critics currently investigating Booker's practice and process include Rocío Aranda-Alvarado, Nick Capasso, Jan Garden Castro, David R. Collens, Christopher Cook, Marion Grzesiak, Matthew Guy Nichols, Valerie Cassel Oliver, Lowery Stokes Sims, Raúl Zamudio.

Leonardo Drew, a Florida-born sculptor who grew up in the north, shares Chakaia Booker's determination to develop an alternative visual language in which to communicate his emotively charged and politically provocative subject matter. He creates highly tactile, intricately textured, and meticulously patterned assemblages and installations on a monumental scale. "I grew up in the P. T. Barnum projects of Bridgeport, Connecticut," he remembers.[40] "The city dump occupied every view of our apartment," Drew recalls regarding its all-pervasive presence in his daily life, "I remember all of it, the seagulls, the summer smells, the underground fires that could not be put out." As a young person, he says, "I would watch the bulldozers troll back and forth over this massive landfill, the dump trucks cart and drop, and the cranes lift, deposit, and bury."[41] Far from consigned to his past, Drew's experience as a child physically and emotionally overwhelmed by the sights, sounds, and smells of the city dump survives into his adulthood. Over the decades, he has translated his memory of the mechanical operations of the industrial machines into his practice as a sculptor in psychologically and physically powerful ways.

The movements of the trucks and cranes of the city dump resonate with Drew's contemporary art practice of creating sculptures: he not only "carts and drops" but "lifts, deposits, and buries" his materials. Drew "came to realize" that the city dump was "'God's mouth' . . . the beginning and the end . . . and the beginning again." He uses this inspiration to create emotionally all-consuming and physically overwhelming sculptures in which he not only visually replicates but artificially manufactures its detritus and debris for his audiences.[42] Drew works to create artworks in which he produces his own versions of "God's mouth." His sculptures are memorials to mortality and icons of immortality. While his sculptures are self-evidently monuments of mourning—as works made from artifacts that all testify to "the

end" by suggesting brokenness, fragmentation, and destruction—they are also testaments to freedom. Drew foregrounds the art of creation as an antidote to the act of destruction, working only with objects he has handcrafted. He signals a new physical, material, spiritual, and imaginative beginning by laboriously creating his sculptures out of materials that resemble salvaged objects but which are in fact artworks that he has beautifully created. As he explains, "I did find something in the discarded . . . 'new life.'" According to Drew, "It's this metaphor and consistent weight of being which drives my work to this day. Though I do not use found objects in my work (my materials are fabricated in the studio) what has remained from early explorations are the echoes of evolution . . . life, death, regeneration."[43] His practice animates the power of discarded materials by undertaking recuperation, recreation, and reimagining. Out of his socially marginalized, economically impoverished, and nihilistically despairing environment, in which a struggle for survival would seem to be the all-defining experience, Drew sustains the "weight of being" by defeating old death in favor of generating "new life." Among the many scholars discussing Drew's practice are Hilton Als, Sarah Jane Cervenak, Rebecca Dimling Cochran, Judith H. Dobrzynski, Xandra Eden, Kate Hunger, Thomas McEvilley, Jessica Morgan, Tim Nye, Valerie Cassel Oliver, Michael O'Sullivan, Claudia Schmuckli, Judith Stoodley, Jeremy Strick, Lisa Jaye Young.

"I grew up in Silver Spring, Maryland, right in the D.C. area," states Jefferson Pinder, a performance and video artist born nearly a decade later in 1970.[44] While he lives and works in an urban area vastly different from that of Drew, he candidly describes the challenges generated by white racism: "the suburbs are a complex battleground for a black man," he admits.[45] This "complex battleground" represents a physical space in which an omnipresent white dominant power maintains a political stranglehold over the lives of all people of color and defines Pinder's practice. "The suburbs are all about control, and I grew up exercising restraint—not getting too mad, and working hard to fit in," Pinder explains.[46] He is an artist who dedicates his life's work to an outright rejection of any and all imposed structures of conformity, and to a no-holds-barred expression of his emotional realities, political beliefs, and historical consciousness. For Pinder, art-making is a liberated space in which he pioneers new strategies of self-representation, self-imagining, and self-creation. More especially, he asks and answers a key question across his performance, installation, and video art: "can I achieve an emotional state by stressing my body out physically?"[47]

In his experimental practice, Pinder's own body is a site not only of corporeal suffering but of psychological and existential struggle. As the catalyst for his provocative aesthetic vision, his body reveals that for Pinder, "what seemed to be truer to me was this physical exertion, using myself and then trying to create a metaphor, a balance within emotional content."[48] He takes his body to its breaking point as a politically powerful way to debate the lives of Black men lived in the "complex battleground" of U.S. mainstream society. Stressed out, exhausted, and traumatized, Pinder's body operates as the language and instrument through which he communicates his powerful subject matter to his audiences. Living out his belief that "there's a contemporary art precedent of being able to use yourself, especially in performance art, as a tool and weapon," Pinder deliberately puts his own body in physical and spiritual danger.[49] In resisting the dehumanizing forces exerted against Black men by a white supremacist society, Pinder's body becomes not only his "tool" but also his "weapon" of liberation.

Working to make a way out of no way, Pinder explains, "I try to embody strength, a black strength of a black power in my pieces."[50] He creates triumph out of tragedy by foregrounding Black survival rather than sacrifice. As testaments to "black strength" and "black power," Pinder's performance, video, and installation pieces operate as declarations of Black liberation. "I embrace blackness in my work because the conversation always seem to hover around race regardless. That is factual," he states.[51] As a Black artist living in a white mainstream U.S. society, he realizes only too well that while "some white artists" may "have that luxury", "I can't separate my work from who I am." For Pinder, a determination to do justice to "who I am," all white racist attempts at annihilating the lives of Black men to the contrary, defines his protest aesthetic. He transforms negative realities into positive possibilities by recognizing that the impossibility of "separating" his practice

from his identity has "given me the chance to really contribute to a variety of conversations about race."[52]

"I do not want to pretend for a moment that I have the same latitude to do work about anything," Pinder admits. Across his bodies of work, he channels his realization regarding the limits he experiences in not being able "to do work about anything" into creating a platform intervening in "conversations about race," especially as they relate to the weighted relationships between Black men's bodies and histories of enslavement, labor, political radicalism, and philosophical resistance.[53] Pinder's practice involves "crawling up into people's psyche." He cultivates these powerful relationships with his audiences in the conviction that "if the work is successful they will be thinking of the work long after they leave the space."[54] His politically hard-hitting and psychologically unflinching artworks represent the Black man's body as a site of strength—corporeal, spiritual, emotional, and philosophical—in order to insist on his audiences' intellectual as well as emotional engagement with his work. While Pinder readily concedes, "I'm not an activist," he insists, "I can at least start a conversation."[55] Among the many leading theorists of Pinder's process and practice are Rachel Beckman, Faedra Chatard Carpenter, Matthew Clay-Robison, Shelly Clay-Robison, Jessica Dawson, Blake Gopnik, Michael T. Martin, Jordana Moore Saggese, Heather S. Nathans, Sam Rappaport, Dorothy Spears, Kurt Shaw, David C. Wall, A. M. Weaver, Susan Zurbrigg.

For Dread Scott, a revolutionary performance and installation artist born in Chicago in 1965, only a few years earlier than Jefferson Pinder, a determination not only to start but to script, structure, and, above all, direct the conversation around issues related to theories of racism, representation, and radicalism defines his life's work. As a contemporary artist who mines U.S. history to condemn centuries of white inhumanity, injustice, and immorality, he insists on questioning first and foremost "the beginning of the U.S. Constitution, which everybody says, *Oh yeah this is the document that talks about freedom.*"[56] A self-appointed activist-artist, Scott reveals that all attempts to interpret the U.S. Constitution as a "document that talks about freedom" can only ever be the work of white supremacist delusion, denial, disrespect, and dehumanization.

Scott debunks and defies white racist dominant mythologies of the United States as a nation founded on liberty. Aware of the overwhelming power held by the United States constitution as the root of white discriminatory systems of racist persecution, inequality, and injustice enacted against Black lives, he insists that "the key thing is, in my perspective, it's a document that's written by slave owners and friends of slave owners." As he emphasizes, this political document has provided, and continues to provide, the "legal and political framework for a system and economy that was founded on slavery." "You get just four paragraphs in," he explains, "and you're already talking about slavery, and in fact specifically the *three-fifths of a man*."[57] Here Scott communicates his outrage against a nation that has always defined white freedoms against Black unfreedoms. His poignant reference to Black men as "*three-fifths of a man*" references a traumatizing reality: white men not only had the rights to enslave but their electoral privileges were expanded or limited directly in relation to the numbers of Black people in their legal possession.

Named Scott Tyler at birth, Dread Scott renamed himself in honor of a man born into slavery in Virginia around 1799. This man, Dred Scott, unsuccessfully sued for legal freedom for himself and his family—his wife Harriet, and their children, Eliza and Lizzie—in 1857. Dred Scott's fight for his own and his family's liberties resulted in an infamous court decision in which the white racist and white supremacist chief justice, Roger B. Taney, stipulated that "slaves were property and were 'so far inferior, that they had no rights which the white man was bound to respect.'"[58] As Scott, the contemporary artist, explains, Taney's statement—which called a moratorium on the hopes for liberty not only for the Scott family but for all enslaved people—endures as "the most well-thought-out, developed, articulated argument for white supremacy I've ever read."[59] The injustice of this "argument for white supremacy" was felt not only by Dred Scott but by all Black radical revolutionaries, including Frederick Douglass.

In 1857, Frederick Douglass, a self-liberated freedom-fighter, denounced the barbarity of this white supremacist court decision that resulted not only in the legal mandate that "slavery may go in safety anywhere under the star-spangled banner" but that "colored persons of African descent have no rights that white men are bound to respect."[60] According to this white supremacist logic, Douglass summarizes, "colored men of African descent are not and cannot be citizens of the United States."[61] Dred Scott's daily fight for existence, no less than that of the self-emancipated Frederick Douglass, was defined by a determination to fight against the "fact" of slavery. Working against white supremacist legislation today, Dread Scott is committed to using every "tool and weapon" available in order to fight the "spirit of slavery" and the rise of the "spirit of mastery." As Douglass himself predicted, and as Dread Scott remains painfully aware, the centuries-long institution of slavery endures as a contemporary reality that possesses the power to destroy, dehumanize, and devastate the lives of all people of color who are fighting to survive the inequalities and injustices of a white supremacist U.S. nation. "While there have been major changes in America since that 1857 Supreme Court case," Scott argues, "the racism and exploitation that led to the ruling which included words to the effect 'there are no rights that a black person has that a white man is bound to respect' hasn't changed much."[62] Frederick Douglass would not be surprised by Scott's harrowing diagnosis of a traumatizing state of unequal race relations, according to which the "form of racism has changed but the basic position of Black people in this society and the rationale for it have remained constant."[63]

Scott dedicates his life no less than his practice to warring against all forms of legal, economic, social, political, corporeal, and philosophical persecution. Working to defeat the discriminatory practices of white racist populations as well as white racist governments, he admits to another motivation undergirding his decision to take on Dred Scott's first name. As a revolutionary activist-artist who is committed to changing white racist mindsets and behaviors by using every resistance strategy at his disposal, Scott's decision to change the spelling from "Dred" to "Dread" introduces a vitally important shift in meaning. As he explains, he made this revision because "I liked the concept of 'dread,' as in fear."[64]

Staging a series of protests against "America's so-called freedoms" that "are nothing to celebrate," Scott creates provocative and transformative works to inspire his white audiences into eradicating their own racism and working for an end to society's inequalities.[65] In recognition of the repeated failures of appeals to safeguard the equal rights of Black people when rooted in moral spiritual, emotional, political, and intellectual arguments alone, he endorses a dissident tactic of cultivating fear in his viewers. For Scott, fear is the only effective mechanism by which it becomes possible to motivate whites to a real and lasting change of heart that will lead to equally real and lasting political and governmental reforms. Among the pioneering critics who discuss the revolutionary power of Scott's work are Bobbi Booker, Will Cameron, Steven C. Dubin, Baldev Duggal, Peter Ferko, Janelle Grace, Patricia Hills, Demetria Irwin, Saul Ostrow, Joey Orr, Angelica Rogers, Michael Slate, Nick Stillman.

Not only are "America's so-called freedoms" "nothing to celebrate" but, according to Lorraine O'Grady, Nari Ward, Chakaia Booker, Leonardo Drew, and Jefferson Pinder, no less than Dread Scott himself, they must be fought using all the tools and weapons that are at a revolutionary Black artist's disposal. As artists despairing of twenty-first-century white racist injustices, these activists understand art-making as a portal of possibility to the realization of revolutionary freedoms. O'Grady's summary of her determination to transform a white dominant art world reads as the rallying cry shared by all these artists: "'NOW IS THE TIME FOR AN INVASION!'"[66]

LORRAINE O'GRADY   *(Born in Boston, Massachusetts, 1934)*

"The invisibility of black women has been much on my mind," Lorraine O'Grady says.[67] Working as a performance and installation artist, she self-consciously visibilizes the invisibilized physical, psychological, emotional, social, cultural, sexual, and political realities experienced by Black women living in the U.S. who fought and continue to fight for their survival. A few years ago, O'Grady delivered a talk that addressed the question "Can women artists take back the nude from a voyeuristic male gaze as a site to represent their own subjectivity?"[68] Her response reveals her despair. "I have to discard the premise," she admits. "From mass culture to high culture, white women may have been objects of the fetishizing gaze, but black women have had only the blank stare."[69] As she realizes, Black women's bodies and subjectivities have been disrespected by white male voyeurism and their existence has been entirely eradicated within the "blank stare" of white supremacy.

O'Grady protests against white dominant systems that have remained focused on the persecution of Black women. She interrogates discriminatory realities facing Black female subjects in their strategies of resistance. She asks a hard-hitting rhetorical question that cuts to the heart of the violations, traumas, and abuses facing Black women. "When even the black woman's ability to survive being raped 'proved' she was less than human (a *true* woman would have committed suicide rather than submit), was it any wonder that black artists wanted, not to take her clothes off, but to keep them on?"[70]

Across O'Grady's eclectic and experimental practice, she names and shames a traumatizing state of affairs. Black women have endured all forms of violence—sexual, spiritual, social, cultural, and political—only to be denied their corporeal existence and even their humanity. She is only too poignantly aware that for past, present, and future Black women the war against the depredations committed against their minds, bodies, and souls by a white racist mainstream society continues. Nothing less than life is at stake for O'Grady in her role as a Black woman artist committed to fight for the right to radical creativity and revolutionary self-expression.

O'Grady responds to the white racist erasures of Black women's lives in mainstream U.S. society by declaring, "My own concern as an artist is to reclaim black female subjectivity so as to 'de-haunt' historic scripts and establish worldly agency."[71] For O'Grady, the only

▶▶ "Black Art Must Take More Risks!"

way to "reclaim," recreate, represent, and reimage Black women's subjectivities and "worldly agency" is to liberate them from the "historic scripts" that perpetuate social, political, cultural, and ideological injustices. She explains that "as a black female artist my work is at the nexus of aggravated psychic and social forces as yet mostly uncharted."[72] O'Grady's revolutionary works radically intervene into these "psychic and social forces" that are "uncharted" and untheorized, unexamined, unrepresented, and unremembered.

"I did a guerilla performance in the early '80s called *Mademoiselle Bourgeoise Noire*, which is French for 'Ms. French Bourgeois,'" recalls O'Grady of a radically confrontational work she performed in white mainstream art galleries and museums from 1980 to 1983 (figure 36).[73] She summarizes her performance as "Ms. French Bourgeois" as follows:

> She wore a gown and a cape made of 180 pairs of white gloves and she carried a whip, a cat-of-nine-tails, made of white macramé that was studded with chrysanthemums and she gave these away during the course of the performance while smiling and saying, 'Won't you help me lighten my heavy bouquet?' When she entered with her crown and her gown and her cape she looked very much like either a debutante or a beauty queen. I was sort of playing off of both of those roles. But then once the flowers were gone and then she was left there with the whip, she took off her cape and beat herself with the whip. The whip was basically a metaphor for external oppression and the gloves were a metaphor for internal repression.[74]

In O'Grady's uncompromising performance, her act of self-flagellation testifies to the atrocities and abuses perpetrated against women of color across the generations that white official histories willfully erased and silenced. She holds Western nations to account for their systematic violence and violations that have not only been integral to, but legally mandated by, centuries of the transatlantic slave trade, slavery, and colonialism.

O'Grady's "flowers are inserted into a white cat-o'-nine tails" to remind readers that the "cat o'nine tails was the whip that made plantations move."[75] While the whip represents white enslavers' torture of enslaved Black people and "a sign of external oppression," the gloves function as "a symbol of internal repression" through the "internalization of those oppressive values" by past and present generations. Together, the objects

testify to the ways in which a white supremacist mindset, ideology, and legal system do irreparable damage to the lives of Black people. "I was combining the external oppression and the internal oppression, in the same way they reinforce each other and keep each other locked in place," she explains.[76] Ultimately, O'Grady's performance in *Mademoiselle Bourgeoise Noire* exposes the enormity of the corporeal and emotional atrocities committed against all people of color, enslaved, self-liberated, and free, by a white racist U.S. society. Over the centuries, Black people have not only been physically assaulted but also psychologically abused: the same system that destroys the body also injures the soul and tears apart the mind.

Mademoiselle Bourgeoise Noire riffs off the icon of the "debutante or a beauty queen" to interrogate the ways in which Black women's bodies have been repeatedly exposed to white mainstream persecution. As she emphasizes, Black women during slavery and in a postemancipation era have been and continue to be subjected to stereotyping, sexualization, objectification, commodification, exoticization, and fetishization. White racist fictions about Black women were perpetuated solely to ensure that the dehumanizing demands of white enslaving and ex-enslaving oppressive classes were met. O'Grady understands the ways Black women were repeatedly caricatured either as maternal nurturers or as sexually available. "If you are simultaneously being seen as the universal prostitute, and at the same time as the sexless matriarch—the Jezebel and the Mammy—neither of which have anything to do with what you are, then sometimes you have to fight for the right not to be either, and sometimes for the right to be both at once," O'Grady declares.[77] Recognizing the psychological toll that the "fight for the right not to be either," as well as to "be both at once," has taken on Black women, she protests against this traumatizing state of affairs. According to her radical practice, Black female agency and artistry rather than objectification and subjugation define her new "lexicon of liberation."

For O'Grady, the only way to account for the absence of Black women's bodies in a mainstream imaginary, and of the Black female nude in Western art history more particularly, is "by referring to the stereotypes of Mammy and Jezebel" and by recognizing the "'synchronous debasement and excision of black female sexuality

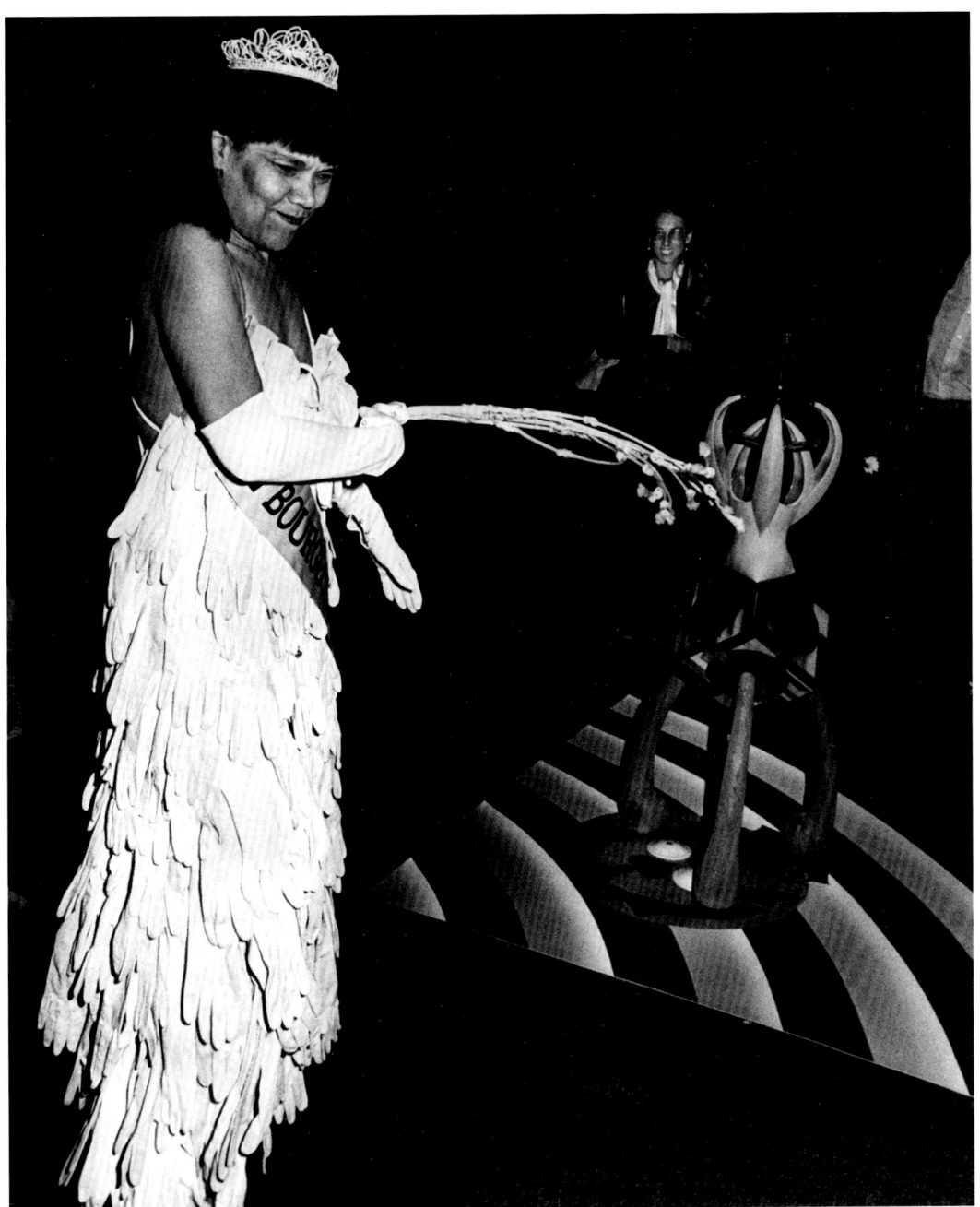

FIGURE 36. Lorraine O'Grady, *Untitled (Mlle Bourgeoise Noire Beats Herself with the Whip-That-Made-Plantations-Move)*, 1980–83/2009. Silver gelatin fiber print 9¾× 7¼ in.; 24.77 × 18.42 cm.). Courtesy of Alexander Gray Associates, New York, © 2022 Lorraine O'Grady / Artist Rights Society (ARS), New York..

though slavery and the cult of 'true womanhood.'"[78] Grady protests against white racist caricatures that artificially dichotomize Black women either as idealized paragons of maternal virtue or as wantonly promiscuous and excessively sexualized. At the same time, she interrogates the "cult of 'true womanhood'" as a white racist Western patriarchal belief system that mythologized elite white women as spiritually pious, sexually pure, and dedicated to moral duty.

As *Mademoiselle Bourgeoise Noire*, O'Grady bears witness to the devastating impact that these traumatizing racist ideologies have had and continue to have on Black women's lives. Recognizing the terrible damage that the "synchronous debasement and excision of black female sexuality" has inflicted on Black women, she reveals the harrowing extent to which "black bourgeois women worldwide were sexually repressed in this era."[79] "What else could they be when they were defined by their surrounding cultures as the universal prostitute?" she asks. "They were desperate for respect."[80] O'Grady employs reused materials to grapple with the extent to which Black women have internalized white racist constructions of their sexualities and identities. "I spent most of that time going to every thrift shop in New York buying white gloves," O'Grady says. "It was very important to me that the gloves should have been worn by women who had actually believed in them." O'Grady visited "every thrift shop" on a quest to seek out the actual white gloves women had worn not only to honor the actual physical object that had adorned their bodies but the beliefs they attached to them: Black women wore these gloves because they believed in their social and political power as objects of status and elite class identity.[81] These gloves come to new life as the adornments on Mademoiselle Bourgeoise Noire's ornate gown. No longer operating as markers of a respectability defined by a white segregated class system, these gloves become symbols for Black female strategies of beautification. A declaration of Black female artistic and political resistance, O'Grady's "guerilla" performances of *Mademoiselle Bourgeoise Noire* holds her white racist audiences morally accountable. At the same time, she celebrates Black female sexuality and beauty.

"*Mlle Bourgeoise Noire* was a critical piece, located at the nexus of race, class, and gender," explains O'Grady.[82]

She recognizes the devastating consequences that white racist myopia has had not only on U.S. society but on mainstream feminism. She protests against this white-led, white-theorized, and white-supported radical movement: "In 1980, when I created it, there were no role models in white feminist art for a tri-partite critique, or at least none that I was aware of," she declares.[83] A key motivation for O'Grady's performance as Mademoiselle Bourgeoise Noire is her commitment to righting these wrongs by providing an interrogation of white patriarchal supremacy, white feminist racism, and white class structures. As part of her improvisational enactment of this imaginary persona, she testifies that "even though black feminists may have admired the energy, even the delirium, of white feminist rhetoric, not to mention the bravery of many of its actions, they still felt alienated by and even a bit derisive toward it."[84] O'Grady responds to feelings of alienation through art-making. *Mademoiselle Bourgeoise Noire* is a beauty icon, feminist avenger, political visionary, and witness to centuries of violence and violation. For O'Grady, she represents a catalyst to acts and arts of self and communal Black female liberation.

Waging a war against white feminist inequalities and in defiance of the ongoing exclusionary practices of a white dominant Western art world, O'Grady staged her first "guerilla performance" as Mademoiselle Bourgeoise Noire at Just Above Midtown Gallery in New York City. As a "response to a Black Abstraction exhibition," her radical alter ego rejects a "mindset among black artists who had had the doors so completely closed in their faces."[85] "They had done what black middle-class people had been doing for generations: trying to make themselves acceptable," she explains. "One of the ways they make themselves acceptable is to make very controlled and beautiful, but very safe, abstract art."[86] She admits, "I was disappointed because I felt that the art on exhibit, as opposed to the people, had been too cautious—that it had been art with white gloves on."[87]

Working to expose the dangers for Black freedoms of expression and self-respect generated by "safe, abstract art," O'Grady takes the view that Black artists have no choice but "to stop that and take risks": to take the white gloves off. During one of many impromptu speeches she gave during her various performances, she issued a rallying cry to all Black artists: "THAT'S

ENOUGH! No more boot-licking . . . No more ass-kissing . . . No more buttering-up . . . No more pos . . . turing of super-ass . . imilates . . . BLACK ART MUST TAKE MORE RISKS!!!"[88] She rejects all survival strategies related to assimilation and conciliation by condemning the artists she understood as pandering to and placating a white racist power structure by creating artworks defined by subjugation and submission rather than by subversion. Aware of her minimal impact in the wake of her performance, she admits that "nobody listened to her, of course." She was left with a poignant and unanswered speculation: "She wondered if the time would ever come when black artists could act with agency—as originators, not recipients."[89]

Now, in 2022, the fate of *Mademoiselle Bourgeoise Noire* appears radically different. O'Grady acknowledges an apparently newly egalitarian art world in which "*Mlle Bourgeoise Noire* herself has been welcomed into the museum."[90] This "welcome," however, comes with no guarantees that anyone listens, even now. O'Grady explains, "Of course, this might be seen as the co-opting of black artists and black artwork by the white art world, the usual form of neutralization."[91] As she realizes, the many guises of white supremacy remain powerful by adapting to shifting political contexts. This white supremacist "neutralization" strategy works to commit very real violences against Black female subjectivities and Black female art practices by endorsing equally deliberate strategies of visibilization to invisibilize and inclusion to exclude.

Black female subjectivities and experiences remain integral to O'Grady's protest aesthetic. She recognizes a danger rooted in the past that shows no sign of losing strength in a white-dominant imaginary. The devastating damage resulting from a white supremacist scopic lens ensures that, "it is the African female who, by virtue of color and feature and the extreme metaphors of enslavement, is at the outermost reaches of 'otherness.'"[92] Aware that, as far as concerns the Black woman's corporeal existence, "we find a body that is always already colonized," O'Grady has developed a revolutionary visual and textual language that equips a "body that has been raped, maimed, murdered" with a "healthy present."[93]

"I want to see myself as a calm reconciler of opposites,"[94] O'Grady admits. She understands, however, that her longing for a resolution remains unfulfilled. She insists, "I am in a state of 'permanent rebellion' against the either/or binaries underpinning Western culture."[95] She theorizes her rejection of these "opposites" and "either/or binaries" and the "tension, and the anger and alertness it provokes" as evidence of "strength in my work" and as a source of emotional power, political persuasion, moral force, and social transformation in her practice.[96] She declares that "if artists and theorists of color were to develop and sustain our critical flexibility, we could cause a permanent interruption in Western 'either:or-ism.'"[97]

For O'Grady, only if "artists and theorists of color" can create and maintain an individual and collective "critical flexibility," via a malleable and multilayered visual, textual, and performative language, will it become possible to "uncover tools of our own with which to dismantle the house of the master."[98] O'Grady reveals her debt to the groundbreaking theoretical work of Audre Lorde, a visionary feminist, political radical, and social justice revolutionary. Lorde knew that the tools of the master would "never dismantle the master's house." O'Grady makes a way out of no way and arrives at her own "loophole" of liberation.[99] She recognizes the failures of the "tools of the master" and hopes that, while these "tools" necessarily fail, perhaps the "tools of our own"—that is, the tools made by centuries of historically enslaved, self-liberated, and free people fighting for freedom—can succeed in liberating Black art from the stranglehold of white supremacist power. Worn out by the difficulties she faces in a prejudicial and persecutory white mainstream U.S. society, she takes heart from the fact that "becoming and being an artist is the only challenge I've never tired of."[100] For O'Grady, "the struggle goes on and on."[101] O'Grady's courageous performances and installations are testaments to her survival and to her rallying battle cry, "I'm still here."[102]

NARI WARD   *(Born in St. Andrew Parish, Jamaica, 1963)*

"I am a storyteller who enjoys conjuring works which are irreconcilable," says Nari Ward. Across his works, he endorses an experimental practice as defined by unsolvable paradoxes and unanswerable complexities. He creates multilayered visual narratives in which he defies exclusionary and dominant parameters of representation. "Celebration, nostalgia, repulsion, danger, abstraction, tragedy, and comedy are all performers within the vision I am creating," he explains, referring specifically to his commitment to representing a range of emotional and corporeal realities.[103] "I build drama from the use of found and everyday objects, merging physical information (materials) with memories, thoughts, experiences and questions."[104] Whereas O'Grady builds drama from the assumption of a fictional persona and repeated performative enactments, Ward generates hard-hitting emotional power by salvaging "found and everyday objects" as fallible emblems of material histories and as spiritual touchstones of memory.

Just as Leonardo Drew foregrounds the social, political, and cultural roles played by labor in his monumental sculptures, so Ward employs a labor-intensive practice. "I need to get involved with the physical aspect of the work first before it can emerge as a catalyst for a kind of mental connection," he explains.[105] While Drew explicitly connects his acts of physical labor with a history of slavery, Ward says, "I also feel my sense of labor has deep roots in my working class upbringing."[106] Ward's installations and assemblages generate a "mental connection" for his viewers by addressing issues related not only to the history of the transatlantic slave trade and slavery but also to the ongoing systems of economic poverty, class disenfranchisement, white racist persecution, and social exclusion facing people of color living in white supremacist dominant nations worldwide.

"Much of my work is about memory and mortality," Ward observes. He complicates this description, however, by noting that he does not "want to say 'death' because that carries too much baggage."[107] He commemorates the corporeal vulnerabilities, emotional complexities, and spiritual conflicts that are integral to the real struggles for existence endured by women, children, and men living and dying across the African diaspora. Ward sheds further light on the psychological rationale undergirding his determination to work with found objects: "I think I always felt that instead of starting with the blank canvas or page it would be simultaneously more problematic and meaningful to use materials or elements which already have a history," he explains.[108] Ward defies the social isolationism and exclusionary bias of the "blank canvas or page," which he interprets as a luxury only white privileged artists can afford. Instead, he endorses a powerful act of resistance by working with used "materials or elements," explaining that "the dysfunctional or discarded hold a sense of hopefulness as well as vulnerability, which appeals to my way of seeing the world."[109] Ward dispenses with the artificiality of the "blank canvas or page," which he criticizes for having no relevance to real lives, to work instead with materials and elements that carry the physical evidence of the history of human struggle. He works respectfully with dysfunctional and discarded objects to memorialize the lives of dysfunctional and discarded people in equally respectful and humanizing ways.

Ward sorrowfully recalls 1990s Harlem as a "desolate and crime-ridden neighborhood."[110] "There was a lot of flight: people were leaving their apartments, buildings were being abandoned," he remembers.[111] As an artist dedicated to developing a recuperative practice to heal a wounded environment, he honors a history of vulnerability across his works. The objects and materials he found on the streets during this period had been discarded by unknown individuals, who had themselves equally been discarded and who did not matter in a white supremacist nation. Ward refused to leave these artifacts to destruction. Instead, he undertook their rescue by "bringing them in" and "dragging them up the five flights of steps" in his apartment block.[112] Almost immediately, however, he faced very real opposition from his neighbors. "Other people in the building felt threatened because they didn't know what I was doing with all this stuff," he recalls.[113] The sense of threat

▶▶ "Pain and Suffering and Transformation"

experienced by his neighbors derived from the fact that "they related my activity to being a homeless person, not an artist."[114] Their misperceptions had immediate and personal consequences for Ward: he was evicted from the building. The collective response of the building's inhabitants to the introduction of a discarded person's pain and trauma into their environment taught him a lifelong lesson. "An artist represented an unknown danger," Ward realized. "It was a revelatory experience for me."[115]

Ward fully embraces the role of the artist as an emblem of the unknown and a symbol of danger. He remains committed through his process of salvage to "finding things on the street that are discarded and in a state of distress" in order to "transform them into something else."[116] At the heart of his practice is his search for an answer to his lifelong question: "How do you talk about connectedness and this element of pain and suffering and transformation without going into specific histories of that representation?"[117] Ward's artworks memorialize the "pain and suffering" of these abandoned objects by resisting all dominant practices that reduce them to their "specific histories" or individual contexts. He deliberately avoids providing a meticulous investigation into each salvaged object's "specific histor[y]." Rather, he reimagines and recreates their emotional realities in order to do justice to their untold stories of human struggle more generally. As he explains, "I was able to look at all these remnants that people left behind and they really inspired me to see the narrative in each of those found objects."[118]

Across his practice, Ward endorses a new visual language in which human dignity, equality, and respect are the defining foundations of his "lexicons of liberation." He creates alternative imaginaries by transforming found objects that are not only abandoned but in "a state of distress" into "something else." His radical protest aesthetic is defined by inclusion rather than exclusion and by an honoring of, and an empathetic engagement with, all human experiences and all lived realities. In his multilayered process, "materials" and elements" that are testaments to "pain and suffering" undergo a process of political and psychological "transformation." Their adaptation and recreation, prior to their insertion into his emotionally powerful assemblages, mean that they no longer circulate solely as signifiers of their previous owner's exposure to trauma in a daily fight for survival. Rather, each of these materials and elements are given a new life by operating as the foundations for radical and transformative acts of agency, artistry, and activism. As the building blocks of his radical artworks in which he foregrounds narratives of possibility, these salvaged materials are no mementos to loss. Instead, they are catalysts to alternative histories. In his reclamatory and revelatory practice, they are testaments to healing rather than wounding, to redemption rather than abandonment, and to creation through preservation rather than destruction.

"A lot of my ideas within the work are really about empowerment," Ward declares.[119] Working to create artworks of survival out of a history of human experiences as defined by destitution and suffering, his practice comes to life from his many questions, "How do you empower yourself as an artist and as a person? How do you claim your own image?"[120] For Ward, there is only one answer: "You create a layered dialogue with a material."[121] At the same time that he self-confessedly memorializes human experiences of emotional suffering and material destitution in his works, Ward creates a "layered dialogue" to liberate their revolutionary and transformative possibilities: "undeniably there is a physicality and a power."[122]

In 1993, Ward installed *Amazing Grace* (figure 37), a site-specific work built from salvaged objects, in a public building in Harlem. Clarifying the origins of his project, he explains, "I decided to collect all the baby strollers that were abandoned, especially those that were used by so-called marginalized people to collect their bottles and cans."[123] This work of artistic salvage reflects his vision of social justice: "For me strollers speak so much about things that are neglected."[124] The reusage and re-creation of the baby stroller in *Amazing Grace* received its inspiration from Ward's realization that it had "gone through being a vessel of potentiality with this new child being placed in it and pushed into the world; and then being used by somebody who's sort of been marginalized and somehow categorized as a failure."[125]

On the one hand, according to Ward's "lexicon of liberation," an abandoned baby stroller signifies as an object of optimism, a "vessel of potentiality" used by parents for a new child. As such, it represents an

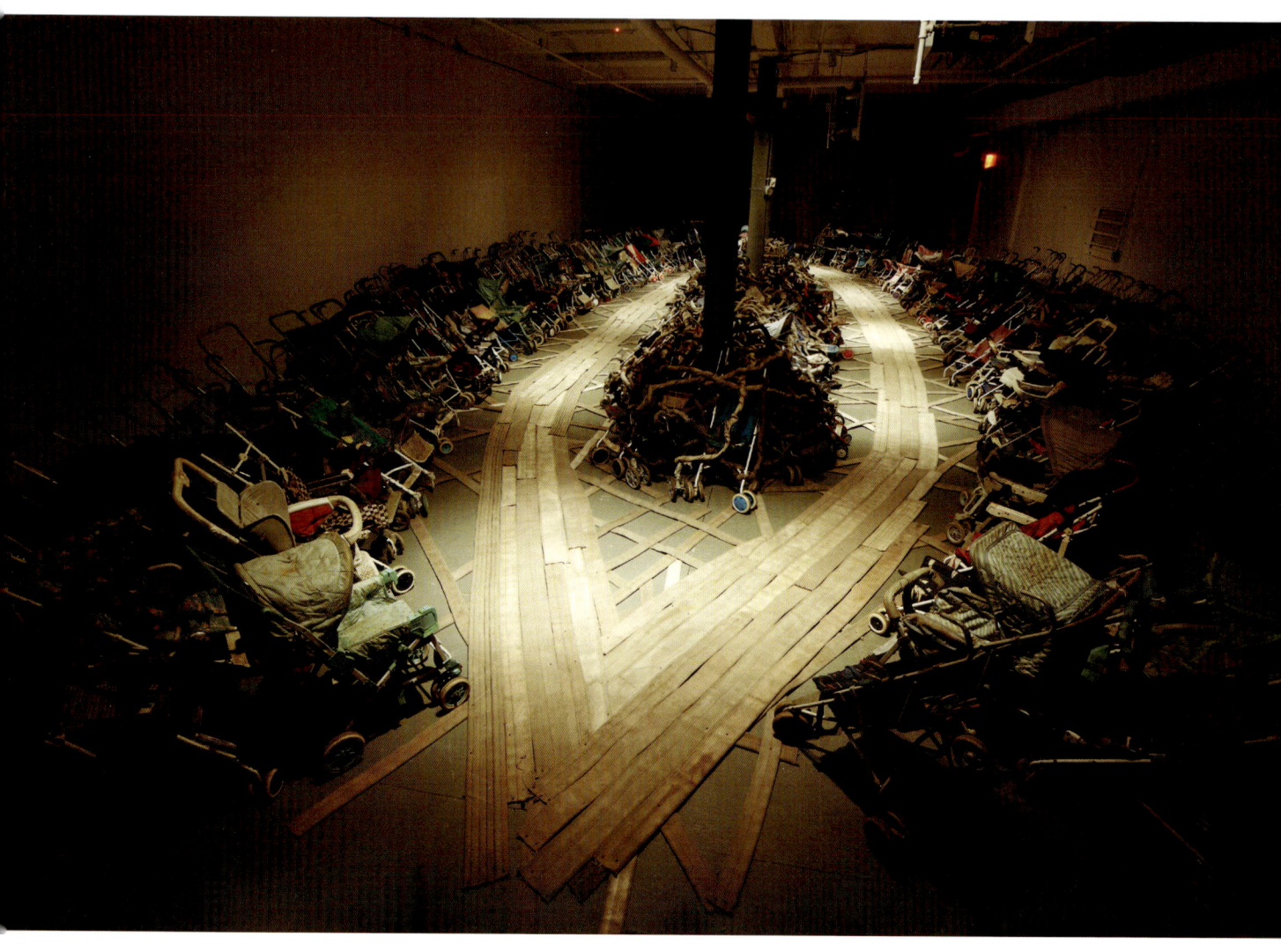

FIGURE 37. Nari Ward, *Amazing Grace*.
Installation view, 1993. Approx. three
hundred baby strollers and fires hoses
(dimensions variable). Private collection.
Photo: Jesse Untracht-Oakner. Courtesy of
the artist, the New Museum and Lehmann
Maupin, New York and Hong Kong.

inspirational celebration of the redemptive power of family and of intergenerational survival. On the other hand, however, the thrown-away baby stroller functions as an artifact of alienation and even annihilation when used by "marginalized" people for the movement not only of their possessions but also of their bottles and cans. These bottles and cans represent a "marginalized" person's courageous means of surviving an unimaginably painful, physically harrowing, and emotionally destitute state of nonexistence. Ward develops an artistic practice in which he visibilizes an invisibilized people and in which he interprets the lives of individuals "categorized as a failure" as successes by honoring their strategies of survival. He relies on these baby strollers "to talk about the crisis in the community, but also the community's potential."[126] In Ward's radical reinterpretation in *Amazing Grace*, the baby stroller is a symbol not only of desolation and deprivation but of the potential for social, political, cultural, and emotional transformation in the promise represented by future generations. He summarizes, "My strategy was not to collect just one or two beat-up strollers, but 365 of them, one for each day to make up a whole year."[127] Ward determined to trace a whole year and comes to grips with natural cycles of birth and death and beginnings and endings across all the seasons of human existence.

Ward's 365 abandoned baby strollers became a source of disruption at the Studio Museum, where he was working on *Amazing Grace*, much like his earlier experience bringing found materials into his apartment building. Just as his neighbors had felt "threatened," Ward admits that the "curators thought I was having a nervous breakdown or something; they came to me and said, 'What are you going to do with these? You can't do anything here, we don't have space for them.'"[128] This time, however, the anxious response to his acts of salvage did not result in personal difficulties. Rather, Ward remembers that the curators' emotional unease had a beneficial result: it made "me realize that I had to think about where I was going to exhibit them."[129] "I thought I needed a church," he recalled.[130] No church being available, Ward compromised and "found a firehouse next to the church."[131] This location not only offered the necessary physical space in which to include all 365 baby strollers but also provided him with additional salvaged materials. He incorporated the surviving remnants of

disused fire hoses into this site-specific work. "Apart from water, a fire hose brings in life," Ward affirms. "It also stands for conduits, passageways, information that passes from one thing to the next."[132] *Amazing Grace* is an installation in which Ward bears witness to all the stages of human existence, encompassing physical journeys, emotional transitions, and imaginative transformations.

Ward creates artworks that communicate their emotional and political connection to an individual's and a community's struggles for existence. He recruits his audiences from the real people fighting for survival in a "desolate and crime-ridden neighborhood." On these grounds, the location of *Amazing Grace* was vitally important, as it allowed him to "get people from the neighborhood involved in the work; because I didn't really feel that comfortable about the white cube" of the gallery space.[133] As he explains, "I wanted to see—bring something that they were somehow familiar with, which is the everyday object; and then build up on that."[134] Ward insists that "it would never have worked in a gallery environment the way it did there."[135] He is an anti-elitist artist who not only rejects the "blank page or canvas" but also the sterile and contextless environment of the "white cube." As an antidote to these dehumanizing contexts, he builds a physically intimate and emotionally accessible relationship with his audiences.

"Once I got into the firehouse—this narrow, long space—it helped me figure out the formation that I wanted," Ward recalls.[136] He arranged the 365 baby strollers in the outline of a boat. In his initial vision for this work, he admits, "I wasn't thinking of a boat form" but "I was actually thinking of a womb."[137] The womb, as an icon of maternal power and familial survival, foregrounds and emphasizes his association of this installation with "potentiality." And yet, when he "started this notion of the womb" and began "articulating it in the drawing of this layout, I started to get depressed, because I thought, 'Oh my God, this piece is so heavy, so sad.'"[138] Two questions burdened him: "How am I going to pull this back? How am I going to bring it into another emotional space?"[139] He admits that "the boat was a good coincidence": it "actually tied into all these other narratives that happened by chance in some respect."[140] According to Ward's aesthetic vision, the boat was no mind-body-and-soul-destroying icon or reductive symbol that closed off meaning but rather one that represented multiple narratives and a myriad of possibilities. For Ward, the decision to replicate the contours of a ship enabled him to fulfill an overall goal: "I was really directed by the redemption of these objects."[141] As he explains, "*Amazing Grace* is about a redemption and transformation."[142]

Amazing Grace endorses an individual's capacity for redemption and transformation. Ward focuses on humanity's spiritual power rather than its mortal fallibility. Concerned that a layer was missing, he chose to add a soundtrack. "I remembered that my father used to always play Mahalia Jackson in our home," Ward recalls. "I wanted to find something from her repertoire and 'Amazing Grace' came to mind," and so this "uplifting" song "entered into the work."[143] An emotional song that eulogizes one person's search for spiritual salvation, *Amazing Grace* was no arbitrary choice for Ward. "The song goes: 'I once was lost, but now I'm found,'" he recites.[144] Here he creates no dystopian installation. Instead, he generates a space for utopian possibility for this work by focusing on *Amazing Grace* as "a song about redemption and change."[145] The song celebrates the promise of being emotionally and spiritually "found," and Ward comments that "it became the necessary element of hope I felt the work needed."[146]

At the heart of Ward's decision to include *Amazing Grace* as the soundtrack to his installation of the same name is the conflicted life story of one historical figure in particular: the song's white British composer, a slave ship captain and enslaver named John Newton. As "a gospel standard that was written by a slave trader," "Amazing Grace" mythologizes Newton's moral transformation and search for spiritual salvation.[147] As Ward summarizes, "The story goes that [Newton] was . . . caught at sea in a storm; and in desperation and in fear of losing his life, he got down on the ground and prayed to God to save him, and that if he . . . was saved he would stop this nasty business of the slave trade."[148] Contrary to any such idealistic interpretation, however, the official records show that Newton experienced only a spiritual epiphany and not a shift in his moral compass during this storm, which occurred during his return from a barbaric, immoral, and inhumane operation in which he had been responsible for enslaving people in West Africa in March 1748. No real change of heart

took place: Newton undertook three more voyages as a captain of ships of enslaved people from 1750 until 1754. While he may have found religion during a storm at sea, it was a religion benefitting white enslaving elites only and in no way prevented Newton's willful and inhumane participation in the "nasty business" of profiting from the enslavement of women, children, and men. If Newton experienced any transformation, it was surface only and the result of self-interest and pragmatic necessity. The details of his biography confirm that Newton did not choose but instead had no choice but to give up his life as an enslaver, due to a sudden illness that confined him to land. Newton became a religious minister years later in 1764 and penned the words for "Amazing Grace" as late as 1772, over two decades after the storm at sea and his widely celebrated moment of redemption that was only a performance and a lie.

Ward's memorialization of a mythologized understanding of Newton's moral conversion and spiritual transformation betrays the political urgency undergirding his preferred focus on this story in his installation. "It's really about transformation. So I felt it was perfect, because I didn't really want this piece to be . . . sad," declares Ward.[149] His self-consciously idealistic imagining of Newton's conversion reintroduces the promise of hope into the installation. According to his perspective, if John Newton—a murderous, torturing, abusive, and human rights violating white enslaver—can experience a spiritual transformation, the implication is anyone can, however morally depraved and emotionally destitute.

Ward's decision to evoke the traumatizing reality of the centuries-long institution of the transatlantic slave trade via his inclusion of *Amazing Grace* ensures that the associations between the "boat form" and a slave ship are incontestable in his installation. In Ward's reimagining, the baby strollers gain heightened psychological power by representing the bodies of enslaved people captured and confined on ships by white murderous enslavers like Newton. Newton himself recorded the position of enslaved people incarcerated on these ships during the Middle Passage: "the slaves lie in two rows, one above the other, on each side of the ship," he wrote, "close to each other, like books upon a shelf. I have known them so close that the shelf would not, easily, contain one more."[150] Ward summarizes his deliberate placement of these baby strollers as follows: "There are some that are on the sides that are on the side that are sort of like [a] witness to these other forms that are sort of in the middle that are tied down."[151] Here he relies on a metaphorical umbilical cord to tie together the violences and traumas endured by Black people during enslavement with the violences and traumas endured by contemporary generations fighting for survival in a white supremacist society. For Ward, the baby stroller is a symbol of past, present, and future acts of torture, murder, persecution, and discrimination as constantly enacted against Black people by white supremacist power structures that refuse to die.

In *Amazing Grace* and elsewhere, Ward prioritizes "my perspective for being part of the minority class or in some ways, the invisible class."[152] He explains, "I have a regard to invest in those kind of things and find a way to give them a moment of importance."[153] In his practice, Ward commits to assuming multiple roles as "a kind of socially conscious artist as well as a liberated artist or trickster."[154] As an idealistic visionary, political protester, and human rights advocate, he remains dedicated to an anti-didactic, anti-explanatory, and anti-self-evident revolutionary aesthetic philosophy.

Ward rejects socially prescriptive and morally doctrinaire art on the grounds that such dogmatic tactics make it too easy for audiences to be alienated, detached, and, if unmoved, entirely unengaged. "It's easy to get people to shut down," he says. "It's really easy: you just get mad and scream."[155] As he realizes, however, "Once you're the screaming guy, it's easy to keep you outside."[156] Searching for a revolutionary antidote to white dominant exclusionary practices, Ward commits to self-reflexive strategies of subversive play and canny subterfuge. He sees "liberated artist" as a "trickster," is the only way to survive inside the white dominant power structure. "If you're the guy who's the mischievous friend, you can come in," Ward maintains, jubilantly declaring, "You can really mess everything up then."[157]

CHAKAIA BOOKER   *(Born in Newark, New Jersey, 1953)*

"I am an abstract, narrative environmental sculptor whose work acknowledges the struggles and the victories in human aspiration and involvement," declares Chakaia Booker.[158] She creates intellectually and politically challenging nonfigurative, highly abstract, and experimental sculptures that foreground a hard-hitting emotional power by refusing to lose sight of her life-defining focus on human struggle. Booker is an activist-artist who remains as committed to subversive strategies of political dissidence as Nari Ward. She explains that "my art focuses on social and cultural issues, on being female, and on the creative diversity of found objects which are metamorphosed into works of art."[159] For Booker, the "creative diversity" of her salvaged materials stimulates her investigation into an array of "social and cultural issues." A determination to work with emotionally charged topics related to the centuries-long struggles for civil rights, economic equality, and political representation by disenfranchised peoples across the world defines her practice. As she explains, "when you're working with found materials, each one comes with its own purpose, history, and use."[160] For Booker, as for Ward, Drew, Pinder, and Scott, "found materials" carry the psychological and spiritually weighted memory of their original purpose, material history, and practical use. More especially, as Ward and Drew foreground the physical intensity of their labor, so Booker admits that the "process of creating the kind of work that I do demands great physical and creative energy."[161]

While Booker confirms the "great physical and creative energy" required by creating artworks that meditate "on social and cultural issues" and "on being female," she insists that the "determining factor" of her art-making practice is not gender": rather "it is commitment." Ultimately, as Booker says, the "actual creation of the work has to do with commitment: understanding the process and finding ways and the means to create it."[162]

▶▶ "Emotional and Physical Scarring"

"I began using discarded pieces of wood, metal, then rubber tires and inner tubes," explains Booker.[163] While she experimented with a wide variety of found objects, "rubber tires and inner tubes" soon became her almost exclusive focus. "Among the reasons for my use of discarded tires is when I began creating larger sculptures I saw that old tires were easily available and easily accessible," she explains.[164] Her prediction that there "will always be rubber," due to the fact that "tires can last up to 2,000 years," suggests that her decision to forge her sculptures from these industrialized materials was by no means only a practical decision.[165] Her works are a consciousness-raising investigation into the damaging relationship between human-made and seemingly invincible objects and a vulnerable natural environment that is highly susceptible to industrial destruction.

For Booker, discarded tires are thematically and symbolically integral to the emotional and political force of her sculptures. In recognition of the fact that "one of the major concerns of my work has been our relationship to the environment and our responsibility for contamination of the environment," she explains, "I saw and still see the recycling of old tires as a contribution to the resolution of the issues involved, both realistically and symbolically."[166] As visual icons, political emblems, and emotional catalysts, Booker's ripped apart, torn, and reworked discarded tires enable her to debate issues related to our collective and individual "responsibility" for the "contamination of the environment."[167] In 2022 these difficulties gain rather than lose momentum. The escalating destruction has resulted in an unprecedented environmental crisis and is caused not only by climate change but also by Western governing bodies whose abusive responses to ecological challenges run a gamut from outright denial to willful ignorance.

"Echoes in Black (Industrial Cicatrization) deals with scarification—the processes of emotional and physical scarring that people go through as they live: class, race, and labor, which are universal problems," summarizes Booker regarding an awe-inspiring work she created in 1997.[168] A monumental sculpture, Echoes in Black is materially, emotionally, and imaginatively overwhelming. This sculpture comes to life from fourteen panels she intimately positioned side by side. The work consists of interlocking and divergent layers of ripped, broken, and re-formed discarded pieces of black rubber tires.

At the same time that Booker relies on an abstract visual lexicon, the textured surfaces are characterized by fracture and fragmentation. Their broken layers provide a hard-hitting visual testament to the "emotional and physical scarring" experienced by individuals experiencing discrimination because of their race and class within capitalist Western societies. A psychologically and physically dominating work, Echoes in Black denies both the artist and her audiences any emotional safe ground. She interrupts the corporeal sterility of the white cube space of the contemporary western gallery by mounting onto its walls a work that pushes herself and her viewers to their spiritual, political, and imaginative limits and emotional breaking points.

On the surface, Booker endorses a nonfigurative visual language in Echoes in Black. If we look more closely, however, the forcibly broken apart and piled-up tire pieces begin to resemble human body parts. The viewer is left with unanswerable questions related to the struggles for human existence. Is Echoes in Black a partially exhumed burial ground? Or a battlefield that is smoldering after brutal conflict? Is it a razed city whose flames are still burning? Or a poisoned landscape in which all the foliage is dead and dying? Could it be that it is the site of a natural disaster? Or is the heaped-up rubble all that is left following a human-made atrocity? Booker's decision to title this sculpture Echoes in Black (Industrial Cicatrization) communicates her protest against the ways in which industrialized, dehumanized manufacturing necessarily results in irretrievable damage or "scarring" not only to the natural environment but to individual lives. Similarly, the phrase "Echoes in Black" underscores her emphasis on the "emotional and physical scarring" that continues to be generated by divides of all kinds, summarized by her reference to "class, race, and labor."

If Echoes in Black is a hard-hitting meditation on the traumatizing effects of wounding via an "emotional and physical scarring," it also provides hope for the possibility of healing. Cicatrization can be defined as the process by which a wound heals via the generation of scar tissue. Booker's practice of ripping tires apart to create an interlocking structure produces her own symbolic form of protective layering. Her shredded tires symbolize the new skin that has the potential to end the pain of a person, a class, and even an entire race. The torn apart, broken, and ruptured surfaces represent her investigation into an individual's responsibility in securing the salvation not only of the natural environment but of society as a whole. As Nari Ward is a trickster with a social conscience, so Chakaia Booker is a radical creator who relies on her revolutionary practice to reenvision new realities and create new worlds.

"People have a tendency to want to touch the work," Booker says of the monumental sculptures she has forged from layers of cascading tire parts.[169] "Touch is important," she explains: "You can't separate intelligence from the hands-on experience."[170] She invites her audiences to engage physically as well as emotionally and intellectually with her sculptures. "You can't live in your head too long because you won't get all the information you need just by thinking it," she insists. "Once you touch your material, it comes alive."[171] This haptic response from her audiences ensures the sculptures become imaginatively, socially, and materially alive. Booker defies all forms of social, political, cultural, emotional, imaginative, and material barriers, insisting, "My quest is always for greater creative freedom with an intention of connection, continuity, and commitment."[172]

LEONARDO DREW   *(Born in Tallahassee, Florida, 1961)*

"My work and my self are not separate," Leonardo Drew states. "They are the same thing."[173] While Chakaia Booker maintains that her "work expresses my observations of life," Drew sees his work as his life.[174] Working with fabricated rather than found materials, he creates psychologically powerful, politically provocative, and imaginatively awe-inspiring sculptures. Across his bodies of work, he does justice to the lived realities within his individual autobiography as well as within the collective biographies belonging to women, men, and children fighting for survival across the African diaspora. "I have studied fine arts, and I'm aware of a tradition and history which has informed my thoughts," he explains. "Being a Black individual talking about a Black experience, there is no way that I can be really true to myself and not speak about being an African-American."[175] Drew accomplishes this not only by speaking but also by reimagining, re-representing, and re-creating a "Black experience" within his sculptures. "I hope when I am no longer here these pieces will stand out as statements on Black historical memory which demanded attention," he declares.[176]

In defiance of his own mortality, Drew's pieces are monuments to immortality. His focus on "Black historical memory" centers on investigating the centuries-long institution of U.S. slavery as a source of violence and violation whose harrowing legacies are far from over. Drew expresses his lifelong hope that his works will "stand out" "in a way which allows everyone to participate and react." While he generates a powerful emotional connection with his audiences in order to stimulate their active engagement with his psychological and political priorities, he refuses to lose sight of the reality that the "weight of my ancestry still continues in my work."[177]

"My days are 16 to 18-hour days; big days are 20-hour days, with four hours of sleep in the room," Drew confides.[178] He takes himself to his physical and emotional breaking point on a daily basis. In an interview in 2019, Drew summarizes his labor: "It's like weight-lifting, I end up with a body cut like a slave. I'm a slave master and slave rolled into one. It is blood, sweat, and tears. And, at 58, I'm surprised that I'm able to keep up with the work, because the sheer physical demands are really monstrous."[179] His commitment to backbreaking labor allows him to honor the generations of physical work undertaken by enslaved people. His physically exhausting practice bears witness to the untold history of the centuries of enslaved labor that made the wealth of Western nations possible. This reality has not only been minimized, distorted, and outright denied by white racist governments but entirely eradicated within

▶▶ *"Weight of My Ancestry"*

white supremacist dominant narratives of nation-building. Drew's commitment to intense physical labor as the foundation for his art-making practices embodies his protest against slavery as a traumatizing reality in which individuals were routinely taken to their physical and emotional limits by being forced to perform mind-body-and-soul-destroying labor. Drew testifies to the "blood, sweat, and tears" that undergirds centuries of enslaved labor: his sculptures exist because he subjects himself to repeated tests of bodily and mental endurance. As enslaved people lived lives of physical and emotional suffering, pain, and trauma, so Drew endorses an artistic process in which suffering is his only defining reality.

Number 25 is one among many psychologically and politically provocative sculptures in which Drew memorializes the sufferings, struggles, and sacrifices embedded within an intergenerational "Black historical memory" (figure 38). An awe-inspiring work he created in 1992, *Number 25* is a "huge cotton wall" Drew forged from numerous handmade cotton bales that he positioned one on top of the other to form a grid.[180] Drew's "epic scale" bears witness to the physical and psychological enormity of cotton as a material that singlehandedly carries the "weight of my ancestry."[181] "You have to be extremely responsible when you pick up material like that," he insists. "You can't just pick it up and use it."[182] He works to gain control of this psychologically weighted and historically burdened material by readily admitting that the dispassionate structure of the grid provides him with "my basis of sanity."[183] "Otherwise it would just be noise," he concedes, explaining, "these things are loud, but if you know what to listen for, they'll speak to you."[184] While he succeeds in ordering his cotton bales into a grid, their patterned textures, unique threads, and loosened ends threaten their stability. Drew relies on corporeally and spiritually charged materials that refuse to be contained within any such rational system to introduce the very real possibility that he as an artist, no less than his audiences, will be overpowered by the unstoppable force of their physical and emotional weight.

"Cotton has a memory," Drew states, all too painfully aware that "it has a history. It is not something that is picked at random, it is something that has a life of its own."[185] If cotton is a material with a memory that has

a "life of its own," then Drew's *Number 25* is a sculpture that has many lives and memories of its own. While the sculpture does not include figurative representations of enslaved bodies, the unique construction and individualized patterning emphasizes the significance of the cotton bales as symbols of and surrogates for the untold lives of untold numbers of enslaved people devastated and destroyed by cotton labor camp production. Burdened by ancestral memory, cotton testifies to the hidden histories of enslaved labor in which Black bodies were broken, bruised, and brutalized. His painstakingly constructed cotton bales show signs of physical stress in an array of material imperfections. For Drew, their material distress speaks to the physical and psychological suffering endured by enslaved people during the processes of cotton manufacture. Drew's *Number 25* is a work on a "heavy subject" he created by "working with material which has memory."[186] He exposes the myopic assumptions of white audiences, stating, "if I weren't standing in front of my work, maybe you wouldn't even consider the idea that this is a Black person dealing with cotton."[187]

For Drew, a lifelong commitment to a labor-intensive practice is the only way in which he is able to begin to interrogate the "emotional weight" of cotton's history.[188] He readily admits to the exhaustion he experienced regarding his handmade process in creating *Number 25*. According to his conviction, the only way to do justice to the historical memory of emotionally burdened materials such as cotton is by undertaking intensive physical labor, through which he replicates and respects the laboring lives of enslaved people of all ages and genders across the African diasporic world.

Number 26, a sculpture Drew created in 1992, is also a monumental work (Figure 39). This sculpture comes to life not from hand-made cotton bales but from canvas, rust, and wood. The work pushes both artist and audiences to come to grips with the enormity of the sufferings of enslaved people who had no choice but to undertake mind-body-and-soul-destroying labor. Here, Drew hangs multiple weathered bags he hand-made in a labor-intensive process from four horizontal wooden bars. In his labor-intensive practice, he painstakingly fabricates each of these aged sacks. As a result, the bags are uniquely stained, individually torn, personally stressed, and hand-damaged. As with *Number 25*, his

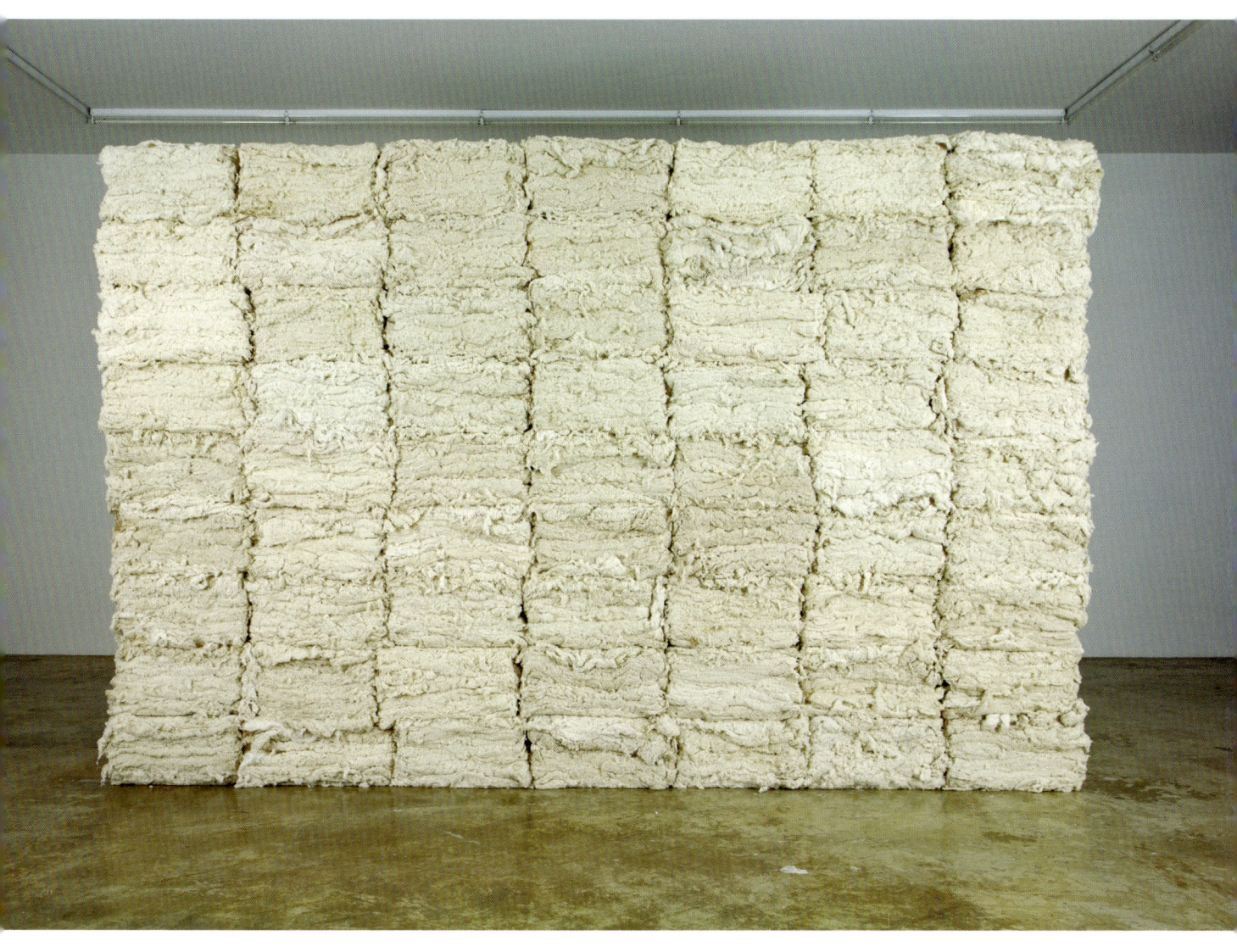

FIGURE 38. Leonardo Drew, *Number 25*, 1992.
Cotton (108 × 120 × 46 in.). Copyright Leonardo
Drew. Image courtesy of Rubell Family Collection,
Miami, and Sikkema Jenkins and Co., New York.

labor intensive practice in creating *Number 26* ensures that the work releases maximum spiritual, emotional, and political power. The psychological and political associations between the injured surfaces of these mutilated and maimed sacks and the injured bodies of enslaved individuals in this traumatized and traumatizing sculpture could not be more self-evident. Their overlapping and interlocking proximity to one another visually signifies the "tight packing" of enslaved peoples of all ages onto ships in which enslaved people were incarcerated by white avaricious enslavers. Similarly, the visual association between the broken bags hanging from wooden bars and the tortured and murdered bodies hanging from trees during lynchings could not be more emotionally unequivocal.

"All this stuff is fabricated in the studio. Very rarely have I actually used actual objects," Drew explains.[189] "They look found, but they only echo found," he adds, admitting the importance of the artist's role. "You can become the weather, you can put things in the process of aging."[190] According to Drew's practice of artificially "aging" his materials, what would seem to be an act of destruction is made possible only by the art of creation. More especially, in *Number 26* Drew employs rust as a tool by which he weathers his cotton sacks, explaining, "Rust is part of the continuum of decay."[191] An especially heavy subject, rust functions as a material burdened by an emotionally and politically loaded memory. Here and elsewhere, Drew relies on rust as a material, metaphor, and practical means by which he grapples with experiences related to the physical loss, mental suffering, and spiritual destruction endured by African diasporic people worldwide.

Drew's refusal to title his works rests the social and political responsibility of interpreting his works firmly on his audiences. Titles like *Number 25* and *Number 26* invite his audiences' empathetic engagement with the emotional realities and political truths of his sculptures on their own terms. Drew insists that "even when we move into abstract painting, there is still the weight and heaviness in the work of most of the Black abstract painters that I've seen and known."[192] For Drew, the emotional power of "Black historical memory" guarantees that the abstract language not only of Black painters but also of Black sculptors is always indivisible from political protest and psychological trauma. "I want to

be there in the moment actually grieving, experiencing, speaking from a place of truth," he explains. "If there is no truth in it, then why bother?"[193]

A defining source of inspiration for Drew's sculptures was his visit to Gorée Island off the coast in Dakar, Senegal. A historical site of centuries of atrocities and abuses during the transatlantic slave trade and slavery, Gorée Island is infamous as one of the geographical locations for the enforced embarkation of untold millions of women, children, and men during the Middle Passage. "He viewed quarters where slaves were held before being shipped to America"—a heartbreaking and mind-body-and-soul-destroying experience.[194] "You start realizing certain things about yourself," he admits, adding "not just as an individual but in terms of your history and your collective history, and where your people are from and how they got here."[195] If interpreted through this psychological lens and experiential reality, Drew's sculptures are unequivocal testaments to his determination to come to grips with the unimaginable scale and unimaginable cost of slavery. He meditates on the enormity, not only of the numbers of the untold millions of individuals who were bought and sold during the transatlantic slave trade and slavery, but of the mental, emotional, and physical suffering that they endured over the generations. In his sculptures, he memorializes the "long history" of enslavement as not only the "very test of the spirit" but also of the mind, imagination, and body. Claudia Schmuckli summarizes the very real impact Drew's visit had on his practice, writing, "Drew left Gorée Island with deeply ingrained images of confinement, of bodies jammed and stuffed into spaces so small that death, not life, was the norm. This notion of suffocating density found its way into his work: layering and stacking, filling and emptying, construction and deconstruction became defining characteristics of Drew's artistic process."[196]

"You tell yourself, and most African Americans tell themselves, when they go to Africa, that they're going back home," Drew states, only to admit that, for himself, this belief was more myth than reality.[197] Rather than experiencing a sense of belonging, he suffered an overwhelming feeling of physical rupture, emotional dislocation, and spiritual loss. He poignantly describes it as "a shock to the system."[198] This overwhelming exposure

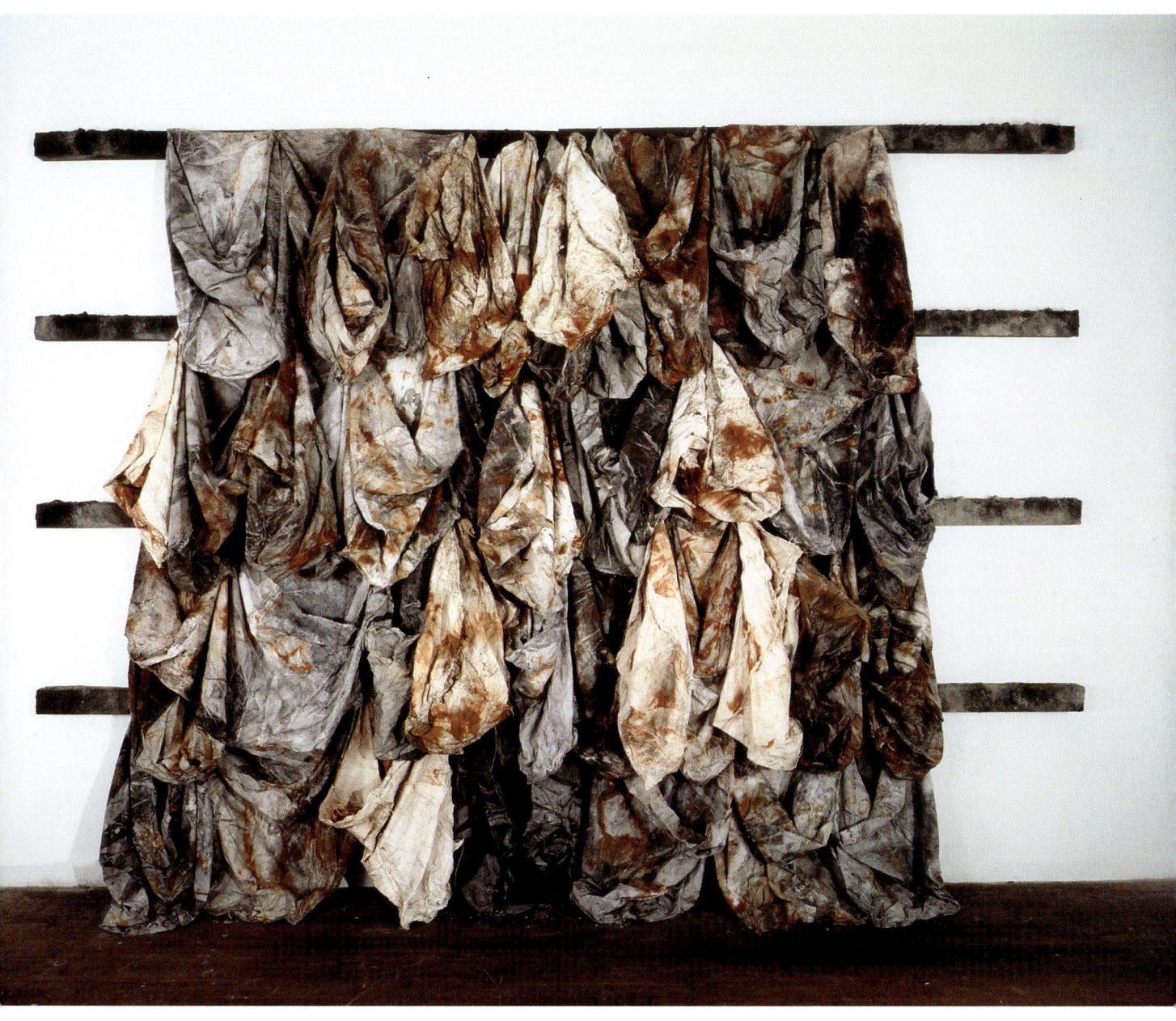

FIGURE 39. Leonardo Drew, *Number 26*, 1992. Canvass, rust, and wood (120 × 168 × 6 in.). Photo: John Berens. Copyright Leonardo Drew. Image courtesy of Sikkema Jenkins and Co., New York.

to suffering defines his practice. While he was fully aware that "our ancestors are from there [Africa]," his monumental works bear witness to the heartbreaking reality, "I was not prepared."[199] Drew bears witness to his sense of urgency in needing "to deal with" this "shock to the system" as an artist.[200] His commitment to "dealing with" this "monster of a history" as an artist defines his life's work. In so doing, he continues to put himself emotionally, physically, philosophically, intellectually, politically, and existentially at risk.[201] In an interview in 2019, Drew reiterated his earlier conviction that his practice is "like weightlifting" and results in "a body cut like a slave. I'm a slave master and slave rolled into one. It is blood, sweat, and tears."[202]

JEFFERSON PINDER   *(Born in Washington, District of Columbia, 1970)*

"Inspired by the symbiosis of music and the moving image, I portray the black body both frenetically and through drudgery in order to convey relevant cultural experiences."[203] So Jefferson Pinder describes his formally eclectic and labor-intensive practice. His own body, like Leonardo Drew's, operates as the site of corporeal and existential struggle. In radical and revolutionary acts and arts of individual and collective liberation, Pinder takes his body to a physical and psychological breaking point. In contrast to Drew's monumental sculptures, however, Pinder communicates his artistic and political vision through collage and video art. "My video work features stylized representations of performers working themselves through exhaustion to unveil genuine emotion," he explains. "My 'action videos' depict physical prowess with the body. The participants, in turn, communicate narratives through the physical tasks they perform."[204] For Pinder, both his own body and the bodies of his "participants," put under extreme physical stress in his performance pieces, provide a means by which he can extrapolate their psychological realities and personal histories.

"As an interdisciplinary artist, I create performances, video work, and objects that challenge viewers to think critically about our highly polarized society," explains Pinder.[205] Grappling with the United States as a nation torn apart by economic, social, and political inequalities, he uses his experimental practice to protest against the abuses generated by the interlocking forces of race, gender, and class oppression. He states, "I place no restrictions on the tools that I employ as an artist, working with materials as disparate as neon lighting and found items in my sculptural stylizations."[206] Pinder sets himself no formal or material limits. He shares Drew's commitment to carrying the "weight of my ancestry." Dedicated to representing the emotional and spiritual power of a "Black historical memory" through the art of salvage, he explains that "I find ways in which reclaimed materials convey rugged histories, relating them to a Black American experience."[207] His practice cuts to the heart of the emotional conflicts, corporeal struggles, and social challenges that are at the heart of a past, present, and future "Black American experience." As an artist turned social commentator, political activist, and radical intellectual, Pinder's sense of his mission is clear: "I explore the tangle of representations, visual tropes, and myths—referencing historical events and invoking cultural symbolism."[208]

Pinder is an intergenerational narrator, political memorialist, and revisionist historian. He describes his practice as "similar to archaeology and anthropology," adding, "I'm excavating pieces of information that will later be reconstructed to form a history, narrative or story."[209] He endorses a self-conscious process of material recreation, psychological reconstruction, and creative reimagining when it comes to generating public and private histories, narratives, and stories of Black lives. He creates artworks that are of the people, by the people, and for the people Pinder says of his video art in particular that "I see myself as a folk video artist."[210] More particularly, he expresses his commitment to "excavating and probing into the essence of black imagery," prompted by one overriding determination: "I'm searching for the heart of black identity."[211]

▶▶ "Heroics through Physical Articulation"

For Pinder, an examination of "black imagery" provides the interpretative lens through which he explores the emotional, social, cultural, and political "heart of black identity." He is a self-appointed interrogator and destabilizer of racially essentialist categorizations. "I play the role of social scientist and specimen" with a view to going "beyond the clichéd ways of looking at ethnicity," Pinder explains.[212] In his practice, he assumes the roles of "social scientist" and "specimen" not to collude in his own objectification, but to establish his ownership over the dehumanizing and derogatory caricatures of Black men that continue to dominate a white racist imaginary. Yet more powerfully, he exposes the reductive foundations of stereotypical formulations of ethnicity by focusing on the lives of Black people not as a homogenous mass but according to their individualized subjectivities and personal experiences. He takes his lived experiences as the psychological point of departure for his performance, video, and collage art: "My science is all about a personal search for history."[213]

"Quilting is an interest of mine," says Pinder. "I did a series of collage-quilts in 2003–2004."[214] "It was around the time when quilts were displayed around the country and it just kind of inspired me to start sewing paper," he explains.[215] The inspiration for Pinder's paper collages emerged from the touring exhibitions of the quilts created by generations of female artists living and working in Gee's Bend, Alabama. He remembers that "in the Quilts of Gee's Bend, one woman," almost certainly Mary Lee Bendolph whose practice is the focus of chapter 3, "used fragments of her dead husband's work clothes" as her source material.[216] Pinder readily recognizes African American women's quilts as a source of physical protection by celebrating their "power to keep you warm at night."[217] He also eulogizes these material objects' sacred status as spiritual carriers of an individual as well as a family's "blood, sweat, and tears."[218] In awe at the psychological and imaginative forces of this centuries-old quilt-making tradition, Pinder admits that a determination to honor the "blood, sweat, tears" of women, children, and men over the generations expresses "what I'm seeking to do with my work."[219] Pinder translates the emotionally charged processes of the Gee's Bend quilt-makers into the spiritual catalysts for his provocative collages.

While Pinder's monochrome collages appear to come to life from entirely abstract designs, he summarizes that "Some of the quilts depict the slave ship."[220] This series of collages he explicitly titled *Slave Ship Quilts* (2003). The emotional power of these paper works derives from his struggle with a sense of loss regarding his biographical origins. "I started thinking about the times I've been asked, 'Where are you from?'" he says. "I couldn't really say."[221] He courageously confronts his lack of knowledge regarding his ancestral roots by admitting, "something about the icon of the slave ship seemed to me representative of where I'm from."[222] Working not only to recuperate but to recreate and reimagine the "icon of the slave ship" as "representative of where I'm from," his *Slave Ship Quilts* consist of sewn together paper collages in which he reproduces this historical image on a monumental scale. Vertical works that hang down gallery walls, they resemble grave memorials in which he does hard-hitting justice to the atrocities and abuses of the Middle Passage. Pinder's psychologically charged and politically provocative *Slave Ship Quilts* represents multiple "icons of the slave ship" in crisscrossing formation. Here the Middle Passage visually overwhelms his viewers as a site of corporeal, emotional, and spiritual mass murder. According to these works, Pinder is from a site of trauma and tragedy in which not thousands but untold millions of people lost their lives.

Pinder does not reproduce just any historical icon in his *Slave Ship Quilts*: "the 156 ships represent voyages made by the slave ship HMS Brooke[s]."[223] The ship represents an enduring historical emblem and political symbol. The white-designed and white-produced eighteenth-century diagrams showing the bodies of enslaved people on board the *Brooks* are no less a source of inspiration for Pinder as they were for Nari Ward in *Amazing Grace*. The mass production of atrocity images of the *Brooks* were white-engineered and white-circulated abolitionist tools, generated to inspire horror and empathy among their white audiences. Images of the *Brooks* were printed with a view to combatting white racist ignorance, apathy, and wholesale abdication of social responsibility regarding the violences and violations of the transatlantic slave trade and slavery.

Pinder's motivations in resurrecting and recreating this barbaric icon reflect his commitment to consciousness-raising and political activism. His reliance on these repeated images of the *Brooks* "draws the viewer in to examine something that they're probably really familiar with," but Pinder also notes that "I move them around in order to create juxtapositions of the ships."[224] Pinder's harrowing decision to insert multiples of this historical icon vertically and horizontally into a grid across his collages has powerful consequences. He relies on visual repetition to overwhelm his audiences with the sheer numbers of white European vessels involved in the centuries-long institution of the transatlantic slave trade and slavery.

"Initially my quilts create a pattern, but upon further examination the viewer begins to recognize the shape of the ships and ultimately, the individual people confined within them," explains Pinder.[225] He provides this visual meditation on the "slave ship designs as a formal element" in order to expose the "cold, calculated manner in which the layout of slave ships was drawn." A "further examination" reveals that what at first appears to be abstract motifs are in fact the very real outlines of enslaved people's bodies. "Packed like sardines, these humans, my ancestors, were cargo," he poignantly comments. He memorializes the unspeakable sufferings, sacrifices, and struggles endured by his ancestors as human cargo by denouncing white immoral greed, avarice, and barbarity. "Each panel has a different substance covering the work—molasses, rum and gunpowder—all materials integral to the trading of slaves," he explains. Pinder's introduction of "molasses, rum and gunpowder" that white European enslavers exchanged for enslaved people shores up his "lexicon of liberation" in which he highlights the traumatizing reality that "the Triangle Trade was a system in which materials were exchanged for human lives." As he summarizes, "These ships left England with the cargo [of] gunpowder and weapons" that were "later traded for slaves in Africa." "Then in the Caribbean, the slaves were traded for molasses and shipped to the United States," he explains, adding, "In the US, the molasses were converted into rum and sent to England—completing the Triangle."[226] "This horrible exchange demonstrates the chilling dehumanization of blacks and marks the beginning of the African-American experience," he says.[227] According to Pinder's "lexicon of liberation," his repetition of the *Brooks* icon, layered through the material substances of "molasses, rum and gunpowder," reinforces the

psychological power and moral force of his memorials to an "African-American experience" defined by physical loss, psychological devastation, and existential annihilation.

Pinder declares, "the Middle Passage is a gateway into a new culture."[228] As he explains, it was only "by working with the formal elements of these patterns" that he made the groundbreaking realization that they were "similar to kente patterns."[229] For Pinder, the visual resonance of this slave ship icon with kente patterns made from interwoven strips of cloth created by the Akan people of Ghana over the generations transforms an act of European destruction into an art of African diasporic creation. As per Pinder's protest aesthetic, artistic agency wills out in the face of white racist attempts at the wholesale annihilation, obliteration, and eradication of Black lives. While his "choice to saturate the quilts in molasses, rum, and gunpowder recalls the trading of human lives for objects," there can be no doubt that, as Pinder himself confirms, his *Slave Ship Quilts* memorialize not only "the story" but the artistic prowess and political dissidence of "my ancestors."[230] "With my series of quilts, bound histories, films, collages and scrolls, I'm communicating the Afro-American experience," he explains, determining to foreground the interpretative agency and radical artistry of all Black people over the generations.[231] "Acting as a filter, all of this information is being processed through me," he says regarding his self-appointed role as an artist turned interpreter, storyteller, and memorialist.[232] His works highlight the hidden histories of ancestral pain and intergenerational wounding as inextricably intertwined with the untold stories of ancestral artistry as activism. Ultimately, for Pinder, art-making operates as a stimulus to empowerment and as a site of healing.

In 2006, Pinder undertook his performance work *Mule* (figures 40, 41, and 42), a provocative piece in which he memorializes individual and collective strategies of past, present, and future acts and arts of Black dissidence and defiance. Pinder is adamant that this work is no testament to white racist subjugation. Instead, he states, "*Mule* is about resistance."[233] "Pulling a three hundred pound log encrusted with pressed tin became my metaphor for struggle," he explains.[234] "In a struggle to move forward, every ounce of energy is utilized to create momentum," Pinder says.[235] "There is no end in sight," he admits, referring to the task's inevitable failure. He fully realizes the futility of his actions: "with my body I pull and submit to the task which lies ahead."[236] Pinder shares Drew's dedication to "bone-breaking" work in honor of the generations of enslaved ancestors who were forced to undertake mind-body-and-soul killing labor. Pinder deliberately evokes the specific context of U.S. slavery which denied enslaved people their humanity by legally ranking them "with horses, sheep, and swine" in white auctioneers' records.[237] He courageously confronts this specific reality in his performance by emphasizing how, "like a mule, I am a beast-of-burden, not focusing on the end, rather pushing forward with blinders and hoping that the poetry of my labor amounts to a pure meditation of what has come before and what lies ahead."[238] Denied his very humanity, he assumes the subjugated position of the mule as a "beast-of-burden" in order to bear witness to his protest against the extent to which the poetry of his and generations of Black men's labor has been stolen by the white enslaving classes to serve their white supremacist agendas. Here, Pinder pushes his body to its corporeal limits in order to illustrate the ongoing emotional, political, material, and social struggles that have faced Black populations historically and that still dehumanize and destroy Black lives today.

"In this performance piece, forward progress on an inner city street becomes damn near impossible," Pinder recalls of the insurmountable challenge he set himself in attempting to pull this "three hundred pound log."[239] His confrontational and visceral performance meditates on the "damn near impossible" difficulties facing all Black people in their fight to survive the violences and violations enacted on a daily basis in white supremacist urban environments in U.S. society. Yet more powerfully, he says, "the object that I move has been weathered by time. [It was d]issected from deteriorating Baltimore homes, [so] I am literally pulling the wreckage of past generations."[240] Warring against white racist discriminatory practices of social exclusion, economic disenfranchisement, and political marginalization Black people have endured over the centuries, he protests against Black lives as wreckage of past and present as well as of future generations. Pinder reinforces the psychological power of his traumatizing

performance by attaching a rusted chain to the massive log. There can be no ignoring the symbolic associations of this chain with centuries of enslavement. For his audiences in Baltimore, the associations between historical slavery and its contemporary legacies of emotional, social, political, and cultural torture and terror for Black lives are immediately palpable. As he explains, "people stopped me on the street. I had conversations with them and it seemed they got it."[241] Like O'Grady, Drew, and Booker, Pinder understands that "physical exertion with the black body has always had layers of significance."[242] They all share his conviction that "we carry a history and our bodies show it."[243]

Pinder makes the politically powerful decision to attire himself not in the everyday clothing of a laborer but in the immaculate and expensive suit for his performance piece *Mule*. "With my identity work, the suit is prevalent in my pieces," he explains, because "it is a connection for me to explore assimilation."[244] Here Pinder investigates the efficacy of resistance strategies endorsed by enslaved, self-liberated, and free people across the generations. As he argues, their survival techniques have encompassed and continue to encompass seemingly capitulatory acts of assimilation that are actually indivisible from outright militant defiance. In this context, he evokes W. E. B. Du Bois's "idea of double consciousness," which says that "on one hand you have the black soul that is free to flourish among your people and, on the other hand, there's a way you have to act."[245] Pinder knows full well that "black souls" are still not free due to the oppressive forces of a white supremacist ideology that continues to deny all equal rights to Black people living in contemporary U.S. society. As he emphasizes of his performance in *Mule*, "I am documenting intense physical tasks as an abstract metaphor for social struggle."[246] For Pinder, these physical tasks speak to the extremities of suffering caused not only by bodily injury but by the social, psychological, and cultural pain generated by white racist strategies of exclusion, erasure, and execution.

Pinder's decision to wear a suit in *Mule* confirms his determination to document a more recent history of resistance. His outfit memorializes Black Civil Rights protesters' formal attire. They typically wore suits as an expression of self-empowerment and a communication of their courageous preservation of personal dignity in the

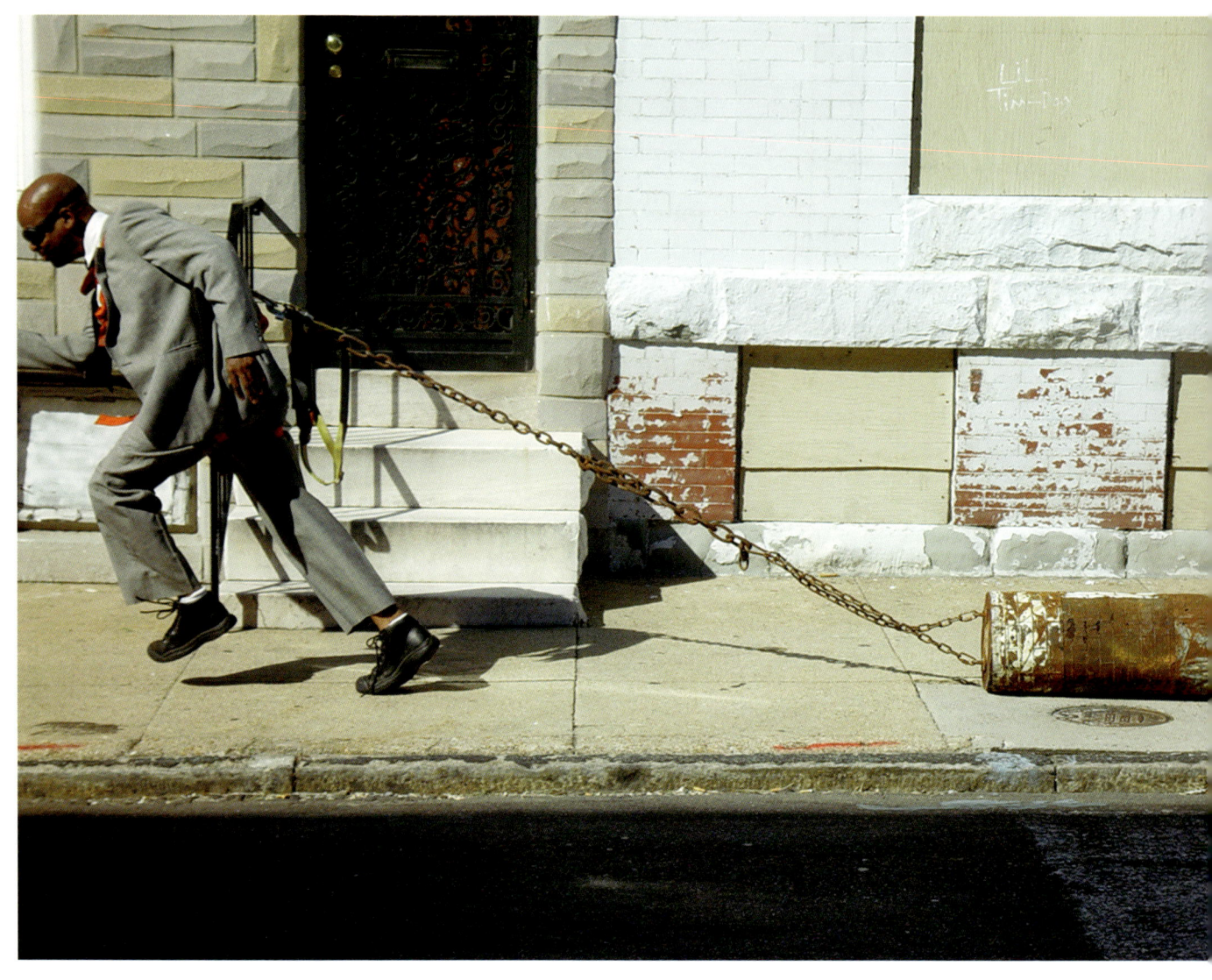

FIGURE 40. Jefferson Pinder, *Mule*,
2006. 8mm film digitally transferred
(two minutes, thirty-five seconds).
Courtesy of the artist.

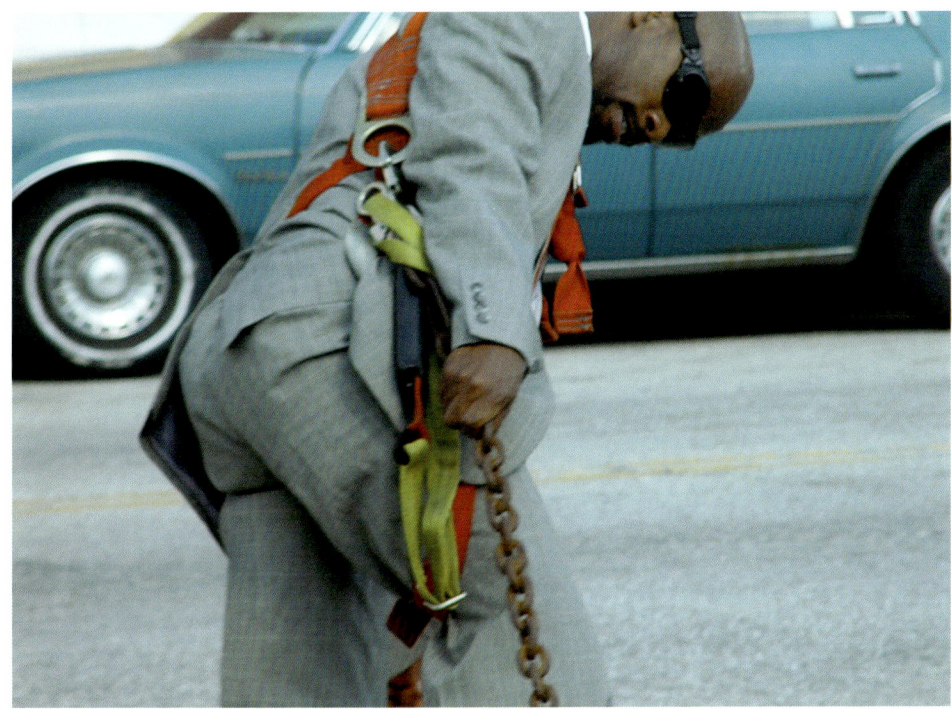

FIGURE 41. Jefferson Pinder, *Mule*, 2006. 8mm film digitally transferred (two minutes, thirty-five seconds). Courtesy of the artist.

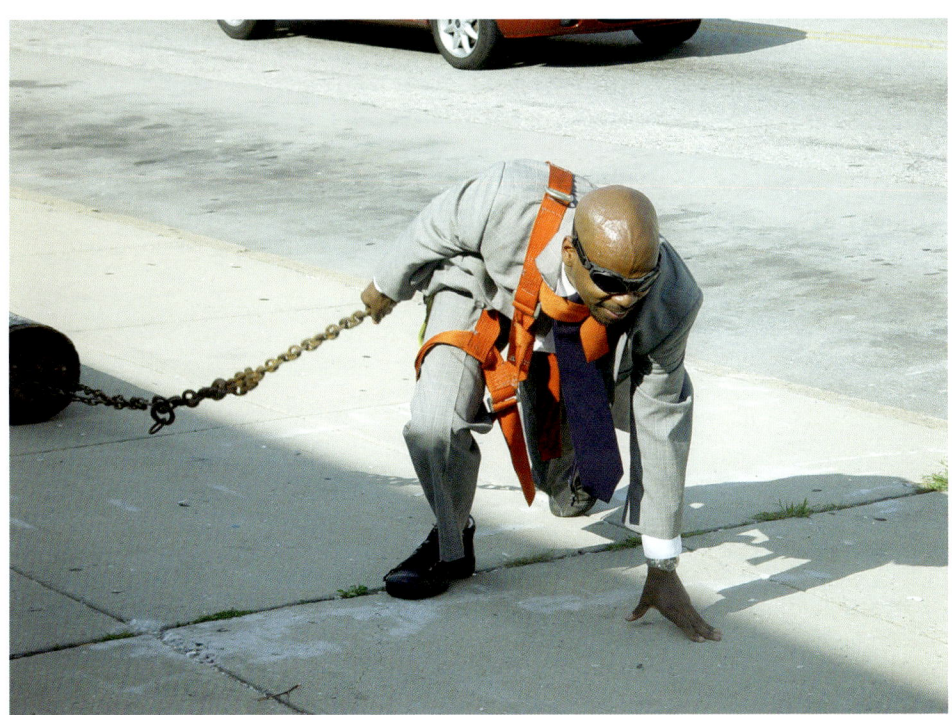

FIGURE 42. Jefferson Pinder, *Mule*, 2006. 8mm film digitally transferred (two minutes, thirty-five seconds). Courtesy of the artist.

face of white racist attacks and abuse. "I love old 1960s era films where the activists are wearing suits," he admits, adding, "it's like their activism is work and the suit is a professional uniform. It's as much about respect as it is style."[247] For Pinder, the suit is a declaration of political radicalism and personal independence, an affirmation of respect and of individual self-fashioning and style. "My grandfather wore a jacket to dinner every night," he recalls. "While there was a formality it was also a reaction to being called a 'boy' all day long."[248] As Pinder readily realizes, for his grandfather it was only "by putting on the suit you became a 'man.'" The fight for the right to wear a suit was a rite of passage for Black men in the reclamation and affirmation of an empowered masculinity. Pinder remains convinced that "there is still a connection between clothes and respectability."[249] Pinder investigates the relationships between identity, masculinity, clothing, and respectability as radical and revolutionary sites not only of artistry but of activism.

"There are hundreds (if not thousands) of unspoken rules of engagement in this never ending fight of racism in the United States," Pinder declares.[250] He refuses to concede defeat by continuing to wage a war against these unspoken rules, insisting, "I'm always trying to find other ways to enter conversations about race."[251] Pinder

generates further conversations about race by putting his own body under physical, emotional, and psychological stress to ask and answer a vitally important question: "How can you express a certain amount of style or heroics through physical articulation?"[252] All too painfully aware that all such questions are "different with a black body," he explains that "I'm trying to highlight life experience through durational tasks and movement."[253] Issues related to the Black body and competing constructions of heroism—encompassing physical endurance, emotional vulnerability, historical reenactment, and imaginative expression—define Pinder's practice.

"We're not yet beyond race," declares Pinder. "I don't want anyone to think that I'm over it."[254] He admits that "it would be nice to have the same autonomy that white artists have and to be able to talk about formal concerns and not have to worry about content at all." He asks, "What would that be like?" only to concede, "That's a particular kind of freedom that is not really a reality for me right now."[255] That "particular kind of freedom" is also "not really a reality" for Lorraine O'Grady, Nari Ward, Chakaia Booker, and Leonardo Drew and very especially for Dread Scott: an artist for whom all acts and arts of resistance are only worthwhile insofar as they are in the service of revolution.

DREAD SCOTT   *(Born in Hyde Park, Chicago, Illinois, 1965)*

"I'm a revolutionary," declares Dread Scott.[256] A fearless performance and installation artist, Scott dedicates his practice to creating art for social change, political transformation, and moral revolution. He readily admits, "I don't think art is a substitute for this sort of revolutionary organizing activism or for the actual revolution." He is an artist turned radical historian, whistle-blowing journalist, powerful witness, antiracist activist, and equal rights campaigner. Scott takes the view that "part of revolutionary politics per se, unlike art, is that you're trying to bring people in an organized way into the movement for revolution." As he maintains regarding the power of revolutionary politics, "It's part of bringing people together and enabling them to develop

the political understanding and organization so they can actually make revolution and seize power and have a different State, a different authority in a different economy." He insists that "the art is part of that process, but it's more about ideas."[257]

For Scott, revolutionary creativity via art-making as opposed to revolutionary activism via political organizing means "just really bringing people to think about things, hopefully in new ways, and hopefully in deeper ways." According to Scott's definition, revolutionary art-making's social justice role differs from revolutionary activism in its focus on political, philosophical, and intellectual ideas and its desire to inspire people to endorse alternative models of thinking that

▶▶ "Do You Believe in Revolution?"

can inaugurate new practices and policies. As he summarizes, "It is part of a process, whereby people can become emancipators of humanity so that collectively, millions of people can make revolution and radically remake the world." For Scott, the sole way in which we can "become emancipators of humanity" is by causing a revolution in social, political, moral, and cultural thought.[258] "What revolutionaries in a country like this need to do, now, is raise people's political consciousness," he advises.[259] Scott issues a rallying cry by instructing his audiences to "do work to help bring about a situation where people are more willing to fight for a radically different situation."[260] He remains optimistic in the face of the atrocities and abuses endemic to a white supremacist U.S. society. "I think there is a real capacity for revolutionary ideas to produce and inspire great art," he declares.[261]

"Given how morally bankrupt and unjust and exploitative this society is, there should be more rebels and outlaws. And I am proud to be one," Scott says.[262] An artist-activist who not only recognizes but lives by the conviction that the only ethical response open to a Black artist fighting for survival in a white supremacist U.S. society is to be a rebel and outlaw, he has only one question for his audiences: "Do you believe in revolution?"[263] He summarizes, "my work is about revolution and humanity getting to a radically different and far better world."[264] For Scott, the ever present reality that his work dedicated to revolution and humanity represents a "perspective" that "is not what most people in the arts and society more broadly are thinking about most of the time," is a hard-hitting testament to the white racist persecutory biases dominant within a white mainstream art world and society.[265] As a result, he expresses no surprise at his invisibilization in a white dominant art world. Scott realizes that his revolutionary art is "sometimes dismissed as 'political art'" because "my work is challenging and it makes some people uncomfortable."[266] Over the decades, he has remained unflinching in his determination to create challenging and uncomfortable art that not only educates his audiences but transforms their lives. "I'm trying to figure out how to get people free," he declares.[267]

Historic Corrections is an emotionally traumatizing and politically provocative mixed-media installation Scott first exhibited in 1998 (figures 43 and 44). In this hard-hitting piece, Scott commits not only to "raising people's political consciousness" but to working out "how to get people free." *Historic Corrections* consists of the following radical elements:

> a 7' × 8' reproduction of a photograph of a 1919 lynching—a Black man on fire with a crowd of white onlookers; a series of translucent Duraclear photographs of Black & Latino "urban youth" framed on one side by prison bars. Centered between the mural and these photographs, a full sized replica of an electric chair. Positioned around the electric chair are four police batons which each strike a cast fiberglass head every 10 seconds with a loud hard blow. Live, un-edited police reports picked up by a police radio accompanies the sound of these headbeatings. Viewers can walk through the piece and view it from different perspectives. Furthermore, given the translucent nature of the Duraclear photographs, viewers can see the "urban youth" either as jailed criminals or they can see the artwork "through their eyes" and be on the same side of the bars as these youth.[268]

Historic Corrections is a socially uncompromising and psychologically confrontational work. Scott's decision to reproduce the "photograph of a 1919 lynching" operates as a visual call to arms in this installation. Scott breaks new ground by undertaking an act not only of historic but of social, political, cultural, and ideological correction. Here he exposes as well as denounces centuries of white racist persecution, torture, and murder enacted against past, present, and future generations of Black people fighting for survival in U.S. society.

This historical photograph is an atrocity image showing the members of the white racist mob that were responsible for the torture, mutilation, and murder of an innocent man called Will Brown in Omaha, Nebraska, on September 28–29, 1919. In an inhumane act of white supremacist annihilation and extermination, Will Brown was murdered during the two days of rioting instigated by white racist protesters who denied the Black man's right to earn a living by his labor. According to Michael L. Lawson, "On September 28 the anger that had been building exploded over an incident in which a black man allegedly raped a 19-year-old white girl."[269] "A manhunt was organized and within a short time a suspect was arrested," Lawson summarizes.[270] The white mob soon found an innocent victim on whom they visited their murderous rage. "Will Brown, a 41-year-old Negro packinghouse worker who suffered from acute rheumatism, was charged with the crime and transported to the courthouse where over 6,000 citizens gathered and permitted themselves to be worked up to the point of frenzy."[271] Abandoned by the hollow mockery and racist injustices of a U.S. legal system that betrayed its white supremacist foundations by diabolically consorting with the villainous white racist murderous mob, Brown had no chance of survival. "When the signal was given, the mob took over and charged the courthouse, set it afire, and raided the jail," Lawson explains. "Frightened prisoners turned Brown over to the mob who stripped him of clothing, severely beat him, dragged him to the street, hanged him, riddled his body with bullets and burnt it."[272]

No less harrowing is the historical account of Will Brown's death provided by historian Orville D. Menard. "Brown was beaten into unconsciousness and his clothes were torn off," he writes.[273] "Hoisted in the air, Brown's spinning body was riddled with bullets. When brought down, his shattered corpse was tied behind a car." Menard reports that Brown's "body was cremated with fuel taken from nearby red danger lamps and fire truck lanterns, while bits of the lynch rope were sold for ten cents each."[274] Brown's heartbreaking declaration, "I am innocent, I never did it, my God, I am innocent" was to no avail against his inhumane and barbaric white racist killers.[275] While Lawson focuses on the mob's barbaric acts of human extermination and execution during the act of the lynching itself, Menard summarizes the horrifying practices that took place in this traumatizing ritual's immediate aftermath. According to Menard's narration, harrowing souvenirs which included "bits of the lynch rope" were circulated among whites as celebratory trophies of their barbarity and in an unrepentant glorifying of their tyrannical and murderous display of power. As understood within the context of centuries of white racist lies and murderous acts, Will Brown was speaking not only for himself but for untold millions when he declared, "I am innocent."

Scott includes this traumatizing photograph showing members from the morally repulsive white mob surrounding Will Brown's mutilated and burning body to strengthen the overwhelming emotional, social, and political power of *Historic Corrections*. His determination to reproduce an enlarged reproduction of this photograph as the backdrop to his installation ensures

that all these figures are life-size in scale. As a result, he succeeds in drawing poignant attention not only to the unspeakable pain that was endured by Will Brown—an innocent man whose body was sacrificed on the altar of white supremacist racist hate—but also to the individual guilt of each of his white killers. There is no mistaking their identities: they are no longer a faceless or anonymous mob. In this photograph, each of the physiognomies of Brown's murderers are clearly visible for the viewer. All of the white male killers wear facial expressions that expose their unapologetic and heinous disassociation from any sense of guilt or wrongdoing at their inhumane acts of torture and murder. Scott transforms this small-scale photograph showing Brown's ritualistic killing at the hands of white supremacist murders into a public education mural. He communicates a never-to-be-forgotten lesson to his viewers regarding centuries of white supremacist persecution, torture, and murder enacted against Black people of all ages, gender, classes, and nations. Ultimately, however, the focus for Scott is not solely on white atrocity but on Black revolution. According to his "lexicon of liberation," Brown is a victim and a martyr to white supremacist terrorism as well as a heroic revolutionary in the centuries-long freedom struggle. In his practice Scott bears witness to a definition of Black revolutionary heroism that encompasses acts of suffering and sacrifice no less than those of struggle and survival.

Scott reproduces the photograph of Will Brown as one among many of his visual strategies in *Historic Corrections*. His revolutionary aim is "to make a real link between lynch mob terror, terror at the turn of the century and jail and the electric chair and the use of the death penalty."[276] He exposes the many devices of white supremacist terrorism by positioning "a full sized replica of an electric chair" in front of this photograph to make incontestable the connection between the history of white racist mob lynchings and the legal "lynchings" of Black people today.[277] The electric chair stands empty. The leather restraints falling down on either side and at the foot of the chair are powerfully suggestive of the missing human presence. Perhaps Scott's refusal to memorialize the execution of any one individual in particular attests to this artifact's power as a memorial to the deaths of untold numbers of Black people in the U.S. nation.

Scott positions "three photographs of Black and Latino men" in the foreground of this installation.[278] He heightens the emotional tension for his viewers by adding a terrifying aural component: Scott surrounds the electric chair with "four police batons which each strike a cast fiberglass head every 10 seconds with a loud hard blow."[279] He emphasizes the sense of threat communicated by the "sound of these headbeatings" by playing "live, un-edited police reports picked up by a police radio." Working to condemn not only historic but also current white racist practices of correction, Scott educates his audiences regarding the violations perpetrated against innocent "Black and Latino men" in present-era police violence.[280] The fact that the portraits are life size and that they are transparencies so that "you can see through them" works to inspire his viewers to empathy and identification rather than detachment and disassociation. As Scott explains, he provides his audiences with an opportunity to choose their perspective, which reveals their moral, social, and political priorities: "viewers can see the 'urban youth' either as jailed criminals or they can see the artwork 'through their eyes' and be on the same side of the bars as these youth."[281] Ultimately, Scott inspires his viewers to reject associations of "urban youth" with jailed criminals. On these grounds, his insistence that his audiences "see it all through their eyes" operates as a declaration of revolutionary art-making as it translates to revolutionary action. Here and across his works, Scott is adamant regarding the urgent necessity of "raising people's political consciousness" not only to encourage them to "think about things, hopefully in new ways," but to become morally responsible agents of social and political change and, as such, "emancipators of humanity."

Only a year later in 1999, Scott took his revolutionary practice beyond the gallery walls to create the site-specific installation, *Jasper the Ghost*, in Socrates Sculpture Park in Queens, New York (figure 45). Working not to memorialize a historic but a modern-day lynching Scott provides the following summary of this emotionally and politically unequivocal work:

> *Jasper the Ghost* recalls the brutal 1998 lynching of James Byrd in Jasper, Texas. James Byrd was dragged to his death behind a pickup truck by three white supremacists. His body was scattered over 10,000' of roadway. *Jasper the Ghost* consists of a 50' section of blacktop the width of a road, a truck bumper, 500 feet of chain ascending from the truck bumper and held in the air by five telephone poles next to this roadway, and many bones hanging from these chains.[282]

Jasper the Ghost is a condemnation of white supremacist atrocity. Here Scott reveals his many "lexicons of liberation" as a revolutionary artist. He honors James Byrd's body as a site of unimaginable suffering and sacrifice by refusing to include any figurative representation of his "brutal 1998 lynching." Instead, he includes only the truck bumper, to which he attaches 500 feet of chain to confirm the traumatizing reality that Byrd's contemporary killing by "three white supremacists" is a direct result of the mind-body-and-soul-destroying damage generated by U.S. slavery.[283] Working to clarify this cause and effect relationship between legal slavery and its ongoing legacies as communicated in widespread racism, prejudice, and persecution, Scott accompanies the many bones that are hanging from chains with cast-iron replicas of neck, leg, and wrist shackles.

"It's a really big piece, and I didn't have nearly enough money to do it. So I had to try to unite with people to do various things so I could get the piece done," declares Scott. "I actually might have had more leg irons and collars in the piece—not a lot more—if I could have."[284] While he worked with salvaged rusted chain, he newly commissioned the neck collars. "I eventually got put in touch with a blacksmith who really loves the history of blacksmithing and who has done work that depicts the history of the craft," he explains. Anxious to communicate to this blacksmith that "a lot of that history also overlaps with slavery," Scott recalls that in their first conversations "I told him a lot about who I am—including my history, that I'm a revolutionary." Inspired by his dialogue with Scott, this blacksmith not only "made the slave neck collars for free" but "he really researched the history of how neck collars were made." As a result, "he made them as close to the way he understood they might have been made in the period of slavery or right after slavery."[285] This blacksmith's commitment to recreating historically authentic replicas of the torture implements of chattel slavery works to collapse the temporal, political, and corporeal boundaries between the historical reality of inhumane bondage and the contemporary era of inhumane lynchings.

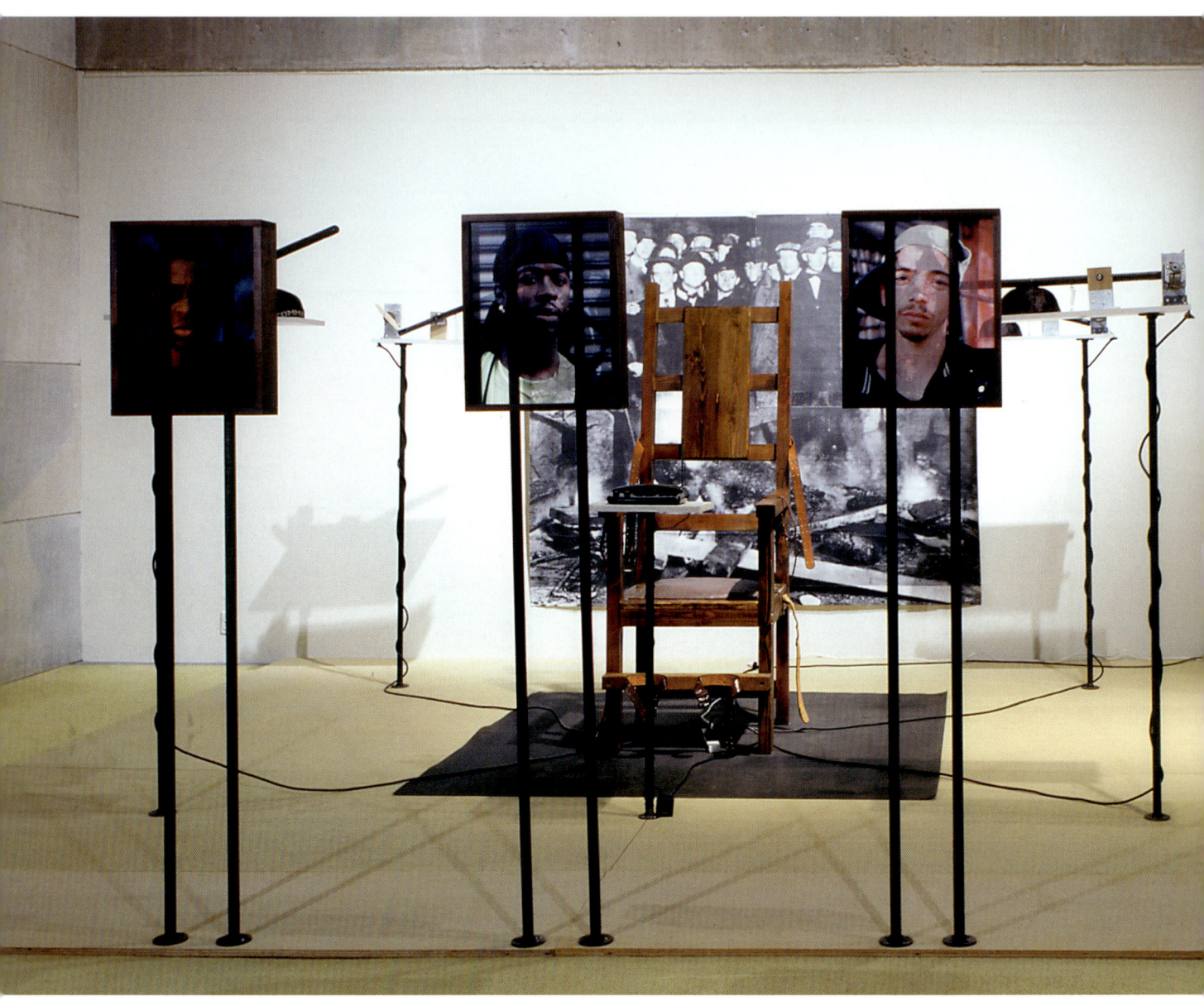

FIGURE 43. Dread Scott, *Historic Corrections*, 1998. Mixed media, including photograph (7 ft. × 8 ft.), Duraclear photographs, audio recordings, and electric chair replica. Courtesy of the artist.

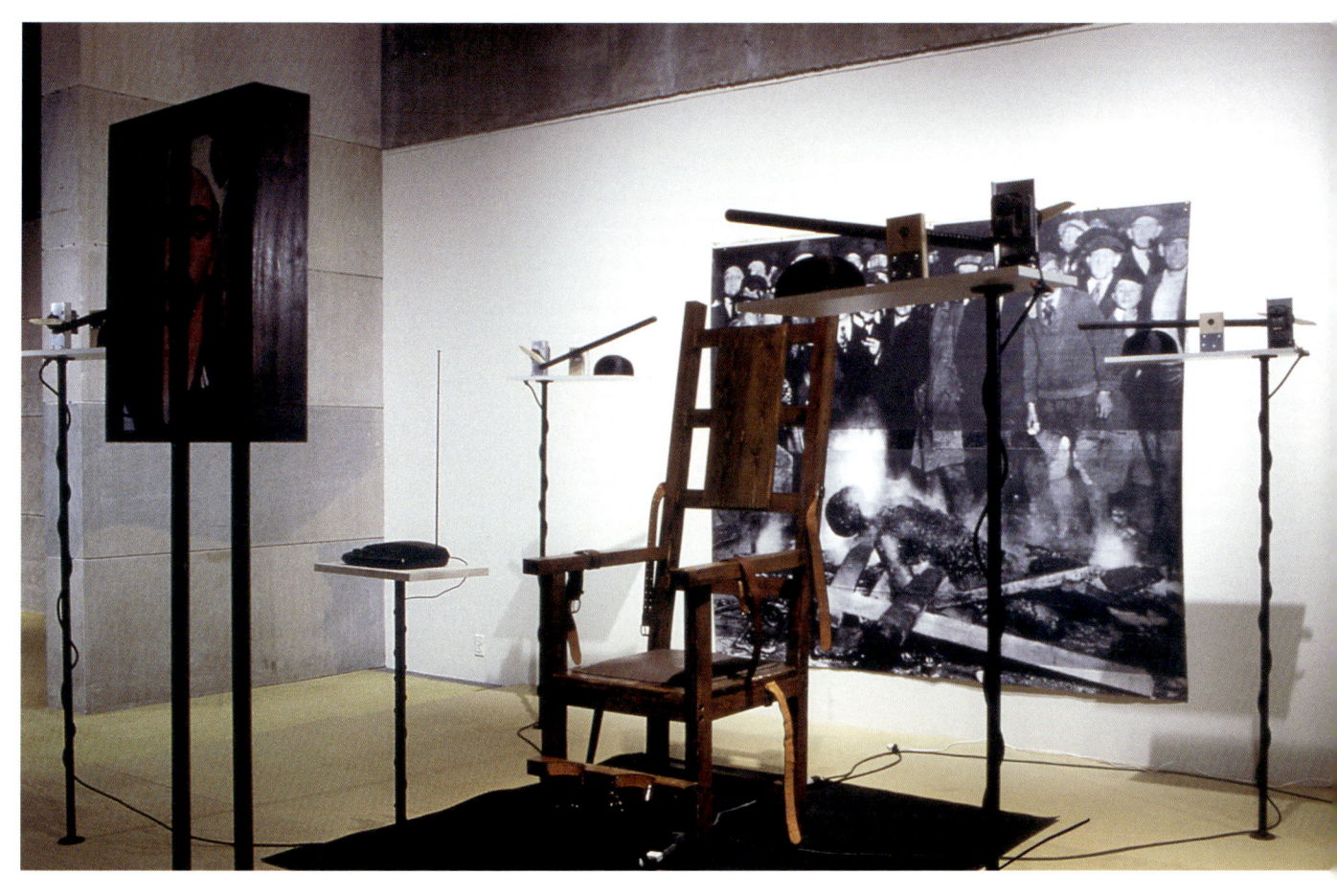

FIGURE 44. Dread Scott, *Historic Corrections*, 1998. Courtesy of the artist.

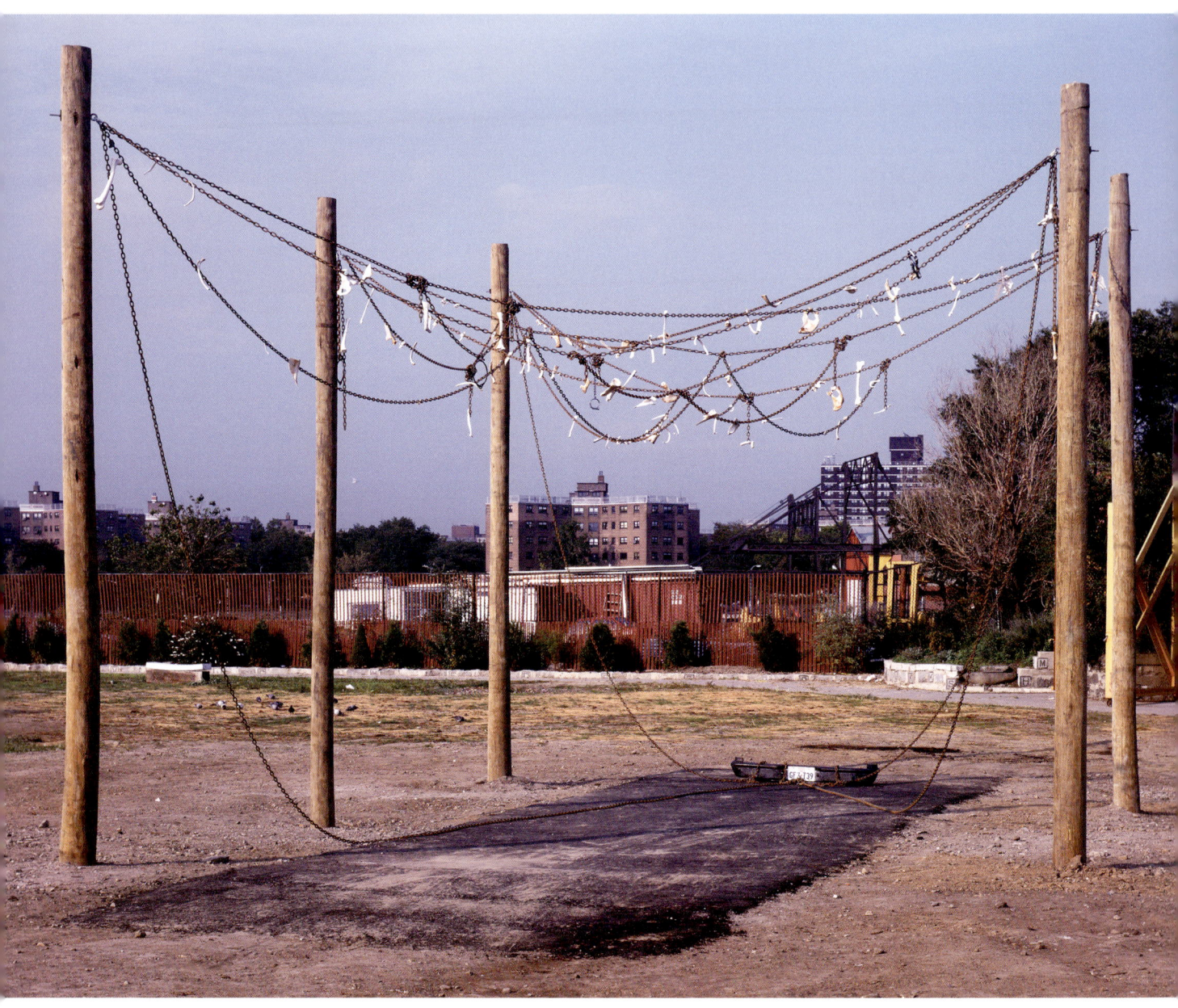

FIGURE 45. Dread Scott, *Jasper the Ghost*, 1999. Asphalt, steel, bones, and wood (20 × 20 × 50 ft.). Courtesy of the artist.

"The leg irons were another interesting story," Scott says. He includes the actual modern day leg irons that are still currently being manufactured by "Hiatt-Thompson," a company based in Birmingham, U.K. He is appalled that "this is a company that is quite proud of its history, as they put it on their web page, of selling some of the best shackles." "They used to call them 'N*gger Collars,'" he states, adding, "this company sold them and sold leg irons and all sorts of restraints for keeping slaves." The piece bears painful witness to the very real material link between these modern day leg irons and the historical shackles that were used in the transatlantic slave trade and slavery. Scott explains, "They made them by using the die that was used to make these leg irons 150 years ago." For Scott, this company's reliance on the same "die" connects the torture and persecution endured by Black people across the centuries. The company has never been out of business in the manufacture of these implements of torture. Scott summarizes their history, saying that "after slavery they sold them to be used on convict labor and all," while in the present day "they sell to prisons and police departments around the world."[286] In his revolutionary practice, Scott relies on materially, spiritually, and emotionally charged objects to expose the relationship between the fact of legal slavery in a historical era and the survival of the "barbarous spirit of slavery" which shows no sign of abating in the present moment.[287]

For Scott, James Byrd's torture and execution at the hands of white supremacists is no aberrant phenomenon but the direct result of centuries of racist persecution, discrimination, and murder. Even now, all freedoms for people of color are still freedoms that are in name only. While Scott is careful to emphasize the particular history of "a person named James Byrd Jr. who was dragged 10,000 feet to his death behind the truck driven by three white supremacists," he does powerful justice to the fact that his experience and tragic life story are "part of a broader history that includes slavery and jail and prison in current days."[288] As he declares, "I wanted to try to have the piece rooted in that particular specific brutal act but try and draw on the whole history of brutality and terror that's been meted out to Black people in our whole history of being here."[289]

Scott's chosen location for *Jasper the Ghost* was no arbitrary decision. "Socrates Sculpture Park is really wonderful. It's in one of the most culturally diverse neighborhoods in the country," he explains.[290] He selected this space and place because it is no white supremacist domain. "There's a huge housing project nearby, and a lot of proletarians come to the park." Among the grounds crew was "one older guy" who played a key role in the erection of Scott's installation. Scott recalls, "He really looked out for this piece and fought to see that it got put up and done right." He also remembers their conversations together: "He talked with me about his experiences with the park and with various racist experiences he faced in his life."

Not only a monument, memorial, consciousness-raising device, and educational weapon, Scott's installation also honors untold oral storytelling traditions and stimulates the sharing of personal experiences as a source of individual and collective empowerment within African American communities. As a "big heavy piece" not only emotionally, politically, and ideologically but also materially and physically, the erection of this installation came at no small personal cost for everyone involved. Just as Ward, Booker, Pinder, and Drew commit to "bone-breaking" labor in the service of creating artworks dedicated to social justice, Dread Scott admitted that for this work in particular, "we had to swing pick axes and all to get it done so it was almost like being on a chain gang."

Jasper the Ghost is the fulfillment of Scott's mission: "because I'm a revolutionary I'm also very consciously trying to do everything I can—as I think all revolutionaries are—to try to help the people change the world." For Scott and all the artists in *Battleground*, a determination to use art to "help the people change the world" defines their "lexicons of liberation." Their lives and works reveal their united understanding of art-making as a battleground in the ongoing fight for equal civil, political, cultural, intellectual, and imaginative liberties.[291]

Scott's practice testifies to his lifelong commitment to using art to "change the world." In 2021, he created a revolutionary project dedicated to mapping hidden histories of enslaved resistance called *Slave Rebellion Reenactment*, a collaborative performance piece conceived on an epic scale and for which he provides the following information:

Slave Rebellion Reenactment is a community-engaged artist performance and film production that, on November 8–9, 2019, will reimagine the German Coast Uprising of 1811, which took place in the river parishes just outside of New Orleans . . . It is a project about freedom. The artwork will involve hundreds of reenactors in period specific clothing marching for two days covering 26 miles. The reenactment, the culmination of a period of organizing and preparation, will take place upriver from New Orleans in the locations where the 1811 revolt occurred—the exurban communities and industry that have replaced the sugar plantations will be its backdrop. The reenactment will be an impressive and startling sight—500+ Black re-enactors, many on horses, flags flying, in 19th-century French colonial garments, singing in Creole and English to African drumming.[292]

If *Historic Corrections* and *Jasper the Ghost* are traumatized and traumatizing investigations into slavery's mind-body-and-soul-destroying social, economic, cultural, legal, and ideological legacies, *Slave Rebellion Reenactment* is unequivocally about freedom. This multidisciplinary "artist performance and film production" which took place in November 2019 was made possible by the participation of "hundreds of reenactors in period specific clothing." Scott's decision to clothe his performers in "period specific clothing" educates both his participants and his viewers regarding the enormity of the German Coast Uprising of 1811 as a historical, social, and political reality that has been eradicated and erased to serve the dominant interests of a white supremacist U.S. national agenda.

Among the priorities of *Slave Rebellion Reenactment* is Scott's commitment to raising awareness regarding an as-yet-unmapped history of Black heroism. "Charles Deslondes, Gilbert, Quamana, Jeesamine, and Marie Rose—some of the leaders of the 1811 uprising—alongside the many enslaved people who were part of the revolt are unsung heroes," he declares. "Their vision, if known about more widely, would inspire many." For Scott, these heroes survive as contemporary role models for future activism. "Their rebellion is a profound 'what if?' story," he says. "It had a small but real chance of succeeding." He adds, "What would that have meant for U.S. and world history?" "Understanding that the past was not predetermined opens the ability for people to dream 'what if?' for the future," he declares. "We hope that this project helps people of all races broaden their vision of what is possible."[293] A testament to what

is possible for "people of all races," *Slave Rebellion Reenactment* is a call to social, political, and cultural revolutionary arms. For Scott and his participant performers, the message of this revolutionary work is rooted in their conviction that "*If our ancestors had a way to get free, we should know that.*"[294]

At the heart of the radical power of Scott's *Slave Rebellion Reenactment* is his call upon "Charles Deslondes, Gilbert, Quamana, Jeesamine, and Marie Rose," no less than the enslaved people whose names are unknown to us, as the unsung heroes not only of a historical rebellion but of a revolution that is still to come. "Part of why this is going to work is because the history that it talks about still exists in the present itself," explains Scott. "It will be a ghost slave army talking about the present looking at the past to talk about the present." As he and everyone participating knows, "this project will work precisely because these issues are still here. The descendants of the enslaved and the descendants of the slave master are still in similar social relations with each other."[295] The "ghost slave army" is a declaration of empowerment for the generations of Black people who refuse, reject, denounce, and defy the enduring white supremacist tyrannies, tortures, and tragedies committed by the descendants of white enslavers. Like O'Grady, Ward, Booker, Drew, and Pinder, Dread Scott and his "ghost army" collectively avow, "Resistance took all sorts of forms."[296]

———

"I'm sure my art will always be political because of who and what I am," declares Lorraine O'Grady. "I seem to get my best political ideas when looking for aesthetic solutions."[297] The experimental artworks of Lorraine O'Grady, Nari Ward, Chakaia Booker, Leonardo Drew, Jefferson Pinder, and Dread Scott, are inspired by their belief in the indivisible relationship between art and politics. Art is politics and politics is art, not only for the artists in this chapter, but for all the artists examined in *Battleground.*. They all commit to using their creativity as a means to effect lasting social change as well as a longstanding moral revolution. "I'm a storyteller, and I'm trying to figure out how to make people think about themselves in a different way," explains Nari Ward. He understands that "to survive, you have to figure out how to express all the different things that make up who you are."[298] Ward is not alone in his convictions. Acts and arts of storytelling are a source of shared solidarity and survival in the face of daily struggle and are at the heart of each of these artists' visual narratives, textual performances, and political memorials.

"My work has allowed me, as an artist, a sculptor, to have a voice that expresses and explores my experiences," says Chakaia Booker.[299] Here, Booker's reflections on the central role played by her own life story eloquently summarize these artists' united commitment to using their personal lives as catalysts for dramatic tension, political relevance, and social urgency. Drew is no less dedicated to having "a voice." He is equally emphatic regarding the significance of his personal history. "I am speaking from an experience," he explains. "I am applying myself to that experience. I am feeling it. I undergo the same preparation each time to deal with each individual piece which comes from my African-American viewpoint."[300] While Drew is dedicated to visualizing his "African-American viewpoint" in his sculptures, Pinder believes that with his performance pieces and installations, "I'm feeding into the Afro-American continuum of art making."[301] Working not in isolation but as part of a social, political, and cultural "continuum" of Black artists and art-making traditions, Pinder is not alone in his "hope to redefine what blackness is."[302] At the heart of this determination is his interrogation of white mainstream audiences' perceptions, assumptions, and expectations: a commitment in evidence across all of these artists' works.

"I think that the intersection of art and political activism should be to help contribute to a situation where people can take that step—both helping to change the social landscape so that there is more upheaval in society, where the powers that be are more isolated and on the defensive, where people are more willing to fight for freedom," proclaims Dread Scott. [303] For Scott, no less than for O'Grady, Ward, Booker, Drew, and Pinder, a practice that is dedicated to inspiring audiences to take the first step to "helping to change the social landscape" provides a moral, political, social, and cultural blueprint for real and lasting revolutionary radicalism. "I have hope for the world. Even with all the horrible, intolerable things going on in the world right now, I still have hope." So Dread Scott maintains in a powerful summary of his "hope for the world" that is also shared by Lorraine O'Grady, Nari Ward, Chakaia Booker, Leonardo Drew, and Jefferson Pinder. For all of these artists, their united conviction that a collective belief in the transformative power of social, political, cultural, and emotional change is possible defines their life's work. As courageous artists-turned-freedom-fighters, they all share Scott's heartfelt determination to "see the world not just as it is, but as it could be."[304]

"HER NAME WAS LAURA NELSON" ART ACTIVISM IS SUFFERING, SACRIFICE, AND SURVIVAL

"I have pictured her clutching her child as she rises from the flames, she looks disdainfully back at her captors as she floats beyond their reach while they clutch after her in vain."[1] So reads Meta Vaux Warrick Fuller's powerful description of her sculpture *In Memory of Mary Turner: As a Silent Protest against Mob Violence*.[2] Renée Ater, who has written extensively on Fuller's work, explains that "Fuller's fifteen-inch, painted plaster sketch" is "one of the first three-dimensional representations of lynching and the only known art work to portray a lynched black woman."[3] Fuller, who was born in Philadelphia as early as 1877 and who died nearly a century later in 1968, created this sole surviving sculpture of a lynched Black woman in 1919. A heartbreaking testament to Black female courage and white male barbarism, the sculpture depicts a white racist mob's harrowing killing of one woman in particular: Mary Turner, a freedom-fighter who experienced unimaginable acts of torture and persecution before she was finally murdered on May 19, 1918.

The death of Mary Turner was one among a "holocaust of lynchings" that took place in Brooks County, Georgia, following the murder of Hampton Smith, an exceptionally barbaric white man who was "the owner of a large plantation."[4] Walter F. White, assistant secretary of the National Association for the Advancement of Colored People (NAACP), confirmed following his investigation into these white mob law atrocities that Smith "bore a very poor reputation in the community because of ill treatment of his Negro employees." Sidney Johnson, one of the many laborers who worked for Smith, was a repeated target of his acts of persecutory violence. "Johnson told Smith that he was sick and

unable to work," White states. "Smith thereupon began to beat him, in spite of the protestations of the victim."[5] A searing indictment of white supremacist brutality, torture, and murder, White's reports on Smith's savagery protest against the horrifying escalation of lynchings perpetrated by vicious and villainous whites against innocent Black lives during this period.

Warring against Smith's barbarity, Johnson took matters into his own hands. "Smith was shot twice through the window near which he was sitting, dying instantly," White writes.[6] Seeking to justify their bloodthirsty vengeance enacted against Johnson and many more individuals whom they had tortured and lynched, this white terrorist mob insisted that there was "a conspiracy among a number of Negroes to kill Smith." As White's investigations reveal, "reports were circulated that the group involved had met at the home of Hayes Turner, another Negro who had suffered at the hands of Smith, and his wife, Mary Turner, whom Smith had beaten on several occasions."[7] A terrible tragedy was the result: "Hayes Turner was captured and lynched near the fork of the Morven and Barney roads."[8]

Traumatized by her husband's wrongful murder and herself the survivor of repeated acts of violence at the hands of Smith, White reports that Mary Turner refused to be silenced in the wake of this atrocity. He writes, "Mrs. Turner made the remark that the killing of her husband on Saturday was unjust and that if she knew the names of the persons who were in the mob that lynched her husband, she would have warrants sworn out against them and have them punished in the courts." The murderers responsible for her husband's execution had only one response to Mary Turner's courageous protest. As White explains, "This news determined the mob to 'teach her a lesson.'" Only one day after her husband's murder, Mary Turner, who "was in her eighth month of pregnancy," was tortured and killed by the same white murderers:

> Her ankles were tied together and she was hung to the tree, head downward. Gasoline and oil from the automobiles were thrown on her clothing and when she writhed in agony and the mob howled in glee, a match was applied and her clothes burned from her person. When this had been done and while she was yet alive, a knife, evidently one such as is used in splitting hogs, was taken and the woman's abdomen was cut open, the unborn babe falling from her woman to the ground. The infant, prematurely born, gave two feeble cries and then its head was crushed by a member of the mob with his heel. Hundreds of bullets were then fired into the body of the woman, now mercifully dead, and the work was over.[9]

"The murder of the Negro men was deplorable enough in itself," White states, but "the method by which Mrs. Mary Turner was put to death was so revolting and the details are so horrible that it is with reluctance that the account is given."[10]

In her work of political defiance and moral denunciation, Fuller refuses to represent her Black female subject's broken and brutalized body in *In Memory of Mary Turner: As a Silent Protest against Mob Violence*. She declares, "I have pictured her clutching her child as she rises from the flames" while "she looks disdainfully back at her captors": a revealing description of this powerful sculpture that bears witness to Mary Turner's death-defying heroism. No voyeuristic spectacle of a subjugated Black woman with her "ankles tied together" as she is "hung to the tree," the sculpture instead represents Turner's standing figure. She appears in a position of dignity while she lays claim to her rights as a mother by protectively holding onto her child. Fuller includes the grotesque, distorted, and dehumanized faces of the white mob wrapped in the folds of Turner's skirts. The men's claw-like hands grasp after Mary Turner to no avail. A vision of liberated Black womanhood defines Fuller's "lexicon of liberation" and Turner "floats beyond their reach."

Shedding light on the source of the emotional and political power of this sculpture, Ater argues that "Fuller created both a symbolic depiction of the horrible violations committed against the black body and a powerful image of transformation that relocates and reclaims the voice, dignity, and honor of the black woman and mother."[11] Ater insists, "Fuller chose to show Mary Turner defiant in her death as she had been defiant in life through her act of speech."[12] Incontestably, Fuller's determination to do justice to Turner's acts of physical, psychological, and political defiance undergirds her provocative reimagining of her life. All too aware of the revolutionary force and power of her radical work, which condemned white racist mob law atrocities and celebrated the agency and authority of Black womanhood, Fuller refused to exhibit it. In a private letter to a friend in 1964, only a few years before she passed, Fuller frankly explained that the sculpture was "too inflammatory for the North where most of the sympathy exists and would never have been received in the South where it should be a lesson."[13]

Living the last decade of her life against a backdrop of civil rights and Black Power activism, Fuller understood the impossibility of exhibiting her sculpture. While she predicted that *In Memory of Mary Turner* would be too emotionally and politically provocative for northern audiences, she painfully realized that its educational message would be entirely lost on white southern viewers simply because they would never allow its exhibition in the first place. Contemporary scholar Caitlin Beach takes the view that "though this sculpture was never publicly exhibited or cast in bronze, it offers much in terms of visual evidence of the artist's activism, countering contemporary racial violence toward African Americans."[14] Beach asks a powerful question, "Might we further understand Fuller's sculpture of Turner not merely as a tribute or documentation of an event, but a work of activism in itself?"[15] Fuller's antiracist, antiviolent, and antipersecution sculpture lives on as a political touchstone, radical symbol, moral lesson, and revolutionary call to arms in the ongoing fight against the modern-day lynchings of people of color in a twenty-first-century white supremacist U.S. society.

Meta Vaux Warrick Fuller lived her life as an artist-educator-protester. She vitally comprehended the centuries-long tradition of African American art-making as a site of political consciousness–raising, historical reinterpretation, and antiracist education. She is not alone. Twentieth- and twenty-first-century artists of color take their practices to their social, political, aesthetic, and imaginative breaking points in recognition of art-making as a battleground in the fight for equal social, political, and civil rights. For Fuller, as for many more artists living and working in 2022, art-making serves as an empowered and empowering space, place, and imaginary in which she is able to honor the sufferings and sacrifices of individuals denied recognition, dignity, and respect. As Julie Buckner Armstrong emphasizes, while "the NAACP used Walter White's findings to persuade President Woodrow Wilson and Georgia's Governor Hugh M. Dorsey to make statements against mob violence," nevertheless, "all attempts to prosecute failed, even though state and national officials had a list of ringleaders' names."[16] Writing in 2008, Armstrong declares, "finding local information about the 1918 lynchings is next to impossible": "white residents, even celebrated community historians, claim no knowledge at all. A limited oral history exists among black residents, but few who know the story will talk about it."[17] Ultimately, Fuller's *In Memory of Mary Turner* survives as a powerful memorial against mob violence. Mary Turner is an individual who was denied all human rights and whose tragic murder has yet to be given justice in both the legal records and U.S. national memory. In Fuller's work, Turner lives on to demand that her hearers not only become witnesses to her pain but also radical activists in the unending fight against white supremacist brutality.

The murder of Mary Turner and the "holocaust of lynchings" that took place in Brooks County, Georgia, in 1918 are not the only atrocities that demand memorialization. As LaShawnda Crowe Storm declares, "There are other stories of women and lynching that must also be remembered."[18] A contemporary artist and activist, LaShawnda Crowe Storm is the founder of the Lynch Quilts Project, "a community based effort which examines the history and ramifications of racial violence in the United States of America through the textile tradition of quilting."[19] Working collaboratively to ensure that "other stories" of "women and lynching" are "remembered," the members of the Lynch Quilts Project inspire participation in their quilting practices by issuing a heartfelt appeal: "Join us in weaving a path towards social justice—past, present and future."[20] Just as

Meta Vaux Warrick Fuller memorialized the atrocities experienced by one lynched Black woman in particular, so LaShwanda Crowe Storm recalls, "the Lynch Quilts Project began with the story of Laura Nelson."[21]

"When I encountered the realization that women and children were also lynched, my research revealed this story and photograph . . . and I was mortified," LaShwanda Crowe Storm explains. The photograph depicted Laura Nelson's killing at the hands of a white murderous mob and was taken by white local photographer, George Henry Farnum. Laura Nelson and her son, Lawrence D. Nelson, were lynched on May 25, 1911, in Okemah, Oklahoma, on the unsubstantiated and unfounded allegation dreamt up by their white supremacist persecutors and murderers that they had been responsible for the shooting of Okemah's Deputy Sheriff. "It's not that in the back of my mind I did not consider this as a natural component of this history," Crowe Storm remembers, "but for some reason, the story of Laura and her son stuck with me."[22] Although "there are several accounts and versions of the events leading up to this atrocity," she explains, "Laura Nelson was murdered on May 25, 1911 in Okemah, OK side-by-side with her son L. D. Lawrence, who was 12 years-old at the time."[23] "There is also documentation that she had a 2 year-old daughter named Carrie in her cell when the lynched mob arrived, as well as a newborn baby girl around 2 months" old, she further reports.[24] In yet another inarguable testament to white barbarity and immorality, LaShwanda Crowe Storm poignantly says of Nelson's children, "Both have been lost through history."[25]

Writing in the wake of these atrocities, an unnamed reporter for the *Crisis: A Record of the Darker Races* lost no time in condemning the deliberate erasure tactics of a white supremacist mainstream media: "The white press of the country gives a few lines to the lynching of a colored woman and her son at Okemah, Oklahoma."[26] Working to rectify the willful omissions generated by white racist newspapers, the *Crisis* published detailed reports of Laura's and Lawrence D. Nelson's final hours, drawing from accounts that had appeared in various publications. According to one of these eyewitness accounts, "there will be no official investigation into the lynching of Laura Nelson, colored, and her sixteen-year-old son, who were taken from the jail here, dragged six miles to the Canadian River, and hanged from a bridge. The woman was the first lynched in the State. She was raped before she was hanged."[27] The *Crisis* also reproduced the harrowing account of these lynchings that originally appeared in the *Muskogee Scimitar*. Here the writer makes an emotional demand of their readers: "Just think of it. A woman taken from her suckling babe, and a boy—a child only fourteen years old—dragged through the streets by a howling mob of fiendish devils, the most unnameable crime committed on the helpless woman and then she and her son executed by hanging."[28] In the next issue of the *Crisis*, the editorial team continued to draw damning attention to the morally unjust, barbaric, and criminal state of affairs in which there is still no sign or hope of justice. "After diligent searching of the newspapers, and after correspondence with friends in Oklahoma, we cannot find that anything has been done to convict the guilty parties," the editors write. Here they testify to the traumatizing reality that "the Negro knows how difficult it is to secure justice on 'simply a question of passion and race prejudice.'"[29]

Working nearly one hundred years later in 2004, LaShwanda Crowe Storm and her artists collective relied on quilting as a radical strategy of commemoration to create *Quilt I: Her Name Was Laura Nelson*.[30] "Quilting is the ideal choice to explore this history because of the great metaphors the quilting process personifies and the communal aspect of quilt making," Crowe Storm explains. "Quilts and the quilting process epitomize reclamation and rediscovery" because they are about "piecing together remnants of fabric and lost history, reclaiming tossed garments and forgotten lives, stitching together all of these fragments into a whole cloth that reflects a more balanced and total view of history, revealing multiple truths along the way."[31] While mainstream official reports distort and deny the trauma and violence experienced by Black people murdered by white supremacist inhumane mobs, revolutionary collectives such as the Lynch Quilts Project rely on collaborative quilting practices to memorialize "forgotten lives" and liberate "multiple truths." They ensure that the experiences of each of these persecuted and murdered individuals are remembered and honored. For Crowe Storm, quilting is not only a way of bearing witness to white racist atrocities but a means to achieving Black spiritual peace and a moral transformation in a still prejudicial and discriminatory white supremacist dominated U.S. society. She believes that "as the fabric can absorb the pain and the needle can guide the way through the process, the act of circling to sew for healing acts as the balancing force in the face of the legacy of lynching, leading the way towards a more tolerant and healed community."[32]

At the center of the Lynch Quilts Project's *Quilt I: Her Name Was Laura Nelson* is a reproduction of the photograph of Laura Nelson's hanging body, originally taken by local white photographer, George Henry Farnum. According to Viola Ratcliffe, "The digital image of Nelson in *Quilt I: Her Name Was Laura Nelson* shares the unique quality of having been developed using twentieth and twenty-first-century photographic technology and nineteenth century quilting techniques."[33] She explains, "LaShawnda Crowe Storm uses digital imaging software to enlarge the photograph so as to render Nelson's figure at human scale, or approximately 5 foot 8 inches."[34] "The image was then divided into squares, each being 5x5 inches, and printed onto fabric transfer paper," and "a chemical compound was used to affix the printed image onto cotton fabric, which was then hand-sewn together to form the quilted image of Laura Nelson."[35] This combination of traditional and modern techniques ensures that the photograph of Laura Nelson dominates this powerful quilt.

The quilt reproduces only a cropped version of this photograph: an intimate focus upon Laura Nelson's broken neck and hanging body. The quilt forces viewers to confront Laura Nelson's individualism and humanity as they receive graphic access to a full view of her face and the detailed pattern of her dress. Ratcliffe explains that the "white quilt squares" that form the backdrop to Laura Nelson's murdered body are made up of "donor's baby bibs, spiritual paraphernalia, and even sections of wedding dresses," allowing the "personal memories of the many members of The Lynch Quilt Project to become part of collective memory."[36] A respectful act of commemoration, this quilt provides the dignified memorial that Laura Nelson was denied in life. The collective's decision to surround her photograph with a black border, onto which they stencil blood red decorative scrolls, visually resonates not only with the gilt-edge frames of family mortuary portraits preserved in precious albums but also resembles the elaborate stone carvings of headstones. As Ratcliffe argues, "In the act of quilting Crowe Storm has removed this image from its original intention, a form of propaganda used to fuel racist ideology, and has now placed it within a context of feminism, activism, and communal art making."[37]

For LaShawnda Crowe Storm, as for all the artists discussed in this book, art is "social work."[38] She declares, "I don't believe my art can necessarily change the world, but it can at least influence the dialogues around me." The statement serves as a powerful summary of the revolutionary philosophy defining all these artists' practices. For the past and present African American artists included in this history, art-making represents a battleground in the fight for individual and collective social, historical, cultural, and imaginative liberation.[39] As Crowe Storm argues, the ultimate power of *Quilt I: Her Name Was Laura Nelson* lies in its hold over contemporary audiences. "Each time the project is exhibited complex discussions on race and lynching occur with many engaging in open conversation about their struggle with race and racism issues as they exist in America," she explains. "Many also talk about the impact this violence had directly on their families, either as victims or perpetrators."[40] As a monument and memorial to past, present, and future white racist abuses and atrocities, *Quilt I: Her Name Was Laura Nelson* is also a history lesson and a revolutionary platform for ongoing discussions about the "struggle with race and racism issues" facing Black people still fighting for survival in white supremacist U.S. society today.

"This history is seldom if ever taught in schools," LaShawnda Crowe Storm observes.[41] She is all too painfully aware that lynching is a centuries-long practice that has been and continues to be perpetrated by white racists against Black people of all ages, genders, classes, and regions, but that remains off-limits in twenty-first-century white supremacist U.S. education. "To talk about this history is unimaginable in the minds of many, as it requires a true examination of our national character and/or one's personal and familial history," she states.[42] For all the artists in this book, the battleground is their shared determination to use art-making to talk about, represent, and reimagine centuries of white racist violence and violation. They do powerful justice to individual and collective strategies of resistance, reclamation, and revolution, no less than of struggle, suffering, and sacrifice, experienced within the personal and familial histories of Black people over the generations. Dramatically to the fore in their radical and revolutionary practices, processes, and philosophies are the ways in which intergenerational trauma visually, politically, historically, emotionally, and socially translates to intergenerational survival. "To make art about lynching and actively place it into the public space requires engagement in forms of racial healing and conflict transformation," declares Crowe Storm, issuing a powerful proclamation to the U.S. nation: "America, we are at a cross roads and now is the time to choose a future based on the reality of history."[43] As LaShawnda Crowe Storm avows, and as all the artists in *Battleground* bear witness, a future that testifies to the "bone-breaking" "reality of history" is "the only way to move forward."[44]

For all the artists.

NOTES

CHAPTER 1 "Can Hate Be Transformed?"

1   Herman, *Fever Within*, 19.
2   For access to a reproduction of Ronald Lockett's work, *Smoke-Filled Sky (You Can Burn A Man's House But Not His Dreams* (1990) see the Souls Grown Deep Foundation website artist's page.
3   Herman, *Fever Within*, 8.
4   See Ronald Lockett's work, *Smoke-Filled Sky (You Can Burn A Man's House But Not His Dreams* (1990).
5   This is the title of a work by Lockett, created in 1996.
6   Sligh, *Transforming Hate*.
7   Ibid.
8   For an in-depth investigation into the "new Jim Crow" see Alexander, *The New Jim Crow*.
9   Sligh, *Transforming Hate*.
10 Ibid.
11 Ibid.
12 Ibid.
13 Ibid.
14 Ibid.
15 Donald Rodney, a Black British artist, coined the phrase "lexicon of liberation" (Bernier, *Stick to the Skin*, xi).
16 Roelstraete, "In Conversation," 26.
17 Ibid.
18 Amos, "Contemporary Views on Racism in the Arts," 206.
19 Ibid.
20 See Doss, *Twentieth-Century American Art* and *American Art of the 20th–21st Centuries*; Joselit, *American Art since 1945*; Pohl, *Framing America*; and Munro, *Originals*.
21 Pioneering volumes have been written by Elsa Honig Fine, James A. Porter, Cedric Dover, Alain LeRoy Locke, Freeman Henry Morris Murray, and Charles C. Seifert. From the mid-twentieth century and into the twenty-first century, key theorists include such scholars as Romare Bearden, Tritobia H. Benjamin, Crystal A. Britton, Eddie Chambers, Floyd Coleman, Lisa Gail Collins, Huey Copeland, Gen Doy, David C. Driskell, Darby English, Lisa Farrington, Elton C. Fax, Jacqueline Francis, Philip B. Harper, Michael D. Harris, Harry Henderson, Bernard L. Herman, bell hooks, Kellie Jones, Leslie King-Hammond, Amy Helene Kirschke, Samella S. Lewis, Lucy R. Lippard, Derek Conrad Murray, Ike Okafor-Newsum, Nell Irvin Painter, Sharon F. Patton, Richard J. Powell, Geoff Quilley, Alan Rice, John W. Roberts, Gwendolyn DuBois Shaw, James Smalls, Shawn Michelle Smith, Lowery Stokes Sims, Krista Thompson, Robert Farris Thompson, Ruth G. Waddy, Michele F. Wallace, Carla Williams, Deborah Willis, Marcus Wood, Elvan Zabunyan.
22 Among the refereed international journals that disseminate cutting-edge research and that constitute an invaluable resource are *International Review of African American Art*, formerly *Black Art: An International Quarterly*, founded in 1976, *Nka: Journal of Contemporary African Art*, and *Callaloo: A Journal of African Diaspora Arts and Letters*.
23 These public institutions include the Schomburg Center for Research in Black Culture, Art and Artifacts Division, the Studio Museum in Harlem, the D. C. Moore Gallery, the Jack Shainman Gallery, the Michael Rosenfeld Gallery, the Bill Hodges Gallery, and the June Kelly Gallery, all in New York City; California African American Museum and Watts Tower Arts Center in Los Angeles; Clark Atlanta University Art Museum, the Souls Grown Deep Foundation, and the Camille Billops and James V. Hatch Archives, Emory University, all in Atlanta, Georgia; David C. Driskell Center for the Study of Visual Arts and Culture of African Americans and the Diaspora, College Park, Maryland; the Ethelbert

Cooper Gallery of African and African American Art, Harvard University, Cambridge, Massachusetts; the Aaron Douglas Gallery and the Carl Van Vechten Gallery, Fisk University Galleries, Nashville, Tennessee; Hampton University Museum, Hampton, Virginia; National Museum of African Art, National Museum of African American History and Culture, Howard University Gallery of Art, and Smithsonian Archives of American Art, all in Washington D.C.; Museum of the African Diaspora, San Francisco; the Walter O. Evans Center for African American Art, Savannah College of Art and Design; the Paul R. Jones Museum, University of Alabama Museums, Tuscaloosa, Alabama.

24 hooks, "Interview with Emma Amos," 40.

25 Jacobs, *Incidents in the Life of a Slave Girl*, 119.

26 Smithsonian Archives of American Art; Widener Library and Fine Arts Library, Harvard University; William R. Perkins Library, Duke University; University of California, Santa Barbara, Library, Art and Architecture Collection; Library of Congress; British Library.

27 Further information on Lipsitz's theory of "engaged scholarship" in Lipsitz, "Breaking the Chains and Steering the Ship."

28 Ibid., 89.

29 Ibid.

30 Kelley, "Black Study, Black Struggle," 156.

31 Lipsitz, "Breaking the Chains and Steering the Ship," 90.

32 Amos, "Contemporary Views on Racism in the Arts," 206.

33 Ibid.

34 Ibid.

35 Ibid.

36 Ibid., 207.

37 Lampe, "Radcliffe Bailey."

38 Ibid.

39 Sheets, "In the Picture: Atlanta, Africa and the Past."

40 McGee, "After an Afternoon," 188.

41 Ibid.

42 Lovell, "Chronology with Notes," 113.

43 Ibid.

44 Ibid.

45 Ibid.

46 Halley, "Lyle Ashton Harris," 7.

47 Ibid.

48 Harris, *Face: Lyle Ashton Harris*.

49 Campbell, "Speaking Out," 83.

50 Ibid.

51 Sims, *Next Generation: Southern Black Aesthetic*, 158.

52 Ibid.

53 Ibid.

54 O'Grady, "Poison Ivy," 8.

55 O'Grady, "Some Thoughts."

56 Ibid.

57 O'Grady, "Poison Ivy," 8.

58 Earnest and O'Grady, "Art in Conversation."

59 O'Grady, "The 1980s."

60 Ibid.

61 Ibid.

62 Martin and Wall, "'Where Are You From?'," 97.

63 Ibid., 102.

64 Ibid.

65 Ibid., 103.

66 Saggesse, "Fade to Black," 43.

67 Marshall and Smith, *Kerry James Marshall: Along the Way*, 17.

68 Alteveer et al., *Kerry James Marshall: Mastry*, 73.

69 Marshall and Smith, *Kerry James Marshall: Along the Way*, 18.

70 Ibid.

71 Choon, "Kerry James Marshall in Conversation with Angela Choon," in Marshall et al., *Look See*, 91.

72 Bernier, *Stick to the Skin*, 2.

73 McDermott, "In Profile."

74 Bernier, *Stick to the Skin*, 6.

75 Ibid.

76 Ryckaert, "Quilt Depicting Horrors of Lynching Stirs Emotions."

77 McGee, "After an Afternoon," 188.

78 Earnest and O'Grady, "Art In Conversation."

79 Davis, "Artist as Art Critic."

80 Clark, "Thinking out Loud," 40.

81 Roberts and Saar, *Body Politics*, 41.

82 Bernier, *African American Visual Arts*, 86.

83 hooks, *Art on My Mind: Visual Politics*, 31.

84 Ibid.

85 Bernier, *Stick to the Skin*, 152.

86 Clark, "Thinking out Loud," 40.

CHAPTER 2   "We Have Power"

1 hooks, "Interview with Emma Amos," 40.

2 Ibid., 34.

3 Ibid.

4 Amos, "Measuring Content," 38.

5 Billops, "Interview of Emma Amos," Billops-Hatch Collection, 47.

6   Lippard, "Floating Falling Landing," 14.

7   Ibid.

8   Murray, "Oral History Interview with Emma Amos."

9   Ibid.

10 Ibid.

11 Flores, "Interview with Alison Saar."

12 Ibid.

13 Ibid.

14 Roberts and Saar, *Body Politics*, 28.

15 Ibid.

16 Ibid., 14.

17 Ibid.

18 MacNaughton, "Spirit in Matter," 6; Amos, "Measuring Content," 38.

19 Flores, "Interview with Alison Saar"; MacNaughton, "Spirit in Matter," 6.

20 Flores, "Interview with Alison Saar."

21 Lampe, "Radcliffe Bailey."

22 Bailey, "Artist Statement," in *Ten Contemporary Artists Explore the Legacy of W. E. B. Du Bois in Our Time*, ed. Yarlow, 144.

23 Feaster, "Soul Man," 46.

24 Ibid.

25 Ibid.

26 Ibid.

27 Bailey, "Artist Statement," in *Ten Contemporary Artists Explore the Legacy of W. E. B. Du Bois in Our Time*, ed. Yarlow, 144.

28 Lampe, "Radcliffe Bailey."

29 Ibid.

30 Ibid.

31 King-Hammond, "Talking through the Mind Fields," 96.

32 Ibid.

33 Nieves, "A Conversation with Willie Cole," 3.

34 Ibid.

35 Lippard, "Floating Falling Landing," 14.

36 Thompson, "Interview," 22.

37 Ibid., 21.

38 hooks, "Straighten Up and Fly Straight," 26.

39 hooks, "Interview with Emma Amos," 45.

40 Mercer, "Emma Amos," 33.

41 Ibid.

42 Ibid., 13.

43 Lippard, "Floating Falling Landing," 16.

44 Throughout this book I use the terms "enslavers" rather than "slaveholders" and "enslaved labor camps" rather than "plantations" as per the terminology endorsed by Edward E. Baptist in his pioneering work, *The Half Has Never Been Told: Slavery and the Making of American Capitalism*. See also Landis, "These Are Words Scholars Should No Longer Use."

45 Lippard, "Floating Falling Landing," 16.

46 Ibid.

47 Ibid.

48 For further information on and an in-depth discussion of her practice, see Amos, "Emma Amos: Skowhegan Lecture archive: 2006."

49 hooks, "Straighten Up and Fly Straight," 26.

50 Ibid., 27.

51 Ibid., 17.

52 Ibid.

53 Lippard, "Floating Falling Landing," 14.

54 Thompson, "Interview: Emma Amos," 23.

55 Patton, "Emma Amos: Art Matters," 43.

56 hooks, "Straighten Up and Fly Straight," 27.

57 Ibid.

58 Amos, "Odyssey," 36.

59 For a detailed investigation into the circulation of the *Brooks* in historic and contemporary visual culture and art history, see Bernier " 'The Slave Ship Imprint.' "

60 Thompson, "Interview: Emma Amos," 23; Lippard, "Floating Falling Landing," 14.

61 Saar, "Lady Lazarus, 1988."

62 Roberts and Saar, *Body Politics*, 15.

63 Ibid.

64 Ibid., 16.

65 Ibid.

66 Saar, "Lady Lazarus, 1988."

67 Lawrence, *Directions: Alison Saar*.

68 Clark, "Thinking Out Loud," 35.

69 Ibid.

70 Ibid., 40.

71 Ibid.

72 Roberts and Saar, *Body Politics*, 18.

73 Ibid., 41.

74 Ibid., 43.

75 Ibid.

76 Ibid., 41.

77 Ibid.

78 Ibid.

79 Ibid., 43.

80 Ibid.

81 Ibid.

82 Ibid.

83 Ibid.

84 Ibid.

85 Ibid.

86 Ibid., 48.

87 Ibid., 49.

88   Ibid., 48.

89   Ibid., 48, 49.

90   Ibid., 49

91   Ibid.

92   Wilson, "Down to the Crossroads," 39.

93   Paysour, "Wonders of the House of Saar," 51.

94   *I'll Bend But I Will Not Break* is the title of a mixed-media work Betye Saar created in 1998.

95   Little, *New Visions*, 16.

96   hooks, *Art on My Mind*, 31.

97   Ibid.

98   Clark, "Thinking out Loud," 36.

99   Ibid.

100 Bailey, "Artist Statement," Bridgette Mayer Gallery.

101 Ibid.

102 Ibid.

103 Caldwell, "Interview with Radcliffe Bailey."

104 Ibid.

105 Ibid.

106 Ibid.

107 Bailey, "Artist Statement," Bridgette Mayer Gallery.

108 Maschke, "Radcliffe Bailey," 17.

109 Ibid.

110 Ibid.

111 Ibid., 19.

112 Dimling Cochran, "Connecting Rhythms," 27.

113 Maschke, "Radcliffe Bailey," 19.

114 Dimling Cochran, "Connecting Rhythms," 27.

115 Aukeman, "Radcliffe Bailey," 112.

116 Dimling Cochran, "Connecting Rhythms," 26.

117 Ibid.

118 Ibid.

119 Ibid.

120 Thompson, *Radcliffe Bailey*, 49; Lampe, "Radcliffe Bailey."

121 Moos, "Conversations," 86.

122 Caldwell, "Interview with Radcliffe Bailey."

123 Lampe, "Radcliffe Bailey."

124 Moos, "Conversations," 88.

125 Caldwell, "Interview with Radcliffe Bailey."

126 Lampe, "Radcliffe Bailey."

127 Ibid.

128 Ibid.

129 Ibid.

130 Bailey, "Radcliffe Bailey's Stunning 'Windward Coast' at the CAC."

131 Ibid.

132 Ibid.

133 Ibid.

134 Thompson, *Radcliffe Bailey*, 106.

135 Ibid.

136 Ibid.

137 Ibid.

138 Ibid.

139 Ibid.

140 Sheets, "In the Picture: Atlanta, Africa, and the Past."

141 Ibid.

142 Thompson, *Radcliffe Bailey*, 107

143 Ibid.

144 Sultan, *Radcliffe Bailey: Tides.*

145 Caldwell, "Radcliffe Bailey."

146 Ibid.

147 Sultan, "Rhapsody in Orange," 27.

148 Thompson, *Radcliffe Bailey*, 20.

149 Bailey, "Radcliffe Bailey: Skowhegan Lecture Archive: 2006."

150 Sultan, "Rhapsody in Orange," 26.

151 Ibid., 29.

152 Moos, "Conversations," 86.

153 Ibid.

154 Thompson, *Radcliffe Bailey: Memory as Medicine*, 20; Maschke, *Out of Bounds*, 17.

155 Ibid.

156 Ibid.

157 Ibid.

158 Ibid.

159 Dimling Cochran, "Connecting Rhythms," 29.

160 Ibid.

161 Caldwell, "Radcliffe Bailey."

162 Amos, *Emma Amos: Paper and Linen.*

163 Silestro, "Willie Cole's BRAND/IDENTITY."

164 Ibid.

165 Gustafson, *Willie Cole.*

166 Silestro, "Willie Cole's BRAND/IDENTITY."

167 Nieves, "A Conversation with Willie Cole," 4.

168 Sims, "The Artist, a Residency, the Museum," 100.

169 Genocchio, "From Newark to . . . Montclair," NJ1.

170 Cole et al., *Afterburn*, 9.

171 King-Hammond, "Talking through the Mind Fields," 94.

172 Ibid., 93.

173 Ibid., 94.

174 Brody, "Every Action Is Political and Spiritual."

175 King-Hammond, "Talking Through the Mind Fields," 94.

176 Ibid.

177 Brody, "Every Action is Political and Spiritual."

178 King-Hammond, "Talking Through the Mind Fields," 94.

179 Ibid.

180 Brody, "Every Action is Political and Spiritual."

181 Silestro, "Willie Cole's BRAND/IDENTITY."
182 Ibid.
183 Brody, "Every Action Is Political and Spiritual."
184 Bernier, "'The Slave Ship Imprint.'"
185 Brody, "Every Action is Political and Spiritual."
186 Bernier, "'The Slave Ship Imprint,'" 1001.
187 Ibid.
188 Ibid.
189 Brody, "Every Action is Political and Spiritual."
190 Ibid.
191 Nieves, "A Conversation with Willie Cole," 4.
192 King-Hammond, "Talking through the Mind Fields," 94.
193 Brody, "Every Action Is Political and Spiritual."
194 King-Hammond, "Talking through the Mind Fields," 94.
195 Brody, "Every Action Is Political and Spiritual."
196 Ibid.
197 Riddle, "Common Objects Uncommon Narratives," 2.
198 Brody, "Every Action Is Political and Spiritual."
199 Riddle, "Common Objects, Uncommon Narratives," 2.
200 Ibid.
201 Ibid.
202 Ibid.
203 Ibid.
204 Hughes, "I'm Still Here."
205 Silestro, "Willie Cole's BRAND/IDENTITY."
206 King-Hammond, "Talking through the Mind Fields," 91.
207 Brody, "Every Action Is Political and Spiritual."
208 Ibid.
209 Ibid.
210 Ibid.
211 King-Hammond, "Talking through the Mind Fields," 90.
212 Ibid.
213 Ibid.
214 Bernard, "Transformer," 69.
215 King-Hammond, "Talking Through the Mind Fields," 96.
216 Amos, "Measuring Content," 38.
217 Amos, *Emma Amos: Paper and Linen.*
218 Amos, "Contemporary Views on Racism in the Arts," 205.
219 Flores, "Interview with Alison Saar."
220 Ibid.
221 hooks, *Art on My Mind*, 31.
222 Flores, "Interview with Alison Saar."
223 Bailey, "Radcliffe Bailey: Skowhegan Lecture Archive: 2006."
224 Thompson, *Radcliffe Bailey*, 20–21.
225 Maschke, "Radcliffe Bailey," 17.
226 Ibid.
227 Aukeman, "Radcliffe Bailey," 112.
228 Ibid; Moos, "Conversations," 87.
229 Lampe, "Radcliffe Bailey."
230 King-Hammond, "Talking through the Mind Fields," 94.
231 Ibid., 95.
232 Ibid.
233 Ibid., 96.
234 Ibid.
235 Ibid., 97.
236 Amos, "Beating the Odds," 74.

CHAPTER 3   Memorials to "My Skin"

1   Alexander, *Nellie Mae Rowe*, 7.
2   For further information, see Haley, *Roots.*
3   Alexander, *Nellie Mae Rowe*, 7.
4   Ibid.
5   Ibid.
6   Arnett, "Nellie Mae Rowe," 298.
7   Ibid.
8   Ibid.
9   Kogan, *The Art of Nellie Mae Rowe*, 31.
10 Ibid.
11 Alexander, *Nellie Mae Rowe*, 7.
12 Ibid., 5.
13 Ibid., 5.
14 Ibid.
15 Ibid.
16 Ibid.
17 Ibid.
18 DeCarlo, "An Artist Who Didn't Know She Was One," 35.
19 Kogan, "Nellie Mae Rowe," 111.
20 Ibid., 115.
21 Kogan, *The Art of Nellie Mae Rowe*, 31.
22 Armstrong, *Nellie's Playhouse.*
23 Ibid.
24 Kogan, *The Art of Nellie May Rowe*, 31.
25 Armstrong, *Nellie's Playhouse.*"
26 Arnett, "Nellie Mae Rowe," 296.
27 Marshall, "Just Because," 245.
28 Paul Arnett et al., *Gee's Bend: The Architecture of the Quilt*, 173.
29 Ibid.
30 Ibid.
31 Cubbs, *Mary Lee Bendolph*, 22.
32 Ibid.
33 Ibid.
34 Ibid.
35 Caldwell, "Mary Lee Bendolph."

36 Cubbs, *Mary Lee Bendolph*, 29.

37 Ibid., 23.

38 Arnett et al., *Gee's Bend*, 14.

39 Cubbs, *Mary Lee Bendolph*, 23

40 Marshall et al., *Kerry James Marshall: Painting and Other Stuff*, 26.

41 Marshall, "A Thousand Words," 232

42 King-Hammond, "Whitfield Lovell," 53.

43 Ibid., 64.

44 Ibid., 59.

45 Bernier, *Stick to the Skin*, 246.

46 Nahas, *Whitfield Lovell*.

47 King-Hammond, "Whitfield Lovell," 54.

48 Nahas, *Whitfield Lovell*, n.p.

49 King-Hammond, "Whitfield Lovell," 56.

50 Ibid.

51 Lovell, "Chronology with Notes," 219.

52 Ibid.

53 Flomenhaft, "Shack Portraiture," 9.

54 Ibid.

55 Ibid., 9, 10.

56 Arnett, "Nellie May Rowe," 296.

57 Phagan, "An Interview with Beverly Buchanan," 17.

58 Flomenhaft, "Shack Portraiture," 14.

59 Ibid., 13.

60 Ibid., 13–14.

61 Ibid., 16.

62 Buchanan, *Parameters*.

63 Buchanan and Amaki, *Beverly Buchanan: Habitats and Shotgun Shacks*, 15.

64 Ibid.

65 Bell, "Small Consolations," 30.

66 Ibid.

67 Yerman, *Women in Art*.

68 Armstrong, *Nellie's Playhouse*.

69 Kogan, *The Art of Nellie Mae Rowe*.

70 Ibid.

71 Alexander, *Nellie Mae Rowe*, 9.

72 Ibid., 11.

73 Ibid., 7.

74 Ibid.

75 Kogan, *The Art of Nellie Mae Rowe*, plate 64.

76 Arnett, "Nellie May Rowe," 307.

77 Kogan, "Nellie Mae Rowe," 111.

78 Arnett, "Nellie Mae Rowe," 304

79 Alexander, *Nellie Mae Rowe*, 11

80 Ibid.

81 Moehringer, "Crossing Over."

82 Alvord, "Memories of Gee's Bend," 22.

83 Ibid., 23.

84 Davis, "The Quilted Word," 21.

85 Cubbs, *Mary Lee Bendolph*, 14.

86 In Paul Arnett et al., *Gee's Bend: The Architecture of the Quilt*, 179.

87 Silvis, "Quilting Artists in Portland."

88 Ibid.

89 In Paul Arnett et al., *Gee's Bend: The Architecture of the Quilt*, 179.

90 Bernier, *Stick to the Skin*, 246.

91 In Paul Arnett et al., *Gee's Bend: The Architecture of the Quilt*, 179.

92 Plocek, "Blanket Statements."

93 In Paul Arnett et al., *Gee's Bend: The Architecture of the Quilt*, 178.

94 Davis, "The Quilted Word," 21.

95 Alvord, "Memories of Gee's Bend," 21.

96 Cubbs, "A History of the Work-Clothes Quilt," 74.

97 Ibid.

98 Ibid.

99 Roulet, "Double Consciousness," 54.

100 Ibid.

101 Arnett, "Wrapped in the Blanket of Time," 39.

102 Ibid.

103 Ibid.

104 McGee, "After an Afternoon," 201.

105 Ibid.

106 Ibid.

107 King-Hammond, "Whitfield Lovell," 61.

108 McGee, "After an Afternoon," 199.

109 Ibid.

110 Ibid.

111 King-Hammond, "Whitfield Lovell," 61.

112 McGee, "After an Afternoon," 199.

113 Ibid.

114 Sandler, Lewis, Quashie, Ottman, Smithgall, and McGee, *Whitfield Lovell: Kin*, 159.

115 Douglass, *My Bondage and My Freedom*, 304.

116 Lovell, "Chronology with Notes," 121

117 Ibid.

118 Ibid.

119 Lovell, "Chronology with Notes," 215.

120 King-Hammond, "Whitfield Lovell," 61.

121 Lovell, "Chronology with Notes," 121.

122 King-Hammond, "Whitfield Lovell," 61.

123 Hazel, "Sanctuary," 103.

124 Douglass, *My Bondage and My Freedom*, 146.

125 Lovell, "Chronology with Notes," 215

126 Gray, *The Confessions of Nat Turner*, 11.

127 Lovell, "Chronology with Notes," 215.

128 Ibid., 219.

129   Lovell and Lippard, *The Art of Whitfield Lovell: Whispers from the Walls*, 11.
130   Lovell, "Chronology with Notes," 217.
131   Ibid., 218.
132   Buchanan, "Artist Statement."
133   Ibid.
134   Ibid.
135   Ibid.
136   Bell, *Small Consolations*, 31.
137   Campbell, "'We're Going To See Blood On Them Next.'"
138   Flomenhaft, "Shack Portraiture," 13.
139   Ibid.
140   Buchanan, *Parameters: Beverly Buchanan*.
141   Bell, *Small Consolations*, 38.
142   Ibid., 39.
143   Wilson, "Beverly Buchanan," 276.
144   Ibid.
145   Buchanan, *Parameters*.
146   Sims, "Home is Where the Heart Is," 43; ellipses in original.
147   Ibid.
148   Clark, "Beverly Buchanan," 42.
149   Vlach, "The Shotgun House," 47.
150   Slesin, "The Shack as Art and Social Comment," C14.
151   Buchanan et al., *Beverly Buchanan 1978–81*.
152   Sims, "Home Is Where the Heart Is," 35.
153   Hughes, "I'm Still Here."
154   Alexander, *Nellie Mae Rowe*, 11
155   Ibid.
156   Ibid.
157   Ibid., 9.
158   In Paul Arnett et al., *Gee's Bend: The Architecture of the Quilt*, 178.
159   Ibid.
160   Nahas, *Whitfield Lovell*.
161   Sandler, Lewis, Quashie, Ottman, Smithgall, and McGee, *Whitfield Lovell: Kin*, 21.
162   Lovell, "Chronology with Notes," 219
163   Ibid.
164   Ibid.
165   Ibid.
166   Slesin, "The Shack as Art and Social Comment," C14.
167   Yerman, *Women in Art*.
168   Ibid.
169   Ibid.
170   Ibid.
171   Buchanan and Flomenhaft, *Beverly Buchanan*, 43.
172   Ibid.

CHAPTER 4   "Sites of Resistance"

1   Hirsch, *Transformational Imagemaking*, 85.
2   Sligh, "Untitled and unpublished Biography Statement," September 16 1993, 1. Clarissa Sligh Papers 1950-2010, Box 37.
3   Sligh, "Reliving my Mother's Struggle," in Zandy, ed., *Liberating Memory*.
4   Ibid.
5   Sligh, "Untitled and unpublished Biography Statement," September 16 1993, 1. Clarissa Sligh Papers 1950-2010, Box 37.
6   Sligh, "It Wasn't Little Rock," 38.
7   Ibid.
8   Ibid.
9   Hirsch, *Transformational Imagemaking*, 85.
10   Ibid.
11   Ibid.
12   Sligh, "Snapshots with family and friends," undated typescript. Clarissa Sligh Papers 1950-2010, Box 14.
13   Ibid.
14   Sligh, *Constructing Black Masculinity: Towards an Iconography of Healing Through Photography*, 1999, 38; Clarissa Sligh Papers, 1950–2010, box 30.
15   Sligh, "On Being an American Black Student," 33.
16   Singer, "Clarissa T. Sligh Interview: Washington Project for the Arts," summer 1991. Clarissa Sligh Papers, 1950–2010, box 8.
17   Williams, *Pat Ward Williams: I Remember it Well*.
18   Ibid.
19   Sims, *Next Generation*, 158.
20   Ibid.
21   Curtis, "Art That Goes Behind the Camera," 286.
22   Campbell, "Speaking Out," 82.
23   Ibid., 82–83.
24   Ibid., 83.
25   Ibid.
26   Ibid.
27   Sligh, "Snapshots with family and friends," undated typescript. Clarissa Sligh Papers 1950–2010, box 14.
28   Campbell, "Speaking Out," 83.
29   Ibid.
30   Ibid.
31   Williams, "Pat Ward Williams: Artist Statement," 10.
32   Ibid.
33   Ibid.
34   Ibid.
35   Harris, "Different, but Not Abnormal" 188.
36   Cohen, "Lyle Ashton Harris," 107.

37 Ibid.
38 McClintock, "Q & A: Lyle Ashton Harris."
39 Ibid.
40 Ibid.
41 Coblentz et al., *Lyle Ashton Harris*, 142.
42 Harris and Harris, "Black Widow," 255.
43 Ibid.
44 Halley, "Lyle Ashton Harris," 9
45 Greene and Shaw, "Conversation Starter."
46 Ibid.
47 Ibid.
48 Ibid.
49 Ibid.
50 Sligh, untitled, undated. Clarissa Sligh Papers, 1950–2010, box 4.
51 Ibid.
52 Sligh, untitled, undated. Clarissa Sligh Papers, 1950–2010, box 6.
53 Sutton, "Art Talk with Clarissa Sligh."
54 Ibid.
55 Sligh, "Interview with Debra Singer," Washington Project for the Arts, Summer 1991, Clarissa Sligh Papers, 1950–2010, box 8.
56 Sligh, "It Wasn't Little Rock," 38.
57 Sligh, *It Wasn't Little Rock*; Sligh, "The Witness Project."
58 Ibid.
59 Sligh, "On Being an Invisible Black Artist."
60 Ibid.
61 Sligh, *Reading Dick and Jane with Me* descriptive copy.
62 Clarissa Sligh website (a number of quotes are from essays no longer posted at the site).
63 Sligh, *Reading Dick and Jane with Me* descriptive copy.
64 Clarissa Sligh website.
65 Sligh, "Reading Dick and Jane with Me," available online here: http://www.clarissasligh.com/essays/2009_readingdick.html.
66 Clarissa Sligh website.
67 Sligh, "A Presence of the Past."
68 Sligh, "Taking the Private Public."
69 Watkins et al., *The Tell Tale Heart*, 1990.
70 Roth and Cobb, "An Interview," 7.
71 Bernier, *Stick to the Skin*, 6.
72 Jones and Roth, "Pat Ward Williams," 20
73 Roth and Cobb, "An Interview," 9.
74 Ibid.
75 Ibid.
76 Jones and Roth, "Pat Ward Williams," 20
77 Roth and Cobb, "An Interview," 6.
78 Ibid.
79 Schwartz, "The Holocaust."
80 Ibid.
81 Roth and Cobb, "An Interview," 6.
82 Ibid.
83 Ibid.
84 Jones and Roth, "Pat Ward Williams," 19.
85 Sims, *Next Generation*, 158, 160
86 Harris, "Lyle Ashton Harris and Chuck Close," 318.
87 Ibid., 316.
88 Ibid., 317.
89 Ibid., 316.
90 Haynes et al., *The Bearden Project*, 91.
91 Harris and Harris, "Black Widow," 253.
92 Ibid., 250.
93 Ibid., 253.
94 Ibid., 250.
95 Ibid., 253.
96 Ibid.
97 Ibid., 255.
98 Ibid.
99 Harris, "Different, but Not Abnormal," 194.
100 Harris and Harris, "Black Widow," 152.
101 Ibid.
102 Cohen, "Lyle Ashton Harris," 107.
103 Ibid.
104 Ibid.
105 Harris, "Different, but Not Abnormal," 192.
106 Ibid., 190.
107 Ibid., 192.
108 Ibid.
109 McClintock, "Q & A: Lyle Ashton Harris."
110 Harris, "Different, but Not Abnormal," 192.
111 McClintock, "Q & A: Lyle Ashton Harris."
112 Haynes et al., *The Bearden Project*, 91.
113 McClintock, "Q & A: Lyle Ashton Harris."
114 Ibid.
115 Ibid.
116 Ibid.
117 Harris, *Lyle Ashton Harris*, 9.
118 Greene and Shaw, "Conversation Starter."
119 Ibid.
120 Ibid.
121 Greene, "*Self Portraits, 2002–2004*."
122 Ibid.
123 Ibid.
124 Ibid.
125 Ibid.
126 Greene, "*Character Recognition, 2006–2007*."
127 Smith et al., *Take Another Look at Race*.
128 Greene and Barrow, "Tom Barrow and Myra Greene," 15.

129   Myra Greene, "*Character Recognition*, 2006–2007."
130   Ibid.
131   Ibid.
132   Ibid.
133   Greene and Shaw, "Conversation Starter."
134   Greene, "*Self Portraits*, 2002–2004."
135   Greene, "*Character Recognition* 2006–2007."
136   Greene, "*Self Portraits*, 2002–2004."
137   Greene, "*Character Recognition* 2006–2007."
138   Ibid.
139   Ibid.
140   Greene and Barrow, "Tom Barrow and Myra Greene: A Conversation," 15.
141   Sligh, "100 Americans: A Presence of the Past in Philadelphia."
142   Lusaka, "Orator (Re)Union: Artist Clarissa T. Sligh Finds her Family," n.d: n.p. Clarissa Sligh Papers, 1950–2010, box 6.
143   Ibid.
144   Frederick Douglass, *The Heroic Slave*, 337.
145   Sutton, "Art Talk with Clarissa Sligh," March 6, 2012.
146   Ibid.
147   Sligh, "A Presence of the Past."
148   Sligh, "Artist Statement," April 1988, n.p. Clarissa Sligh Papers 1950-2010, box 1.
149   Williams, "Pat Ward Williams: Artist Statement," 10.
150   Roth and Cobb, "An Interview," 6.
151   Ibid.
152   Ibid.
153   Jones and Roth, "Pat Ward Williams," 22.
154   McClintock, "Q & A: Lyle Ashton Harris."
155   Ibid.
156   Harris, *Lyle Ashton Harris*, 9.
157   Greene and Shaw, "Conversation Starter."
158   Ibid.
159   Ibid.
160   Ibid.

CHAPTER 5   "Prepared to Die"

1   McNally, "A Life on Leather."
2   Ducat, *All Me.*
3   Ibid.
4   Ducat, *All Me*; King, "A Lifetime Patiently Etched Into Leather," CN14.
5   Ducat, *All Me.*
6   Ibid.
7   Ibid.
8   Ibid.
9   Ibid.
10   King, "A Lifetime Patiently Etched into Leather," CN14.
11   Ducat, *All Me.*
12   Oppenheimer and Oppenheimer, "Indelible Images."
13   Ibid.
14   Ducat, *All Me.*
15   Ibid.
16   Oppenheimer and Oppenheimer, "Indelible Images."
17   Ibid.
18   Ibid.
19   Rembert et al., *Don't Hold Me Back*, 27.
20   Ibid.
21   Ibid.
22   Ibid.
23   Holder, "Amazing Grace."
24   Ibid.
25   Rembert et al., *Don't Hold Me Back*, 27.
26   Ducat, *All Me.*
27   Ibid.
28   Ibid.
29   Rembert et al., *Don't Hold Me Back*, 27.
30   Ibid.
31   Ibid.
32   Ducat, *All Me.*
33   Ibid.
34   McNally, "A Life on Leather."
35   Ibid.
36   Ibid.
37   Ducat, *All Me.*
38   Rembert, "The n-Word Project."
39   Ducat, *All Me.*
40   Oppenheimer and Oppenheimer, "Indelible Images."
41   Douglass, *My Bondage and My Freedom*, 202
42   Ibid.
43   Ibid.
44   Rembert et al., *Don't Hold Me Back*, 27.
45   Douglass, *Life and Times*, 363.
46   Ducat, *All Me.*
47   Oppenheimer and Oppenheimer, "Indelible Images."
48   Marshall, "Just Because," 242.
49   Ibid.
50   Ibid., 237.
51   Ibid., 244.
52   Marshall, Sultan, and Jafa, *Kerry James Marshall*, 123.
53   Ibid.
54   Reid, "Kerry James Marshall," 45.
55   Ibid.
56   Marshall, Sultan, and Jafa, *Kerry James Marshall*, 12.
57   Marshall and Smith, *Kerry James Marshall: Along the Way*, 18.

58 Ibid.

59 Meyer, *In The Tower.*

60 Marshall et al., *Kerry James Marshall: Painting and Other Stuff*, 26.

61 Ibid.

62 Marshall et al., *Kerry James Marshall: Mastry*, 79.

63 Ibid.

64 Ibid.

65 Queens College, CUNY, *Queen's College Art Faculty*, 39.

66 Ibid.

67 Ibid.

68 Ibid.

69 Debra Priestly, "Preserves," 29.

70 Ibid.

71 Marshall, Sultan, and Jafa, *Kerry James Marshall*, 12.

72 Thomas, "Mickalene Thomas."

73 Ibid.

74 Marshall et al., *Kerry James Marshall: Mastry*, 79.

75 Maerkle, "Mickalene Thomas."

76 Ibid.

77 Ibid.

78 Meyers, "Material Girl."

79 Booth, "In Mickalene Thomas's Awe-Inspiring Portraits."

80 Ibid.

81 Ibid.

82 Ibid.

83 Williams, "Mickalene Thomas."

84 Ibid.

85 Ibid.

86 Rembert et al., *Don't Hold Me Back*, 28.

87 Ibid.

88 Ibid., 28–30.

89 Ibid., 30.

90 Ibid.

91 Ibid.

92 Ibid.

93 Ibid.

94 Ducat, *All Me.*

95 Oppenheimer and Oppenheimer, "Indelible Images."

96 Rembert et al., *Don't Hold Me Back*, 30.

97 Douglass, *My Bondage and My Freedom*, 76.

98 Ibid.

99 Ducat, *All Me.*

100 Oppenheimer and Oppenheimer, "Indelible Images."

101 Ibid.

102 Ducat, *All Me.*

103 Ibid.

104 Rembert et al., *Don't Hold Me Back*, 34.

105 Ducat, *All Me.*

106 McNally, "A Life on Leather."

107 Ducat, *All Me.*

108 Oppenheimer and Oppenheimer, "Indelible Images."

109 Ibid.

110 Ibid.

111 Rembert, *Winfred Rembert: Amazing Grace*, 106.

112 Ibid.

113 Ibid.

114 Ibid.

115 Rembert et al., *Don't Hold Me Back*, 24.

116 Ibid.

117 Ibid.

118 Rembert, *Winfred Rembert: Amazing Grace*, 100.

119 Ibid.

120 Ibid.

121 Rembert et al., *Don't Hold Me Back*, 26.

122 Ducat, *All Me.*

123 McNally, "A Life on Leather."

124 Ducat, *All Me.*

125 Rembert et al., *Don't Hold Me Back*, 26.

126 Ibid.

127 Gray, *The Confessions of Nat Turner*, 11.

128 Douglass, *The Lessons of the Hour*, 17.

129 Ibid.

130 Ibid.

131 Ibid.

132 Rembert et al., *Don't Hold Me Back*, 26.

133 McNally, "A Life on Leather."

134 Rembert et al., *Winfred Rembert: Memories of My Youth*, 72

135 Ibid.

136 Ducat, *All Me.*

137 Rembert, *Winfred Rembert: Amazing Grace.*

138 Rembert et al., *Winfred Rembert: Memories of My Youth*, 64

139 Ducat, *All Me.*

140 Ibid.

141 Ibid.

142 Rembert et al., *Don't Hold Me Back*, 36.

143 Ibid.

144 Ibid.

145 Ibid.

146 Ibid.

147 Ibid.

148 Rembert, *Winfred Rembert: Amazing Grace*, 16.

149 Rembert et al., *Don't Hold Me Back*, 22.

150 Marshall and Smith, *Kerry James Marshall: Along the Way*, 18.

151 Ibid.

152 Marshall, "Kerry James Marshall, Interview."

153 Storr and Choon, *Kerry James Marshall*, 92.

154 Ibid., 99.

155 Ibid.

156 Marshall and Smith, *Kerry James Marshall: Along the Way*, 19.

157 Ibid.

158 Neff, " Kerry James Marshall Interviewed by John Neff: Part I."

159 Douglass, *The Lessons of the Hour*, 32.

160 Marshall, "Kerry James Marshall, Interview."

161 Ibid.

162 Neff, " Kerry James Marshall Interviewed by John Neff: Part II."

163 Storr and Choon, *Kerry James Marshall*, 92.

164 Sultan, *Kerry James Marshall*, 118.

165 Ibid.

166 Ibid.

167 Ibid.

168 Storr and Choon, *Kerry James Marshall*, 99

169 Sultan, *Kerry James Marshall*, 118.

170 Ibid.

171 Ibid.

172 Rowell, "An Interview with Kerry James Marshall," 266.

173 Ibid., 268.

174 Ibid., 266.

175 Ibid.

176 Ibid.

177 Ibid., 263.

178 Ibid., 265.

179 Ibid.

180 Ibid.

181 Ibid., 263.

182 Ibid.

183 Ibid.

184 Ibid.

185 Storr and Choon, *Kerry James Marshall*, 92

186 Meyer, *In the Tower*.

187 Ibid.

188 Marshall, Sultan, and Jafa, *Kerry James Marshall*, 22.

189 Marshall et al., *Kerry James Marshall: Painting and Other Stuff*, 27.

190 Ibid.

191 Bernier, *Stick to the Skin*, 6.

192 Marshall, Haq, Enwezor, Roelstraete, and Vermeiren, *Kerry James Marshall: Painting and Other Stuff*, 21.

193 Ibid.

194 Ibid., 21–22.

195 Ibid., 27. Marshall's painting of Harriet Tubman is titled *Still-Life with Wedding Portrait*, 2015.

196 Marshall, Haq, Enwezor, Roelstraete, and Vermeiren, *Kerry James Marshall: Painting and Other Stuff*, 27.

197 Ibid.

198 Rowell, "An Interview with Kerry James Marshall," 266.

199 Walker, *Appeal*.

200 Ibid., 18.

201 Ibid., 20.

202 Ibid., 23.

203 Ibid.

204 Gray, *The Confessions of Nat Turner*, 10

205 Ibid., 11.

206 Ibid., 7.

207 Marshall et al., *Kerry James Marshall: Mastry*, 248.

208 Marshall, "Kerry James Marshall Interviewed by John Neff: Part II."

209 Priestly, "Preserves," 30.

210 Ibid.

211 Ibid.

212 Ibid.

213 Ibid.

214 Douglass's *Narrative*, 81.

215 Priestly, "Preserves," 30.

216 Ibid.

217 Douglass, *My Bondage and My Freedom,* 53.

218 Priestly, "Preserves," 31.

219 Ibid.

220 Ibid.

221 Ibid.

222 Hewitt, "Betye Saar," 16.

223 Priestly, "Preserves," 31.

224 Ibid.

225 Ibid.

226 Ibid.

227 Ibid.

228 Ibid.

229 Ibid.

230 Melandri, *Mickalene Thomas*, 39.

231 Ibid.

232 Ibid., 40.

233 Felsenthal, "Mickalene Thomas."

234 Williams, "Mickalene Thomas."

235 Ibid.

236 Booth, "In Mickalene Thomas's Awe-Inspiring Portraits."

237 Ibid.

238 Thomas, "I am HM."

239 Clark, "Beautiful Photos."

240 Ibid.

241 Ibid.

242 Ibid.

243 "Brooklyn Museum: A Little Taste Outside of Love: Mickalene Thomas," 4.

244 Bruney, "Mickalene Thomas."

245 Meyers, "Material Girl."

246 Ibid.

247 Bruney, "Mickalene Thomas."

248 Tinson, "Making Up."

249 Meyers, "Material Girl."

250 Ibid.

251 Oates, "BeDazzled."

252 Thomas, "I am HM."

253 Thomas et al., *Mickalene Thomas*, 79.

254 Sargent, "Mickalene Thomas."

255 Ibid.

256 Clark, "Beautiful Photos."

257 Ibid.

258 Oppenheimer and Oppenheimer, "Indelible Images."

259 Rembert et al., *Don't Hold Me Back*, 36.

260 Rembert et al., *Winfred Rembert: Memories of My Youth*, 105.

261 Ibid.

262 Rembert, *Winfred Rembert: Amazing Grace*, 96.

263 Oppenheimer and Oppenheimer, "Indelible Images."

264 Rembert et al., *Don't Hold Me Back*, 4.

265 Ibid., 7.

266 Ibid.

267 Rowell, "An Interview with Kerry James Marshall," 270.

268 Ibid., 266.

269 Ibid.

270 Ibid.

271 Marshall, "A Thousand Words," 232.

272 Ibid.

273 Ibid.

274 Ibid.

275 Hunt, "Rhinestones and Oprah."

276 Clark, "Beautiful Photos."

277 Booth, "In Mickalene Thomas's Awe-Inspiring Portraits."

278 Ibid.

279 Truth, "Women's Rights Convention."

280 Sargent, "Mickalene Thomas."

281 Thomas, "Hotter Than July."

282 Melandri, *Mickalene Thomas*, 28.

283 Thomas, "Hotter Than July."

CHAPTER 6   "A Tool and Weapon"

1   O'Grady, "Performance Statement #1," 38.

2   Ibid.

3   Ibid., 37, 38.

4   Ibid., 38.

5   O'Grady, "Performance Statement #3."

6   Ibid.

7   O'Grady, "Performance Statement #3," 45, 44.

8   O'Grady, "Performance Statement #2"; O'Grady, "The Space Between."

9   Ibid.

10 O'Grady, "Performance Statement #2," 41.

11 O'Grady, "The Space Between."

12 O'Grady, "Performance Statement #2,"

13 O'Grady, "The Space Between."

14 Wyma, "22 Questions."

15 Ibid.

16 Ibid.

17 Pace, "Nari Ward."

18 Ibid.

19 Ward, *Togli il fermo/Let It Go*.

20 Ibid.

21 James, "Sun Splashed," 30.

22 Pace, "Nari Ward."

23 Ibid.

24 Ibid.

25 Ward and Bui, "Nari Ward with Phong Bui."

26 Ward, "Work in Progress."

27 James, "Sun Splashed," 30.

28 Ibid.

29 O'Grady, "Performance Statement #1"; James, "Sun Splashed," 34.

30 Ward, *Nari Ward: Rite Of Way*, 32.

31 Oliver, "A Conversation," 73.

32 Ibid.

33 Castro, "The Language of Life," 25.

34 Oliver, "A Conversation," 74.

35 Castro, "The Language of Life," 25.

36 Ibid.

37 Oliver, "A Conversation," 74.

38 Zamudio, "Reading between the Treads," 17.

39 Oliver, "A Conversation," 76.

40 Drew and Schmuckli, *Existed*, 20.

41 Ibid.

42 Ibid. [ellipses in original]

43 Ibid.

44 Pinder and Zurbrigg, *Jefferson Pinder*, 10.

45 Ibid.

46 Ibid.

47 Martin and Wall, "'Where are you from?'" 77.

48 Ibid.

49 Ibid., 81.

50 Ibid., 83.

51   Clay-Robison, "Conversation with Jefferson Pinder."
52   Ibid.
53   Ibid.
54   Ibid.
55   Rappaport, "HPAC Exhibition."
56   Scott et al., *Fragments*, 6.
57   Ibid.
58   Scott, *Dread Scott: Decision*.
59   Scott et al., *Fragments*, 6.
60   Douglass, "Speech on the Dred Scott Decision."
61   Ibid.
62   Scott, "Dread Scott: FAQ."
63   Ibid.
64   Ibid.
65   Grace, "Honoring US Freedoms Through Dissent."
66   O'Grady and Butler, "Chat about *WACK!*"
67   O'Grady, "The Cave."
68   Ibid.
69   Ibid.
70   O'Grady, "On Being the Presence."
71   O'Grady, "Olympia's Maid"
72   Ibid.
73   O'Grady and Butler, "Chat about *WACK!*"
74   Ibid.
75   Cottingham, "Interview of Lorraine O'Grady."
76   Ibid.
77   Earnest and O'Grady, "Art in Conversation."
78   O'Grady, "On Being the Presence."
79   O'Grady, "*Mlle Bourgeoise Noire* and Feminism."
80   Ibid.
81   O'Grady, "Lorraine O'Grady," 404.
82   O'Grady, "*Mlle Bourgeoise Noire* and Feminism."
83   Ibid.
84   Ibid.
85   O'Grady and Butler, "Chat about *WACK!*"
86   Ibid.
87   O'Grady, "Lorraine O'Grady", 403
88   Williams, "'Frame Me.'"
89   O'Grady, "The 1980s: An Internet Conference Moderated by Maurice Berger."
90   Earnest and O'Grady, "Art In Conversation."
91   Ibid.
92   O'Grady, "Olympia's Maid."
93   Ibid.
94   O'Grady, *Work Development*, 25.
95   Ibid.
96   Ibid.
97   O'Grady, "Olympia's Maid."
98   Ibid.
99   Lorde, "History is a Weapon"; Jacobs, *Incidents*, 173.
100   O'Grady, "Job History."
101   Ibid.
102   Ibid.
103   Ward, " Nari Ward: St. Peter's Odyssey Salon."
104   Ibid.
105   Ward and Bui, "Nari Ward with Phong Bui."
106   Ibid.
107   Ward and Ilesanmi, *Nari Ward*.
108   Ward, "Artist Statement," 871.
109   Ibid.
110   Ward and Bui, "Nari Ward with Phong Bui."
111   Ibid.
112   Ward and Ilesanmi, *Nari Ward*.
113   Ibid.
114   Ibid.
115   Ibid.
116   Vergne, "It's Ok to Disagree," 69
117   Ibid.
118   Ward and Bui, "Nari Ward with Phong Bui."
119   Lemon, "A Conversation with Nari Ward," 77–80.
120   Ibid., 80.
121   Ibid.
122   Ibid.
123   Ward and Bui, "Nari Ward with Phong Bui."
124   Pace, "Nari Ward."
125   Ward, "Nari Ward: Skowhegan Lecture archive: 2003,"9.
126   Vergne, "It's Ok to Disagree," 65.
127   Ward and Bui, "Nari Ward with Phong Bui."
128   Vergne, "It's Ok to Disagree," 67.
129   Ibid.
130   Ibid.
131   Pace, "Nari Ward."
132   Ibid.
133   Ward, "Nari Ward: Skowhegan Lecture archive: 2003," 9.
134   Ibid.
135   Ibid.
136   Vergne, "It's Ok to Disagree," 67.
137   Ibid.
138   Ibid.
139   Ibid.
140   Ibid.
141   Ibid.
142   Pace, "Nari Ward."
143   Vergne, "It's Ok to Disagree," 67.
144   Pace, "Nari Ward."
145   Omachi, "Installation View."
146   Ibid.
147   Ward, "Nari Ward: Skowhegan Lecture archive: 2003," 9.

148 Ibid.
149 Ibid.
150 Newton, *Thoughts*, 33–34.
151 Ward, "Nari Ward: Skowhegan Lecture archive: 2003," 9.
152 Lemon, "A Conversation," 80.
153 Ibid.
154 Ward and Ilesanmi, *Nari Ward*.
155 Vergne, "It's Ok to Disagree," 74.
156 Ibid.
157 Ibid., 74–75.
158 Aranda-Alvarado, "Chakaia Booker," 5.
159 Ibid.
160 Castro, "The Language of Life," 26.
161 Oliver, "A Conversation," 77.
162 Ibid.
163 Castro, "The Language of Life," 26.
164 Oliver, "A Conversation," 78.
165 Castro, "The Language of Life," 30.
166 Oliver, "A Conversation," 78.
167 Ibid.
168 Castro, "The Language of Life," 25.
169 Oliver, "A Conversation," 77.
170 Booker and Stokes Sims, *Chakaia Booker*.
171 Ibid.
172 Oliver, "A Conversation," 79.
173 Dobrzynski, "Leonardo Drew," E8.
174 Aranda-Alvarado, "Chakaia Booker," 5.
175 Nye, "Leonardo Drew," 6.
176 Ibid.
177 Dobrzynski, "Leonardo Drew," E8.
178 Ibid.
179 Kunitz, "In Public and In Color."
180 Dimling Cochran, "Epic Mythologies of Detritus," 36.
181 Dobrzynski, "Leonardo Drew," E8.
182 Nye, "Leonardo Drew," 7.
183 O'Sullivan, "Leonardo Drew," G01.
184 Ibid.
185 Nye, "Leonardo Drew," 7.
186 Ibid., 6–7.
187 Ibid.
188 Kunitz, "In Public and In Color."
189 Weiss, "Dust to Dust," 27.
190 Dobrzynski, "Leonardo Drew," E8.
191 Drew and Schmuckli, *Existed*, 11.
192 Nye, "Leonardo Drew," 6.
193 Ibid., 7.
194 Dobrzynski, "Leonardo Drew," E8.
195 Drew and Schmuckli, *Existed*, 12.
196 Ibid., 12.
197 Drew, *Leonardo Drew: Journal*.
198 Ibid.
199 Ibid.
200 Ibid.
201 Ibid.
202 Kunitz, "In Public and In Color."
203 Clay-Robison, "Conversation with *Jefferson Pinder*."
204 Pinder, "Jefferson Pinder: FADO Performance Centre."
205 Ibid.
206 Pinder, "Jefferson Pinder: Dark Matter."
207 Ibid.
208 Pinder, FADO Performance Art Center.
209 Nathans, "Visualizing August," 79.
210 Gopnik, "Folk Video Artist Jefferson Pinder."
211 Hess, "Pillars of Learning," 27.
212 Dawson, "Jefferson Pinder."
213 Nathans, "Visualizing August," 79.
214 Martin and Wall, "'Where are you from?'" 76.
215 Ibid.
216 Roulet, "Double Consciousness," 54.
217 Ibid.
218 Ibid.
219 Ibid.
220 Martin and Wall, "'Where are you from?'" 76.
221 Ibid.
222 Ibid.
223 Nathans, "Visualizing August," 83.
224 Martin and Wall, "'Where are you from?'" 76.
225 Nathans, "Visualizing August," 83.
226 Ibid.
227 Ibid., 84.
228 Ibid., 83.
229 Martin and Wall, "'Where are you from?'" 76.
230 Nathans, "Visualizing August," 82.
231 Ibid., 79.
232 Ibid.
233 Martin and Wall, "'Where are you from?'" 104.
234 Ibid.
235 Ibid.
236 Ibid.
237 Douglass, *Narrative*, 120.
238 Pinder and Frank, *Jefferson Pinder: Anthology*.
239 Martin and Wall, "'Where are you from?'" 104.
240 Pinder and Frank, *Jefferson Pinder: Anthology*.
241 Martin and Wall, "'Where are you from?'" 81.
242 Saggese, "Fade to Black," 45.
243 Ibid.
244 Martin and Wall, "'Where are you from?'" 77.
245 Ibid.

246 Ibid., 104.
247 Ibid., 89.
248 Ibid., 90.
249 Ibid.
250 Ibid., 103.
251 Clay-Robison, "Conversation with Jefferson Pinder."
252 Pinder and Zurbrigg, *Jefferson Pinder: Action*, 10
253 Ibid., 25.
254 Martin and Wall, "'Where are you from?'" 103.
255 Ibid.
256 Scott et al., *Fragments*, 93
257 Ibid.
258 Ibid.
259 Scott, "Make Revolutionary Art."
260 Ibid.
261 Ibid.
262 Ibid.
263 Ibid.
264 Grace, "Honoring U.S. Freedoms Through Dissent."
265 Ibid.
266 Ibid.
267 Scott et al., *Fragments*, 93
268 Scott, *Historical Corrections.*
269 Lawson, "Omaha," 413
270 Ibid., 413–15.
271 Ibid. 415.
272 Ibid.
273 Menard, "Tom Dennison," 160
274 Ibid.
275 Ibid.
276 Slate, "Dread Scott."
277 Scott, *Historical Corrections.*
278 Ibid.
279 Ibid.
280 Ibid.
281 Ibid.
282 Scott, *Jasper The Ghost.*
283 Ibid.
284 Slate, "Dread Scott."
285 Ibid.
286 Ibid.
287 Douglass, *Life and Times*, 363.
288 Slate, "Dread Scott."
289 Ibid.
290 Ibid.
291 Ibid.
292 Scott, *Slave Rebellion Reenactment.*
293 Ibid.
294 Scott et al., *Fragments*, 91 Italics in original.
295 Ibid.

296 Ibid., 76.
297 O'Grady, "Performance Statement #1."
298 Vergne, "It's Ok to Disagree, ", 73.; Lemon, "A Conversation with Nari Ward," 71.
299 Oliver, "A Conversation," 79.
300 Nye, "Leonardo Drew," 6.
301 Nathans, "Visualizing August," 79.
302 Dawson, "Jefferson Pinder."
303 Slate, "Dread Scott."
304 Irwin, "Controversy and Conversation," 19.

CHAPTER 7   "Her Name Was Laura Nelson"

1 Ater, "Race, Gender, and Nation," 33
2 This sculpture is held in the collections of the Museum of African American History in Boston.
3 Ater, "Race, Gender, and Nation," 126.
4 White, "The Work of a Mob," 221.
5 Ibid.
6 Ibid.
7 Ibid.
8 Ibid., 222.
9 Ibid., 223
10 Ibid.
11 Ater, "Race, Gender, and Nation," 149.
12 Ibid., 154.
13 Ibid., 155.
14 Beach, "Meta Warrick Fuller's Mary Turner and the Memory of Mob Violence," 16.
15 Ibid., 18.
16 Armstrong, "'The People,'" 115, 114.
17 Ibid., 114.
18 Crowe Storm, "Laura Nelson's Story."
19 Ibid.
20 Ibid.
21 Ibid.
22 Crowe Storm, "Laura Nelson's Story," ellipses in original.
23 Ibid.
24 Ibid.
25 Ibid.
26 "Along the Color Line," 99.
27 Ibid.
28 Ibid., 100.
29 "The Oklahoma Lynching," 154.
30 See LaShawnda Crowe Storm, *Quilt I: Her Name Was Laura Nelson*, 2004.
31 Ibid.
32 Ibid.

33 Ratcliffe, "To Be a Witness," 25.

34 Ibid.

35 Ibid.

36 Ibid., 31.

37 Ibid., ii.

38 Crowe Storm, "The Accidental Artist."

39 Ibid.

40 Ibid.

41 Crowe Storm, "The Project."

42 Ibid.

43 Ibid.

44 Ibid.

RESOURCES

ARCHIVES, MUSEUMS, AND GALLERIES

The Aaron Douglas Gallery, Fisk University Galleries, https://www.fisk.edu/galleries

ACA Galleries, http://www.acagalleries.com

African American Museum of Dallas, http://www.aamdallas.org

African and Asian Visual Artists Archives, https://www.vad.ac.uk/digital/collection/AAVAA

Art Institute of Chicago, http://www.artic.edu

Bill Hodges Gallery, http://billhodgesgallery.com

Birmingham Museum of Art, African American Art, https://www.artsbma.org/tag/african-american-art/

California African American Museum, http://www.caamuseum.org

The Carl Van Vechten Gallery, Fisk University Galleries, https://www.fisk.edu/galleries

Clark Atlanta University Art Museum, https://www.cau.edu/art-museum/

David C. Driskell Center for the Study of Visual Arts and Culture of African Americans and the African Diaspora, http://www.driskellcenter.umd.edu

D. C. Moore Gallery, http://www.dcmooregallery.com

Detroit Institute of Visual Arts, General Motors Center for African American Art, https://www.dia.org/art/collection/dia-collection

The Ethelbert Cooper Gallery of African and African American Art, https://coopergallery.fas.harvard.edu

Hampton University Museum, http://museum.hamptonu.edu

Houston Museum of African American Culture (HMAAC), http://hmaac.org

Howard University Gallery of Art, https://art.howard.edu/gallery-art

Jack Shainman Gallery, http://www.jackshainman.com

June Kelly Gallery, http://www.junekellygallery.com

Michael Rosenfeld Gallery, http://www.michaelrosenfeldart.com

Museum of the African Diaspora, http://www.moadsf.org

National Gallery of Art, The Collecting of African American Art series, http://www.nga.gov/content/ngaweb/audio-video/collecting-african-american-art.html

National Museum of African American History and Culture, http://nmaahc.si.edu

Smithsonian National Museum of African Art, http://africa.si.edu

Neil L. and Angelica Zander Rudenstine Gallery, The Hutchins Center for African & African American Research, https://hutchinscenter.fas.harvard.edu/our-cores/rudenstine-gallery

New York Public Library, Schomburg Center for Research in Black Culture, Art and Artifacts Division, http://www.nypl.org/locations/divisions/art-and-artifacts-division#about

North Carolina Central University Art Museum, https://www.nccu.edu/nccu-art-museum

The Paul R. Jones Museum, University of Alabama Museums, Tuscaloosa, Alabama, https://paulrjones.museums.ua.edu/paul-jones/

Smithsonian American Art Museum, Artworks by African Americans from the Collection, http://americanart.si.edu/collections/aaa

Smithsonian Archives of American Art, http://www.aaa.si.edu

Souls Grown Deep Foundation, http://soulsgrowndeep.org

Studio Museum in Harlem, http://www.studiomuseum.org

University of California, Santa Barbara Library, Art and Architecture Collection, https://www.library.ucsb.edu/art/art-architecture-collection

SCAD Museum of Art, The Walter O. Evans Collection of African American Art, https://www.scadmoa.org/about/permanent-collection?active=0

Watts Towers Arts Center, http://www.wattstowers.us

Emma Amos

https://ryanleegallery.com/artists/emma-amos/
https://maryryangallery.com/artists/emma-amos/
http://www.flomenhaftgallery.com/emma-amos.html

Radcliffe Bailey

http://www.jackshainman.com/artists/radcliffe-bailey
http://www.bridgettemayergallery.com/artists/radcliffe
    -bailey/biography

Mary Lee Bendolph

http://www.soulsgrowndeep.org/artist/mary-lee-bendolph
http://www.gregkucera.com/geesbend_prints.htm#mary
    _lee_bendolph

Chakaia Booker

https://chakaiabooker.com
https://nmwa.org/art/artists/chakaia-booker
https://www.metmuseum.org/art/collection/search/492175
https://stormking.org/artist/chakaia-booker

Beverly Buchanan

http://beverlybuchanan.com
https://www.edlingallery.com/artists/beverly-buchanan
http://www.barbaraarcher.com/artists/buchanan/exhibition
    .html

Willie Cole

http://www.williecole.com
https://www.alexanderandbonin.com/artist/Willie_Cole
    /biography/
http://www.mauscontemporary.com/beta_pictoris_Maus
    _Contemporary_Art_gallery_Willie_Cole.html

Leonardo Drew

https://www.sikkemajenkinsco.com/leonardo-drew-2016
https://vigogallery.com/artists/1
http://rosenfeldporcini.com/artists/5-leonardo-drew/works
https://crownpoint.com/artist/leonardo-drew

Myra Greene

http://www.myragreene.com
http://patrongallery.com/exhibition/68/myra-greene

Lyle Ashton Harris

http://www.lyleashtonharris.com
http://davidcastillogallery.com/artist/lyle-ashton-harris
http://www.albertmerolagallery.com/lyle-ashton-harris
    .html

Whitfield Lovell

http://www.dcmooregallery.com/artists/whitfield-lovell

Kerry James Marshall

http://www.jackshainman.com/artists/kerryjames-marshall

Lorraine O'Grady

http://lorraineogrady.com
https://www.alexandergray.com/artists/lorraine-o-grady
Lorraine O'Grady Papers, 1952–2012, http://academics
    .wellesley.edu/lts/archives/MSS.3.html

Jefferson Pinder

http://www.jeffersonpinder.com
http://www.patriciasweetowgallery.com/artists/jefferson
    -pinder

Debra Priestly

http://www.debrapriestly.net
http://www.junekellygallery.com/priestly/index.html

Winfred Rembert

https://adelsongalleries.com/winfred-rembert

Nellie Mae Rowe

http://www.soulsgrowndeep.org/artist/nellie-mae-rowe
http://www.barbaraarcher.com/artists/rowe/index.html
https://www.judithalexander.org/about-nellie-mae-rowe
https://americanart.si.edu/artist/nellie-mae-rowe-4170

Alison Saar

http://www.lalouver.com/artist.cfm?tArtist_id=263
http://www.phylliskindgallery.com/artists/as

Dread Scott

http://www.dreadscott.net

Clarissa T. Sligh

http://clarissasligh.com
Clarissa Sligh Papers, 1950–2010, https://archives.lib.duke
    .edu/catalog/slighclarissa

LaShawnda Crowe Storm

https://www.lashawndacrowestorm.com
http://www.thelynchquiltsproject.com

Mickalene Thomas

http://mickalenethomas.com
http://www.lehmannmaupin.com/artists/mickalene-thomas
http://kavigupta.com/artist/mickalene-thomas

Nari Ward

http://www.nariwardstudio.com
http://www.lehmannmaupin.com/artists/nari-ward
https://www.galleriacontinua.com/artists/nari-ward-76

Pat Ward Williams

http://www.umich.edu/~ws483/pww.htm

Journals

Callaloo: A Journal of African Diaspora Arts and Letters,
    https://www.press.jhu.edu/journals/callaloo
International Review of African American Art (formerly *Black
    Art: An International Quarterly*) webzine archives, http://
    iraaa.museum.hamptonu.edu
*Kalfou: A Journal of Comparative and Relational Ethnic
    Studies*, https://tupjournals.temple.edu/index.php/kalfou
Nka: Journal of Contemporary African Art, https://read
    .dukeupress.edu/nka

BIBLIOGRAPHY

Alexander, Judith. *Nellie Mae Rowe: Visionary Artist, 1900–1982*. Southern Arts Federation, 1983.

Alexander, Michelle. *The New Jim Crow*. The New Press, 2012.

Allen, Jane Ingram. "Making Chaos Legible: A Conversation with Leonardo Drew." *Sculpture*, vol. 36, no. 9, 2017, 22–29.

"Along the Color Line." *The Crisis: A Record of the Darker Races*, vol. 2, no. 3, 1911, pp. 99–100.

Altman, Rebekah. "Identity in the Balance: The Iconic Works of Alison Saar." Atkinson Gallery, Santa Barbara City College, 2009.

Alvord, Ellen M. "Memories of Gee's Bend: A Conversation with Rubin Bendolph Jr." *Piece Together: The Quilts of Mary Lee Bendolph*, edited by Mary Lee Bendolph, et al. Mount Holyoke College Art Museum, 2018, pp. 16–23. https://moodle.swarthmore.edu/pluginfile.php/436811/mod_resource/content/1/Gees%20Bend%20CatalogFINAL_1.16.18_small.pdf

Amos, Emma. "Beating the Odds." *Heresies #25*, vol. 7, no. 1, 1990, p. 74.

———. "Contemporary Views on Racism in the Arts." *M/E/A/N/I/N/G: An Anthology of Artists' Writings, Theory and Criticism*, edited by Susan Bee and Mira Schor. Duke University Press, 2000, pp. 204–33.

———. "Dos and Don'ts for Black Women Artists." *Heresies #15*, vol. 4, no. 3, 1982, p. 17.

———. "Emma Amos: Skowhegan Lecture archive: 2006." New York; Skowhegan, M.E.: Skowhegan School of Painting and Sculpture, 2006.

———. "Measuring Content." *Looking Forward, Looking Black*, edited by Jo Anna Isaack. Hobart and William Smith Colleges Press, 1999, pp. 38–39.

———. "Odyssey." *Emma Amos Paintings and Prints, 1982–92*, edited by Thalia Gouma-Peterson. College of Wooster Art Museum, 1993, pp. 35–44.

———. *Emma Amos: Paper and Linen: Drawings, Etchings and Weavings*. National Urban League, 1981.

Andersson, Andrea, and Julie Crooks. *Mickalene Thomas: Femmes Noires*. Goose Lane Editions, 2019.

Annenberg/CPB. "Episode 5: Beverly Buchanan." *A World of Art: Works in Progress*. Annenberg Media, 1997.

Aranda-Alvarado, Rocío. "Chakaia Booker: Jersey Ride." *Chakaia Booker: Jersey Ride*, by Chakaia Booker and Rocío Aranda-Alvarado. Jersey City Museum, 2004, pp. 5–16.

Armstrong, Julie Buckner. *Mary Turner and the Memory of Lynching*. University of Georgia Press, 2011.

———. "'The people . . . took exception to her remarks:' Meta Warrick Fuller, Angelina Weld Grimke, and the Lynching of Mary Turner." *Mississippi Quarterly*, vol. 61, no. 1–2, 2008, pp. 113–41.

Armstrong, Linda Connelly, dir. *Nellie's Playhouse*. Center for Southern Folklore, 1983. https://www.judithalexander.org/about-nellie-mae-rowe/nellie-s-playhouse-video-parts-i-ii.

Arnett, Matt. "Gee's Bend Quilts and Beyond." *El Palacio*, vol. 112, no. 4, 2007, pp. 30–37.

———. "Wrapped in the Blanket of Time." *Mary Lee Bendolph: Gee's Bend Quilts, and Beyond*, edited by Joanne Cubbs, et al. Tinwood Books, 2006, pp. 39–54.

Arnett, Paul, et al. *Gee's Bend: The Architecture of the Quilt*. Tinwood Books, 2006.

Arnett, Paul, Joanne Cubbs, and Eugene W. Metcalf, Jr. *Thornton Dial in the 21st Century*. Tinwood Books, 2005.

Arnett, William. "Nellie May Rowe: Inside the Perimeter." *Souls Grown Deep: African American Vernacular Art of the South*, vol. 1, edited by Paul Arnett and William Arnett. Tinwood Books, 2000, pp. 290–307.

Ater, Renée. *Race, Gender, and Nation: Rethinking the Sculpture of Meta Warrick Fuller*. University of Maryland, PhD dissertation, 2000.

———. *Remaking Race and History: The Sculpture of Meta Warrick Fuller*. University of California Press, 2011.

Atkins, Robert. "Up and Coming: Lyle Ashton Harris." *New York Times*, 25 September 1994, p. 40.

"A.T. & T. Sponsors U.S. College Tour by Gee's Bend Quilters." *Michigan Chronicle*, 19 September 2007, p. C7.

Aukeman, Anastasia. "Radcliffe Bailey: Railroad Spikes, Tintypes, and African Votives." *Art News*, November 1995, p. 112.

Backer, Yona, and Naomi Beckwith, et al. *Radical Presence: Black Performance in Contemporary Art*. Contemporary Arts Museum, 2013.

Bagneris, Mia. "Mickalene Thomas: An Interview." *Mickalene Thomas: Waiting on a Prime-Time Star: 18 January – 9 April 2017*. Newcomb Art Museum, 2017, pp. 4–13. https://www.vianolavie.org/wp-content/uploads/sites/52/2017/02/MT_Brochure.pdf.

Bailey, Radcliffe. "Artist Statement." Bridgette Mayer Gallery. http://www.bridgettemayergallery.com/artists/radcliffe-bailey/biography

———. "Artist Statement." *Ten Contemporary Artists Explore the Legacy of W. E. B. Du Bois in Our Time*, edited by Loretta Yarlow. University of Massachusetts Press, 2014, p. 144.

———. "Radcliffe Bailey: Skowhegan Lecture Archive: 2006." Skowhegan School of Painting and Sculpture, 2006.

Bailey, Radcliffe, and David Moos. *The Ocean Between: Radcliffe Bailey*. Maruani Mercier Gallery, 2019.

Bailey, Stephanie. "Basel: Mickalene Thomas's 'Better Days' Absolute Art Bar." *Whitewall*, 12 June 2013. https://whitewall.art/art/basel-mickalene-thomasbetter-days-absolut-art-bar.

Baker, Courtney. "Courtney Baker Interviews Lorraine O'Grady." Unpublished email exchange, 1998. https://lorraineogrady.com/wp-content/uploads/2015/11/Courtney-Baker-Lorraine-OGrady_Email-Interview_Unpublished.pdf

Baptist, Edward E. *The Half Has Never Been Told: Slavery and the Making of American Capitalism*. Perseus Books, 2014.

Barber, Jarrette. "The Quilt Makers of Gee's Bend: History Is Still in the Making!" *Westside Gazette*, 20 September 2007, 8A.

Barned-Smith, St. John. "Through 12 Black Boxes, Young Artists Speak." *Philadelphia Inquirer*, 6 May 2009. https://www.inquirer.com/philly/entertainment/20090506_Through_12_black_boxes__young_artists_speak.html.

Bartels, Kathleen S., and Jeff Wall, eds. *Kerry James Marshall*. Vancouver Art Gallery, 2010.

Beach, Caitlin. "Meta Warrick Fuller's Mary Turner and the Memory of Mob Violence." *Nka: Journal of Contemporary African Art*, issue 36, 2015, pp. 16–27.

Beardsley, John, ed. *The Quilts of Gee's Bend*. Tinwood Books, 2002.

Beardsley, John, et al. *Gee's Bend: The Women and Their Quilts*. Tinwood Books, 2004.

Beckman, Rachel. "Pinder's 'Ships' Have Sailed." *Washington City Paper*, 25 April 2006, pp. 13–14.

Belcher, Max. *House and Home: Spirits of the South*. University of Washington Press, 1994.

Belefski, Erin. "Is My Shoe Art?" *Arts and Activities*, vol. 153, no. 4, 2013, 28–29.

Bell, Nicholas Robin. *Small Consolations: Miniature Architecture of Memory in Contemporary American Art*. University of Delaware, MA thesis, 2008.

Bendolph, Mary Lee. *Husband Suit Clothes (Housetop Variation), 1990*. https://www.artsy.net/artwork/mary-lee-bendolph-gees-bend-husband-suit-clothes-housetop-variation

Bendolph, Mary Lee, et al. *Piece Together: The Quilts of Mary Lee Bendolph*. Mount Holyoke College Art Museum, 2018.

Bernard, Catherine. "Transformer: The Work of Willie Cole." *NKA: Journal of Contemporary African Art*, issue 15, 2001, pp. 64–69.

———. *Willie Cole: Iron Works*. Avran Gallery, 1999.

Bernier, Celeste-Marie. *African American Visual Arts: From Slavery to the Present*. University of North Carolina Press, 2008.

———. "'The Slave Ship Imprint:' Representing the Body, Memory, and History in Contemporary African American and Black British Painting, Photography, and Installation Art." *Callaloo*, vol. 37, no. 4, 2014, pp. 990–1022.

———. *Stick to the Skin: African American and Black British Art (1965–2015)*. University of California Press, 2019.

Bernier, Celeste-Marie, and Hannah Durkin, eds. *Visualizing Slavery: Art across the African Diaspora*. Liverpool University Press, 2016.

Billops, Camille. "Interview of Emma Amos." Hatch Billops Collection, 1995.

Blanch, Andrea. "Mickalene Thomas: Seurat's Rhinestones." *Musée Magazine*, vol. 5, no. 1, 2013, pp. 65–80. http://mickalenethomas.com/press_pdfs/2013/Mickalene%20Thomas_Musee%20Magazine_2013.pdf.

Booker, Bobbi. "Youths' Dreams Come Alive with Artist's Aid." *Philadelphia Tribune*, May 17, 2009, p. 4C.

Booker, Chakaia, and David R. Collens. *Chakaia Booker*. Storm King Art Center, 2004.

Booker, Chakaia, and Hallie Ringle. *Speakeasy*. Kniznick Gallery, Women's Studies Research Center, Brandeis University, 2016.

Booker, Chakaia, and Lowery Stokes Sims. *Chakaia Booker*. Marlborough Gallery, 2008.

Booker, Chakaia, and Rocío Aranda-Alvarado. *Chakaia Booker: Jersey Ride*. Jersey City Museum, 2004.

Booth, Katie. "In Mickalene Thomas's Awe-Inspiring Portraits, a Meaningful Reflection of Black Women in Art." *New York Times*, 29 January 2016. https://kavigupta.com/press/430-in-mickalene-thomass-awe-inspiring-portrait-a-meaningful-reflection/

Borgatti, Jean. "Willie Cole's Africa Remix Trickster and 'Tribe.'" *African Arts*, vol. 42, no. 2, 2009, pp. 12–23.

Bremer, D. Neil, ed. *Inside Out: Chakaia Booker*. Elmhurst Art Museum, 2008.

Brenson, Michael. "Beverly Buchanan: Evocations of Poor Black Southern Life." *New York Times*, 24 May 1991, p. C26.

Bright, Deborah, ed. *The Passionate Camera: Photography and Bodies of Desire*. Routledge, 1998.

Brock, Glenny. "Meaning Pieced Together: Discovering the Quiltmakers of Gee's Bend." *Birmingham Weekly*, 27 May 2004, p. 4.

Brody, Jacqueline. "Every Action Is Political and Spiritual: An Interview with Willie Cole." *Artnet*, 14 February 1997. http://www.artnet.com/magazine_pre2000/features/brody/brody97-2-14.asp.

Brooklyn Museum. "A Little Taste Outside of Love: Mickalene Thomas." Brooklyn Museum, 2007. https://www.brooklynmuseum.org/opencollection/objects/5044.

Brotherton, Elizabeth. "Patchworks of Tradition; for Gee's Bend, Quilting Was More than Art." *Roll Call*, 18 February 2004.

Bruney, Gabrielle. "Mickalene Thomas Is Celebrating Our Skin: Studio Visits." *The Creators Project*, 4 May 2016. https://creators.vice.com/en_us/article/mickalene-thomas-studio-visit.

Buchanan, Beverly. "Artist Statement." Barbara Archer Gallery. http://www.barbaraarcher.com/artists/buchanan/about.html.

———. *Beverly Buchanan: Drawings and Sculpture*. Truman Gallery and Soter Gallery, 1978.

———. *Beverly Buchanan: Sculpture, 7 February–5 March 1982*. University of Alabama, Visual Arts Gallery, 1982.

———. *Home Space Place Memory: The Work of Beverly Buchanan*. St. Louis Community College, 2012.

———. *Parameters: Beverly Buchanan*. Chrysler Museum, 1992.

———. *Southern Expressions: A Sense of Self*. High Museum of Art, 1988.

Buchanan, Beverly, and Amalia K. Amaki. *Beverly Buchanan: Habitats and Shotgun Shacks*. Bureau of Cultural Affairs, 2000.

Buchanan, Beverly, and Eleanor Flomenhaft. *Beverly Buchanan: Shackworks; A 16-Year Survey*. Montclair Art Museum, 1994.

Buchanan, Beverly, et al. *Beverly Buchanan, 1978–81*. Athenee Press, 2015.

Burak, Stephanie. "About the Artists and Art Featured in the Exhibition, *Mary Lee Bendolph, Gee's Bend Quilts, and Beyond*." September 2012. http://www.venturamodernquiltguild.com/wp-content/uploads/2012/09/Exhibition-Mary-Lee-Bendolph-Gees-Bend-Quilts.pdf.

Busia, Abena P. A., and Alison Saar. "Fashioning a Self in the Contemporary World: Notes toward a Personal Meditation on Memory, History, and the Aesthetics of Origin." *African Arts*, vol. 37, no. 1, 2004, pp. 54–63.

Byard, Carole M., and Clarissa T. Sligh. *Ancestors Known and Unknown: Box Works*. Coast to Coast National Women Artists of Color, 1991.

Cahan, Susan. *Mounting Frustration: The Art Museum in the Age of Black Power*. Duke University Press, 2016.

Caldwell, Kenneth. "Interview with Radcliffe Bailey." *OKTP*, 1 March 2007. http://paulsonfontainepress.com/wp-content/uploads/Radcliffe-Bailey-2007-OKTP.pdf.

———. "Mary Lee Bendolph." *OKTP*, 1 July 2008. http://paulsonfontainepress.com/wp-content/uploads/Bendolph-2008-OKTP-Mary-Lee.pdf.

Cameron, William. "Dread Scott Interview with Will Cameron." *Fragments of the Peculiar Institution*, edited by Dread Scott, et al. CPInPrint Cameron + Brown, 2016.

Campbell, Andy. "'We're Going to See Blood on Them Next': Beverly Buchanan's Georgia Ruins and Black Negativity." *Rhizomes*, vol. 29, 2016. http://rhizomes.net/issue29/campbell/index.html.

Campbell, Mary Schmidt. "Speaking Out: Some Distance to Go." *Art in America*, vol. 78, no. 9, 1990, pp. 78–85.

Capasso, Nick. *Chakaia Booker: In and Out*. DeCordova Sculpture Park and Museum, 2010.

Carey, Celia, dir. *The Quiltmakers of Gee's Bend*. Richland County Public Library Foundation, 2011.

Carpenter, Faedra Chatard, ed. *Coloring Whiteness: Acts of Critique in Black Performance*. University of Michigan Press, 2014.

Cash, Floris Barnett. "Kinship and Quilting: An Examination of an African-American Tradition." *Journal of Negro History*, vol. 80, no. 1, 1995, pp. 30–41.

Castro, Jan Garden. "The Language of Life: A Conversation with Chakaia Booker." *Chakaia Booker: Jersey Ride*, by Chakaia Booker and Rocío Aranda-Alvarado. Jersey City Museum, 2004, pp. 23–31.

———. "Serendipity and Faith: A Conversation with Nari Ward." *Sculpture*, vol. 32, no. 5, 2013, pp. 50–55.

Cervenak, Sarah Jane. "Black Gathering: 'The Weight of Being' in Leonardo Drew's Sculpture." *Women and Performance: Journal of Feminist Theory*, vol. 26, no. 1, 2016, pp. 1–16.

Chambers, Eddie, ed. *The Routledge Companion to African American Art History*. Routledge, 2019.

Chambers, Jesse. "Brand Conscious." *Birmingham Weekly*, 19 April 2007, p. 25.

Chew, Cassie M. "Out of Necessity: Stitching Freedom, Stitching Art." *The Crisis: A Record of the Darker Races*, vol. 111, no. 4, 2004, pp. 51–53.

Childs, Adrienne L., et al. *Riffs and Relations: African American Artists and the European Modernist Tradition*. Skira Rizzoli Publications, 2019.

Chou, Kimberly. "Nari Ward: Reclaiming a Moment of Grace." *Wall Street Journal*, 15 January 2013, p. A20. https://www.wsj.com/articles/SB100014241278873235962045782 43913182814872

Clark, Erin. "Thinking Out Loud: Alison Saar." *Artworks Magazine*, winter 2008, pp. 33–40.

Clark, Meredith. "Beautiful Photos of Women Take on Stereotypes through High Art." *Refinery29*, 2 November 2015. http://www.refinery29.com/2015/11/96793/mickalene -thomas-muse-photos.

Clark, Trinkett. "Beverley Buchanan." *Beverly Buchanan: Shackworks, A 16-Year Survey*, by Beverly Buchanan and Eleanor Flomenhaft. Montclair Art Museum, 1994, pp. 40–44.

Clay-Robison, Matthew. "Conversation with Jefferson Pinder." *Jefferson Pinder: Dark Matter*, by Jefferson Pinder. York College Galleries, 2014.

Cohen, Michael, "Lyle Ashton Harris." *Flash Art*, May–June 1996, p. 107.

Cole, Willie. *Game Show: Installations and Sculptures by Willie Cole*. Bronx Museum of the Arts, 2001.

———. *Perspectives: Willie Cole*. Birmingham Museum of Art, 1998.

———. *Sources and Metamorphoses*. Tampa Museum of Art, 2004.

Cole, Willie, and Charles Wylie. *Willie Cole*. Saint Louis Art Museum, 1992.

Cole, Willie, and Dorit Yaron. *Willie Cole: On Site*. David C. Driskell Center, University of Maryland, 2016.

Cole, Willie, et al. *Afterburn: Willie Cole: Selected Works: 1997–2004*. Worcester Art Museum, 2005.

Cole, Willie, and Mark Richard Leach. *Willie Cole: From Our House to Your House*. Mint Museum of Art, 1991.

Cole, Willie, and Mason Riddle. *Willie Cole: New Prints*. Highpoint Editions, 2012.

Cole, Willie, and Patterson Sims. *Complex Conversations: Willie Cole Sculptures and Wall Works*. Gwen Frostic School of Art, Western Michigan University, 2012.

Collins, Lisa Gail. "Economies of the Flesh: Representing the Black Female Body in Art." *Skin Deep, Spirit Strong: The Black Female Body in American Culture*, edited by Kimberly Wallace-Sanders. University of Michigan Press, 2002, pp. 99–127.

Cook, Christopher. *RubberMade: Sculpture by Chakaia Booker*. Kemper Museum of Contemporary Art, 2008.

Cook, Greg. "Mickalene Thomas: The Seduction of Blackness." *WBUR News*, 3 January 2013. http://legacy .wbur.org/2013/01/03/mickalene-thomas-ica.

Cooks, Bridget R. *Exhibiting Blackness: African Americans and the American Art Museum*. University of Massachusetts Press, 2011.

Cooper, Ashton. "Q&A: Mickalene Thomas in Finding Meaning in Material Things." *Blouin ArtInfo*, 7 October 2014.

Copeland, Huey. "Darks Mirrors: Theaster Gates and *Ebony*." *Artforum International*, vol. 52, no. 2, 2013, pp. 222–29.

Corcoran, Heather. "Mickalene Thomas's Elegy." *Interview Magazine*, 10 December 2012. http://www .interviewmagazine.com/art/mickalene-thomas -lehmann-maupin#_.

Cotter, Holland. "The Topic is Race; the Art is Fearless." *New York Times*, 30 March 2008. http://www.nytimes .com/2008/03/30/arts/design/30cott.html.

Cottingham, Laura. "Interview of Lorraine O'Grady." Hatch Billops Collection, 1996. http://lorraineogrady.com /writing/interview-by-laura-cottingham-1995.

Crawford, Margo Natalie. *Black Post-Blackness: The Black Arts Movement and Twenty-First-Century Aesthetics*. University of Illinois Press, 2017.

Crisell, Luke. "Body and Soul." *Nylon*, April 2009, p. 148. http://images.exhibit-e.com/www_lehmannmaupin _com/72377384.pdf.

Crowe Storm, LaShawnda. "Creative Power for Social Change!" LaShawnda Crowe Storm, n.d. https://www .lashawndacrowestorm.com/biography.

———. "Laura Nelson's Story." *The Lynch Quilts Project*. LaShawnda Crowe Storm, n.d. https://www .thelynchquiltsproject.com/laura-nelsons-story.

———. "The Lynch Quilts Project: A Community Drive Project by Artist LaShawnda Crowe Storm. Our Story." LaShawnda Crowe Storm, n.d. https://www .thelynchquiltsproject.com/about-us.

———. *Quilt I: Her Name Was Laura Nelson, 2004.* https://www.thelynchquiltsproject.com/her-name-was-laura-nelson

Cubbs, Joanne. "A History of the Work-Clothes Quilt." *Gee's Bend: The Architecture of the Quilt*, edited by Paul Arnett, et al. Tinwood Books, 2006, pp. 67–89.

Cubbs, Joanne, et al., eds. *Mary Lee Bendolph: Gee's Bend Quilts, and Beyond.* Tinwood Books, 2006.

Curtis, Cathy. "Art That Goes behind the Camera: Photography: Pat Ward Williams tries to show what is outside the frame—or what is invisible on the surface." *Los Angeles Times*, 6 June 1991. https://www.latimes.com/archives/la-xpm-1991-06-06-ca-478-story.html.

Dailey, Meghan. "Leonardo Drew." *Nka: Journal of Contemporary African Art*, issue 6–7, 1997, p. 69.

Dallow, Jessica. *Family Legacies: The Art of Betye, Lezley, and Alison Saar.* Ackland Art Museum, University of North Carolina at Chapel Hill in association with University of Washington Press, 2005.

———. "Reclaiming Histories: Betye and Alison Saar, Feminism, and the Representation of Black Womanhood." *Feminist Studies*, vol. 30, no. 1, 2004, pp. 74–113.

Davis, Chris. "The Quilted Word." *Memphis Flyer*, 25 February 2005. http://www.memphisflyer.com/memphis/the-quilted-word/Content?oid=1116161.

Davis, Noah. *Seventy Works.* Underground Museum, 2014.

Davis, Olga Idriss. "The Rhetoric of Quilts: Creating Identity in African-American Children's Literature." *African American Review*, vol. 32, no. 1, 1998, pp. 67–76.

Davis, Theo. "Artist as Art Critic: An Interview with Conceptualist Lorraine O'Grady." *Sojourner: The Women's Forum*, November 1996, pp. 25–28.

Dawson, Jessica. "Jefferson Pinder 37, Video Artist." *Washington Post*, 14 September 2008. https://www.patriciasweetowgallery.com/press/jefferson-pinder-37-video-artist/

Deavere Smith, Anna. *Lyle Ashton Harris.* Gregory R. Miller & Company, 2002.

DeCarlo, Tessa. "An Artist Who Didn't Know She Was One." *New York Times*, 3 January 1999. https://www.nytimes.com/1999/01/03/arts/recordings-an-artist-who-didn-t-know-she-was-one.html

Dimling Cochran, Rebecca. "Connecting Rhythms: A Conversation with Radcliffe Bailey." *Sculpture*, vol. 31, no. 5, 2012, pp. 24–29.

———. "Epic Mythologies of Detritus." *Sculpture*, vol. 29, no. 3, 2010, pp. 34–39.

———. "Radcliffe Bailey." *NKA: Journal of Contemporary African Art*, issue 15, 2001, p. 84.

———. "Willie Cole: The Other Side." *Sculpture*, vol. 25, no. 2, 2006, pp. 24–29.

Dobrzynski, Judith H. "Leonardo Drew: Extracting Metaphors from 'Life's Detritus.'" *New York Times*, 2 February 2000, E1–E8.

Doherty, Donna. "City Artist Winfred Rembert's Story Comes to light in 'All Me.'" *Tribune Business News*, 29 April 2012. http://www.nhregister.com/article/NH/20120427/NEWS/304279964.

Doss, Erika. *American Art of the 20th–21st Centuries.* Oxford University Press, 2017.

———. *Twentieth-Century American Art.* Oxford University Press, 2002.

Douglass, Frederick. "The Heroic Slave." *My Bondage and My Freedom*, edited by Celeste-Marie Bernier. Oxford University Press, 2019, pp. 332–369.

———. *The Lessons of the Hour.* Thomas and Evans, 1894. https://archive.org/details/09359080.4757.emory.edu.

———. *Life and Times of Frederick Douglass, Written by Himself.* De Wolfe & Fisk Co., 1892.

———. *My Bondage and My Freedom*, edited by Celeste-Marie Bernier. Oxford University Press, 2019.

———. *Narrative of the Life of Frederick Douglass, An American Slave*, edited by Celeste-Marie Bernier. Broadview Press, 2018.

———. "Speech on the Dred Scott Decision." *Two Speeches*, C. P. Dewey, 1857, pp. 27–46. https://teachingamericanhistory.org/document/speech-on-the-dred-scott-decision-2/.

"Dread Scott and Progressive Art Exhibit under Attack." Revolution, 13 July 2016. http://revcom.us/a/448/interview-with-artist-dread-scott-en.html.

Drew, Leonardo. *Leonardo Drew.* Threading Wax Space, 1992.

———. *Leonardo Drew: Journal.* Contemporary Art Museum, 2017.

———. "Untitled." *Bomb*, vol. 41, 1992, pp. 84–85.

Drew, Leonardo, and Claudia Schmuckli. *Existed: Leonardo Drew.* Giles, 2009.

Drew, Leonardo, and Lorenzo Fusi. *Leonardo Drew: Existing Everywhere.* Gli ori, 2006.

Drew, Leonardo, and Xandra Eden. *Leonardo Drew.* Charta, 2013.

Dubin, Steven C. *Arresting Images: Impolitic Art and Uncivil Actions.* Routledge, 1992.

Ducat, Vivian, dir. *All Me: The Life and Times of Winfred Rembert.* Filmmakers Library, 2012.

Duncan, Sally Anne. "From Cloth to Canvas: Reinventing Gee's Bend Quilts in the Name of Art." *Museum Anthropology*, vol. 28, no. 1, 2005, pp. 19–34.

Earnest, Jarrett, and Lorraine O'Grady. "Art in Conversation: Lorraine O'Grady with Jarrett Earnest." *Brooklyn Rail*, 3 February 2016. http://brooklynrail.org/2016/02/art/lorraine-ogrady-with-jarrett-earnest.

Enwezor, Okwui, and Henry Louis Gates Jr. *Lyle Ashton Harris: Excessive Exposure*. Gregory R. Miller & Company, 2010.

Esleck, Emily. "Sculptor Willie Cole Tells Art Students to 'Always Look Forward.'" *University Wire*, 2 October 2015.

Farrington, Lisa E. *African-American Art: A Visual and Cultural History*. Oxford University Press, 2016.

——— . "Conceptualism, Politics and the Art of African American Women." *Source: Notes in the History of Art*, vol. 24, no. 4, 2005, pp. 67–75.

——— . "Emma Amos: Art as Legacy." *Women's Art Journal*, vol. 28, no. 1, 2007, pp. 3–11.

Feaster, Felicia. "Soul Man: Radcliffe Bailey." *Atlantan*, December 2009.

Felsenthal, Julia. "Mickalene Thomas on Her Photographic Muses." *Vogue*, 28 January 2016. http://www.vogue.com/article/mickalene-thomas-muse-aperture.

Finkel, Jori. "Mickalene Thomas up Close and Very Personal." *Los Angeles Times*, 20 April 2012. http://articles.latimes.com/2012/apr/20/entertainment/la-ca-mickalene-thomas-20120422.

Fischman, Lisa. *Radcliffe Bailey: Notes*. Bridgette Mayer Gallery, 2013.

Fleetwood, Nicole R., et al. *Mickalene Thomas: I Can't See You without Me*. Wexner Center for the Arts, 2018.

Flomenhaft, Eleanor. "Shack Portraiture: An Interview with Beverly Buchanan." *Beverly Buchanan: Shackworks, A 16-Year Survey*, edited by Beverly Buchanan and Eleanor Flomenhaft. Montclair Art Museum, 1994, pp. 9–16.

Flores, Gabe, "Interview with Alison Saar." PORT: Portlandart.net, 20 November 2010. http://www.portlandart.net/archives/2010/11/interview_with_13.html.

Foster, Hal, and Teju Cole. *Kerry James Marshall: History of Painting*. David Zwirner Books, 2019.

Frazier-Booth, Kimberly. "Shack Attack Comes to Phillips Art Gallery." *Bay State Banner*, 23 June 1994, p. 16.

Freeman, Linda, dir. *Emma Amos: Action Lines*. L & S Video, 1999.

Fuller, Meta Vaux Warrick. *In Memory of Mary Turner: As a Silent Protest against Mob Violence*, 1919. https://artsandculture.google.com/asset/in-memory-of-mary-turner-as-a-silent-protest-against-mob-violence/6AGtTaPw-CH_Bg

Genocchio, Benjamin. "From Newark to . . . Montclair: The Artist Willie Cole Is the Man of the Moment." *New York Times*, 12 March 2006, p. NJ1.

Gioni, Massimiliano, and Gary Carrion-Murayari, eds. *Nari Ward: We the People*. Phaidon, 2019.

Golden, Thelma, and Christine Y. Kim, eds. *Freestyle*. Studio in Harlem, 2001.

Gopnik, Blake. "Folk Video Artist Jefferson Pinder Seeks to Cast Off 'Black Art.'" *Washington Post*, 24 January 2010. http://www.washingtonpost.com/wp-dyn/content/article/2010/01/21/AR2010012105237.html.

Gouma-Peterson, Thalia, ed. *Emma Amos Paintings and Prints, 1982–92*. College of Wooster Art Museum, 1993.

Grace, Janelle. "Honoring U.S. Freedoms through Dissent: Interview with Dread Scott." *Hyperallergic*, 4 July 2010. https://hyperallergic.com/7791/dread-scott-honoring-freedoms-thru-dissent.

Gray, Thomas R. *The Confessions of Nat Turner, The Leader of the Late Insurrection in Southampton, V.A.* Thomas R. Gray, 1831.

Greene, Myra. "*Character Recognition*, July 13–July 26, 2009." Center for Photography at Woodstock, 2009. https://www.cpw.org/past-exhibitions/myra-greene.

——— . "*Character Recognition*, 2006–2007." Myra Greene, n.d. https://www.myragreene.com/charaacterrecognition.

——— . *My White Friends*. Kehrer, 2012.

——— . "*Self Portraits*, 2002–2004." Myra Greene, n.d. https://www.myragreene.com/selfportraits.

Greene, Myra, and Tate Shaw. "Conversation Starter." *My White Friends*, by Myra Greene. Kehrer, 2012.

Greene, Myra, and Tom Barrow. "Tom Barrow and Myra Greene: A Conversation." *Exposure*, vol. 40, no. 1, 2007, pp. 4–15.

Griffey, Randall R., et al. *My Soul Has Grown Deep: Art from the Black South*. Yale University Press, 2018.

Grossberg, Michael. "Hides to Seek." *Columbus Dispatch*, 23 January 2011.

Gustafson, Elaine D. *Willie Cole: Sources and Metamorphoses*. Tampa Museum of Art, 2005.

Guy Nichols, Matthew. "Willie Cole: The Energy of Objects." *Art in America*, vol. 95, no. 5, 2006, pp. 146–52.

Haley, Alex. *Roots: The Saga of an American Family*. Doubleday, 1976.

Halley, Peter. "Lyle Ashton Harris Interviewed by Peter Halley." *Lyle Ashton Harris*, by Lyle Ashton Harris, Tommy Gear, and Peter Halley. Knokke: Gallery Maruani and Mercier, 2014.

Harris, Frank, III. "The n-Word Project." http://n
-wordproject.tumblr.com/post/95185593219/if-theres-a
-nigga-in-the-building-stand-up.

Harris, Lyle Ashton. "Different, but Not Abnormal: 'Out' in
Africa." *Nka: Journal of Contemporary African Art*, issue
38–39, 2016, pp. 186–95.

———. *Face: Lyle Ashton Harris.* New Museum of
Contemporary Art, 1993.

———. "Lyle Ashton Harris and Chuck Close: A
Conversation." *Lyle Ashton Harris: Excessive Exposure*,
edited by Okwui Enwezor and Henry Louis Gates Jr.
Gregory R. Miller & Company, 2010, pp. 313–329.

Harris, Lyle Ashton, et al. *Lyle Ashton Harris: Blow Up.*
Gregory R. Miller & Company, 2008.

Harris, Lyle Ashton, and Johanna Burton. *Lyle Ashton Harris:
Today I Shall Judge Nothing That Occurs.* Aperture, 2017.

Harris, Lyle Ashton, Tommy Gear, and Peter Halley. *Lyle
Ashton Harris.* Knokke: Gallery Maruani and Mercier,
2014.

Harris, Lyle Ashton, and Thomas Allen Harris. "Black Widow:
A Conversation." *The Passionate Camera: Photography
and Bodies of Desire*, edited by Deborah Bright. Routledge,
1998, pp. 248–62.

Harris, Melissa. "South Side Artist's Latest Project: Saving
Long-Abandoned Bank." *Chicago Informer*, 5 August 2012.
https://www.chicagotribune.com/business/ct-xpm-2012-08
-05-ct-biz-0805-confidential-theaster-20120805-story
.html.

Harris, Shawnya L., and David C. Driskell, eds. *Expanding
Tradition: Selections from the Larry D. and Brenda A.
Thompson Collection.* Georgia Museum of Art, 2017.

Harris, Thomas Allen, dir. *Through a Lens Darkly: Black
Photographers and the Emergence of a People.* Chimpanzee
Productions, 2014.

Hayes, Jeffreen M. "Myra Greene." *International Review of
African American Art*, vol. 22, no. 2, 2008, p. 11.

Haynes, Lauren, et al., eds. *The Bearden Project.* Studio
Museum in Harlem, 2012.

Hays, Constance L. "Teenager Shot in Quarrel Says He'll
Continue to Oppose Drugs." *New York Times*, 8 August
1992, p. 23.

Hazel, Carla. "Sanctuary: The Great Dismal Swamp." *The Art
of Whitfield Lovell: Whispers from the Walls*, edited by
Whitfield Lovell and Lucy R. Lippard. Pomegranate, 2003,
pp. 102–109.

Herman, Bernard L., ed. *Fever Within: The Art of Ronald
Lockett.* University of North Carolina Press, 2016.

———. "The Quilts of Gee's Bend: How Great Art Gets Lost."
Journal of Modern Craft, vol. 2, no. 1, 2009, pp. 9–15.

Hess, Whitney. "Pillars of Learning." *Pittsburgh City Paper*, 9
June 2004, p. 27.

Hewitt, Mary Jane. "Betye Saar: An Interview." *International
Review of African American Art*, volume 10, no. 2, 1992, pp.
7–23.

Hills, Patricia. *Whitfield Lovell.* D. C. Moore Gallery, 2000.

Hirsch, Robert. *Transformational Imagemaking: Handmade
Photography since 1960.* Focal Press, 2014.

Hobbs, Robert. *30 Americans: Rubell Family Collection,
December 3, 2008–May 30, 2009.* Contemporary Arts
Foundation, 2013.

Holder, Sarah. "The Amazing Grace of Winfred Rembert."
Yale Herald, 8 April 2016. https://www.uwire.com/2016
/04/08/the-amazing-grace-of-winfred-rembert.

hooks, bell. "An Aesthetic of Blackness: Strange and
Oppositional Aesthetic Inheritances." *The Object of Labor:
Art, Cloth, and Cultural Production*, edited by Joan
Livingstone and John Ploof. MIT Press, 2007, pp. 315–32.

———. *Art on My Mind: Visual Politics.* Norton, 1995.

———. *Emma Amos: Changing the Subject.* Art in General,
Inc., 1994.

———. "Interview with Emma Amos." *Artist and Influence*,
vol. 14, no. 1, 1995, pp. 33–46.

———. "Straighten Up and Fly Straight: Making History
Visible." *Emma Amos Paintings and Prints, 1982–92*,
edited by Thalia Gouma-Peterson. College of Wooster Art
Museum, 1993, pp.15–28.

Hoover, Paul. "Pair of Figures for Eshu: Doubling of
Consciousness in the work of Kerry James Marshall and
Nathaniel Mackey." *Callaloo*, vol. 23, no. 2, 2000, pp.
728–48.

Hotton, Julia. "Emma Amos: Woman of Substance." *Black
American Literature Forum*, vol. 19, no. 1, 1985, pp. 24–25.

Hughes, Langston. "I'm Still Here," 1957. https://
cosmolearning.org/books/im-still-here-589/poem

Hunger, Kate. "Leonardo Drew: 'Rust in Peace.'" *San Antonio
Express-News*, 26 March 2000.

Hunt, Kenya. "Rhinestones and Oprah." *Metro*, 30 March–1
April 2007.

Hunter, Clementine, and Nellie Mae Rowe. *Two Black Folk
Artists: Clementine Hunter, Nellie Mae Rowe.* Miami
University Art Museum, 1987.

Indrisek, Scott. "Nari Ward." *Modern Painters*, vol. 24, no. 1,
2012, pp. 34–35.

Irving, David K., dir. *Betye and Alison Saar: Conjure Women
of the Arts.* L & S Video, 1998.

Irwin, Demetria. "Controversy and Conversation for
MOCADA Art Exhibit." *New York Amsterdam News*, 20
March–26 March 2008, p. 19.

Jackson, Candace. "Southern Past, Modern Present." *Wall Street Journal*, 8 July 2011. https://www.wsj.com/articles/SB10001424052702303544604576429941552270 56

Jacobs, Harriet Ann. *Incidents in the Life of a Slave Girl. Written By Herself. Ed. L. Maria Child*. Published for the Author, 1861.

James, Curtia. "3 Works of Art." *Essence*, vol. 25, no. 9, 1995, p. 96.

James, Erica Moiah. "Sun Splashed." *Nari Ward: Sun Splashed*, edited by Naomi Beckwith, et al. Prestel, 2015, pp. 30–42.

Jones, Kellie. "Pat Ward Williams Photography and Social/Personal History." *Eyeminded: Living and Writing Contemporary Art*. Duke University Press, 2011, pp. 207–14.

———. "Personal Public Portraits: The Art of Whitfield Lovell." *Black American Literature Forum*, vol. 19, no. 1, 1985, pp. 46–47.

Jones, Kellie, and Moira Roth, "Pat Ward Williams: A Narrative Chronology." *Pat Ward Williams: Probable Cause*, edited by Pat Ward Williams, Kellie Jones, and Moira Roth. Goldie Paley Gallery. 1992.

Joselit, David. *American Art since 1945*. Thames and Hudson, 2003.

Kapplow, Heather. "A Walk through the World of Lorraine O'Grady." *Hyperallergic*, 31 December 2015. http://hyperallergic.com/265223/a-walk-through-the-world-of-lorraine-ogrady.

Kelley, Robin D. G. "Black Study, Black Struggle." *Ufahamu: A Journal of African Studies*, vol. 40, no. 2, 2018, pp. 153–168.

Kerry James Marshall. Art21, 2017. http://www.art21.org/artists/kerry-james-marshall/videos

King, Carol. "A Confidence Highlighted in Rhinestones." *New York Times*, 12 April 2009, p. 23.

King, Chris. "A Lifetime Patiently Etched into Leather." *New York Times*, 24 December 2000, p. CN14. http://www.nytimes.com/2000/12/24/nyregion/art-a-lifetime-patiently-etched-into-leather.html.

King-Hammond, Leslie. "Talking through the Mind Fields: A Conversation Between Willie Cole and Leslie King-Hammond." *Anxious Objects: Willie Cole's Favorite Brands*, edited by Patterson Sims, Montclair Art Museum, 2006, pp. 90–99.

———. "Whitfield Lovell in Conversation with Leslie King-Hammond." *The Art of Whitfield Lovell: Whispers from the Walls*, by Whitfield Lovell and Lucy R. Lippard. Pomegranate, 2003, pp. 53–102.

King-Hammond, Leslie, ed. *Gumbo Ya Ya: Anthology of Contemporary African-American Women Artists*. Midmarch Arts Press, 1995.

Kinnahan, Linda A. "'Bodies Written Off:' Economies of Race and Gender in the Visual/Verbal Collaborative Clash of Erica Hunt's and Alison Saar's *Arcade*." *We Who Love to Be Astonished: Experimental Women's Writing and Performance Poetics*, edited by Laura Hinton and Cynthia Hogue. University of Alabama Press, 2002, pp. 165–78.

Klassen, Teri. "Representations of African American Quiltmaking: From Omission to High Art." *Journal of American Folklore*, vol. 122, no. 485, 2009, pp. 297–334.

Knowles, Solange. "Solange Interviews Mickalene Thomas." *Opening Ceremony*, 19 March 2013. http://blog.openingceremony.com/entry.asp?pid=7590.

Kogan, Lee. *The Art of Nellie Mae Rowe: Ninety Nine and a Half Won't Do*. Marquand, 1998.

———. "Nellie Mae Rowe: Multiple Contexts, Multiple Meanings." *Sacred and Profane: Voice and Vision in Southern Self-Taught Art*, edited by Carol Crown and Charles Russell. University Press of Mississippi, 2007, pp. 111–27.

Krajewski, Sara. *Leonardo Drew*. Madison Art Center, 1999.

Kuennen, Joel. "Naomi Beckwith in Conversation with Solange and Mickalene Thomas." ArtSlant.com, 18 September 2015. https://www.artslant.com/ny/articles/show/43980-naomi-beckwith-in-conversation-with-solange-and-mickalene-thomas.

Kunitz, Daniel. "In Public and in Color: A Conversation with Leonardo Drew." *Sculpture: A Publication of the International Sculpture Center*, vol. 38, no. 5, 2019, pp. 20–27. https://sculpturemagazine.art/in-public-and-in-color-a-conversation-with-leonardo-drew.

Lampe, Lilly. "Radcliffe Bailey." *Bomb*, 16 July 2013. http://bombmagazine.org/article/7278/radcliffe-bailey.

Landers, Sean. "Mickalene Thomas." *Bomb*, vol. 116, 2011, pp. 30–38. http://bombmagazine.org/article/5105/mickalene-thomas.

Landi, Ann. "Dressing for Excess." *ARTnews*, June 2012, p. 66.

Landis, Michael Todd. "These Are Words Scholars Should No Longer Use to Describe Slavery and the Civil War." *History News Network*, Columbian College of Arts and Sciences, George Washington University, 4 September 2015. https://historynewsnetwork.org/article/160266

Lash, Miranda, and Trevor Schoonmaker, eds. *Southern Accent: Seeking the American South in Contemporary Art*. Duke University Press, 2016.

Laster, Paul. "A Window on Art: Mickalene Thomas's Shiny Sex Appeal Paintings." *New York Observer*, 21 April 2010. http://observer.com/2010/04/a-window-on-art.

Lawrence, Sidney. "The Color of Art." *American Art*, vol. 11, no. 1, 1997, pp. 2–9.

———. *Directions: Alison Saar*. Smithsonian Institution, 1993.

Lawson, Michael L. "Omaha, a City in Ferment: Summer of 1919." *Nebraska History*, vol. 58, no. 3, 1977, pp. 395–417.

Leigh Brown, Patricia. "From the Bottomlands, Soulful Stitches." *New York Times*, 21 November 2002, p. F1. http://www.nytimes.com/2002/11/21/garden/design-notebook-from-the-bottomlands-soulful-stitches.html.

Lemon, Ralph. "A Conversation with Nari Ward." *The Refinery X: A Simple Twist of Fate*, edited by Marco Pierini, et al. Gli Ori, 2006.

Leonardo Drew. Art21, 2017. http://www.art21.org/artists/leonardo-drew.

Letiche, Hugo. "Doubling: There's an Escape from Commodification . . . ?" *Society and Business Review*, vol. 4, no. 1, 2009, pp. 8–25.

Lewis, Desiree. "Against the Grain: Black Women and Sexuality." *Agenda*, vol. 19, no. 63, 2005, pp. 11–24.

Lippard, Lucy R. "Floating Falling Landing: An Interview with Emma Amos." *Arts Paper*, vol. 15, no. 6, 1991, pp. 13–16.

———. "Spirits Moving in the Pictures." *Chronicle of Higher Education*, 24 March 2000, p. B108.

Lipsitz, George. "Breaking the Chains and Steering the Ship: How Activism Can Help Change Teaching and Scholarship." *Engaging Contradictions: Theory, Politics, and Methods of Activist Scholarship*, edited by Charles R. Hale. University of California Press, 2008, pp. 88–112.

Little, James. *New Visions: James Little, Whitfield Lovell, Alison Saar*. Queens Museum, 1988.

Lockett, Ronald. *Once Something Has Lived It Can Never Really Die, 1996*. The Souls Grown Deep Foundation. https://www.soulsgrowndeep.org/artist/ronald-lockett/work/once-something-has-lived-it-can-never-really-die.

———. *Smoke-Filled Sky (You Can Burn A Man's House But Not His Dreams)*. The Souls Grown Deep Foundation, 1990. http://www.soulsgrowndeep.org/artist/ronald-lockett/work/smoke-filled-sky-you-can-burn-mans-house-not-his-dreams.

Lorde, Audre. "History is a Weapon: The Master's Tools Will Never Dismantle the Master's House," 1979. https://www.historyisaweapon.com/defcon1/lordedismantle.html

Lovell, Whitfield. "The Dream Described." *New York Times*, 1 January 2010. http://www.nytimes.com/interactive/2010/01/18/opinion/20100118-OPART.html?_r=0.

———. "Leslie Hewitt by Whitfield Lovell." *Bomb*, issue 104, 1 July 2008, p. 64–65.

———. *Mercy, Patience, and Destiny: The Women of Whitfield Lovell's Tableaux*. Savannah College of Art and Design, 2009.

———. *Whitfield Lovell: Kith and Kin*. D. C. Moore Gallery, 2008.

Lovell, Whitfield, and Judy Collischan, ed. *Whitfield Lovell: Portrayals*. Neuberger Museum of Art, 2000.

Lovell, Whitfield, Lowery Stokes Sims, and Bartholomew F. Bland. *Whitfield Lovell: All Things in Time*. Hudson River Museum, 2008.

Lovell, Whitfield, and Lucy R. Lippard. *The Art of Whitfield Lovell: Whispers from the Walls*. Pomegranate, 2003.

———. "Chronology with Notes by Whitfield Lovell." *The Art of Whitfield Lovell: Whispers from the Walls*, by Whitfield Lovell and Lucy R. Lippard. Pomegranate, 2003, pp. 63–73.

Lovell, Whitfield, and Nandini Makrandi Jestice. *Whitfield Lovell: Deep River*. Hunter Museum of American Art, 2013.

Lusaka, Jane. "(Re)Union: Artist Clarissa T. Sligh Finds her Family." *Orator*, vo. 2, no. 1, 1994, pp. 5 and 11.

MacNaughton, Mary Davis. "Spirit in Matter: Works by Alison and Lezley Saar." *Alison and Lezley Saar*, edited by Mary Davis MacNaughton. Ruth Chandler Williamson Gallery, Scripps College, and Perpetua Press, 2000.

Maerkle, Andrew. "Mickalene Thomas: Models of Agency." *ART iT*, 15 August 2011. http://www.art-it.asia/u/admin_ed_itv_e/XsWaKLhzjmeVwCA6rx2v.

Manchanda, Catharina, et al. *Figuring History: Robert Colescott, Kerry James Marshall, Mickalene Thomas*. Yale University Press, 2018.

Marshall, Kerry James. "American Artist: A Portfolio and Interview." *Callaloo*, vol. 21, no. 1, 1998, pp. 253–62.

———. *Believed to be a Portrait of David Walker, c.1830*. https://www.muhka.be/programme/detail/71-kerry-james-marshall-painting-and-other-stuff/item/3667-believed-to-be-a-portrait-of-david-walker-ca-1830

———. "Kerry James Marshall, Interview: Putting Black Artists into the Textbooks." *Independent*, 17 October 2014. https://www.independent.co.uk/news/people/kerry-james-marshall-interview-putting-black-artists-textbooks-9801055.html.

———. *Kerry James Marshall: Mementos*. University of Chicago, 1998.

———. "Just Because from Chris Ofili." *Kerry James Marshall: Mastry*, edited by Kerry James Marshall, et al. Rizzoli, 2016.

———. *One True Thing: Meditations on Black Aesthetics*. Museum of Contemporary Art, 2003.

———. "'Rhythm Mastr' Kerry James Marshall." *Art21*, November 2011. https://art21.org/read/kerry-james-marshall-rythm-mastr.

———. *Still-Life with Wedding Portrait*, 2015. https://www.metmuseum.org/art/collection/search/701471

———. "A Thousand Words: Kerry James Marshall Talks About Rythm Mastr." *Kerry James Marshall: Mastry*, edited by Kerry James Marshall, et al. Rizzoli, 2016.

———. "Young Artist to Be." *Kerry James Marshall: Mastry*, edited by Kerry James Marshal, et al. Rizzoli, 2016.

Marshall, Kerry James, and Deborah Smith. *Kerry James Marshall: Along the Way*. Camden Arts Centre, 2005.

Marshall, Kerry James, et al. *Kerry James Marshall*. Harry N. Abrams, Inc., 2000.

———. *Kerry James Marshall: Inside Out*. Konig, 2018.

———. *Kerry James Marshall: Look See*. David Zwirner, 2016.

———. *Kerry James Marshall: Mastry*. Skira Rizzoli Publications, 2016.

———. *Kerry James Marshall: Painting and Other Stuff*. Ludion, 2014.

Martin, Courtney J. "Emma Amos in Conversation." *Nka: Journal of Contemporary African Art*, issue 30, 2012, pp. 104–13.

———. *Four Generations: The Joyner/Giuffrida Collection of Abstract Art*. Gregory R. Miller, 2016.

Martin, Michael T., and David C. Wall. "'Where are you from?' Performing Race in the Art of Jefferson Pinder." *Black Camera*, vol. 2, no. 1, 2010, pp. 72–105.

Maschke, Kathy L., ed. "Radcliffe Bailey." *Out of Bounds: New Work by Eight Southeast Artists*. Nexus Contemporary Art Center, 1996.

Maxwell, Claire. "Interview with Lyle Ashton Harris: Exploring Both Ghanaian Tradition and Modernity in *Accra My Love*." Burnaway, 24 April 2013. https://burnaway.org/magazine/interview-with-lyle-ashton-harris-exploring-both-ghanaian-tradition-and-modernity-in-accra-my-love.

McClintock, Dinah. "Q & A: Lyle Ashton Harris on His Kennesaw State University Show and His Love Affair with Ghana." *ArtsAtl*, 22 March 2013. https://www.artsatl.org/qa-lyle-ashton-harris/.

McDaniels, Pellom, III. *Still Raising Hell: The Art, Activism, and Archives of Camille Billops and James V. Hatch*. Stuart A. Rose Manuscript Archives and Rare Book Library, 2017.

McDermott, Emily. "In Profile: Abigail DeVille." *Frieze*, 3 July 2017. https://www.frieze.com/article/profile-abigail-deville

McGee, Julie L. "After an Afternoon: Whitfield Lovell in Conversation with Julie L. McGee." *Whitfield Lovell: Kin*, edited by Irving Sandler, et al. Rizzoli, 2016, pp. 183–202.

———. "Field, Boll, and Monument: Toward an Iconography of Cotton in African American Art." *International Review of African American Art*, vol. 19, no. 3, 2003, pp. 37–48.

———. "Whitfield Lovell: Autour du Monde." *Nka: Journal of Contemporary African Art*, issue 26, 2010, pp. 48–59.

McLeod, Carmen. "Tête à Tête: Mickalene Thomas in Conversation with Carmen McCleod." *Art Papers*, November/December 2012, p. 10. https://davidcastillogallery.com/wp-content/uploads/2019/10/1-Art-Papers-Dec-2012.pdf.

McNally, Owen. "A Life on Leather." *Hartford Courant*, 17 September 2000. http://articles.courant.com/2000-09-17/entertainment/0009170135_1_hanging-jail-lynching.

McNatt, Glenn. "Lawsuits Tinge Quilter's Fame." *McClatchy–Tribune Business News*, 28 June 2007, p. 1.

Melandri, Lisa, ed. *Mickalene Thomas: Origin of the Universe*. Santa Monica Museum of Art, 2012.

Menard, Orville D. "Tom Dennison, the *Omaha Bee*, and the 1919 Omaha Race Riot." *Nebraska History*, vol. 68, 1987, pp. 152–65.

Mercer, Kobena. "Kerry James Marshall: The Painter of Afro-Modern Life." *Afterall: A Journal of Art, Context, and Enquiry*, vol. 24, 2010, pp. 80–88.

Mercer, Valerie J. "Emma Amos: A Skillful and Imaginative Printmaker." *Emma Amos Paintings and Prints, 1982–92*, edited by Thalia Gouma-Peterson. College of Wooster Art Museum, 1993, pp. 29–34.

Meyer, James. *In The Tower: Kerry James Marshall*. National Gallery of Art, 28 June–7 December 2013. http://www.nga.gov/content/dam/ngaweb/exhibitions/pdfs/2013/nga-kjmarshall-brochure.pdf.

Meyers, Suze. "Material Girl: An Interview with Mickalene Thomas." *Columbia Spectator*, 1 May 2014. http://spc.columbiaspectator.com/eye/2014/05/01/material-girl.

Miller-Keller, Andrea. *Lorraine O'Grady: Matrix 127*. Wadsworth, 1995.

Millsom, Carol. "Winfred Rembert Exhibits at New York's Adelson Gallery." *Folk Art Messenger*, vol. 22, no. 1, 2010, pp. 13–14.

Moehringer, J. R. "Crossing Over: Chapter 1 / Mary Lee's Vision." *Los Angeles Times*, 22 August 1999. https://www.latimes.com/archives/la-xpm-1999-aug-22-mn-21385-story.html.

Mooney, Amy. "Mementos: Kerry James Marshall." *Nka: Journal of Contemporary African Art*, issue 9, 1998, pp. 24–27.

Moore, Madison. "Q+A: Mickalene Thomas' Photographic Funk." *Art in America*, 17 February 2011. https://www.lehmannmaupin.com/press/art-in-america69.

Moos, David. "Conversations Between Radcliffe Bailey and David Moos and Manual Jordan." *Radcliffe Bailey: The Magic City*, edited by David Moos. Birmingham Museum of Art, 2001.

Morrison, Toni. *Beloved: A Novel*. Alfred A. Knopf, 1987.

Munro, Eleanor C. *Originals: American Women Artists*. Simon and Schuster, 1979.

Murray, Albert. "Oral History Interview with Emma Amos." Archives of American Art Oral History Program, 3 October 1968. https://www.aaa.si.edu/interviews/oral-history-interview-emma-amos-11451.

Murray, Derek Conrad. "Mickalene Thomas Afro-Kitsch and the Queering of Blackness." *American Art*, vol. 28, no. 1, 2014, pp. 9–15.

Myers, Terry R. "Kerry James Marshall's Tempting Painting." *Afterall: A Journal of Art, Context, and Enquiry*, vol. 24, 2010, pp. 72–79.

Nahas, Dominique. *Whitfield Lovell: Embers*. D. C. Moore, 2000.

Nathans, Heather S. "Visualizing August: Wilson's Gem of the Ocean." *New England Theatre Journal*, vol. 19a, 2008, pp. 75–86.

Neff, John. "Kerry James Marshall Interviewed by John Neff: Part I." Studio Chicago, 3 May 2010. http://studiochicago .blogspot.com/2010/05/kerry-james-marshall -interviewed-by.html.

———. "Kerry James Marshall Interviewed by John Neff: Part II." Studio Chicago, 5 May 2010. http://studiochicago .blogspot.com/2010/05/kerry-james-marshall-interviewed -by_05.html.

Newsum, Horace (H. Ike Okafor-Newsum). *SoulStirrers: Black Art and the Neo-Ancestral Impulse*. University of Mississippi, 2016.

Newton, John. *Thoughts upon the African Slave Trade*. J. Ruckland, 1788.

Nichols, Matthew Guy. "Chakaia Booker: Material Matters." *Art in America*, vol. 92, no. 6, June–July, 2004, pp. 164–69.

———. "The Taxonomy of Ruin." *Art in America*, vol. 96, no. 1, January 2008, pp. 112–15.

Nieves, Marysol. "A Conversation with Willie Cole." *Game Show: Installations and Sculptures by Willie Cole*, by Willie Cole. Bronx Museum of the Arts, 2001.

Nola.com. "Radcliffe Bailey's Stunning 'Windward Coast' at the CAC." *The Times-Picayune Video in HD*, https://www .youtube.com/watch?v=QUC07YjvjXw.

Nye, Tim. "Leonardo Drew Interviewed by Tim Nye." *Sculpture: Leonardo Drew, Lisa Hoke, Brad Kahlhamer: 16 January – 28 February 1992*, edited by Leonardo Drew, et al. Thead Waxing Space, 1992.

Oates, Leah. "BeDazzled: Mickalene Thomas Interviewed by Leah Oates." *NY Arts*, Fall 2009, inside cover, pp. 6–7.

O'Brien, John. "Alison Saar: Exalting Ambiguity." *Sculpture*, vol. 26, no. 1, 2007, pp. 28–31.

O'Grady, Lorraine. "The 1980s: An Internet Conference Moderated by Maurice Berger." *Issues in Cultural Theory, vol. 10*. Center for Art, Design, and Visual Culture, University of Maryland, and Georgia O'Keefe Museum Research Center, 2007. http://lorraineogrady.com/writing /the-1980s-an-internet-conference-2005.

———. "Black Dreams." *Heresies* #15, vol. 4, no. 3, 1982, pp. 42–43. Reprinted in *Writing in Space, 1973–2019*, edited by Aruna D'Souza, Duke University Press, 2020, pp. 69–76.

———. "The Cave: Lorraine O'Grady on Black Women Film Directors." *Artforum*, vol. 30, no. 5, 1992, pp. 22–24. http:// lorraineogrady.com/wp-content/uploads/2015/11/Lorraine -OGrady_The-Cave-Lorraine-OGrady-on-Black-Women -Film-Directors_Artforum-International-Magazine.pdf.

———. "Cutting Out the New York Times (CONYT)." *Writing in Space, 1973–2019*, edited by Aruna D'Souza. Duke University Press, 2020, pp. 6–7.

———. "Job History (from a Feminist "Retrospective")." *Writing in Space, 1973–2019*, edited by Aruna D'Souza. Duke University Press, 2020, pp. 260–68.

———. "Lorraine O'Grady." *Contemporary Art and Multicultural Education*, edited by Susan Cahan and Zoya Kocur. New Museum of Contemporary Art and Routledge, 1996, p. 142.

———. *Lorraine O'Grady / MATRIX 127*. Wadsworth Athenaeum, 1995.

———. "Lorraine O'Grady." *Performance Artists Talking in the Eighties*, edited by Linda M. Montano. University of California Press, 2000, pp. 400–406.

———. *Lorraine O'Grady: Where Margins Become Centers*. Carpenter Center for the Visual Arts, 2016.

———. "*Mlle Bourgeoise Noire*, 1955." *High Performance*, vol. 4, no. 2, 1981, p. 56. Reprinted in *Writing in Space, 1973–2019*, edited by Aruna D'Souza. Duke University Press, 2020, pp. 8–10.

———. "*Mlle Bourgeoise Noire* and Feminism." *Writing in Space, 1973–2019*, edited by Aruna D'Souza. Duke University Press, 2020, pp. 110–14. https://www. dukeupress .edu/Assets/PubMaterials/978-1-4780-1113-2_601.pdf.

———. "Nefertiti/Devonia Evangeline." *High Performance*, vol. 17–18, no. 5, 1982, p. 133. Reprinted in *Writing in Space, 1973–2019*, edited by Aruna D'Souza. Duke University Press, 2020, pp. 50–52.

———. "Olympia's Maid: Reclaiming Black Female Subjectivity." *Writing in Space, 1973–2019*, edited by Aruna D'Souza. Duke University Press, 2020, pp. 94–109. https:// www.dukeupress.edu/Assets/PubMaterials/978-1-4780 -1113-2_601.pdf.

———. "On Being the Presence That Signals an Absence." *Writing in Space, 1973–2019*, edited by Aruna D'Souza. Duke University Press, 2020, pp. 115–19. https://www. dukeupress.edu/Assets/PubMaterials/978-1-4780-1113 -2_601.pdf.

———. "Performance Statement #1: Thoughts about Myself, When Seen as a Political Artist." *Writing in Space,*

1973–2019, edited by Aruna D'Souza. Duke University Press, 2020, pp. 37–39.

———. "Performance Statement #2: Why Judson Memorial? or, Thoughts about the Spiritual Attitudes of My Work." *Writing in Space, 1973–2019*, edited by Aruna D'Souza. Duke University Press, 2020, pp. 40–42.

———. "Performance Statement #3: Thinking out Loud: About Performance Art and My Place in It." *Writing in Space, 1973–2019*, edited by Aruna D'Souza. Duke University Press, 2020, pp. 43–49. https://www.dukeupress .edu/Assets/PubMaterials/978-1-4780-1113-2_601.pdf.

———. "Poison Ivy," letter to the Editor. *Artforum*, vol. XXXVII, no. 1, 1988, p. 8. https://www.alexandergray.com /attachment/en/594a3c935a4091cd008b4568 /TextTwoColumnsWithFile/594a3c945a4091cd008b46b0].

———. "*Rivers* and Just above Midtown." *Writing in Space, 1973–2019*, edited by Aruna D'Souza. Duke University Press, 2020, pp. 213–18.

———. "*Rivers*, First Draft: working script, cast list, production credits." 1982. https://lorraineogrady.com/wp-content /uploads/2015/11/Lorraine-OGrady_Rivers-First-Draft _Working-script.pdf.

———. "Some Thoughts on Diaspora and Hybridity: An Unpublished Slide Lecture." *Writing in Space, 1973–2019*, edited by Aruna D'Souza. Duke University Press, 2020, pp. 119–25.

———. "The Space Between." *Lorraine O'Grady /Matrix 127*. Wadsworth Athenaeum, 1995, pp. 8–9. http://lorraineogrady .com/writing/the-space-between-1995.

———. "Thinking out Loud: About Performance Art and My Place in It," 1983. http://lorraineogrady.com/wp-content /uploads/2015/11/Lorraine-OGrady_Thinking-out-loud -About-performance-art-and-my-place-in-it_Unpublishe -for-Tony-Whitfield.pdf

———. "Work Development: A non-chronological mapping of the newly completed website, lorraineogrady.com, to accent the emergence of the work's motifs through a back-and-forth interweaving across time." *Lorraine O'Grady: Concept-based Art*. Lorraine O'Grady, 2022. http://lorraineogrady.com /wp-content/uploads/2015/11/Lorraine-OGrady_Work -Development.pdf.

O'Grady, Lorraine, and Connie Butler. "Lorraine O'Grady and Connie Butler Chat about *WACK! Art and the Feminist Revolution*." WPS1 Art Radio, 28 January 2008. http://lorraineogrady.com/writing/wps1-chat-with-connie -butler-2008.

"The Oklahoma Lynching." *The Crisis: A Record of the Darker Races*, vol. 2, no. 4, 1911, pp. 153–54.

Oliver, Valerie Cassel. "A Conversation with Chakaia Booker." *RubberMade: Sculpture by Chakaia Booker*, by Christopher Cook. Kemper Museum of Contemporary Art, 2008.

Ollman, Leah. "Alison Saar Gives Her Sculptures an Inner Life." *Los Angeles Times*, 26 March 2011. http://www.lalouver.com /html/gallery-history-images/other-resources/AS-LAT -Ollman-2011.pdf.

Omachi, Christopher. "Installation View: Nari Ward's 1993." *Whitewall*, 1 February 2013. https://www.whitewall.art/art /installation-view-nari-wards-1993.

Oppenheimer, William, and Ann Oppenheimer. "The Indelible Images of Winfred Rembert." *Folk Art Messenger* online, vol. 16, no. 2, 2003. http://folkart.org/mag/winfred -rembert.

Orr, Joey. "Radical View of Freedom: An Interview with Dread Scott." *Journal of American Studies*, vol. 52, no. 4, 2018, pp. 913–28.

O'Sullivan, Michael. "Leonardo Drew: A Trash Course in Sculpture." *Washington Post*, 26 March 2000, p. G01. http:// www.washingtonpost.com/wp-srv/WPcap/2000–03 /26/004r-032600-idx.html.

Pace, Alessandra. "Nari Ward: The Inside of a Sunshower." *Flash Art*, October 1996. https://www.lehmannmaupin.com/ko /bodo/flash-art.

Patterson, Troy. "The New Heroes of Civil Rights." *Southern Living*, September 2013, pp. 75–79.

Patton, Sharon. "Emma Amos: Art Matters." *Nka: Journal of Contemporary African Art*, issue 16–17, 2002, pp. 40–47.

Paysour, Fleur. "Wonders of the House of Saar." *International Review of African American Art*, vol. 20, no. 3, 2005, pp. 51–53.

Pendleton, Tonya. "A Witness of Our Times: Politics and Commemoration in the Art of Pat Ward Williams." *Philadelphia Tribune*, 24 January 1992, p. 5D.

Peterson, Karin E. "Discourse and Display: The Modern Eye, Entrepreneurship, and the Cultural Transformation of the Patchwork Quilt." *Sociological Perspectives*, vol. 46, no. 4, 2003, pp. 461–90.

Phagan, Patricia. "An Interview with Beverly Buchanan." *Art Papers*, vol. 8, no. 1, 1984, pp. 16–17.

Pierini, Marco, et al. *The Refinery X: A Simple Twist of Fate*. Gli Ori, 2006.

Pinder, Jefferson, and Susan Zurbrigg. *Jefferson Pinder: Action*. Duke Hall Gallery of Fine Art, James Madison University, 2015.

Pinder, Jefferson. "Artist Statement." http://www.jeffersonpinder .com/bio.

———. "Jefferson Pinder." FADO Performance Art Centre. http://www.performanceart.ca/index.php?m=people _details&id=423.

———. *Jefferson Pinder: Dark Matter*. York College Galleries, 2014.

———. "Jefferson Pinder: Dark Matter." Patricia Sweetow Gallery, December 29, 2015. https://www.artsy.net/partner /patricia-sweetow-gallery/overview.

———. *New [New] Corpse*. Green Lantern Press, 2014.

———. *Onyx Odyssey*. Hyde Park Art Center, 2016.

Pinder, Jefferson, and Nicholas Frank, eds. *Jefferson Pinder: Anthology*. Peck School of the Arts, 2009.

Pinder, Kimberly N. *Painting the Gospel Black: Public Art and Religion in Chicago*. University of Illinois Press, 2017.

Plocek, Keith. "Blanket Statements." *Houston Press*, 24 August 2006. http://www.houstonpress.com/arts/blanket -statements-6545565.

Pohl, Frances K. *Framing America: A Social History of American Art*. Thames and Hudson, 2002.

Pollack, Barbara. "Rhinestones Odalisques: Mickalene Thomas." *ARTnews*, vol. 110, no. 1, 2011. https://www.artnews.com/art -news/retrospective/archives-mickalene-thomas-work-goes -beyond-black-esthetic-2011-10971/.

Priestly, Debra. *Preserves*. June Kelly Gallery, 2002.

———. "Preserves." *Visualising Slavery: Art Across the African Diaspora*, edited by Celeste-Marie Bernier and Hannah Durkin. Liverpool University Press, 2016.

Prokopow, Michael J. "Material Truths: The Quilts of Gee's Bend at the Whitney Museum of Art: An Exhibition Review." *Winterthur Portfolio*, vol. 38, no. 1, 2003, pp. 57–66.

Quashie, Kevin E. "More Than You Know: The Quiet Art of Whitfield Lovell." *Massachusetts Review*, Spring 2011, pp. 58–71.

Queens College, CUNY. *Queens College Art Faculty*. Gowin-Ternbach Museum, 2014. http://qcpages.qc.cuny.edu /godwin_ternbach/godternb_exhibitions/exhibitions_images /QC_Faculty_catalogue.pdf.

Raiford, Leigh, and Heike Raphael-Hernandez, eds. *Migrating the Black Body: The African Diaspora and Visual Culture*. University of Washington Press, 2017.

Rappaport, Sam. "HPAC Exhibition Explores African American Identity." 11 November 2015. http://www .patriciasweetowgallery.com/press/hpac-exhibition-explores -african-american-identity.

Ratcliffe, Viola. "To Be a Witness: Lynching and Postmemory in LaShawnda Crowe Storm's 'Her Name Was Laura Nelson.'" MA thesis, Bowling Green State University, 2015.

Raynor, Vivien. "Sculpture Full of Visual Puns: Cross-Cultural Implications abound in Works by Willie Cole." *New York Times*, 14 June 1992, p. NJ13.

Reid, Calvin. "Kerry James Marshall." *Bomb*, vol. 62, 1998, pp. 40–47.

Rembert, Winfred, et al. *Winfred Rembert: Amazing Grace*. Hudson River Museum, 2012.

———. *Winfred Rembert: Another View*. Adelson Galleries, 2015.

———. *Don't Hold Me Back: My Life and Art*. Chicago: Cricket Books, 2003.

———. *Winfred Rembert: Caint to Caint*. Adelson Galleries, 2013.

———. *Chasing Me to My Grave: An Artist's Memoir of the Jim Crow South*. London: Bloomsbury Publishing, 2021.

———. Rembert, Winfred, et al. *Winfred Rembert: Memories of My Youth*. Adelson Galleries, 2010.

———. "Works and Reminiscences." *Winfred Rembert: Amazing Grace*. Hudson River Museum, 2012.

Riddle, Mason. "Common Objects, Uncommon Narratives: New Prints by Willie Cole." *Willie Cole: New Prints*, by Willie Cole and Mason Riddle. Highpoint Editions, 2012.

Roach, Hadley. "Thread to the World: Alison Saar." *Bomb*, 17 November 2011. https://bombmagazine.org/articles /thread-to-the-word-alison-saar.

Roberts, Mary Nooter, and Alison Saar. *Body Politics: The Female Image in Luba Art and the Sculpture of Alison Saar*. Fowler Museum of Cultural History, 2000.

Roberts-Burton, Angela Lynette. "Out of the Land: The Quilts of the Bendolph Family." MA thesis, Howard University, 2009.

Roelstraete, Dieter. "An Argument for Something Else: Dieter Roelstraete in Conversation with Kerry James Marshall, Chicago, 2012." *Kerry James Marshall: Painting and Other Stuff*, edited by Nav Haq. Ludion, 2014.

Rogers, Angelica. "Does This Flag Make You Flinch?" *New York Times*, 14 July 2016, p. SR11. https://www.nytimes .com/2016/07/15/us/artist-flag-protests-lynching-by-police .html?_r=0.

Rosenberg, Karen. "How Lorraine O'Grady Transformed Harlem into a Living Artwork in the '80s—And Why It Couldn't Be Done Today." *Artspace*, 22 July 2015. http://www .artspace.com/magazine/interviews_features/in_focus /lorraine-ogrady-on-the-making-of-her-1980s-parade -performance-harlem-52996.

Rosenfeld, Austen. "Rhinestones Are a Woman's Best Friend." *Style.com*, 6 March 2015.

Roth, Moira, and Portia Cobb. "An Interview with Pat Ward Williams." *Afterimage*, vol. 16, 1989.

Roulet, Laura. "Double Consciousness: A Conversation with Jefferson Pinder." *Sculpture*, vol. 37, no. 6, 1 July 2018. https://sculpturemagazine.art/double-consciousness-a -conversation-with-jefferson-pinder/.

Rowe, Nellie Mae. *Picking Cotton*. The Souls Grown Deep Foundation, 1981. http://www.soulsgrowndeep.org/artist /nellie-mae-rowe/work/picking-cotton.

Rowe, Nellie Mae, and J. Richard Gruber. *Nellie Mae Rowe*. Morris Museum of Art, 1996.

Rowell, Charles H. "An Interview with Kerry James Marshall." *Callaloo*, vol. 21, no. 1, 1998, pp. 263–72.

"Rural Quiltmaker's Handy Work Subject of New Postal Stamp." *Westside Gazette*, 21 September 2006, p. 1B.

Ryckaert, Vic. "Quilt Depicting Horrors of Lynching Stirs Emotions." *USA Today*, 28 January 2013. https://eu .usatoday.com/story/news/nation/2013/01/28 /quilt-depicts-lynching-draws-mixed-emotions /1869923.

Saar, Alison. *Alison Saar: Artist-in-Residence*. Dartmouth College Studio Art Exhibition Program, 2003.

———. *Alison Saar: Breach*. Lafayette College Art Galleries, 2017.

———. "Lady Lazarus, 1988." *In a Dark Vein*, by Mary Ann Unger. Sculpture Center, 1989.

———. *Myth, Magic, and Ritual: Figurative Work by Alison Saar*. Freedman Gallery, Albright College, 1993.

Saar, Betye. *I'll Bend But I Will Not Break*. Los Angeles County Museum of Art, 1998. https://collections.lacma.org /node/2261898.

Saggese, Jordana Moore. "Fade to Black: An Interview with Jefferson Pinder." *International Review of African American Art*, vol. 25, no. 3, 2015, pp. 43–48.

Salley, Raél Jero. "Kerry James Marshall: Ultra Black Light." *Chicago Art Journal*, vol. 19, 2009, pp. 50–62.

Sandler, Irving, et al. *Whitfield Lovell: Kin*. Rizzoli, 2016.

Sargent, Antwaun. "Mickalene Thomas on Muses, Models, and Mentors." *Interview Magazine*, 10 March 2016. http://www .interviewmagazine.com/art/mickalene-thomas.

Scala, Mark, ed. *Creation Story: Gee's Bend Quilts and the Art of Thornton Dial*. Vanderbilt University Press, 2012.

Scheper-Hughes, Nancy. "Anatomy of a Quilt: The Gee's Bend Freedom Quilting Bee." *Anthropology Today*, vol. 19, no. 4, 2003, pp. 15–21.

Schor, Mira, et al. "Contemporary Feminism Art Practice, Theory, and Activism: An Intergenerational Perspective." *Art Journal*, vol. 58, no. 4, 1999, pp. 8–29.

Schulz, Mike. "Heavy Ideas with Elements of Play: Alison Saar, Still . . ." *River Cities' Reader*, 1 February 2013. http://www .lalouver.com/html/gallery-history-images/other-resources /AS-RCreader-Schultz-2013.pdf.

Schwartz, Terese Pencak. "The Holocaust: Non-Jewish Victims." *Jewish Virtual Library: A Project of AICE*. https://www .jewishvirtuallibrary.org/non-jewish-victims-of-the-holocaust.

Scott, Dread. "The Art of Red Lining." *Revolution*, 30 August 2009. http://revcom.us/a/174/redlining-en.html.

———. "Darwin: Discover the Man and the Revolutionary Theory that Changed the Course of Science and Society." *Revolution*, 8 January 2006. http://revcom.us/a/029/darwin -discover-man-theory.htm.

———. *Dread Scott: Decision*. Dreadscott.net, 2012. https:// www.dreadscott.net/works/dread-scott-decision.

———. "Dread Scott: FAQ." https://www.dreadscott.net/faq/

———. "Dread Scott on a Racist System." *Prison Photography*, 15 October 2009. https://prisonphotography.org/2009/10/15 /dread-scott-on-a-racist-system.

———. *Historical Corrections*, 1998. https://www.dreadscott .net/works/historic-corrections

———. "An Interview with Roy De Carava." *A Gathering of the Tribes*, 23 February 2007. http://web.archive.org /web/20050223050109/http://www.tribes.org/cgi-bin/form .pl?karticle=539.

———. *Jasper The Ghost*, 1999. https://www.dreadscott.net /works/jasper-the-ghost.

———. "Make Revolutionary Art to Propel History Forward . . . Confront the World as It Is and Radically Dream about How It Could Be Different." *Liberator Magazine*, June 2011.

———. "Outrage and Controversy at NY Museum Art Show Depicting Police Brutality." *Alternet*, 28 March 2008. http:// www.alternet.org/story/80640/outrage_and_controversy_at _ny_museum_art_show_depicting_police_brutality.

———. "Slave Rebellion Reenactment." https://www.slave-revolt .com.

Scott, Dread, et al., *Fragments of the Peculiar Institution: A Project by the Artist Dread Scott*. C and B Publications, 2016.

Scott, Dread, and Patricia Hills. *Dread Scott: Welcome to America*. MoCADA, 2008.

Shaw, Gwendolyn DuBois. *Represent: 200 Years of African American Art in the Philadelphia Museum of Art*. Yale University Press, 2014.

Shaw, Kurt. "Jefferson Pinder: Black and White Issues." *Pittsburgh Tribune Review*, 3 January 2004. http://www .patriciasweetowgallery.com/press/jefferson-pinder -black-and-white-issues.

Sheets, Hilarie M. "In the Picture: Atlanta, Africa, and the Past." *New York Times*, 3 July 2011, p. AR19. http://images .bridgettemayergallery.com/www_bridgettemayergallery _com/Bailey_NY_Times_July_2011.pdf.

Shepherd, Elizabeth. *Secrets, Dialogues, Revelations: The Art of Betye and Alison Saar*. Wight Art Gallery, University of California, 1990.

Silestro, Sarah. "Willie Cole's BRAND/IDENTITY." *Gatepost*, 21 November 2015. http://fsugatepost.com/2015/11/21 /willie-coles-brandidentity.

Silver, Leigh. "Interview: Mickalene Thomas Discusses Creating a Different Kind of Portrait for Her New Show 'I Was

Born to Do Great Things." *Complex Art +Design*, 1 October 2014. http://www.complex.com/style/2014/10/interview-mickalene-thomas.

Silvis, Helen. "Quilting Artists in Portland." *Skanner*, 6 July 2005.

Sims, Lowery Stokes. "The Artist, a Residency, the Museum: Willie Cole at the Studio Museum in Harlem." *Anxious Objects: Willie Cole's Favorite Brands*, by Patterson Sims. Montclair Art Museum, 2006, pp. 100–101.

———. "Home Is Where the Heart Is: Beverly Buchanan's Shack Sculpture in Context." *Beverly Buchanan: Shackworks, A 16-Year Survey*, by Beverly Buchanan and Eleanor Flomenhaft. Montclair Art Museum, 1994, pp. 33–36.

Sims, Lowery Stokes, ed. *Next Generation: Southern Black Aesthetic*. University of North Carolina Press, 1990.

Sims, Patterson. *Anxious Objects: Willie Cole's Favorite Brands*. Montclair Art Museum. 2006.

Slate, Michael. "Dread Scott: Making Art and Revolution." *Revolutionary Worker #1107*, 17 June 2001. http://revcom.us/a/v23/1100-99/1107/dread_scott.htm.

Slesin, Suzanne. "The Shack as Art and Social Comment." *New York Times*, 18 January 1990, p. C14.

Sligh, Clarissa T. "100 Americans: A Presence of the Past in Philadelphia." http://www.clarissasligh.com/selected_works/install/100.html.

———. *Clarissa Sligh Papers, 1950-2010*. David M. Rubenstein Rare Book & Manuscript Library, Duke University.

———. *Clarissa Sligh: The Presence of Memory*. Robert B. Menschel Photography Gallery, 1991.

———. *Curator's Eye I: National Gallery of Jamaica, January 18–June 19, 2004*. National Gallery of Jamaica, 2004.

———. "It Wasn't Little Rock." *Potomac Review*, vol. 38, 2004–5, pp. 7–25.

———. *It Wasn't Little Rock*. Visual Studies Workshop Press, 2005.

———. *My Mother, Walt Whitman and Me: A Recollection*. Clarissa Sligh, 2019.

———. "On Being an American Black Student." *Heresies*, vol. 7, no. 1, 1990, pp. 29–33.

———. "On Being an Invisible Black Artist." *Art and Artists*, vol. 17, no. 1, February/March 1988.

———. "A Presence of the Past: My Work as a Storyteller in the Artists' Book Medium." *Hand, Voice, and Vision: Artists' Books from Women's Studio Workshop*, edited by Kathleen Walkup. Women's Studio Workshop, 2010. http://www.clarissasligh.com/essays/2010-presenceofthepast.html.

———. *Reading Dick and Jane With Me*. Visual Studies Workshop, 1989. http://www.clarissasligh.com/essays/2009_readingdick.html.

———. "Taking the Private Public." *She Who Was Lost Is Remembered: Healing from Incest through Creativity*, edited by Louise M. Wisechild. Seal Press, 1991, pp. 147–151.

———. *Transforming Hate: An Artist's Book*. 2016.

———. "The Witness Project: Remembrance and Struggle." https://clarissasligh.com/themes/social-injustice/witness-project.

———. *Wrongly Bodied Two*. Women's Studio Workshop, 2004.

Smith, Shawn Michelle, et al. *Take Another Look at Race: Myra Greene and Carla Williams*. Visual Studies Workshop, 2009.

Smith, Wes. "The Ladies of Gee's Bend: The Fabric of Many Lives Runs through Their Quilts." *Orlando Sentinel*, 29 January 2007. http://articles.orlandosentinel.com/2007-01-29/news/GEESBEND_1_bend-quilts-gee-bend-orlando-museum.

Snodgrass, Susan. "Heroes and Martyrs: Kerry James Marshall's New Work." *Art in America*, vol. 86, no. 11, 1998, pp. 92–95.

Sohan, Vanessa Kraemer. "'But a quilt is more': Recontextualizing the Discourse(s) of the Gee's Bend Quilts." *College English*, vol. 77, no. 4, 2015, pp. 290–312.

Son, Angela. "Interview with Beverly Buchanan." *Art Animal: A Women's Art Magazine*, 8 November 2012. http://www.artanimalmag.com/beverly-buchanan.

South, Will. *Remix: Themes and Variations in African-American Art*. Columbia Museum of Art, 2016.

Soutif, Daniel, ed. *The Color Line: Les Artistes africains-américains et la ségrégation, 1865–2016*. Flammarion, 2016.

Souza, Gabriella. "New Project from the Contemporary Explores Our Relationship with History." *Baltimore Magazine*, 5 May 2016. http://www.baltimoremagazine.net/2016/5/5/new-project-from-the-contemporary-explores-our-relationship-with-history.

Spears, Dorothy. "'60s Legacies, Personal Histories." *New York Times*, 1 June 2008.

Stanislaus, Grace C. *Instill and Inspire: The John and Vivian Hewitt Collection of African-American Art*. University of Pittsburgh, 2017.

Stillman, Nick. "Dread Scott." *Bomb*, 23 September 2009. http://bombmagazine.org/article/4234/dread-scott.

Strick, Jeremy. *Leonardo Drew*. Saint Louis Art Museum, 1996.

Sultan, Terrie. *Kerry James Marshall*. Johnson County Community College Gallery of Art, Johnson County Community College, 1995.

———. "Rhapsody in Orange." *Radcliffe Bailey: The Magic City*, edited by David Moos. Birmingham Museum of Art, 2001, pp. 26–29.

Sultan, Terrie, ed. *Radcliffe Bailey: Tides*. Blaffer Gallery, 2002.

Sutton, Rebecca. "Art Talk with Clarissa Sigh." National Endowment for the Arts blog, 6 March 2012. https://www.arts.gov/art-works/2012/art-talk-clarissa-sligh.

Tallman, Susan, et al., eds. *Mirror, Mirror: The Prints of Alison Saar.* Jordan D. Schnitzer Family Foundation, 2019.

Thomas, Mickalene. "Hotter Than July," *American Visions, n.d., n.p.*

———. "I am HM." *Flourodigital.com*, 28 March 2013. https://fluorodigital.com/2013/03/mickalene-thomas.

———. *Mickalene Thomas.* Kavi Gupta, 2014.

———. "Mickalene Thomas." *Trace Magazine*, April 2008. https://www.lehmannmaupin.com/ch/mei-ti-bao-dao/trace.

———. *Mickalene Thomas: Happy Birthday to a Beautiful Woman.* 2012. https://www.eastman.org/mickalene-thomas-happy-birthday-beautiful-woman.

———. *Muse: Mickalene Thomas Photographs.* Aperture, 2015.

Thomas, Mickalene, et al. *Mickalene Thomas.* Rhona Hoffman Gallery, 2008.

Thompson, Carol, ed. *Radcliffe Bailey: Memory as Medicine.* High Museum of Art, 2011.

Thompson, Mildred. "Interview: Emma Amos." *Art Papers*, vol. 19, no. 2, 1995, pp. 21–23.

Tinson, Teddy. "Making Up with Mickalene Thomas." *Interview Magazine*, 26 June 2014. http://www.interviewmagazine.com/art/mickalene-thomas-tete-de-femme.

Truth, Sojourner [Marius Robinson Transcription], "Women's Rights Convention: Sojourner Truth," *The Anti-Slavery Bugle*, 21 June 1851, p. 160. https://chroniclingamerica.loc.gov/lccn/sn83035487/1851-06-21/ed-1/seq-4/.

Tuymans, Luc. "Kerry James Marshall in Conversation." *Bomb*, vol. 92, 2005, pp. 52–61.

Twigs, Ruth. *Tangible Spirits with Alison Saar.* Virginia Museum of Fine Arts, 1996.

Unger, Mary Ann. *In a Dark Vein.* Sculpture Center, 1989.

Vartanian, Hrag. "Dread Scott Is Bringing the Wars Home." *Hyperallergic*, 17 August 2011. https://hyperallergic.com/32470/dread-scott-is-bringing-the-wars-home.

———. "'A Man Was Lynched by Police Yesterday:' Flag Goes Up in New York City." *Hyperallergic*, 8 July 2016. https://hyperallergic.com/310037/a-man-was-lynched-by-police-yesterday-flag-goes-up-in-new-york-city.

Vergne, Philippe. "It's Ok to Disagree: A Conversation with Nari Ward." *Nari Ward: Sun Splashed*, edited by Naomi Beckwith, et al. Prestel, 2015, pp. 62–76.

Vlach, John Michael. "The Shotgun House: An African Architectural Legacy. Part I." *Pioneer America*, vol. 8, no. 1, 1976, pp. 47–56.

Waddell, Edward W. "Life Ain't Been No Crystal Stair." *Art Papers*, vol. 9, no. 6, 1985, pp. 13–14.

Walker, David. *Walker's Appeal, in Four Articles; Together With A Preamble, To The Coloured Citizens of the World.* Revised and published by David Walker, 1830.

Walker, Kara. "Mickalene Thomas." *Bomb*, vol. 107, 2009, pp. 72–73.

Ward, Nari. "Artist Statement." *Callaloo*, vol. 37, no. 4, 2014, pp. 871–73.

———. *Nari Ward: Attractive Nuisance.* Hopefulmonster, 2001.

———. *Nari Ward: G.O.A.T.* Socrates Sculpture Park, 2017.

———. "Nari Ward: Skowhegan Lecture Archive: 2003." New York; Skowhegan, M.E.: Skowhegan School of Painting and Sculpture, 2003. Transcript by Judith Stoodley.

———. "Nari Ward: St. Peter's Odyssey Salon September 10–October 16, 2004." Deitch Projects, Jeffrey Deitch Curatorial Projects, 2004. https://www.deitch.com/archive/deitch-projects/exhibitions/st-peters-odyssey-salon.

———. *Togli il fermo/ Let it go.* Silvano, 2013.

———. "Work In Progress." *V Magazine*, vol. 15, 2002. https://www.lehmannmaupin.com/press/v-magazine.

Ward, Nari, and Brian Keith Jackson. *Rooted Communities: the Art of Nari Ward.* Louisiana State University School of Art, 2014.

Ward, Nari, and Olukemi Ilesanmi, *Nari Ward: Rite of Way.* Walker Art Center, 2001.

Ward, Nari, and Phong Bui. "Nari Ward with Phong Bui." *Brooklyn Rail*, 3 May 2012. http://www.brooklynrail.org/2012/05/art/nari-ward-with-phong-bui.

Watkins, Mel. "Pat Ward Williams Interview with Mel Watkin." *The Tell Tale Heart: Washington Project for the Arts, March 9–May 5, 1990: Ken Little, James Luna, Judy Southerland, Pat Ward Williams*, by Mel Watkins, et al. Washington Projects for the Arts, 1990.

Watkins, Mel, et al. *The Tell Tale Heart: Washington Project for the Arts, March 9-May 5, 1990: Ken Little, James Luna, Judy Southerland, Pat Ward Williams.* Washington Project for the Arts, 1990.

Way, Jennifer. "Reterritorialization and *Whispers from the Walls*." *Journal of Material Culture*, vol. 9, no. 3, 2004, pp. 219–36.

Weaver, A. M. "In the Studio: Jefferson Pinder, from Cosmonaut to Escape Artist." *Art Voices Magazine*, 6 November 2012.

Weinberg, Lauren. "Mickalene Thomas Jet Set." *Time Out Chicago*, 26 November 2008, p. 72.

Weiss, Allen S. "Dust to Dust: Drew in Conversation with Weiss." *Existed: Leonardo Drew*, by Leonardo Drew and Claudia Schmuckli. Giles, 2009.

Wells, Georgina. "Color Theory: Making Connections, Both Personal and Public." *Modern Painters*, vol. 25, no. 4, 2013, p. 26.

Wells-Barnett, Ida B. "Southern Horrors: Lynch Law in All Its Horrors." *Selected Works of Ida B. Wells-Barnett*, edited by Trudier Harris. Oxford University Press, 1991, pp. 14–45.

White, Walter F. "The Work of a Mob." *Crisis: A Record of the Darker Races*, vol. 16, no. 5, 1918, pp. 221–23.

Wilcox, Chloe. "Beverly Buchanan: *And You May Find Yourself*" *Brooklyn Rail*, June 2015. https://brooklynrail.org/2015/06/artseen/beverly-buchanan-and-you-may-find-yourself.

Williams, Carla. "Clarissa Sligh and Zanele Muholi in Conversation with Carla Williams." *Exposure*, vol. 42, no. 1. 2009, pp. 4–17.

———. "Mickalene Thomas: A Presence Impossible to Reproduce." *Aleim Magazine*, 26 June 2014. http://aleim.com/issue4/mickalene-thomas.

Williams, Pat Ward. "Pat Ward Williams: Artist Statement." *Constructed Images: New Photography*, edited by Deborah Willis and Kellie Jones. Schomburg Center for Research in Black Culture, 1989, p. 10.

———. "Pat Ward Williams Commission for Rosa Parks Park." Department of Art, College of Fine Arts, Florida State University, 26 May 2011. http://art.fsu.edu/pat-ward-williams-commission-for-rosa-parks-park-debuted.

———. *Pat Ward Williams: I Remember It Well*. Smith College Museum of Art, 1993.

———. *Pat Ward Williams: Probable Cause*. Goldie Paley Gallery. 1992.

———. *The Tell Tale Heart*. Washington Projects for the Arts, 1990.

———. "Two Installations." *Reframings New American Feminist Photographies*, edited by Diane Neumaier. Temple University Press, 1995, pp. 142–45.

Williams, Rachel. "Society: Artists' Challenge to Stop and Search: Young People in Liverpool and New York Use Graphic Depictions to Explore the Similarities in How They Are Treated by the Police." *Guardian*, 14 March 2012, p. 38.

Williams, Stephanie Sparling. "'Frame Me': Speaking Out of Turn and Lorraine O'Grady's Alien Avant-Garde." *Stedelijk Studies*, issue 3, Fall 2015. http://www.stedelijkstudies.com/journal/frame-me-speaking-out-of-turn-and-lorraine-ogradys-alien-avant-garde.

Williams-Gibson, Jessica. "Quilts Hold Gee's Bend Community Together." *Recorder*, 13 October 2006, p. 10.

Williamson, Chet. "Myth of the Lawn Jockey: Willie Cole Examines Race Relations and an Icon of Kitsch." *Worcester Magazine*, vol. 31, no. 10, 2005, p. 18.

Willis, Deborah. *Convergence, 8 Photographers*. Photographic Resource Center, 1990.

———. *Personal Narratives: Women Photographers of Color*. Southeastern Center for Contemporary Art, 1993.

———. "A Search for Self: The Photograph and Black Family Life." *The Familial Gaze*, edited by Marianne Hirsch. University Press of New England, 1999, pp. 107–23.

———. "Women's Stories/ Women's Photobiographies." *Reframings: New American Feminist Photographies*, edited by Diane Neumaier. Temple University Press, 1995, pp. 84–92.

Willis Thomas, Hank, and Deborah Willis, et al., eds. *All Power: Visual Legacies of the Black Panther Party*. Minor Matters Books, 2016.

Wilson, Judith. "Beverly Buchanan Sculptor." *Beverly Buchanan Sculpture*. UAB Arts Gallery, 1982.

———. "Down to the Crossroads: The Art of Alison Saar." *Secrets, Dialogues, Revelations: The Art of Betye and Alison Saar*, by Elizabeth Shepherd. Wight Art Gallery, University of California, 1990, pp. 32–46.

———. "Hexes, Totems and Necessary Saints: A Conversation with Alison Saar." *Real Life*, vol. 19, 1988–89, pp. 36–44.

———. "Lorraine O'Grady: *Critical Interventions*." *Lorraine O'Grady: Photomontages*, by Lorraine O'Grady. INTAR Gallery, 1991. http://lorraineogrady.com/wp-content/uploads/2015/11/Judith-Wilson_Lorraine-OGrady-INTAR-Gallery_Lorraine-OGrady-Critical-Interventions.pdf.

Wooden, Isaiah Matthew. "Jefferson Pinder and the Art of Black Endurance." *PAJ: A Journal of Performance and Art*, vol. 40, no. 1, 2018, pp. 74–82. https://www.jeffersonpinder.com/the-art-of-black-endurance.

Wyma, Chloe. "22 Questions for Multimedia Sculptor Nari Ward." *Blouin Artinfo*, 27 March 2012. https://www.lehmannmaupin.com/press/22-questions-for-multimedia-sculptor-nari-ward.

———. "Mickalene Thomas." *Modern Painters*, vol. 24, no. 8, 2012, pp. 23–24.

Yau, John. "In Conversation: Whitfield Lovell with John Yau." *Brooklyn Rail*, 10 July 2006. http://www.brooklynrail.org/2006/07/art/whitfield-lovell.

Yerman, Marcia G. *Women in Art: Interview between Marcia Yerman and Beverly Buchanan*. Time Warner, 1993. https://archive.org/details/XFR_2013-09-05_2A_01.

Young, Lisa Jay. "Spiritual Minimalism." *Young Performing Arts Journal*, vol. 18, no. 2, 1996, pp. 44–52.

Zamudio, Raúl. "Reading between the Treads." *Chakaia Booker: Jersey Ride*, by Chakaia Booker and Rocío Aranda-Alvarado. Jersey City Museum, 2004, pp. 17–24.

Zandy, Janet, ed. *Liberating Memory: Our Work and Our Working-Class Consciousness*. Rutgers University Press, 1995.

Zed, Xenia. "Makin' a way Outta No Way: Nellie Mae Rowe." *Raw Vision*, vol. 32, 2000, pp. 24–31.

Zimmer, Lori. "Reconstructing the Glittering Female Gaze: A Conversation with Revolutionary Artist." *PMc Magazine*, December 2011. http://pmc-mag.com/2011/11/mickalene-thomas.

Zimmer, William. "Sculptures of Shacks Make Up a Small Village." *New York Times*, 1 May 1994, p. 12.

INDEX